Management Consulting

Fifth Edition

Management Consulting

Delivering an Effective Project

Louise Wickham

Jeremy Wilcock

Harlow, England • London • New York • Boston • San Francisco • Toronto • Sydney
Auckland • Singapore • Hong Kong • Tokyo • Seoul • Taipei • New Delhi
Cape Town • São Paulo • Mexico City • Madrid • Amsterdam • Munich • Paris • Milan

PEARSON EDUCATION LIMITED
Edinburgh Gate
Harlow CM20 2JE
United Kingdom
Tel: +44 (0)1279 623623
Web: www.pearson.com/uk

First published 1999 (print)
Second edition 2004 (print)
Third edition 2008 (print)
Fourth edition 2012 (print and electronic)
Fifth edition published 2016 (print and electronic)

ISBN: 978-1-292-12760-6 (print)
         978-1-292-13016-3 (PDF)
         978-1-292-13009-5 (ePub)

British Library Cataloguing-in-Publication Data
A catalogue record for the print edition is available from the British Library

Library of Congress Cataloging-in-Publication Data
Names: Wickham, Louise, author. | Wilcock, Jeremy, author.
Title: Management consulting : delivering an effective project / Louise
    Wickham, Jeremy Wilcock.
Description: Fifth Edition. | New York : Pearson, 2016. | Revised edition of
    the authors' Management consulting, 2012. | Includes bibliographical
    references and index.
Identifiers: LCCN 2016002742| ISBN 9781292127606 (print) | ISBN 9781292130163
    (pdf) | ISBN 9781292130095 (ePub)
Subjects: LCSH: Business consultants. | Industrial management.
Classification: LCC HD69.C6 W53 2016 | DDC 001—dc23 LC record available at
    http://lccn.loc.gov/2016002742

10 9 8 7 6 5 4 3 2 1
20 19 18 17 16

Print edition typeset in 9.5/12.5 pt ITC Charter by Lumina Datamatics, Inc.
Print edition printed in Slovakia by Neografia

NOTE THAT ANY PAGE CROSS REFERENCES REFER TO THE PRINT EDITION

To Amelia, Annabelle, Constance, Henry, Louis and Mabel

Brief contents

Contents

Part Three Undertaking the project

8 Working with the client

9 Creative approaches for developing solutions

10 Decision making in the client context

Lecturer Resources

For password-protected online resources tailored to support the use of this textbook in teaching, please visit **www.pearsoned.co.uk/wickham**

Preface

If you can't explain what you're doing in simple English, you're probably doing something wrong.

Alfred Kazin

Being a consultant shares many similarities with being a manager but there are important differences. Doing a student consulting project is a good way for the uninitiated to experience what it is like and more importantly practise the key skills required. This book aims to offer comprehensive support to students undertaking a consulting exercise as part of their course. It will be of value to undergraduates and higher degree students, offering a range of insights, tools and practical advice appropriate for both levels. Although the book is primarily aimed at those studying management, we recognise that students studying many other disciplines undertake consulting projects, such as those on engineering, IT or creative courses, so it is relevant for them as well.

The first four editions of *Management Consulting* have occupied an almost unique niche in providing students with the tools to undertake a consulting project, while at the same time providing a framework for new professional practitioners to use. For the fifth edition, we have added some new material, particularly case studies and reflected the way in which the world of management consulting is evolving. The businesses the consultant works for are changing, as new technologies play a greater role in the way they operate. In addition, as more businesses use external consultants they have become more demanding as clients and expect more concrete evidence of success. Gone are the days when the seasoned operator could just say, 'Trust me, I'm a consultant'. Our favourite cartoon depicted in Figure 3.2 is perhaps becoming a thing of the past but it serves as a useful reminder that successful consulting is about both the client and the consultant working together as equal partners.

Both authors have many years of experience in the world of business and consulting in particular and this 'real world experience', we hope, provides a counterbalance to the more academic literature on management consulting in other texts. In addition Jeremy Wilcock is the Business Engagement Manager at the Business School, University of Hull, working to strengthen the school's relationships with its corporate partners and the business community in general. He has lectured in strategic management at undergraduate and MBA level at Hull, supervised and assessed student teams working on management consulting projects and has acted as academic supervisor for successful Knowledge Transfer Partnerships.

This book can be used both as a reference point to check on tools and techniques and used sequentially to manage a consulting project. Part One (Chapters 1–4) is concerned with consulting in its managerial and business context and also looks at key skills required to be an effective consultant. These are divided into: analysis skills, project management skills and relationship building skills. Part Two, on project definition and analysis (Chapters 5–7), considers the factors that a student should look at to successfully start a project, including vital people and analysis skills. Part Three, on undertaking the project (Chapters 8–11), considers the key project management and relationship-building skills required for successful delivery. The final part of the book (Chapters 12–14), delivering the product to the client, considers communicating the outcome of the project and learning from it. It also looks at consulting as a profession and some of its recent developments in the industry. Furthermore, it provides a guide to major consulting firms and the career structures they offer to those who are considering consulting as a future career.

Another way to use the book is to divide the sections into the 'consulting experience' and the 'consulting process'. Figure P.1 shows the two areas. The 'experience' is about what is consulting, what it can do for a business and the skills required. The 'process' is the mechanics by which the reader can achieve a successful project.

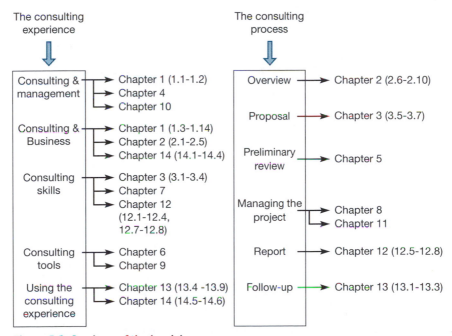

Figure P.1 Sections of the book by area

We also recognise that this book is being used by a wide variety of students, ranging from undergraduates who are doing their first consulting project to experienced managers who have had some experience of consulting but wish to know more. Whilst it would be impossible to identify which parts of the book are relevant for each individual student, we have instead created some 'pathways' (see Table P.1) for four 'typical' users to help readers navigate and get the most out of the book:

- 3rd year undergraduate (principally business) students doing first project (A)
- Masters or PhD students without business experience (B)
- MBA and other Masters students with business experience (C)
- Business managers working with consultants or starting out in consulting themselves (D)

Table P.1 Sections of book relevant for each student type to follow

	A	B	C	D
Chapter 1	All	All	All	All
Chapter 2	All	All	All	All
Chapter 3	3.1–3.4, 3.6–3.7	All	All	All
Chapter 4	–	–	All	All
Chapter 5	5.1–5.3, 5.5	All	All	All
Chapter 6	6.1–6.2	All	All	All
Chapter 7	–	–	All	All
Chapter 8	8.9–8.10	8.1–8.2, 8.9–8.10	All	All
Chapter 9	9.1–9.3	All	All	All
Chapter 10	–	–	All	All
Chapter 11	11.1–11.2, 11.5–11.9	All	11.4	–
Chapter 12	12.1–12.7	All	12.4–12.5, 12.8	12.4–12.5, 12.8
Chapter 13	13.7–13.8	All	13.1–13.5	–
Chapter 14	14.5	All	All	14.5–14.6

This is a large subject and students should look at the suggestions for key and further reading to explore the ideas further. At the end of each chapter there is a short case exercise. Many of these are new and based on real cases (though names have been changed to protect the guilty!). In addition, there is a new longer case study that runs throughout the book on a strategic consulting exercise undertaken at the Apollo Tech Solutions company. The latter is designed for the student to use the knowledge learned in the preceding chapters. All of these changes are in a large part in response to the reviewers of the fourth edition, who gave us many valuable comments and feedback as to how we could improve the text. We would like to thank them for their contributions as well as Margaret Dewhurst and David Bishop. Finally, we would like to thank the team at Pearson for all their help and support, without whom this book would not be possible.

We hope that this book will both aid your consulting project and make it more interesting and rewarding, whether as a student exercise or in real life.

Louise Wickham
Jeremy Wilcock
September 2015

Acknowledgements

We are grateful to the following for permission to reproduce copyright material:

Cartoons
Figure 3.2 from Copyright © Scott Adams, Inc./Dist by UFS, Inc. Reproduced by permission. Scott Adams, Inc.

Figures
Figure 2.2 from The Institute of Risk Management. *A Risk Management Standard* © AIRMIC, ALARM, IRM 2002. Reproduced with permission; Figure 4.2 from *Marketing Management*, 11th edn, Pearson Education, Inc. (Kotler, P.) p. 395, Prentice Hall © 2003. Reprinted and electronically produced by permission of Pearson Education, Inc., Upper Saddle River, New Jersey; Figure 5.5 from *Business Process Change: A Guide for Business Managers and BPM and Six Sigma Professional*, 2nd edn (Harmon, P. 2007) p. 171, with permission from Elsevier; Figure 5.6 from *Exploring Public Sector Strategy*, Pearson Education, Ltd. (Johnson, G. and Scholes, K. 2001) p. 301, © Pearson Education, Ltd. Used by permission; Figure 6.9 from *The Delta Project: Discovering New Sources of Profitability in a Networked Economy*, Palgrave Macmillan (Hax, A.C. and Wilde, D.L. 2001) Figure 1.1, p. 10. Republished with permission of Palgrave Macmillan; Figure 6.11 from 'Using the balanced scorecard as a strategic management system', *Harvard Business Review*, Adapted from Figure 1.1: Translating Vision and Strategy – Four Perspectives (Kaplan, R.S. and Norton, D.P.), Copyright © 1996 by the Harvard Business School Publishing Corporation, all rights reserved. Reprinted by permission of Harvard Business Review; Figure 6.12 from 'Strategies of diversification', *Harvard Business Review*, Issue No. 25(5) (Ansoff, H.I 1957), Copyright © 1957 by the Harvard Business School Publishing Corporation, all rights reserved. Reprinted by permission of Harvard Business Review; Figure 6.13 from © Boardroom Associates, 2011. Used by permission; Figure 6.15 from Bruce D. Henderson, The Product Portfolio Matrix (1970). The Star, the Dog, the Cow and the Question Mark – The Growth Share Matrix, used by permission; Figure 6.17 from *Crossing the Chasm*, HarperCollins Publishers (Moore, G. A.) Adaptation of figure [p. 17: 'The Revised Technology Adoption Life Cycle'] Copyright ©1991 by Geoffrey A. Moore. Reprinted by permission of HarperCollins Publishers; Figure 7.3 from *Introduction to Type* ®, 6th, CPP, Inc. (Myers I.B. 1998) Characteristics Frequently Associated with Each Type Table, p. 13, Copyright 1998, 2012 by CPP, Inc. All rights reserved. Reproduced with permission from the publisher, CPP, Inc. Further reproduction is prohibited without the Publisher's written consent; Figure 8.2 from The Uncertain Management Consulting Services Client, *International Studies of Management & Organization*, 43(3), 35 (Pemer, F. and Werr, A. 2013), reprinted by permission of the publisher (Taylor & Francis Ltd, http://www.tandfonline.com); Figure 10.3 from Four styles of strategic planning, *Long Range Planning*, 26(6), 132–7 (Idenberg, P.J. 1993), with permission from Elsevier.

Tables
Table 5.3 from Tools and Templates>Cause and effect>The Cause and Effect a.k.a. Fishbone diagram. http://www.isixsigma.com/tools-templates/cause-effect/cause-and-effect-aka-fishbone-diagram/, iSixSigma. Used by permission; Table 8.1 from The Uncertain Management Consulting Services Client, *International Studies of Management & Organization,* 43(3), 33 (Pemer, F. and Werr, A. 2013), reprinted by permission of the publisher (Taylor & Francis Ltd, http://www.tandfonline.com).

Acknowledgements

Text

Epigraph on page 157 adapted from *Man's Search For Meaning*, ISBN-13: 978-1844132393, Penguin Random House UK (Frankl, V.) p. 86 ; Extract on page 194 adapted from *The Seven Cs of Consulting*, Chapter 4, 3rd edn, Pearson Education, Ltd (Cope, M. 2010) © Pearson Education, Ltd. Used by permission; Extract on page 202 adapted from *Flawless Consulting: A Guide to Getting Your Expertise Used*, 3e, John Wiley & Sons (Block, P. 2011) pp. 130–136, reproduced with permission of John Wiley & Sons, Inc.; Epigraph on page 189 from The Gathering Storm: The Second World War, Volume 1 by Winston S. Churchill, Rosetta Books. ISBN: 0795308329 page 565. Reproduced with permission of Curtis Brown, London on behalf of The Estate of Winston S. Churchill; Extract on page 246 adapted from Coping with Uncertainty: A Naturalistic Decision-Making Analysis. *Organizational Behavior and Human Decision Processes*, 69(2), 149–163 (Lipshitz, R. and Strauss O. 1997), with permission from Elsevier; Extract on page 310 from *Management Consulting: A Complete Guide to the Industry*, 2e, John Wiley & Sons (2001) Table 6.2, page 180, reproduced with permission of John Wiley & Sons, Inc.

Management consulting in context and how it adds value

Chapter 1

The nature of management consulting and how it adds value

Ninety per cent of the consultants give the other 10 per cent a bad reputation.

Henry Kissinger

Learning outcomes

The main learning outcomes from this chapter are to:

- understand the nature of management consulting as a managerial role;
- appreciate the nature of the client–consultant role relationship;
- recognise the responsibilities of the consultant;
- understand what *motivates* a business manager to bring in a consultant;
- recognise the ways in which a consultant can *add value* for a client business;
- explore why businesses fail and *need* a consultant;
- understand the things a consultant can *offer* a client business by way of value-creating support.

What *is* a management consultant? The MCA (Management Consultancies Association Ltd) defines management consulting as 'the creation of value for organisations, through improved performance, achieved by providing objective advice and implementing business solutions'. This sentence encompasses some very critical points: the client organisation expects value for its investment. It needs high-quality and practical advice that it can use. This advice, when implemented, should lead to a measurable improvement in the organisation's fortunes. But this advice should be dispassionate and impartial – the consultant should not simply aim to please. If it requires major changes to the way the client operates, the advice should be communicated without fear or favour. This needs skill, competence and confidence.

> **The management consultant's expertise must deliver value to the client organisation.**

From figures provided by the MCA, the UK consulting industry has grown from its early beginnings in the 1950s to a business worth around £8.1 billion, employing around 40,000 consultants. The industry is also said to contribute just under £1 billion to the UK's balance of payments by employing its talents overseas. So by any measure, consultancy is valuable and valued. The management consultant should therefore live up to high expectations. For a more sceptical, yet even-handed, assessment of the management consultancy industry, the student is recommended O'Shea and Madigan's *Dangerous Company*. This contains some useful case studies and, in the authors' words, 'has ripped back the curtain and exposed the practices of this secretive industry to the light of day. It has changed the formula of the consulting relationship, putting power back where it belongs, into the hands of the people who pay the bills'.

1.1   What a management consultant does

> **Management consulting is a special form of management activity.**

A management consultant is paid for going into an organisation and undertaking a special project on its behalf. This can be for a profit-motivated commercial venture, non-profit organisations such as charities or government and other public sector bodies, whether local, national or international. Of late, however, there has been a challenge mounted against what has been alleged as the wasteful over-use of consultants in the public sector. In the new era as budgets come under increasing scrutiny the management consultant will be challenged more than ever to deliver real value for the cost of being hired, especially when public money is used.

The types of project undertaken by consultants are as varied as management itself. They may be very specific or wider in scope. They may involve the proffering of specialist technical expertise, such as the development of IT systems. Some projects may be 'softer' and aim at facilitating cultural change within the organisation. In some cases they may have the objective of resolving internal conflicts within the organisation. They may be concerned with helping the organisation build relationships with outside parties. In other instances, they may aim to help the organisation gain a critical resource. Often they will be focused on a specific issue that has been recognised by the organisation's management and has been well defined. In many instances, though, they are of a broad 'business strategy' nature. The extent to which the client organisation has specific objectives in mind varies greatly. Most projects will involve gathering and analysing information and sharing findings with the organisation. A management consulting project can vary from a matter of weeks to a year or more.

A management consultant offers their management abilities, expertise and insights to the client business in order to *create value for it*. However, it is a cost for the client business and competes with all the other factors a business needs if it is to grow: money for investment; people and their skills; raw materials and equipment. The client will find the service the consultant is offering attractive only if it is something that the business cannot provide for itself. Further, it must be the *best* investment option on offer given all the other things the business could buy in.

This means that a consultant must understand a number of things from the outset. The consultant must know why what they are offering will be of value to the client business and that it represents a good *investment opportunity* for the business given the opportunity cost of other investment options. This forms the basis of what the consultant can 'sell' to the business. The consultant must recognise what they will enable the business to do in its marketplace, why the business cannot do this for itself and how the individuals who make up the business can unify around the project.

Although management consultancy is seen as a specialist management role, the consultant must have the skills of a general manager. The consultant must not only be able to undertake specific (and often technical) projects, they must also be able to market what they offer (not forgetting that marketing includes the development of the actual consulting 'product' as well as its promotion), sell the product to clients and manage a relationship with them. This is a challenge. Experience in consulting provides a fast 'learning curve' in management skills, though consultants should not lose sight of the fact that their credibility will only be defined by the quality of the advice and recommendations that they put forward.

1.2 Consulting and management roles

> To be a management consultant requires a thorough and fundamental understanding of the scope of management.

Managerial functions

A traditional approach defines management in terms of the *functions* the manager undertakes. For example, Henri Fayol, a management thinker of the early twentieth century, decided there were five such basic functions: planning, organising, staffing, directing and controlling. This echoes the strategic planning acronym APIC (analysis, planning, implementing and controlling).

Planning

Planning is concerned with defining the business's vision (its desired future state) and mission (reason for being in business) and identifying the courses of action and projects needed to move the organisation in that direction. Planning varies greatly in its level of formality. A simple project with few tasks and low resource requirements will demand only a minimum of consideration and documentation. A major project with complex, and perhaps risky, outcomes will require a considerable degree of time and effort in its planning. Its implementation will involve complex communication networks drawing together a large number of managers.

Formal planning techniques may be advantageous if project organisation is to be effective. Different businesses differ in their approach to planning and the degree to which it is formalised as a management activity. As well as the nature and complexity of the project and the significance of its outcomes, organisational style, culture and individual management traits will be important determinants in the approach to planning.

Organising

The organising function relates to the overall structuring of the business. Roles, responsibilities and reporting relationships are defined for individuals and subgroups. In strategic terms this means ensuring that the organisation's structure is appropriate for its strategy and environmental situation. The organisation's structure and business processes dictate the way in which it will work and how it will use its capabilities. This is sometimes referred to as the strategy–structure–process fit. This topic is reviewed well by Van de Ven and Drazin (1985).

Staffing

Staffing is the function concerned with making sure that the business has the right people in place. People, their skills, abilities and experience are assets the business undervalues at its peril. The staffing function ensures that people have the right skills in order to undertake the projects the business needs to carry out to be successful. In modern organisations the staffing function is often integrated into a broader human resource management function. Key elements of the human resource strategy are recruitment, appraisal, personal development and skills training. Additional elements will include establishing remuneration, career development and coaching and staff motivation policies.

Directing

Directing relates to the process of encouraging people to implement efficiently the tasks necessary to deliver the business or project goals. Originally it referred to the management function of instruction or delegation to subordinates. A modern interpretation would be broader and would include a manager's responsibilities as a leader and motivator of individuals and teams and the creator of a supportive organisational culture.

Controlling

Managers use resources. Resources, be they money, people or productive assets, must be utilised in the best way possible. Controlling is the function that is concerned with making sure that the right resources are in place, that they are being used effectively and that their use is properly accounted for. Traditionally, controlling was largely about *budgeting* – that is, financial control. Now a broader interpretation would regard it as the process of focusing the business towards its goals through the implementation of an appropriate *strategy*. This strategy will direct the optimal utilisation of all the business's resources and the development of its capabilities. A strategic perspective sees resources more broadly than the traditional 'money–labour–machinery' view. Dynamic aspects like organisational knowledge and learning are regarded as resources as well. The consultant engages directly at this resource level.

This traditional approach to the nature of management has been challenged as it may be seen to offer an idealised image of what the manager actually does. It pictures the manager as 'above' the organisation, coordinating its activities in a detached way and progressing it towards some well-defined, rational end. In fact, most organisations are not like this at all. Managers cannot detach themselves from their organisations; they are very much part of them. The organisation defines the manager as much as the manager defines the organisation. They must work with limited information and make decisions using intuition, their skills and experience as much as formal analysis. The ends they work towards may be motivated as much by implicit and emotional drives as explicit and rational ones.

Managerial roles

Henry Mintzberg has suggested that a more productive approach is to look at the *roles* managers actually undertake rather than the *functions* they are supposed to undertake. He believes that there are ten such roles in three groups: *interpersonal* roles, *informational* roles and *decisional* roles.

Interpersonal roles relate to the ways in which managers interact with other organisational members. It is through interpersonal roles that managers draw their power and authority. The three key interpersonal roles are the *figurehead*, the *leader* and the *liaison*.

The figurehead

The figurehead role is the one in which the manager represents the organisation, or the part of it for which he or she is responsible, in a formal manner. The figurehead role is especially important for entrepreneurs and managers of small businesses.

The leader

The leader role refers to the manager's interaction with subordinates. It is the role the manager is playing when delegating tasks, motivating people to undertake these tasks and supporting them in achieving them. Leadership differs from authority. Authority arises from a position within an organisational hierarchy. It makes leadership possible, but does not guarantee it.

The liaison

Many managers have a responsibility for representing the business to the outside world. The liaison role is the one in which managers interact with people from other organisations. The critical responsibility is one of gaining some resource for the business such as customer goodwill, essential productive factors or investment capital.

Managers must make decisions on behalf of their organisations. Accurate and incisive analysis, wise judgement and a decisive bias for action are the fundamental qualities of a manager. To be effective decision makers, managers need access to timely and accurate information on the business itself as well as its immediate task environment. *Informational roles* are concerned with obtaining and manipulating the information the business needs. The three critical informational roles are the *monitor*, the *disseminator* and the *spokesperson*.

The monitor

The monitor role leads the manager to identify and acquire information on behalf of the organisation. It may involve the processing and storage of information so that it is readily available for use by decision makers. Analysis is a critical task for the monitor.

The production of sales statistics, accounts and market intelligence are important tasks for the monitor.

The disseminator

Managers do not work in isolation. Information of itself is useless: it must be shared with others in the organisation. The disseminator is concerned with ensuring that available information is passed on within the organisation to information processors and decision makers. Reports, meetings and presentations represent formal means of dissemination. Unofficial 'grapevines' are often an influential way of disseminating information informally.

The spokesperson

The spokesperson is also involved in disseminating information, but to the outside world rather than internally. Important spokesperson roles are taken on by sales and marketing staff, who inform customers about the company's offer; purchasing managers, who let suppliers know what the company needs; and financial managers, who apprise investors of the company's status and prospects.

Third, *decisional* roles are involved in identifying a future direction for the organisation, defining the projects and strategic imperatives to take it there and resolving the crises that may impede its progress. These roles are the *entrepreneur*, the *disturbance handler*, the *resource handler* and the *negotiator*.

The entrepreneur

The entrepreneur is concerned with shaping and making decisions that lead the organisation forward in a significant way. Mintzberg uses the term entrepreneurial in a broader sense than it is used in traditional management theory. In Mintzberg's sense, the entrepreneur need not be an owner or founder of the organisation – any manager can take on the entrepreneurial role. An entrepreneurial decision is one that aims to exploit an opportunity or address a threat. Such a decision may be significant, but it may not be especially pressing at the time. It encompasses the activities of conventional entrepreneurs and what have come to be known as *intrapreneurs*, managers who take an entrepreneurial approach within an established business.

The disturbance handler

Organisations tend to establish and follow set patterns of behaviour. They find their own ways of doing things and abide by them. This can be considered organisational culture, but is better viewed as organisational inertia. A fixed pattern of working will produce satisfactory results provided that there is no change in either the organisation's internal state or its external condition. If change does occur, the organisation's way of doing things may no longer produce the desired results. Such a change is known as a disturbance.

Disturbances demand immediate attention. The business will suffer a reduced performance or even fail if they are not addressed promptly. A disturbance is often referred to as a management crisis. Organisational inertia conditions management's response to a crisis. Often, the first reaction of managers when faced with a crisis is to try to replace any missing resource so as to keep the organisation in its original state. Maintaining the status quo when the organisation has been impacted by a disturbance is the responsibility of the disturbance handler.

Disturbance handling is not a continuous role. It comes into play only when a crisis happens. Some managers may be predisposed to deal with certain crises as a consequence of their roles: sales managers, for example, will be in the front line if an important customer is lost; purchasing managers will lead the way in finding a new supplier. If the crisis is significant enough, conventional relationships can be driven into a state of flux. Recrimination and organisational politics can arise. But the organisation may well need to make functional and structural changes in order to survive in the changed circumstances it faces.

The resource allocator

Businesses consume resources. They do so to be able to pursue the opportunities that present themselves. These resources are valuable and must be used in the best way possible if the business is to be successful. Few businesses face a simple yes or no answer when considering future possibilities. It is not the cost of investing in a project that matters so much as its opportunity cost: the returns that might have been gained if the resources invested in the project had been invested elsewhere.

Managers must decide which of the opportunities that offer themselves is the best one at a particular time. They must prioritise and allocate resources across a variety of options. For example, should the business invest in that advertising campaign or would the money be better spent on a new sales representative? Should export efforts be directed at the Far East, or are the transitional economies of central Europe likely to offer a better return? Should investment be directed at a new product, or might it be more profitable to acquire that competitor? Managers must address such questions every day. In doing so they are taking on the resource allocator role. As with the entrepreneurial role, the resource allocator is dependent on the informational role in order to make good decisions about where resources are best placed.

The negotiator

People collaborate in organisations because value can be created by separating and coordinating tasks. The extra value created must be shared both within organisations and between the different organisations that come into contact with each other. Individuals and organisations must advocate their right to a share of resources available. This advocacy is reflected in the negotiator role. Sometimes this role is concerned with sharing resources with outside organisations. The sales manager will negotiate with customers. The purchasing manager will negotiate with suppliers. Finance managers will negotiate with investors. Inside the operation, personnel managers will negotiate remuneration packages with employees.

Many negotiations take on an informal character. They may manifest themselves as unofficial 'understandings' between managers about how resources will be shared. Organisational politics is a consequence of (and limited by) unofficially negotiated outcomes. Not all negotiations are a 'zero-sum' game: that if one party wins, the other must lose. Effective negotiators look for win–win solutions. Nor is effective negotiation a matter of taking a stance and holding to it. It is more about identifying what is required from a situation and then being flexible in finding ways to achieve what is wanted.

Any one management role will have a profile that combines some or even all of these ten roles in a particular way. The way in which these roles define the profile of management responsibilities within the organisation will depend on a range of factors. The organisation's size will be a critical determinant. The bigger the business and the more managers it employs, the greater will be the latitude for managers to specialise. In a small business, a single entrepreneur may take on most, if not all, of the roles at some time or other. In a large multinational corporation, managers may be in a position where their roles will be more narrowly defined.

The complexity of the organisation and its environment will also be important. Complexity refers to the amount of information managers must process before making a decision. If complexity is high, informational roles will be important and it may be necessary to have managers dedicated to these roles. A fast-growing organisation undergoing rapid change may present a special leadership challenge and demand that particular attention be paid to interpersonal roles. The profile of management roles will reflect the organisation, the stage in its evolution and its environmental situation.

1.3   The client–consultant interaction

The consultant's tasks are management tasks.

The consultant *is* a manager. Like any manager, the consultant will at times take on many, if not all, of the ten roles defined by Mintzberg. The consultant's role parallels and integrates with that of managers within the client organisation. Through this interaction the client–consultant relationship is built.

Managers work in a network of relationships. These relationships exist between managers working within a particular organisation and between the managers in different

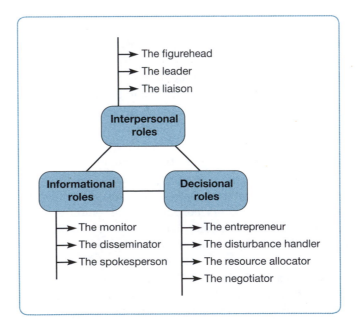

Figure 1.1 The managerial role profile

organisations who come into contact with each other. The consultant who moves into an organisation must define the relationship they wish to create with the managers who already work in the client business and possibly with some of those in other organisations with which the client comes into contact. Two considerations will determine what sort of relationship this will be. These are: the nature and structure of management roles in the client organisation and the objectives of the consulting exercise.

Every organisation is different, as is every manager. It is possible to see consistent patterns in the way in which managerial roles take shape. Different organisations will require a different profile of management roles. But every organisation will demand that managers carry out the interpersonal, informational and decisional roles in a way that is right for the business. These roles must be carried out with the correct degree of competence and in balance with each other.

The motivation to call in a consultant arises because managers have identified issues or challenges, which, when resolved, will benefit the organisation but which they recognise they are not in a position to deliver a solution themselves. This inability may well be due to resource or skill gaps. In filling these gaps, the consultant is offering to complement and develop the role profile within the organisation. The ways in which the consultant can interact with and develop the business management role profile are directly related to the roles Mintzberg has identified. There are five primary types of consultant–management role interaction: *supplementing, complementing, differentiating, integrating* and *enhancing*.

Supplementing

Supplementing involves the consultant adding to the existing skill profile to increase its capability but not alter its overall shape. The consultant is an additional resource who takes on a project that could well have been taken on by an existing manager had time been available. This type of consulting role offers a way of enabling the business to manage demand fluctuations in a low-risk way. The consultant allows the business to add and subtract human resources in a flexible manner. The consultant is neutral in development terms and does not aim to make any fundamental changes in the organisation.

Complementing

Complementing occurs when the organisation realises it has a deficiency in its profile of management roles which the consultant can fill. This may require the consultant to introduce a role specialism to complement such a weakness in the client business role profile. Projects that enhance the business's marketing approach or develop presentations to financial backers are important examples. Consultants can play an important role in supporting existing managers to improve leadership by helping them to develop a unifying organisational mission.

The consultant may complement the informational role. Important examples might include marketing research and the setting up of management information systems. These projects will make demands on both the monitoring and the disseminating aspects of the informational role. The consultant may also be active in supporting the spokesperson role. Developing communications aimed at customers and investors is the task of the public relations expert. Lobbyists may be employed to communicate and influence decision makers in government.

The consultant can contribute to the decisional role in a variety of ways. Speculative business development projects, which explore a range of possibilities for the business in the future, complement the *entrepreneurial role*. A consultant may be called in as a *disturbance handler* to help the business's management deal with a crisis. The setting up of budgeting management control systems is an example of the consultant complementing the work of the *resource allocator*. Some consultants specialise in *negotiating* and can contribute to the way in which the business approaches important customers, suppliers or investors. The complementing role can be considered as the consultant filling in a gap in the management's existing role profile.

Differentiating

The overall profile of management roles will depend on a number of factors. The size of the organisation will be critical. The larger the business, the greater the latitude for allowing managers to specialise their roles. One aspect of the process of organisational growth will be an increasing tendency towards role specialisation. Differentiating involves the consultant helping the client business to differentiate its management roles and allow managers to specialise.

This process of role differentiation is critical if the organisation is to grow successfully. It is only through such specialisation that the business can not only grow but also improve its performance as it grows. However, such differentiation is not always easy. Managers (not least successful entrepreneurs) often resist giving away areas of responsibility. They would rather use the organisation's growth to 'build their empire'. This can result in the manager having too large an area of responsibility, too much information to analyse and not enough time. Invariably, the quality of decision making suffers.

Integrating

Mature organisations are characterised by well-defined organisation structure and role responsibilities. These become established and may be subject to organisational inertia. They may persist even when they are no longer appropriate. If the business's environment and competitive situation change, then an evolution in the way the business does things may be called for. If environmental change is particularly fast, the occasional revolution may be called for. Such changes demand that the old role profile be broken down and a new profile allowed to emerge. The new roles may combine or integrate a number of aspects of the old roles.

Integrating involves the consultant helping the client business to reorganise its management roles and build a new set of manager relationships and responsibilities. As with differentiating, the consultant called in to integrate roles into a new, more flexible structure must address both hardware and software issues. A new structure must be invented and the change management issues needed to motivate managers to work within it must be addressed.

Enhancing

Enhancing is the most general type of role development process. It demands not so much that the role profile of the organisation be changed but that the manager's overall level of performance be improved. Enhancing involves the consultant helping the client management team improve the effectiveness of their overall management role profile. There are a variety of ways this might be achieved. Training of individual managers is usually an important part. This training may be directed towards improving technical and functional skills or may develop interpersonal skills such as motivation and leadership. Training may be supplemented through structural changes such as improved communication systems and attention to overall strategic understanding.

1.4 The responsibilities of the management consultant

The consultant must take on the responsibilities of being a manager not just for the organisation they work for but also the organisation they work with.

All managers have responsibilities both to the organisations and to the individuals who work in them. At one level, organisations are collections of individuals, so it is individual managers who must take on responsibilities on behalf of the organisations they work for. It has been suggested (Carroll, 1979) that managerial and organisational responsibilities operate at four levels. These may be referred to as the economic, the legal, the moral and the discretionary.

Economic responsibilities

The fundamental economic responsibility of the manager is to act in a way which is consistent with the long-term health of their business and maximises its value for its investors. This is not to suggest that the manager, like the economist's perfect entrepreneur, simply tries to maximise short-term profits. Real-world managers do not have the information to behave like this. Short-term profits to investors may be diverted in order to fund reinvestment projects aimed to achieve growth and so deliver more profits in the future. Potential profits may be compromised if other responsibilities are given priority. In economics, *agency theory* suggests that the interests of managers and investors differ and that, under certain circumstances, managers will act in their own best interests. Given these constraints, it may still be properly said that the consultant's economic responsibility is to advocate only projects which genuinely seem, in light of the information available, to be in the best interests of the business as a whole, given its stated strategic objectives and the concerns of the stakeholders who have an interest in it.

Legal responsibilities

All businesses have a responsibility to operate within the rule of law. Laws provide the official rules through which businesses interact with each other. Most legal systems have two codes: the *criminal*, which the state takes responsibility for implementing, and the *civil*, in which the responsibility for initiating proceedings lies with individuals. Business activity is subject to both. Nowadays, most governments try to minimise the impact of legislation on business as it is recognised that unnecessary legal restrictions impede business activity. Consideration of the impact of a new law on business is taken into account in the legislative process.

The consultant has a legal responsibility to ensure that the activities of the organisation he or she is working for, and any activities he or she may advocate on its behalf, are legitimate in light of the criminal and civil laws to which the business is subject. The exact nature of this legal responsibility, and the extent to which the consultant may face recrimination if it is breached, will depend on the law involved, the consultant's contractual obligations and the degree of culpability for outcomes. Ensuring that this condition is met, especially when the business is operating in a highly technical area, or in a part of the world with a different legal system, can be quite challenging. In this case, taking legal advice from experts (not least about one's own responsibilities) may be an important part of the consulting exercise.

Moral responsibilities

Moral responsibilities go one step beyond legal ones. In societies there are a whole complex of rules, norms and expectations. Some of these rules are written down in the form of laws or contractual agreements (which are often subject to civil law). But many are unwritten or even unspoken. They are merely an understanding about what is 'right' and what is 'wrong'. They are expectations about how people should behave towards each other. These rules may not even be noticed – until they are broken!

Though it is not always made explicit, every society, and to some extent every distinct grouping within a society, has its own code of morality. These codes often relate to the way in which stakeholders will be treated, above and beyond simple contractual rights. For example, most managers feel a higher degree of responsibility to employees than their contracts of employment dictate. Losing people is painful, so a business may retain people who are not absolutely necessary. Entrepreneurs who own their business may allow family members greater performance latitude than non-family members.

Many cultures have their own distinct rule systems. In displaced ethnic groups, networking may be supported by moral expectations about the responsibilities of members of the community towards each other. Edicts on the way in which debt is structured are common, as are rules about reciprocity of favours. Recognising such moral codes is an important aspect of the consultant's job. The consultant must recognise that he or she is as subject to these moral responsibilities as to the legal ones. Moral responsibilities are not merely 'nice to have'. Ignoring them will limit the effectiveness of the consulting exercise. Outcomes which go against the moral expectations of the client will, at best, not be implemented. Outright rejection can often occur.

Discretionary responsibilities

Discretionary responsibilities are those the consultant decides to take on as part of a personal moral order. They are not responsibilities the industry would normally be expected to observe. Discretionary responsibilities usually relate to a refusal to work in certain project areas, or to work towards project outcomes of which the consultant does not approve. This may mean avoiding certain industry sectors or types of project. Typically, such discretionary responsibilities arise as a result of the consultant's personal concerns about a range of domestic political issues, the environment or business activity in the developing world.

Although this may mean that the consultant must occasionally turn down valuable projects, it can also be a means of differentiation from the values other (perhaps competing) consultants advocate. Discretionary values may make a consultant more attractive to certain individuals and organisations. There is nothing inconsistent in using discretionary responsibilities as a means of gaining an edge in the marketplace.

1.5   Types of clients

The consultant needs to appreciate that there will be multiple stakeholders whether inside the organisation or external to it.

Edgar Schein (1997) suggested that process consulting can be enhanced by an appreciation of the different types of clients involved. He suggested that the consultant interacts with a number of individuals within the client organisation and that the concept of the individual client may be problematic. Rather, the consultant interacts with a network of individuals who play subtly different roles. Schein proposed six such client types.

Contact clients

The contact client is the person, or persons, who first approach the consultant and propose the consultant addresses a problem or issue on behalf of the organisation. Sometimes contact clients may themselves be from outside the organisation; for example, other consultants, business advisers or venture capitalists.

Intermediate clients

Intermediate clients are members of the organisation who become involved in the consulting project. They will work with the consultant and provide information, attending meetings and influencing the way the project unfolds.

Primary clients

The primary client is the person or persons who have identified the problem or issue the consultant has been called in to address and who will be most immediately affected by it. It is they who must own the project and be willing to pay in order to have the issue resolved.

Unwitting clients

Unwitting clients are members of the organisation who will be affected by the intervention of the consultant. They do not initiate the project and have no direct or formal control over it. They are not aware that they will be affected by the project.

Indirect clients

Indirect clients are members of the organisation who will be affected by the intervention of the consultant and who are aware that they will be affected. However, the consultant is not aware that the project will have an impact on them. Indirect clients may feel positive or negative about the consultant's intervention. They can be very influential behind the scenes and can facilitate or hinder the progress of the project.

Ultimate clients

Ultimate clients are the total community, those stakeholders who will be affected by the consultant's intervention. This will include members of the organisation and, possibly, members of the organisations which come into contact with the client organisation. The ultimate client group forms the universe of interests the consultant must take into account when progressing the project.

1.6 Modes of consulting

> Consulting is characterised by different approaches which reflect fundamental assumptions about the consultant's role.

All managers have their own approach to the tasks they face and the way they deal with people. This determines the manager's style. A critical element here is the perception the manager has about their fundamental role in the organisation. These are referred to as *modes*. In his book *Process Consultation*, Edgar Schein characterised three basic modes based on the relationship between the consultant and the client: the expert, the doctor–patient and the process consulting modes.

The expert mode

In the expert mode the client identifies a particular problem with the business, analyses the problem and articulates it to the consultant. The consultant then uses their expertise to identify a solution to the problem. This form of consulting is often found in areas where the consultant has a specialist knowledge which the client organisation recognises that it lacks.

The doctor–patient mode

The doctor–patient mode is also characterised by the consultant acting as an expert. In this mode, however, the consultant also takes responsibility for diagnosing the problem in the first place. The client may just express an opinion that the business 'could be better' in some way or that 'something is not quite right'. Again, the consultant is expected to contribute specialist knowledge and insights to the business.

The process consulting mode

Both the expert mode and the doctor–patient mode demand that the consultant, an outsider, offers a well-considered, expert solution – a prescription – to address the problems that the business faces. Process consulting takes a different stance. It is based on the premise that the only people who can help the business are the people who make it up. The consultant, as an outsider, cannot impose a solution on the organisation. What the consultant can do is assist those who make up the organisation to recognise problems and then discover the solutions to them. The consultant is not so much an expert, more a facilitator of change.

Schein makes a strong case of the process mode. Consultants can recommend better ways of doing things but these will become reality only if the people who make up the organisation feel that they have ownership of the new approach. A process approach to consulting helps ensure that the client organisation feels it is identifying its own solutions – solutions which are right for its business. Consultants bring expertise and the client will often expect the consultant to 'take charge' of the issues the business faces. 'After all,' it is often heard said, 'that's what they are being paid for!' An over-reliance on a process approach can sometimes leave clients feeling that they have done all the work themselves. Indeed, by the very nature of the process mode, the more proficient the consultant is in using it, the greater the risk that the client will feel that the consultant has not made a 'real' contribution.

In their paper 'Choosing a Consulting Role' (1990) Champion, Kiel and McLendon propose nine different roles the consultant may need to play: hands-on expert, moderator, partner, coach, teacher/trainer, technical adviser, counsellor, facilitator or effective observer. Without discussing the individual definitions at this point the message is clear: the consultant needs an ability to wear one or more of several hats. The appropriate role needs to be established from the outset. An individual consultant should possess the necessary flexibility. In larger consultancies, staff with the right skills for the specific role should be deployed.

1.7	The decision to use a consultant

> Hiring a consultant is not a decision to be taken lightly.

Why should a business manager ask the advice of an independent consultant? The decision is a significant one for a number of reasons. There may be an immediate financial cost. Even if the consulting is 'free' because it is being undertaken through an undergraduate consulting team, or the cost is being borne by a small business support agency, there may still be significant indirect costs such as marketing research.

There will also be a cost due to the need to dedicate management time to the consulting exercise. If a consulting project is to be successful, the consultant team must be supported in their activities. They will need briefing sessions and regular review meetings. The management time that must be dedicated to this is valuable, especially in a small business. The activities of consultants, if not managed effectively, can raise suspicions and lead to political infighting between managers. The decision to call in consultants occurs after a consideration of the costs and benefits involved and a conclusion that the potential benefits should outweigh the costs of the necessary investment. This is not a one-off decision. It is something that the client business constantly assesses. Maintaining the client's confidence and the belief that the consultancy exercise has something of value to offer is a critical responsibility for the consultant.

This presents a particular challenge for *management* consultants. Consultants who work in highly technical areas such as computing and engineering clearly offer the business an expertise the business itself may not have. However, every business will have *management* expertise. The business may *feel* that this expertise is greater than that offered by outsiders who have no knowledge of the business, its customers and its markets. Even if the business recognises the need for additional management resources, why should consultants be used? Why not just employ more managers?

The management consultant must therefore constantly ask three fundamental questions:

1 What can I offer the client business that will enhance its performance and help it achieve its objectives?

2 Why will my contribution be more valuable than that which existing managers, and potential recruits, can contribute?

3 How can I communicate to the client business that what I offer is valuable?

Answering these three questions involves the application of analytical, project management and relationship-building skills, which are discussed further in Chapter 3. This chapter aims to show how these skills may be developed and applied by considering what a management consultant has to offer the client business. The actual outputs of a consulting exercise centre on providing one or more of six things: information, specialist expertise, a new perspective on problems, support for internal arguments, support in gaining a critical resource and the creation of organisational change. These are considered in more depth in Sections 1.9–1.14.

1.8   Why do businesses fail?

> **Very often a consultant is engaged because the business is experiencing a potentially terminal crisis.**

It can happen to all types of company whether great or small, long-established or relative newcomers. Everything seems to be going fine to everyone working to deliver the organisation's plans and goals, yet seemingly from nowhere comes traumatic news without warning: factory closures, job losses, boardroom resignations, even going into receivership. How can it be that what works well one moment is suddenly unable to keep the operation in business?

Admittedly there may be unavoidable external factors such as unforeseen economic recession, war, loss of strategic raw materials or a sudden hike in input costs, but researchers such as Jeff Cornwall, Gustav Berle, Michael Ames, Moya Mason, Rob Holland, Scott Clark, Mike Myatt, Patricia Schaefer and Dave Lavinsky ascribe business failure to shortcomings within the company itself, specifically its management. As Moya K. Mason writes (2011), 'The short answer is, regardless of the industry, failure is the result of either the lack of management skills or lack of proper capitalization, or both'. Most of the problems identified by these researchers fall under seven headings:

Business model

The company may lack vision or clarity as to why it is in business – what is its primary purpose and what are the key skills it needs. Its owner may have gone into business for egotistical personal reasons rather than in pursuit of a clear opportunity. Expectations may be unrealistic. The company may become over-generalised, trying to compete in too many markets as an average player rather than focusing on one or two as the category leader. It may be that the company simply cannot grasp what is needed to aspire to sustainable competitive advantage in the longer term.

Markets and customers

One contributory factor may be a failure to understand and react to change: all customers are human and their habits, tastes and preferences can change. It is critical to monitor, ideally to anticipate, such changes. The company may become over-dependent on a single customer or a few key ones and be held a hostage to fortune by them. It may be critically dependent on the public sector, only to find budgets have been severely cut back. Competitors may change the market landscape with innovations and unforeseen initiatives. There can be significant changes in the macro-environment. If the company does not respond, it risks being left behind. Thorough market research and a proper understanding of market circumstances is vital if the company is not to risk engaging in an ill-conceived new venture: 'look before you leap' is indeed a wise aphorism. Simply copying what others do is to court disaster, yet many are the cases of firms launching precipitately into new areas to enjoy a piece of the action without conducting their homework, only to experience costly failure.

Cash management

Failure to manage cash flow is one of the commonest causes of business failure. The firm may over-borrow, spend its cash before it is flowing positively, have a capital structure carrying too much debt, have inadequate cash reserves and poor credit arrangements. It may manage its debtors ineffectively. It may become over-reliant on a critical source of finance that suddenly dries up. It may be the case that the company's managers lack financial awareness and responsibility. Then there are those who, blinded or dazzled by short-term success, make irresponsible personal use of business funds. Entrepreneurs who treat the company as their own personal piggy-bank without paying proper heed to sound financial governance are often behind their business's demise.

Financial management

Similarly, shortcomings in managers' financial competence may land the company in difficulty. There may be poor inventory management, with working capital tied up unnecessarily in fixed assets. Poor forecasting may lead to unsatisfied demand. Controllable costs may be allowed to increase without challenge. There may be unnecessary over-investment in fixed costs, such as buildings or people. Alternatively, a company with negligent or incompetent financial management may fail to prepare contingency plans to address volatility in its uncontrollable costs.

Business planning and performance

At worst, there may be no formal business plan, with the business simply reacting to events as and when they occur. Proper planning should lead to effective resource allocation, the definition of clear and realistic targets and appropriate prioritisation. There may be uncontrolled or unexpected growth which will lead to the business 'overheating' – slow and steady growth is infinitely preferable to rapid over-expansion. Another error may be a focus on short-term profits at the expense of creating sustainable value for the long term, risking under-investment in marketing and promotion. Alternatively, companies may diversify and add new product areas or new divisions which dilute overall profitability. On the downside, the ability to manage low sales, inadequate profitability, and failure to price correctly or respond to aggressive retaliation from competitors will demand sound business planning.

Processes

Although much was made of business process re-engineering in the late 1990s, it remains a truism that the successful business, like any well-oiled machine, should have effective and consistent business processes and internal controls, as well as the discipline to use them. These processes must be user-friendly and not over-engineered; otherwise they will risk being ignored or bypassed. If there is no performance monitoring, or if such performance monitoring as there may be is not understood, is ignored or used incorrectly, the company may risk 'flying blind', failing to see the warning signs before it is too late. Processes are needed across every facet of business, whether it is new product development, signing off advertising copy, authorising price changes, reviewing personal performance, planning career development or writing marketing plans, to name but a few. Especially for young companies experiencing rapid growth, it has to be appreciated that the informal teamwork and spirit of adventure that brought them success hitherto will not be able to bring them success in a more complex organisation: there has to be a set 'way of doing things' which needs to be documented. Yet it is remarkable how such an arguably mundane topic can be neglected even in well-established multinational businesses. Those who should know better still manage to launch new products without research, and have defective budgetary control systems, or lamentable production scheduling.

Management

But above all, it is poor management at the top of the organisation which will bring it down. Owner managers can fail to delegate, they may try to go it alone without seeking professional external advice – or worse they may seek uninformed help or financial support from friends and family. They may tolerate inadequate, inexperienced or downright poor management because it is cheap and compliant and may be unable to attract and retain the right talent. They may experience poor feedback and 'white lies' from ingratiating subordinates or they may be in denial, refusing to accept there are problems with the business they have grown and which they love. Their pride will not let them separate ego from business, heart from head, and they will fail to recognise their strengths and weaknesses. This is borne out by a recent study by Professors Sivanathan and Fast who state that power can go to the head of a senior manager if they are surrounded by yes-men, adding, 'power is an elixir, a self-esteem enhancing drug that surges through the brain telling you how great your ideas are. This leaves the powerful vulnerable to making overconfident decisions' (*Daily Telegraph*, 3 March 2012). Life at the top can indeed be tough and a business owner may experience 'burn-out' or be subjected to family pressures and other life distractions. Finally, in Dave Lavinsky's colourful phrase, 'maybe the owner is just a jerk' whom staff, suppliers and customers will not wish to support wholeheartedly.

Knowledge of these likely causes of failure will be invaluable to the management consultant. In a document titled 'Planning Against a Business Failure' (1998) Rob Holland of the University of Tennessee recommends that the chances of success will be improved if companies pay heed to ten basic items:

1 Develop a business plan.
2 Obtain accurate financial information about the business in a timely manner.
3 Profile the target customer.
4 Profile the competition.
5 Go into business for the right reasons.
6 Do not borrow family money and do not ask the family for advice.
7 Network with other business owners in similar industries.
8 Remember someone else will always have a lower price.
9 Realise that consumer tastes and preferences change.
10 Become better informed of the resources that are available.

A consultant's first diagnosis of a business experiencing difficulty could do well to focus on these areas initially.

1.9	Provision of information

> **Good management decisions require an informed understanding of the business and its situation.**

Some areas of information that are critical to a business are:

- the business's customers: their needs and buying behaviour;
- the business's products: their design, technology and development;
- the markets in which the business operates: their size, growth and dynamics;
- outside organisations that can offer support: who they are, what they offer and how they can be contacted;
- the business's competitors: who they are, their strengths and the threat they pose.

Information is valuable to a business and has a cost, either direct (such as that purchased from market research companies) or indirect in terms of the management time needed to gather it. Information is a resource that must be managed. Even if managers are willing to accept the cost involved, they can do so only if they know what information is available and where it is. The consultant can offer the small business manager a service in providing information that can help the business. However, this is only the start of the consultant's service. Decisions are not made on the basis of hard data alone. The consultant will add value by analysing and presenting information in a way that enables the business manager to make effective decisions. Analytical skills considered in Part Two are therefore needed.

1.10 Provision of specialist expertise

Managers can be generalists without particular expertise in specific management disciplines.

The demands of managing a small business are such that managers cannot afford to specialise in a narrow area of management such as marketing, operations or finance. They must do all these things at once and so at times they need to seek the advice of people with specialist knowledge.

Some important areas of management that can benefit from the insights and ideas of a specialist are: business strategy, marketing strategy development, marketing research, new product development programmes, developing proposals for financial support, information systems development, planning exporting and international marketing. Projects such as these benefit from the application of technical knowledge and an ability to use specialist analysis techniques. Rather than having to learn these themselves managers will often call upon the support of consultants. The key to successful consulting in this area is not to make decisions on behalf of the manager but to *help* the manager in making their own. It is their business; they have a detailed knowledge of what it is about and know what it aims to achieve. This knowledge of the business is much greater than any the consultant can develop in the short time he or she will be working with the business. The consultant adds value by bringing along a 'tool-kit' of conceptual frameworks and idea-generating models that can be used to make sense of the information and knowledge the manager already has. This then enables the manager to make better decisions. The management of projects involving the provision of specialist expertise will be discussed further in Chapter 2.

1.11 Provision of a new perspective

The consultant will add value by helping the manager to step back from a problem, to see it in a different way and to identify new means to its solution.

Managers are not decision-making automata. They are human beings who must analyse complex environments, use well-developed but necessarily limited cognitive skills and then make decisions in the face of uncertainty. Managers use 'cognitive maps', 'mind-sets' or 'dominant logics' through which they see their managerial world. These act to focus the manager's attention on certain aspects of their environment, select particular facts as relevant, link causes to effects and then suggest courses of action. Such cognitive schemes are not rational decision-making devices. They manifest themselves as the manager's interests, priorities, prejudices and judgement. They become established and resist change. They determine the way managers see their organisations and competitors, and they can have a bearing on the way joint ventures are managed. In a study of what he refers to as 'groupthink', Irvin Janis (1982) examined in great depth decisions by US presidents and close advisory groups that led to far-reaching policy errors in international affairs. He concluded that seven defects in decision making can arise when a group becomes over-coherent and begins to share expectations and norms:

- The group's considerations are limited to a narrow range of options – possibilities outside this set are rejected out of hand or not considered at all.
- The initial objectives to be fulfilled by the course of action are not reviewed or challenged.
- Newly discovered risks are not used to challenge the initially preferred course of action.
- Courses of action initially rejected by the group are not reconsidered in the light of new information.
- The experience and expertise of external experts are not sought or considered.
- When new information comes to light, the group emphasises and prioritises information that backs its initial hypotheses and ignores information that contradicts them – this is sometimes referred to as a 'myside bias'.
- The group spends little time considering how bureaucratic inertia or organisational resistance might inhibit the implementation of chosen policies.

While Janis's examples are drawn from political decision making, their relevance to organisational decision making in general is not in doubt. The effective consultant should be aware of these factors and be prepared to challenge group thinking. Managers limit their problem-solving ability because they often get too close to an issue, seeing it only in terms of their existing expectations, understanding and 'way of doing things'. Indeed, the consultant should ultimately aim to help managers see 'problems' really as opportunities to do things differently and perhaps better.

To do this the consultant may simply offer a fresh mind to an issue. Better still, the consultant can contribute some conceptual frameworks that open up thinking. Consultants can also offer support in helping individuals and groups become more innovative in their thinking by using the creativity techniques described in Chapter 9.

1.12   Provision of support for internal arguments

> **The consultant is responsible for delivering findings and advice to individuals and must be sensitive to the interests of those individuals and their objectives.**

Managers do not always agree with each other. Disagreements arise over a wide range of issues. Conflicts of opinion take a variety of forms. They range from open, honest exploration of different options to often quite nefarious political intriguing. They can be seen as a refreshing opening of possibilities or they may lead to smouldering resentment. A manager may be tempted to use a consultant not so much to provide an impartial view but to back up his or her position in a debate. How should a consultant react to being used in this way?

The first thing to note is that the existence of different perspectives and a tolerance of dissent that allows them to be expressed are healthy. Managers should be paid to think and express themselves and must be free to do so. In a competitive environment (in which ideas compete for resources) they should also be free to marshal whatever resources they can to make their case. This can include external consultants. A consultant must recognise that they are employed not by a company in the abstract but rather by *individuals* within a company. The decision to use consultants is made by a group or 'decision-making unit' within the business. This may involve supporting them in internal debates. However, the consultant must be careful.

If the consultant is too obviously in the camp of a particular manager, his or her impartiality will be impaired. Other management groups may become suspicious and will find grounds on which to reject the consultant's advice. If the consultant is seen to be twisting facts to fit a particular position, his or her credibility will be damaged.

A few useful ground rules are as follows:

- Understand the 'politics' of the consulting exercise.
- Be sensitive as to who is supporting different positions in the organisation.
- Recognise who will benefit and who will lose from the different options under discussion.
- Make sure the objectives of the consulting exercise are clear and in the open.
- Make sure any information used can be legitimated and any analysis undertaken justified.
- Build rapport with the client and be honest with the client about the strengths and weaknesses of their argument.
- Introduce and explore options which reconcile different positions in a win–win way.
- Provide the client manager with information and insights but allow him or her to make a particular case within the business by themselves.
- If put in a position where credibility might be lost, remind the manager that a loss of impartiality and credibility will defeat the point of using independent consultants in the first place!

1.13   Provision of support for gaining a critical resource

The consultant can offer the client valuable support in gaining the resources it needs.

An organisation must attract resources in order to survive. One of the manager's most critical functions is attracting resources on behalf of the firm. Some important resources for the business include:

- the goodwill of customers;
- capital from investors;

- capital from government support agencies;
- people with particular skills and knowledge;
- specialist materials, equipment and services.

Key tasks involve identifying who can supply the particular resources, how they might be contacted and the issues involved in working with them. The consultant can be particularly valuable by working with the client and developing a communication strategy, which helps the business to be successful in its approach to suppliers of critical resources.

Gaining the goodwill of customers is the function of marketing in its broadest sense. While it may be argued that this should be a central part of the business's competences, the consultant can assist in the developing of marketing plans, communication strategies and promotional campaigns.

People, especially those with special knowledge and skills, are a critical – if not *the* critical – resource for businesses. Consultants can add much value by advising a business on its people requirements, developing an understanding of the market for such people and developing advertisements to attract them. The consultant may also advise on the interview and selection procedures. A business may have identified suppliers of the materials and services it needs to undertake its activities. It is increasingly recognised that a business can improve its performance by actively *reverse marketing* itself to suppliers. This ensures that suppliers are aware of the business's needs and are responsive to them. It may, for example, encourage suppliers to innovate and make their offerings more suited to the buyer's requirements. This demands communication with both existing and potential suppliers, a process a consultant can assist greatly.

Many businesses will benefit from further cash injection. Different stages of growth create different capital requirements. An important type of consulting activity is the assistance given in helping businesses gain the support of investors such as banks and venture capitalists. This involves developing a picture of the potential of the firm and why it might offer an attractive investment opportunity, identifying suitable investment organisations, preparing a business plan and even formally presenting it.

1.14   Facilitating organisational change

> The consultant must be aware of the human dimensions to the change they are advocating and be competent in addressing the issues it creates.

All organisations are undergoing change all the time. Sometimes this is a 'natural' response to the internal dynamics of organisational growth. At other times it may be in response to an external impetus or shock that forces the organisation to modify the way in which it does things. All of the types of project above may, if they are to be implemented successfully, demand some degree of change in the structures and operating practices of the business. They may also demand that managers change their roles and responsibilities.

Change usually meets resistance. Managers, like most human beings, tend to be conservative when it comes to altering the way things are done. This is only to be expected. Although change may offer new possibilities, it also presents uncertainties. It is only natural that managers try to hold on to what they know to be reliable and rewarding. How can they be certain that a different future will offer the satisfactions achieved at present? Are the changes in their best interest? Even if change *seems* to offer the possibility of greater satisfaction, what are the risks? What happens if the manager is dissatisfied with the outcomes? What 'insurance' against unwanted consequences can they call on? It is concerns such as these which can lead to distrust of consultants operating in a business. The effective management of organisational change demands that these questions be addressed. Sometimes organisations call for change as the primary goal of the consulting exercise. In response to this, *change management* has developed as a specialist consulting area. More often, though, change management is required as a subsidiary area in order to effect the implementation of more specific organisational projects, such as business expansion or structural reorganisation.

Team discussion points

1 Do the external and the internal consultant add value in different ways?

2 How might the client/employer's expectations of how they add value differ?

3 How might specialisation of roles within the consulting team influence the way in which it might add value for the client?

4 Consider the way in which your team is adding value for your client based on the six platforms for value addition discussed above.

Summary of key ideas

- Consulting is a special type of management activity.
- The consultant can be understood to provide ten types of managerial roles to the client business. These are placed into three groups:
  - the interpersonal (featuring the roles of the figurehead, the liaison and the leader);
  - the informational (featuring the roles of the monitor, the disseminator and the spokesperson);
  - the decisional (featuring the roles of the entrepreneur, the disturbance handler, the resource allocator and the negotiator).
- The consultant must integrate these roles with those already operating in the client business. This can happen in one of five ways:
  - supplementary (adding extra skills to those already present);
  - complementary (adding a missing role);
  - differentiating (helping managers distinguish roles among themselves);
  - integrating (helping managers build a new order of roles and individual responsibilities);
  - enhancing (helping managers make their existing roles more effective).
- The consultant must operate with four levels of managerial responsibility. These are:
  - economic (a responsibility to ensure that the projects advocated are in the best interests of the client business);

- legal (a responsibility to ensure that projects operate within the law);
- moral (a responsibility to ensure that project outcomes meet with the moral and ethical expectations of the client);
- discretionary (the right of the consultant to select or reject projects on the basis of personal ethical considerations).

- Consultants must be able to do something for a business that it is unable to do for itself.
- This must genuinely offer new value to the client business.
- Businesses fail due to inadequacies in their business model, problems (including neglect) relating to their markets and customers, poor cash and financial management, ineffective planning and performance monitoring, and inefficient processes – but mainly through the failings of top management.
- Important areas of value addition include the provision of:
  - information;
  - specialist expertise;
  - a new and innovative perspective;
  - support for internal arguments;
  - support in gaining critical resources such as capital, people or productive factors;
  - driving organisational change.
- Many consulting projects involve a combination of a number of these elements.
- The consultant must constantly communicate to the client the new value he or she is creating through these outputs.

Key reading

Mintzberg, H. (2011) *Managing*. Harlow, Essex: Financial Times Prentice Hall.

Newton, R. (2010) *The Management Consultant: Mastering the Art of Consultancy*. Harlow, Essex: Financial Times Prentice Hall.

Further reading

Carroll, A. (1979) 'A three-dimensional model of corporate performance', *Academy of Management Review*, 4 (4), 497–505.

Champion, D., Kiel, D. and McLendon, J. (1990) 'Choosing a consulting role', *Training and Development Journal*, Feb. 1990.

Cornwall, C. (date unknown) 'The entrepreneurial mind', Nashville, TN: Belmont University.

Drucker, P.F. (2007) *The Practice of Management* (2nd rev. edn). Oxford: Butterworth-Heinemann.

Golembiewski, R.T. (ed.) (2000) *Handbook of Organizational Consultation* (2nd edn). New York: Marcell Decker.

Holland, R. (1998) 'Planning against a business failure', ADC Info. No. 24 Paper, University of Tennessee.

Janis, I.L. (1982) *Groupthink*. Boston, MA: Houghton Mifflin Company.

Lavinsky, D. (2008) 'The 6 untold reasons why businesses fail'. www.growthink.com/content/6-untold-reasons-why-businesses-fail [accessed 24 November 2015]

Lundberg, C.C. (1997) 'Towards a general model of consultancy', *Journal of Organisational Change Management*, 10 (3), 193–201.

Maister D.H., Galford R., Green C.W. (2002) *The Trusted Advisor*. London: Simon and Schuster.

Mason, Moya K. (2011) 'What causes small businesses to fail', www.moyak.com/papers/small-business-failure.html [accessed 24 November 2015]

O'Shea, J. and Madigan, C. (1999) *Dangerous Company* (2nd edn). Boston MA: Nicholas Brealey Publishing.

Schein, E.H. (1997) 'The concept of "client" from a process consultation perspective: a guide for change agents', *Journal of Organizational Change Management*, 10 (3), 202–216.

Schein, E.H. (1987) *Process Consultation*, Vol. II. Reading, MA: Addison-Wesley.

Schein, E.H. (1988) *Process Consultation*, Vol. I (revised edn). Reading, MA: Addison-Wesley.

Schein, E.H. (2010) *Organizational Culture and Leadership* (4th edn). San Francisco, CA: Jossey-Bass.

Van de Ven, A.H. and Drazin, R. (1985) 'The concept of fit in contingency theory', *Research of Organizational Behaviour*, 7, 333–365.

Case exercise

Go Global

Go Global was a tour operator founded by Dirk Schuyster and a couple of partners in the early 1990s. All three of them had learnt their trade with one of the UK's premier tour firms, but they believed they could prosper rather more if they took their business and customer knowledge with them and set up on their own.

They had identified a valid point of difference. By advertising in the regional press, collecting their passengers from locations close to their homes and using regional embarkation points they could offer a more customer-friendly service than larger, traditional operators. Their business aimed to be low cost and was targeted at customers who were retired or on lower incomes – customers who may not have travelled frequently, did not have high service expectations and who wanted someone else to do the planning and organisation for them. 'Your holiday begins from the moment you board our coach', claimed the Go Global brochures. Destinations included proven favourites such as the Dutch bulb fields, the Channel Islands, the Italian lakes and German Christmas markets. Tours were of short duration with accommodation in low-cost, family-run hotels.

Schuyster and his partners set up business in rented premises in Epping, recruiting local Essex staff. Go Global's business model proved successful. There was a real excitement, commitment and sense of teamwork as the business grew, new tour destinations were added and customer numbers steadily increased. Schuyster in particular took a very close interest in all aspects of the company's operations, including the tour details, the choice of regional titles in which they advertised and the brochure copy.

But as the business grew, things started to change. In a boardroom coup Schuyster insisted that his partners resign. Their settlement cost the business £3 million. He then extended the business's operations into additional market sectors such as ocean cruises, flights and long-haul destinations where established competitors were very strong. The business flourished and Schuyster relocated into large new premises near Chelmsford that he had bought at a cost of £8 million. To manage the increasing scale and complexity of his business he recruited senior managers from other tour operators, at least two of which had collapsed. The fact that they were associated with failed operations did not concern Schuyster: they would be grateful to be employed by him and could be relied upon to comply with his wishes.

In the office, staff felt increasingly apprehensive about Schuyster and his personal style. A large, burly individual, he was frightening when angered and micro-managed the business obsessively. He could be abusive towards staff, manhandled and made lewd comments about female employees who were too frightened to complain and coerced them into falsifying records. He talked about them as 'people I pay' rather than team members whose services and skills he needed to purchase. His style was to control through fear and intimidation. A compensation of £45,000 had to be paid to a director to dissuade her from prosecuting him for sexist abuse. Yet the personal favourites he had recruited were spared such conduct and at the annual staff parties it was Schuyster who led the horseplay and merry-making.

Schuyster's aggressive behaviour also extended to customers and competitors. On one occasion he strode from his personalised BMW on to a quayside and harangued a group of complaining passengers who had suffered an ocean cruise in appalling weather, accusing them of plotting against him. He described his customers as 'horrid little people' and happily admitted he would never stay at the types of hotel into which they were booked, let alone go on one of his own holidays. Complaints were contemptuously dismissed with the comment 'there are plenty more little punters where they came from'. When competitors went out of business' he rubbed his hands with glee and telephoned his suppliers to ensure they knew.

Thus as Go Global was prospering and was winning accolades for its growth, including being featured as a Local Business of the Year, the methods its belligerent and increasingly dysfunctional owner was employing were starting to put the company at risk. The travel industry is incestuous and prone to gossip, so people were well aware of Schuyster's behaviour and he started to make enemies. A takeover offer came when the company was at the height of its success, but he rejected it out of hand. By now Schuyster was also drawing large sums of money out of the business as personal loans to buy property in Chingford and to fund the tasteless and extravagant lifestyle of his estranged wife Cheryl. This was against the advice of his finance director as well as his non-executive chairman, a wealthy former school friend with no travel industry experience whom he had asked to take on the role. Schuyster's view was that he could do as he liked, as he was the sole shareholder. Board meetings became screaming sessions at which Schuyster insisted he was in the right: he would not listen to opinions or advice he did not like.

Eventually his cavalier methods and conviction of his infallibility brought him one enemy too many. He cancelled a substantial contract with a cruise ship owner, who successfully sued him for several millions in compensation. This, together with the money Schuyster had taken out of the business, put an intolerable strain on the cash flow. In desperation he doubled the salary he was drawing and re-mortgaged his home and the Chingford properties, but the banks would not help him. On Good Friday 2002 the business went into administration. 'Go Global Goes Gurgle!' trumpeted the tabloids as 30,000 holidaymakers lost their money and suppliers and hoteliers were left being owed millions. The entire staff lost their jobs. Schuyster took Cheryl and the family away to a pre-arranged luxury holiday in the Seychelles, but on his return he defaulted on his loans, the business went into receivership and in due course he was declared bankrupt.

It could all have been so different. It could all have been so much happier.

1 How many of the common causes of business failure can you identify in the Go Global case?

2 Could they have been avoided – and if so, how?

3 If you had been hired as a consultant by Dirk Schuyster, how would you have gone about giving him advice on his operation?

Chapter 2

Consulting: the wider context and consulting process

Success is a science; if you have the conditions, you get the result.

Oscar Wilde

> ## Learning outcomes
>
> The learning outcomes from this chapter are to:
>
> - recognise the types of projects consultants are called upon to undertake within the business environment;
>
> - appreciate the ways in which those projects add value;
>
> - recognise the sequence of activities that characterise the typical consulting project;
>
> - appreciate the management issues that each of these stages presents to the consultant;
>
> - understand how the challenges of each stage may be approached to ensure the success of the consulting project.

In the previous chapter we looked at what management consulting actually is and how it adds value for the client. Now we relate it to the firm's lifecycle and main processes to show how a consultant can identify, sell and implement a successful consulting project. There is inevitably much overlap with the study of how businesses operate and students should integrate their knowledge of this while thinking about their consulting project. Consulting projects are not done as an esoteric exercise. They are about the very real issues that businesses face. The previous discussion about the management role of consultants and the ways in which they add value makes it clear that the challenges consultants face, are as wide as management itself. However, when consultants are called in to undertake work on behalf of a business, it is with a specific project in mind. If it is not, then the consultant should be worried!

Many large consulting firms, for example McKinsey, are typically split into 'industry' and 'functional' practices. The aim of this is to offer deep knowledge of the industry in which a potential client operates, together with a wide experience of consulting in a particular business function. It also has the advantage of ensuring that the consulting team, with a mix from both sides, offers both the best expertise and enough 'distance' to remain objective. However, for many smaller consulting firms and especially independents, it is not possible to put together such a team and they have to decide where they want to position themselves (this is discussed further in Section 3.5). If their main experience is within one industry, then they need to seek work in functional areas where this is more important: interim management being an example. However, if they have a lot of experience in a particular function, say finance or marketing research where technical knowledge is key, then industry experience is less critical. There are no hard and fast rules on this balance between industry and technical knowledge. The most important thing is that the client has confidence in your ability to successfully undertake the assignment.

2.1 Lifecycle of a business and the role of consulting

When assessing a new consulting proposal, consider lifecycle stage and parts of the business to focus on.

Businesses go through a lifecycle from their inception, beginning with the start-up phase through ultimately to its exit from the market (or rebirth into another market). There has been much discussion (Levie and Lichtenstein, 2010) about the way businesses grow as they move through this lifecycle and whether indeed the path is linear. However, it is useful when considering a consulting project to understand where a business may be in terms of its lifecycle and what issues may be involved as a result. Using Greiner's model, that he developed in 1972 and revised in 1998, we can build a simple framework to explore this (Table 2.1).

The framework represents represents a linear model i.e. firms progress smoothly through the stages or die. Churchill and Lewis (1983) were among the first to think about the consequences of businesses not completely overcoming the crises they faced. They showed that as firms moved through the lifecycle, they had more options than just selling the business or folding, if they failed to progress from Stage 1 and 2. This also provides some more opportunities for consultants to help the business such as:

- In Stage 3 – growth strategies for current business models, looking for partners or buyers or adapting the business by finding new markets
- In Stage 4 – adapting the business model for new markets or looking for buyers for the firm and helping with the sales process

	Stage 1 - Creativity	Stage 2 - Direction	Stage 3 - Delegation	Stage 4 - Co-ordination	Stage 5 - Collaboration
Stage of lifecycle	Start-up	Rapid growth/ Survival	Growth/ Establishment	Consolidation	Maturity
Crises	Leadership (People)	Autonomy (Systems)	Control (People & Systems)	Red tape (People & Systems)	Personnel fatigue (People)
Possible consulting projects	Identify current skill shortages	Develop systems for delegation	Build networks to improve control	Implement new ways of working	Focus on team work and behavioural skills

31

A more recent work by Furlan and Grandinetti (2011) has looked at the types of growth that a firm can experience:

- Size (increasing physical capacity through internal investment or acquisition)
- Relationship (improving links with suppliers, customers, partners and other external organisations)
- Capability (working 'smarter' through better systems and training of workforce)

Analysing the business's opportunities for growth in this way may also offer clarity on the consulting project required.

2.2   Management consulting: strategic processes of a business

Management consulting looks at the strategic processes of a firm including strategy, sales, marketing, marketing research, business development and finance (see Figure 2.1). For many this would be the classic view of consulting. It is in this manner that the large, well-known firms such as Bain & Company operate.

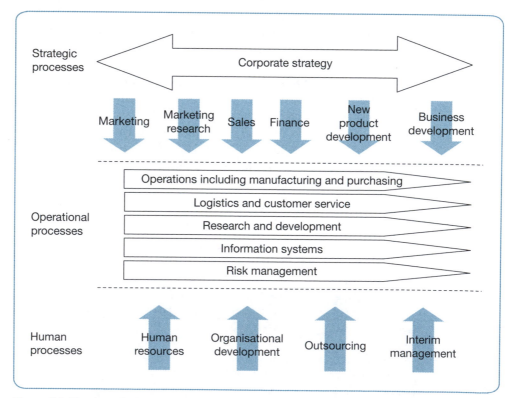

Figure 2.1 Firm's main processes

Strategy

One of the broadest project types is working with a firm on the development of its strategy, either at a corporate level, or at a business unit level, the latter being sometimes referred to as 'business planning' or 'business development'. A new consulting brief is likely to have been triggered by what Johnson et al. (2014) refer to as 'intended strategy development', that is, a planned change in strategic direction by a firm. A project of this type is a great opportunity. It offers the consultant a broad remit to contribute to the development of the business. However, some care is called for in interpretation. The first task the consultant faces is to establish exactly what the client wants from a 'strategy' project. Sometimes the client has something specific in mind, as a result of a detailed strategic planning exercise, but often not. Common outcomes desired from such assignments include:

- growth of the business within its core markets by capitalising on market growth or market share increase;
- expansion of the business into new market sectors;
- development of new products;
- increasing profits through cost-reduction programmes;
- internal structural reorganisations.

The client may simply state that he or she wants to 'grow the business'. If this is so then the consultant will need to step back, evaluate the possible options for growth and propose the best path to the client, bearing in mind the lifecycle stage that the business is at (see Section 2.1). At this stage many 'strategy' projects resolve themselves into one or more of the project types listed above. An effective consultant can use the project proposal to establish exactly what the client wants and to manage his or her expectations about what can realistically be achieved. The role that a consultant can play in a strategy assignment can vary from challenging existing strategic issues, providing 'best practice' from knowledge derived from their experience on strategic choices to helping implement strategic change. On a positive note, strategy consulting assignments are prized by consultants as they are often used as a 'foot in the door' to develop a longer working relationship with clients. However, they are also the most visible and people tend to remember the failures rather than the successes, which can easily tarnish the reputation of a consulting company.

Marketing research

Marketing research is the process through which managers discover the nature of the competitive environment in which they are operating. The objective of marketing research is to obtain information that managers can use to support their decision making. Information reduces risk and enables managers to dedicate valuable resources in a more reliable way. Marketing research falls into two types based on the sort of questions it aims to answer and the source of the answers. First there is *primary research*, which is information collected for the specific project. This is further subdivided as follows:

- *Quantitative research* provides answers to questions when those answers need to be expressed in statistical or numerical form. It aims to answer the 'how much, how often and how many' questions that managers pose.

- *Qualitative research* provides answers to questions that do not demand a quantified answer. It provides the insights that answer managers' 'who, what and why' questions.

Secondary research is based on information that has been collated earlier for reasons other than the project at hand. It takes the form of existing reports, articles and commentaries that just prove to be relevant to the project. At one level it is 'market intelligence': an ongoing review of articles, reports and customer gossip about a market. At another level it might be an in-depth study collating the opinions of managers across an industry or functional area.

Both types of research can demand the use of complex statistical techniques or sophisticated psychometric methodologies to develop a complete picture. At this level marketing research demands a high degree of expertise on the part of the researcher. Good consultants recognise their limitations. They know when it is time to call in the expert marketing researcher. This does not mean they cannot add value for the client. While marketing research specialists are often used to undertake the work, a consultant can develop a brief for a professional marketing research exercise and can help the client understand what the results mean.

Marketing

Marketing research is a powerful approach to identifying business opportunities. Exploiting them, though, requires a *marketing strategy* and a *marketing plan*. A marketing strategy defines the approach the business will take in order to get the customers' attention and critically get them to spend their money on the business's products or services. The marketing mix dictates the key elements of a marketing strategy. The marketing strategy will be built on the answers to the following questions:

- What products do customers want from a sector's producers?
- In what way are competitors failing to provide these products?
- What price are customers expecting or willing to pay?
- What channels are available for getting the product to the customer?
- Who might be the partners in the distribution process?
- How might they be approached?
- In what ways can customers be informed that the product is available?
- How can the customers' interest be stimulated through promotion?

In developing a marketing strategy the consultant is answering these questions. Often, getting the answers will demand the contribution of experts such as marketing researchers and communication specialists. If this is the case the consultant can be involved in a number of ways. He or she might simply be asked to highlight these needs so that the client can pick up the project. Alternatively, he or she may be invited in to support the client in working with such experts. In some cases, the client may give the consultant complete control and have him or her subcontract work with specialists as an integral part of the consulting project. Implementing a marketing strategy (i.e. a marketing plan) involves a range of activities. The implementation can resolve itself into the product development, promotional and sales activity projects detailed below. Clearly, an effective, well-presented marketing strategy project creates follow-up opportunities for the consultant.

The key part of the marketing plan is the promotional campaign. This is any programme of activities dedicated to informing customers about a product, stimulating their interest and encouraging purchase. Examples include advertising and public relations campaigns, web marketing, social media, sales drives, direct mailings, exhibitions and in-store demonstrations. Though each of these approaches is different, the consultant faces a common profile of tasks when developing such campaigns. The key questions the client will be asking will be:

- What methods will prove to be cost effective?
- What will be the mechanics of running the campaign?
- How can it be monitored?

The consultant must develop an understanding of how much it will cost, using each technique available, to contact a potential customer, the impact each is likely to have on the potential customer, the likelihood that they will make a purchase, how much they will spend if they do and over what period. A comparison of the techniques can then be made which, in light of the client's promotional objectives and available budget, provides the basis for designing an effective promotional plan.

Sales

For many businesses, especially small and medium-sized ones, the sales team is the primary promotional tool. Detailed and thoughtful planning of sales force activity is a process which offers real returns. Some of the projects that a consultant might be asked to look at include the following:

- overall organisation of the team to optimise the resources available, based on the customers' geographical spread;
- sales team training in order to be more effective; for instance, focusing on customer service rather than 'short-term' sales;
- other activities that a sales team could undertake, such as obtaining market intelligence while out selling and the use of their knowledge of customers to contribute more directly to new product development;
- sales team motivation and rewards that can be used to align the thrust of the sales with the firm's overall strategic objectives;
- planning sales campaigns for either ongoing activity or short-term periods of special activity to support, say, a new product launch, the firm's entry into a new geographic area or a move into a new customer sector. The important decision elements of a sales campaign include:
  - Which members of the sales force will be involved?
  - What products will be given priority?
  - Which customers will be targeted?

- In what geographic area?
- The sales literature that will be used.
- The special prices and deals that can be used to motivate purchase.
- Bonuses and rewards for sales performance.
- Other marketing and PR activity that will support the sales drive.

The decision about each of these elements will affect not only the cost of the promotion but also its overall success. Clearly, there is an opportunity for the consultant to add considerable value here, through their experience with other organisations.

New product development

It is a business's products (which can include services as well as tangible products) that the customer ultimately buys. A well-designed product that addresses the customer's needs in an effective manner is only part of a business success story but it is an *essential* part. New product development (NPD) represents a complex project that draws in most, if not all, of the firm's functions. Research and development, marketing and sales, production, purchasing and human resources will all be called upon to make a contribution. New product development is often undertaken by interdisciplinary teams, which cut across departmental boundaries. Where the costs of NPD are relatively high such as in the pharmaceutical or high-tech industries, firms often look to external organisations. The consultant can offer support to the new product development programme in a number of ways. The most important include:

- Identifying new products from third parties and negotiating a licence arrangement or takeover of firm with new product;
- ensuring the firm's new product development process is as efficient as possible (set against benchmarks of other leading companies);
- understanding the customer's needs through marketing research;
- technical advice on product development;
- identifying and working with suppliers of critical components;
- development of marketing and PR campaigns to support the launch;
- developing promotion campaigns to get retailers or distributors on board;
- financial planning and evaluation of the return on new product investment.

The consultant may also be invited in to facilitate change management programmes designed to integrate the new product development team and enhance its performance.

Finance

Businesses often need injections of capital. New start-ups and high-growth businesses in particular need funds – in addition to those provided by customers – in order to ensure they reach their potential. Investment capital can be obtained from a number of sources. Banks, 'investment angels' (wealthy individuals) and venture capital companies are important to new and high-growth businesses, with private equity houses offering finance to all sectors. Government grants may be available to small businesses in some areas. More mature firms can obtain funds from stock market flotations. Consultants are often called in to offer advice in four critical areas:

- evaluation of the business's investment needs;
- identification of funding providers and how they might be contacted;
- developing an understanding of the criteria employed by funding providers and how these might be addressed;
- developing communications with funding providers, particularly in relation to proposals and business plans.

Though general in form, these project areas will vary in their details according to the business and the fund provider it is approaching. Potential investors such as private equity houses also use consultants to conduct 'commercial due diligence' on a proposed purchase. Here the consultant's specialist knowledge of the market sector will help the potential investor to answer some of their key questions:

- What is the market situation for this company, i.e. what are the growth prospects?
- What is the competitive arena in which the company finds itself and how is this likely to change?
- Is the business plan put forward by the proposed new management team credible in light of the above?
- In particular are the forecasts for sales and profits given by the new team realistic?
- Will I get the required return on my investment when I come to exit (sell) in the required timeframe (typically five years)?

> A consultant can add value by helping the business improve how it undertakes its strategic processes.

2.3 'Hard' side consulting: operational processes of a business

Whilst it is evident that a successful business needs good strategic processes, it also requires well-run operational processes (see Figure 2.1). Products or services need to be delivered correctly and on time to the customers in order for the business to remain competitive. As business becomes more complex in terms of manufacturing and distribution, there are more areas where the process may fail or be suboptimal. This is where consultants have helped businesses for a long time, starting with the first consultancy, Arthur D. Little, in the late nineteenth century. A.D. Little's mission was to help firms to benefit from the new technologies available to the businesses of the time, notably the railway for transport and the telegraph for communication. While new technologies, particularly IT, continue to change the way firms can operate, consultants can look at the operational processes of a business and recommend (and often implement) better ways of working.

Operations management

Consulting in the area of operations management often involves large complex assignments engaging a variety of disciplines including manufacturing, logistics (distribution of products or services), purchasing (the buying in of raw materials and services) and customer service. Consultants can help answer the following questions that a business may pose:

- Where, in the manufacturing process, do most of my products fail (or are rejected on quality grounds, i.e. quality bottlenecks) and how can I rectify it?
- Can my manufacturing process be ordered in a better way to improve productivity (i.e. more products delivered quicker or at lower cost)?
- Why some of my manufacturing are lines more efficient than others and can I raise all of them to the standard of the best?
- Is there a more cost-effective way to deliver products to customers?
- Can I buy my raw materials more cost effectively and reduce waste?
- How can I improve customer service, so customer retention is increased?

Answers to the above offer a platform for very tangible consulting projects where outputs can be measured: the percentage of products rejected on quality grounds or the number of customers retained over a defined period.

> Many of today's popular consulting tools, such as Six Sigma's DMAIC process (see Chapter 5), have been developed from operations management projects.

Information technology management

Managers need information if they are to make good decisions. They need information on both the business's external situation (its competitive environment) and its internal state. Management information systems aim to collect and organise such information and present it to managers in a usable form. The consultant can add value, in developing an understanding of the information needs of the business, the way in which information flows around the organisation and the competitive advantage that might be gained through investment in IT. Management information is not just about managers *having* information; it is about them *using* it effectively.

One example of the above is customer relationship management or CRM systems. Firms that have a large number of customers are looking for ways to improve the relationship that they have with individual customers. Tesco in the UK, for example, with its Clubcard system, has been very successful in identifying customer trends from the data they collect every time one of the Clubcard holders makes a purchase. It helps them decide on the range of products to be stocked in an individual store, for instance. It also enables them to send out targeted mailings to customers based on historic purchases; for example, those who have bought dog food in the past could be sent a voucher for a new range of treats for dogs. Many believe this is a much more cost-effective way to target potential customers than the traditional methods of, say, TV or press advertising. Consultants have an important role here as they can:

- Look at the process by which data is collected and analysed, as this is critical to make it useful.
- Interpret the findings of the analysis and recommend how the data should be used for targeting.
- Look at measures to evaluate how well the CRM system is performing in terms of increased sales and profits.

Risk management

While firms take the health and safety of their workers very seriously, in today's world there are many other risks that have be managed. The Institute of Risk Management has defined four main areas: financial, strategic, operational and hazard (see Figure 2.2).

Companies providing a public service (e.g. transport, leisure facilities, retail outlets or products consumed by the public) also have to consider risks to their customers either from accidents or, increasingly, from deliberate sabotage. A consultant can help a firm assess the likelihood of certain events happening and put in place contingency plans to deal with them. For publicly quoted companies (those whose shares are traded on the stock exchange), there are risks associated with 'corporate governance', i.e. the way in

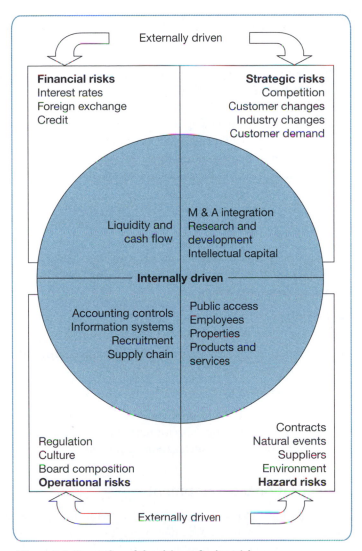

Figure 2.2 **Examples of the drivers for key risks**

Source: The Institute of Risk Management. *A Risk Management Standard* © AIRMIC, ALARM, IRM 2002. Reproduced with permission.

which the firm operates and specifically how it reports information to its shareholders. There have been many high-profile cases, most notably Enron in the US, that have highlighted the issues associated with poor (or indeed illegal) corporate governance. Consultants can help firms either prior to a flotation (launching of shares on the stock exchange) or when the rules change (i.e. post-Enron) to ensure they have the appropriate systems in place.

> Consultants add value by helping optimise the firm's operational process through bringing outside expertise and perspective.

2.4 'Soft' side consulting: human processes of a business

Whilst both the strategic and operational processes are key in the functioning of a well-run business, most firms rely heavily on their human capital. In terms of consulting, this has often been regarded as the most difficult to quantify in terms of benefits to an organisation. However, that does not mean that it is not important and a good consultant in this area can be highly effective if the major issues of a company are around the actions of its people. In today's complex organisations, dysfunctional teams at any level can be highly destructive. The best consultants in any field are also able to understand the human dynamics of a project. This is discussed further in Chapter 7.

Human resources

Attracting the right sort of people to contribute to the business is an important challenge managers must address, especially those in high-growth businesses. A consultant can be of value in this area in several ways:

- assessing the firm's human resource requirement and identifying skill and knowledge gaps, both currently and predicting for the future;
- developing assessment criteria, interview procedures and, possibly, psychometric testing of candidates;
- advice on the reimbursement packages new recruits will expect.

Staff retention is equally important and consultants can advise firms on their human resources policies in terms of remuneration packages (pay, pensions, holiday and sickness benefits and other 'perks' such as company cars).

Organisational development

This is a long and established area for consulting, having begun in the early part of the twentieth century with advocates attempting to define the 'best' way to organise a workforce, just as machines could be ordered in the mass production era. Over the next hundred years, the ideas evolved as the notion that there was one optimal way to organise a firm was shown to be wrong. The situation that a firm found itself in was more relevant in determining its organisational structure. Consultants can:

- work with individuals as a personal coach to improve their ways of working and motivation levels;
- work with groups to improve their collective performance and productivity;
- look at the whole organisation to advise on its structure;
- discuss the organisational culture and its leadership styles.

In all of these it is the very fact that consultants are outsiders and so deemed to be 'neutral' that enables them to address issues which a boss or colleague may feel unable to do.

Organisational development projects can arise when the firm is facing a crisis of leadership (see Section 2.1). Many successful entrepreneurs want to sell their business but they are not only the owner but also the leader of the firm. The existing management team therefore operates with a very strong leader whose opinions are of major importance. When that leader decides to leave, the team can lack this strong focus and may find it difficult to carry on operating in the same way. Here a consultant can help the team assess their strengths and weaknesses and identify solutions to the problem. Perhaps they need another strong leader/owner or one of them could 'step up' to the post of leader: it would depend on the personalities involved.

Most firms have 'boards' made up of its legal directors plus often its senior managers. They fulfil an important management role and if a board is dysfunctional, this will have serious consequences for the ability of the firm to operate effectively. To resolve this, a consultant may be called in to look at the reasons why the board is not functionally effective and offer solutions. Common symptoms of the former are:

- not being able to see 'the big picture' and/or getting bogged down in detail;
- not ensuring that the management plans are being carried out effectively;
- not challenging the management in their growth plans and pushing forward the business;
- not understanding the risks the business faces and allowing the organisation to make serious mistakes.

The cause of the above may lie in the make-up of the team. Are they the right people in the right roles? Are they communicating effectively with one another? This is sometimes an issue with multicultural teams. Are there gaps, for example, not enough independent directors (non-executives) to balance the executive directors? Only once a consultant has got to the bottom of these issues, can he or she make a recommendation. It will be one of the hardest tasks that a consultant may face, as it will involve senior people being critically evaluated and some may even lose their position as a result. Some very large egos could be crushed and such an assignment is not for the faint-hearted!

Interim management

Interim managers can either undertake a change programme or project, or take on a specified role that had been filled by a permanent employee. How does an interim manager differ from a management consultant? It is sometimes difficult to differentiate between these two roles as the lines can be blurred and the task the same. A consultant usually, though, is an 'outsider' making recommendations to an organisation's management team whereas an interim manager has explicit responsibility to deliver as an employee would do. Firms would use interim managers for temporarily vacant positions either because a restructuring of the organisation has caused a gap or someone has left and a permanent replacement has not been found. They may also have the short-term requirement for a position relating to an internal project that cannot be filled by their existing personnel. Many management consultants are also interim managers and vice versa, as they need similar skills.

Outsourcing

This is a rapidly developing area for many businesses, where processes that tradition-ally have been done by the company themselves are given to another organisation to carry out. In 2014, the outsourcing market worldwide accounted for $104.6 billion (TPI Information Services Group). There are two main areas: ITO, or information technology outsourcing, and BPO, or business process outsourcing. The former became popular as information technology became more complex and the degree of skill required favoured specialists. They would effectively take over and run the IT processes of a company. The information technology outsourcing market in 2014 was estimated to be worth $76.1 bil-lion (ibid.).

Business process outsourcing covers all the areas outside IT. In 2014, the market for BPO was worth $28.5 billion (ibid.). The most common example is customer care centres that are often run by specialist call centre companies. However, many other business pro-cesses are now regularly conducted by third parties. These include many finance functions such as accounts, customer billing and cash management; human resource functions, e.g. management of employee records and recruitment, procurement or purchasing of goods and services and research and development. All are specialist functions and for many firms it is more cost effective for someone else to do them. Consultants working for outsourcing companies can offer added value by advising their clients on the best ways to carry out the processes based on their experience.

> Consulting involving 'human processes' is often the most demanding but can have the most impact.

2.5 Consulting to the non-profit and public sectors

In Europe, consulting to the public sectors accounted for 14 per cent of the total in 2012 and continued to be a dominant client sector in the United Kingdom and Ireland (FEACO Survey 2011–12). However, with the large-scale austerity packages in many countries and the cutback of government spending, this proportion has fallen from 20 per cent in 2009. Some government services have been transferred to the non-profit sector, largely charities that rely on public donations. They provide goods and services that our society believes should be provided without making a profit; for example, care of historical buildings and landscapes or the provision of housing for low-income people. Although they do not make a profit, the non-profit organisation does operate in the business world and so faces many similar challenges. So a consultant in the non-profit sector may find the actual work the same as in the profit sector, such as the identification of a strategy or delivery of a marketing plan, for example. However, there are a few specialist areas that a consultant may get involved with. The first is fundraising, which is where many of these organisations derive their income. Another may be the management of endowments and legacies that can critically affect the ability of the non-profit organisation to operate.

Consulting to the public sector or government organisations again has many similarities to the private (or profit) sector. The government is a major employer, particularly in healthcare, so many of the human consulting projects described in the section above are applicable. In addition, public sector projects such as urban regeneration also require the type of consulting skills described in the section above on operational processes. The main difference between consulting in the profit sector and for government is the financial aspect. As the key objectives of a public project do not include a profit target, the cost of managing a project can sometimes be difficult to handle. This is due to getting a balance between achieving the government's policy aims and getting the best value by keeping costs to a minimum. There is also the possibility of 'political interference' where projects are hampered by a change of government policy: large IT projects are particularly prone to this.

2.6   Overview of the consulting process

A consulting project will be successful only if the right actions are carried out in the right order. A client will not accept a solution to a problem he or she does not yet recognise exists. It is premature to decide on the best options for a business if no analysis of what that business is about has been carried out.

Most consulting projects go through nine stages. The process starts with an initial contact between the consultant and the client. This is followed by recognition that the consultant can help the business in some way and a project is initiated. In the third stage the consultant will suggest further investigation into and analysis of the issues facing the client's business before proposing a set of formal objectives that both should work towards. Fourthly, the consultant will then document those objectives in a formal proposal. This constitutes the 'contract' between the consultant and client. The fifth stage requires developing a project charter that supports this contract. The development of the project can only be undertaken on the basis of a sound understanding of the business and its context. The sixth stage of the project involves undertaking this analysis. This stage never really ends, as further analysis may be required as the project progresses, even in the final follow-up stage.

The seventh stage is the implementation of the project. This stage will demand further information gathering, evaluation of the business issues, analysis and evaluation of options and formulation of recommendations. When this is complete, the eighth stage involves

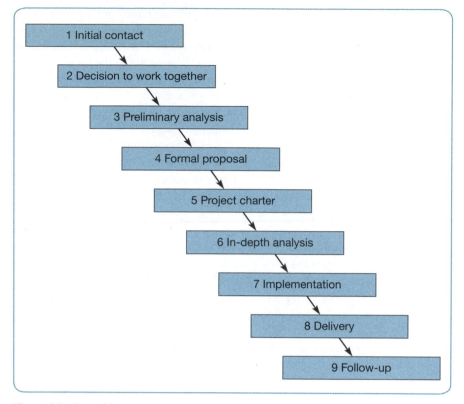

Figure 2.3 Consulting process

communicating those findings and recommendations back to the client in some way. This communication will aim to encourage and facilitate implementation. In the final stage, the consultant may maintain contact with the client if this can in some way benefit one or preferably both parties. This process is illustrated in Figure 2.3. The consultant's approach to each stage will differ depending on the nature of the consulting project and the client with whom he or she is working. Every successful consulting project achieves its aims because the consultant has managed each stage effectively.

> Every successful consulting project goes through a set process, the length and complexity of which is determined by the type of project being undertaken.

2.7 Initial contact and initiating the project

Consultants meet with potential clients in numerous different forums. In principle, there are four mechanisms by which the consultant and client meet and decide they should work together.

- The consultant and client meet in an impromptu way.
- The consultant proposes his or her services to a client.
- The client seeks out the services of a particular consultant.
- A third party brings the consultant and client together.

Business networks bring together people seeking ways to help each other. This is often an important forum for consultants to make contact and present what they have to offer. Business networks exist in and between business sectors. One of the most popular ways now to network is through social media sites such as LinkedIn. Professional bodies, such as the Chartered Management Institute set up conferences and seminars. Consultants, like any other business service providers, are responsible for promoting the service they offer to customers. This may be through professional bodies, such as the Institute of Consulting, which provide some endorsement for the service on offer and support its promotion. Consultants can also promote themselves via advertising, particularly in specialist industry publications or on their website. Direct marketing to potential clients may also be a useful tool. Clients may sometimes approach a consultant for advice. This may be in response to the consultant's promotional activities or be a result of recommendations from another satisfied customer.

The client is making the decision to invest in his or her business through buying the insights and advice of an outside expert. The consultant is deciding to offer his or her expertise to the client. This demands a considerable commitment and means the consultant cannot pursue other projects. Taking on a particular project represents an *opportunity cost* to the consultant. Project initiation may occur with both consultant and client sharing a clear understanding of what the client wants. Often the client is unclear as to specific objectives. He or she may just feel that things could be better with the business. In this case, the consultant must be adept at probing the client and getting him or her to reveal something about the business. Such probing must be undertaken with subtlety if it is not to be seen as obvious and invasive. This demands effective use of the questioning techniques detailed in Section 7.4.

Both client and consultant must be clear on exactly what is being initiated. It could be the entire project. It is more likely, though, that it is actually an invitation by the client to the consultant to make a *formal proposal* for the project (stage four of the process). This will certainly be the case if the consultant is being invited to make a proposal or pitch in competition with other consultants. Even if no competition is involved and the client is inviting the consultant to move straight on to the full project, an interim proposal is still a good idea. It is an effective means of managing the client's expectations about the project's outcomes. The actual initiation of the project can take a variety of forms. It may be a simple verbal agreement to go ahead. It may take the form of an informal note or letter. In other cases the project may be initiated by a formal and detailed contract. The formality of the initiation will reflect the interests of both client and consultant and will depend on the following points.

How well the consultant and client know each other

If the consultant and client know each other very well, the project can be initiated with a low degree of formality. If there is a good deal of trust between both parties to the exercise, then both will rely on the fact that the details of the project can be adjusted through mutual agreement as understanding develops.

Expectations from the project

The agreement to initiate the project will reflect the expectations of the client as to the outcomes of the project. If those expectations have been thoroughly thought through by the client and have been well defined, the client may use the initiation of the project as an opportunity to articulate those outcomes and communicate them to the consultant. In this case the initiation may take a more formal guise.

Level of resources committed to the project by the client

The more the client is likely to invest in the consulting exercise (by way of money, people and time), the more likely it is that he or she will want to document the decision in some way and to formalise the initiation.

Investment by the consultant in making the formal proposal

Preparing the formal proposal demands time, energy and possibly direct expenditure on the part of the consultant. How much commitment is made here will depend on the nature (and value) of the project, the need to collect information, the level of detail in the proposal and the mechanism of delivering it to the client. A great deal of preparation may be needed, especially if the pitch for the project is a competitive one. In this case, the consultant may require the client to offer a degree of commitment to undertaking the project and to make this commitment explicit in the terms of the proposal.

The need to communicate within the client business

If the client business is quite large, a manager in the middle of the organisational hierarchy may initiate the consulting exercise. If so, such a person may want to record the decision to initiate a consulting exercise. He or she may need to do so in order to inform superiors and to comply with internal decision-control procedures.

The need to inform third parties

The delivery of the exercise may be of interest to a number of people outside the client organisation. Institutional investors such as banks and venture capitalists may demand the opinions of outside experts before committing capital. If the business is the subject of a possible acquisition, the acquirer may require that a consultant evaluate the business. In these cases the initiation may be formalised so as to keep the third party informed.

> A proposal at the start, even an interim or informal one, is essential for a successful consulting project.

2.8 Preliminary analysis of the issues and defining objectives

The consultant must make a decision about what can be achieved by the consulting exercise. It is this that will be offered to the client in the formal proposal. This decision must be based on an understanding of the business and its situation. Background research and an evaluation of the business will be called for. This stage calls on the analytical approaches discussed in Chapter 6.

There are three key questions to be answered by this preliminary analysis:

1 What are the major opportunities and issues the business faces?
2 What prevents the business capitalising on the opportunity or dealing with the issues?
3 How can the consultant's service help the business overcome this block?

The formal proposal will be made around the answers to these questions.

It should not be forgotten that this is a *preliminary* analysis. This investment must be of the right order for the project. It should be sufficient so that a proposal can be made which is relevant, meaningful and, critically, attractive to the client. If the consultant is in a competitive situation, then investing in this understanding may offer good dividends. The investment should though not be too high in relation to the final scope of the project. Clients rarely pay the consultant for making the initial proposal. The costing of this preliminary evaluation must, ultimately, be included in the overall bill for the exercise. If the pitch is competitive, the consultant will not see any return on the investment if the proposal is not successful.

If the information is needed to develop an understanding of how the client *potentially* may be helped, it may be useful. If it will be used only for *delivering* that help, it can safely be left until a commitment has been made to the full project. A management project of any significance should be defined around its *objectives*. A critical element in the success of the consulting exercise is that its objectives are well defined and understood by all involved. It is the objectives of the project that the client is 'buying' and they represent the link between where the business is now and where it might be with the consultant's help.

> A preliminary analysis of the business's issues is a useful way of ensuring the proposal will deliver the client's requirements.

2.9 Pitching the project: the formal proposal and project charter

The formal proposal represents the consultant's statement of what he or she can achieve on behalf of the client business. A full exploration of the details to be included in and the structuring and writing of a formal proposal is given in Chapter 3. An important point to be made at this stage is that the proposal operates at a number of levels.

- It provides a concise and efficient means of communicating the objectives of the project to the client.
- It guides analysis and ensures that investment in information gathering is at an appropriate level.
- It gives the consulting team a common focus when differentiating tasks and organising the project delivery.
- It provides a fixed point of reference which can be referred back to if it is felt the project is drifting.
- It can be used to manage the expectations of the client.

If properly written and presented, the proposal prevents expectations of the outcomes becoming unrealistic. This can easily happen and if expectations get too high, even a good project will disappoint the client. The project charter is the key document and provides the 'ground rules' for the team. It is very useful, not just for the client but for the consulting team as well, as it acts as an anchor for the project and manages the expectations of both parties. It is always agreed by the project team at the start. It can change only if all members of the team agree and they have very strong reasons for changing it.

> **The proposal defines what the client will be paying for. Investing time and effort in the preparation and communication of a good proposal always pays dividends.**

2.10 Project progression and follow-up

At this stage the consultant applies his or her insights, expertise and knowledge to create a new understanding for the client. Every consulting project has its own character but also includes some essential activities.

Information gathering

Information is needed to understand the opportunities and issues the business faces and its capabilities in relation to them. Information gathering is an ongoing activity that is assisted by the techniques discussed in Chapter 6. The need for information must always be challenged in relation to its cost and the objectives of the project.

Analysis and interpretation

The consultant must interpret the information and create a new perspective from it. Developing this can be aided by the creative approaches described in Chapter 9 and the auditing techniques in Chapter 6. Analysis does not occur in isolation from information gathering: it is iterative with it. Information prompts analysis and analysis highlights information gaps.

Interaction with the client business

The consultant needs to keep the client informed of the progression of the project and perhaps obtain further information about the business. Interacting with the client is an opportunity not just to give and obtain information but also to build a relationship with the client, which can lead to a more effective project. Approaches to building this relationship are discussed in Chapter 7.

Project management and monitoring

The project proposal and charter commit the consultant to three things: a set of *agreed objectives* that will be delivered at a *specified time* for a *given budget*. Slippage in any one of these aspects can lead to unsatisfactory outcomes for the client, the consultant or both. Monitoring will involve ensuring that key events are happening on time and that expenditure is in line with that anticipated. Effective monitoring procedures ensure that if slippage does occur, remedial action can be taken to get the project back on track.

Keeping records

Consultants should invest time in keeping a good record of the progression of a project, such as a file of important documents and notes on communications. A project log such as that discussed in Section 11.8 may supplement this. It may involve more formal records such as plans and budgets. Keeping records is good practice as it enables progression of the project to be monitored. Queries may be resolved quickly by reference back to communications. A good set of records allows the consultant to reflect on the project, learn from the experience and so enhance performance in the future.

> During the project, do not forget to monitor progress and keep records. Although time-consuming, they pay dividends later.

The client and consultant might want to keep in touch after the formal outputs of the project have been delivered for the following reasons.

Advice on implementation

It is usually up to the client to put the consultant's recommendations into practice. However, the client may feel the need to call further upon the skills and insights of the consultant for clarification of points in the final report and for guidance on how implementation might be effected. An agreement to support the client in this way may be a feature of the project proposal.

Preparing ground for new project

Even if the consultant has not made an explicit agreement to support the client after the final report has been delivered, it may be judicious to do so. If the client is satisfied with the outputs of the project, then there is the possibility that the client and consultant may both gain by working together on a future project.

Seeking an endorsement

A consultant builds his or her career on reputation. The endorsement of a satisfied client or a statement that he or she has benefited from the advice of the consultant can be very valuable. Confidentiality is important and some care may be needed in referring to a particular project.

Project review and evaluation

Consultants are always alert to the possibility of improving their performance, through learning from their experiences. Reviewing how the project went, in terms of both positives to be repeated and negatives to learn from, is an important part of this. The views of the client may be sought, either through informal discussion or by means of a more formal questionnaire.

Networking

The consultant may seek to maintain a relationship with the client merely to build his or her presence in the business network. The benefits may not be immediately clear, but awareness of the consultant and what he or she can offer is built. There is always the possibility that new business will emerge if the client recommends the consultant to a contact.

> A consulting project does not necessarily end when the report is presented to the client.

Team discussion points

1 Chapter 1 discussed the mechanisms by which consultants can create value for their clients. In summary, these were:
   - the provision of information;
   - the provision of specialist expertise;
   - the provision of a new perspective;
   - the provision of support for internal arguments;
   - the provision of support in gaining a critical resource;
   - the creation of organisational change.

   Each member of the team should select one of the project types listed in this chapter. Using the framework in Chapter 1, each team member should prepare and deliver a short (one-page) presentation detailing how each means of value creation can support the project type selected and ensure that its outcomes will be satisfactory for the client.

2 Most consulting teams differentiate individual roles within the team. In this way they get the best out of a team effort. The exact profile of roles varies. Often the following roles make an appearance:

- a team coordinator;
- an information gatherer;
- an information analyser;
- a report writer;
- a report presenter;
- a client contactor;
- a team counsellor.

These roles are discussed more fully in Section 11.1.

Discuss, as a group, how each role might contribute to each stage of the consulting process. You may care to set up a grid summarising your ideas (stages vertically and roles horizontally). Retain this for planning individual involvement in the project when the project charter is developed.

Summary of key ideas

Consultants' projects can be split into those looking at the strategic processes of a firm, those dealing with the operational processes and those dealing with the human processes. Many that would be considered typical 'management consulting' are those involved with the processes such as strategy or business development, marketing and sales. Operations management and IT management are examples of areas where consultants are used to improve the firm's performance. Human resource and organisational consulting has traditionally been strong but related areas of interim management and outsourcing are now providing the growth in this type of consulting.

A consulting exercise is a project that moves through a number of distinct stages. The key stages are:

- Initiation: the consultant and client meet and decide to work together.
- Preliminary analysis: development of an understanding of what the consultant can do for the client.
- Formal proposal: a statement by the consultant to the client of what the project will achieve for the business.
- Progression of project: actual undertaking of the project.
- Delivery of results: communicating the findings to the client.
- Following up: post-delivery activities.

Different projects move through these stages in different ways but each represents a distinct management challenge that can be met by using analysis, project management and relationship-building skills.

Key reading

Biswas, S. and Twitchell, D. (2002) *Management Consulting: A Complete Guide to the Industry* (2nd edn). New York: John Wiley and Sons Inc. (Chapters 1–4).

Block, P. (2011) *Flawless Consulting: A Guide to Getting Your Expertise Used* (3rd edn). San Francisco, CA: Jossey-Bass (Chapter 3).

Further reading

Bradley, N. (2013) *Marketing Research: Tools and Techniques* (3rd edn). Oxford: Oxford University Press.

Czerniawska, F. and May, P. (2006) *Management Consulting in Practice*. London: Kogan Page (Chapters 4 to 9).

Greiner, L.E. and Poulfelt, F. (eds) (2010) *Management Consulting Today and Tomorrow: Perspectives and Advice from 20 Leading World Experts*. Abdingdon, Oxon: Routledge.

Housden, M. (2010) *CIM Coursebook – Marketing Research and Information* (2nd edn). Oxford: Butterworth Heinemann.

Johnson, G., Scholes, K. and Whittington, R. (2014) *Exploring Corporate Strategy* (10th edn). Harlow, Essex: FT Prentice Hall (Chapter 12).

Kellett, T. (2010) *Board Dynamics: Managing the Battle in the Boardroom*. Guildford, Surrey: Grosvenor House Publishing Ltd.

Lippitt, G. and Lippitt, R. (1994) *The Consulting Process in Action* (2nd edn). Chichester, West Sussex: Pfeiffer Wiley.

Lynch, R. (2009) *Strategic Management* (5th edn). Harlow, Essex: FT Prentice Hall (Chapters 8 to 12).

Newton, R. (2010) *The Management Consultant: Mastering the Art of Consultancy*. Harlow, Essex: FT Prentice Hall (Chapters 1 to 4).

Case exercise

Waterton Performing Arts Festival

The Warterton Performing Arts Festival (WPAF) is a long and well-established charity that has been in operation for over 50 years. Culminating annually in a series of stage-based performances (including drama, speech, singing, and dance), it offers individuals and groups the opportunity to participate in a competition and be professionally assessed by world-class judges. The charity is one of a large group of such festivals based in the UK and Europe and is struggling to keep its head above water. Annually it has some 2,500 entries, distributed among some very different sections ranging from the very traditional – such as hymn singing – to the more contemporary creative dance.

The last seven years have been difficult for the Festival. It is continually running at a loss and is only able to continue with the financial support of a few individuals who have an emotional and historical attachment to WPAF.

One of WPAF's more enlightened officers, Lucy, has taken the decision to use some of the monies donated to the Festival to seek some help in putting the Festival back on a better footing. In particular, she wants the organisation to be more in-line with the requirements of younger people, and open to new developments, for example. She knows that the prime benefactor will not continue to donate as he has done in the past without some major improvements.

She calls you in and outlines the many problems facing WPAF:

- Overtime 'sales' (comprising entry fees and admissions to the events) are slowly decreasing. Not all sections are affected; 'dance' is quite buoyant, but the overall downward trend is clear.

- Attempts have been made to cut costs – such as altering the venues and reducing judging costs (though the latter of which is fixed by the Festival's governing body). The biggest single remaining cost, however, is stationery; the Festival has always used the same printer which can work with the quirkiness of the section secretaries, some of whom have only a rudimentary knowledge of the use of computers.

- The main benefactor tends to impose his own views on the WPAF based on his own historical perspective (he took part as a child).

- The age profile of the key people is quite old and does not reflect the target audiences that the Festival serves. Each of the eight sections is led by someone over 60. Despite numerous attempts, there is no succession planning as the Festival is run by a small number of stalwarts and no one is coming forward to help or replace them.

- As all are volunteers, and without anyone in real authority, it is difficult to make the group behave as a team. Each section secretary runs his or her own show and only matters of common interest, like health and safety, require them to turn to the central group for help.

- Apart from a recently introduced website created by a student from a local university, IT systems are non-existent. Attempts have been made to introduce automated systems but not enough of the participants are using the system for this to be valuable.

- The chairman is world-class in his field (opera singing) but he knows little or nothing of running an organisation. His idea of chairing a meeting is to ask the various secretaries to read out prepared statements. There is no discussion and decisions are taken unilaterally causing regular dissension in the group.

- With time, there are more and more demands placed on the WPAF by its governing body (the UKIGF). WPAF has to be a member the UKIGF to protect itself in many legal ways, as the requirements of health and safety, child safeguarding and care of the disabled increase annually. The body, which is international, imposes its own rules about the number of participants per section, choice of adjudicators etc. The links with UKIGF and coordination of the group are dealt with by one over-stretched lady.

- The treasurer, James, who has been in post for over 20 years, also works for five other charities and has little time to devote to the WPAF. He is perceived by some to cut corners. James has always considered that producing an accurate picture of which sections are or are not profitable would be 'divisive'.

- WPAF as a charity is registered with the Charities Commission though little is understood in the group of what requirements that imposes on WPAF.
- There have been some disagreements between the sections about a range of topics, such as contestants entering more than one class within a section. Guidelines are very informal.
- The Festival is suffering from local and regional competition. Slowly some of the sections are being eroded as they are seen as dated, even elitist.

1 From the long list of problems above, consider some of the consulting projects that might help the organisation. Hint – Which are strategic, which are operational and which are 'people issues'?

2 Consider what questions you would ask Lucy to try to understand what are WPAF's greatest priorities, as you cannot solve everything at once. Which do you see as WPAF's most pressing problem?

3 Choose one of what you believe to be the highest priorities and consider the stages you might go through using the consulting process outlined above.

Chapter 3

The skills of the consultant and the project proposal

You must be the change you wish to see in the world.

Mahatma Gandhi

Learning outcomes

The learning outcomes from this chapter are to:

- appreciate the skills effective management consultants bring to the job and in particular recognise the importance of the:

  - *project management skills* necessary to keep the consulting project on schedule and on budget;

  - *analysis skills* needed to understand the client business, identify the opportunities it faces and develop strategies to exploit them;

  - *relationship-building skills* needed to relate ideas, to positively influence decision makers and to make the project happen in real organisations.

- understand the selling process of a consulting project.

- recognise the key elements of the project proposal and how they may be articulated in order to have an impact and to influence the recipient.

What does it take to become a successful consultant? Certainly, many of the skills listed in this chapter could equally apply to an internal managerial role. To those new to consulting, the list may also seem very daunting but fear not; a lot of the skills can be learnt and honed with experience. The key is to recognise what you are good at and improve upon the ones that you are not. Often you will work in a team and so your relative weaknesses can be compensated by other's strengths and vice versa. Nobody's perfect and has all the required skills: we are human, after all! To try and help the novice consultant, those skills that are essential and those which are still important but less critical will be identified on page 56.

Skill set	Essential	Important
Project management	• define objectives • develop formal plans • sequence and prioritise tasks	• manage finances • recognise the expertise needed • manage one's own time
Analysis	• process information and draw conclusions • recognise the external opportunities and challenges the business faces • assess the business's internal condition	• identifying what information is available and what is needed • assessing the business's financial situation • evaluating the business's markets • analysing the firm's decision-making process
Relationship building	• building rapport and trust • communicating ideas effectively • negotiating objectives and outcomes	• effective questioning • working effectively as a team • demonstrating leadership

A consultant would not be able to survive in business for long without being able to 'sell a project'. In large consultancies, this is often a specialised task done by the senior directors or business development managers and so other members of staff may not feel part of this process. Experience shows that even the most junior members of a potential consulting team should get involved in the selling of a project. Why is this important? Getting involved in a project after the proposal has been accepted and the work starts, is difficult. The reason is that the junior consultant could not have any input on the overall structure, the objectives and the required outcomes of the project, so it is like starting something with one hand tied behind your back. A good salesperson does not just sell anything for the sake of revenue. They ensure that the sale is appropriate.

> **The leader of a consulting project should involve and get input from every member of the team who may be working on the project during the sales process.**

3.1 The effective consultant's skill profile

Consulting represents a particularly challenging management task for a number of reasons. First, the consultant is not working within his or her 'own' organisation. He or she is, in the first stages of the consulting exercise at least, an 'outsider'. In some ways this offers advantages. It may allow the consultant to ask questions and make recommendations that an 'insider' feels they cannot. Managers within a business tend to adopt the organisation's way of seeing things – a kind of 'groupthink', which limits the way both problems and opportunities are seen. The consultant might well see opportunities in a fresher, more responsive way. As the consultant ultimately leaves the organisation, he or she can afford a more dispassionate approach. Painful 'home truths' may be recognised more readily (or at least not denied!) by the consultant. For this reason, the consultant will be in a stronger position to advocate difficult courses than someone who does not wish to compromise an open-ended and long-term position within the business. In the back of the consultant's mind at the end of a project, though, is often the thought of 'repeat business', which is getting more work with the client. Such temptation to abandon your independence for the sake of potential further work should be avoided.

However, being an outsider presents some challenges. It means that the consultant must actively build relationships and create a sense of trust. Established managers can often take these for granted. Consultants may formally be employed by an organisation, but often they must operate some distance from it. The employing organisation offers support in a variety of ways but the consultant is 'out on their own' in a way the conventional manager is not. The consultant must be both self-supporting and self-starting. The consultant is often involved in 'strategic' projects that have significant consequences and affect the future of the whole business. They cut across the interests of the managers of established parts or functions within the business. Managers may resist what they see as interference in 'their' areas and challenges to 'their' interests. Managing such projects demands an ability to deal with such organisational politics in a firm, sensitive and responsible way.

In order to meet the challenge of managing the consulting project the consultant must develop a skill profile that allows him or her to call upon abilities in three key areas:

- managing the consulting exercise as a *formal project*;
- employing the *analytical skills* necessary to gain an understanding of the client business and the possibilities it faces;
- *communicating* ideas and positively *influencing* others.

> **A successful consultant has to be independent-minded but needs to be trusted by the client.**

3.2   Project management skills

A consulting exercise is essentially a self-contained project within a business environment. Therefore the best results are achieved if the consulting exercise is managed as such.

> **Essential skills are the ability to define objectives, develop formal plans and be able to sequence and prioritise tasks. If these are not done well, the project will inevitably fail.**

Define objectives

Objectives state what the project is going to achieve for the client. However, not every statement is a good objective. A stated objective must be subject to a critical review.

- Is it well defined?
- Will the organisation know when it has achieved the objective?
- Is the objective achievable, given the external market conditions that face the business?

- Is it realistic, given the business's internal resources?
- How is the objective to be phrased?
- Will those who will play a part in achieving it readily and clearly understand it?
- Is the objective one that all involved in the business can commit to? If not, why not? How will this matter?

These questions will be explored fully in Chapter 5.

Develop formal plans

A plan is a course of action specified in order to achieve a certain objective. Critical aspects of planning include defining tasks, ordering them and understanding the resource implications of the task sequence. In particular, the consulting team will need to identify who will be responsible for carrying out the tasks and the financial implications of their activities. A plan must be properly articulated and communicated if it is to work. A variety of project planning techniques are discussed in Chapter 11.

Sequence and prioritise tasks

Even a simple plan will demand that different people carry out a number of tasks at different times. Those tasks must be coordinated within the shape of the overall project. Time-tabling will be important. It will be possible to carry out some tasks only after others have been carried out first. Some tasks may be performed alongside each other. Some tasks must be given priority over others if resources are to be used effectively. Prioritisation must be undertaken both *by* individuals and *between* individuals on the project team. A project in which task order and priority have been well defined will be delivered in a shorter time period and at a lower cost. A number of methods have been developed to assist managers in organising complex task sequences. These are reviewed in Chapter 11.

Manage the financial resources that are spent during the consulting project

The client will not want to see unexpected bills at the end of the project. Budgets must be set before the project starts so that the resource requirements may be understood. Actual expenditure must be monitored against anticipated expenditure. An effective approach to managing the budget for a consulting project is discussed in Section 11.2.

Recognise the human expertise necessary to deliver the project

It is important to understand how the specialist skills of the various members of the consulting team can be put to best use. Productive teamworking is crucial for consulting success. (This issue is discussed in detail in Chapter 7.) One area where teamworking and project management skills meet is in deciding who will do what. Not every member of the team can or should attempt to undertake every task. It is unlikely, given people's individual preferences that they would wish to. The range of individual roles in the project is considered in Section 11.1.

Manage personal time

The management of personal time is an important aspect of project management. Time management skills are discussed in detail in Chapter 11. They allow time to be used productively and mean last-minute panics are avoided, reducing stress. Relaxed management is more effective and engenders confidence.

3.3	Analysis skills

A consulting exercise must do something for the client business. It must offer the business the chance of moving from where it is 'now' to somewhere 'new and better'. This demands both an analysis of the business's current situation and an analysis of the opportunities open to it. Analysis involves taking information about the business and its situation and processing that information so that effective decisions may be made from it.

> For a consultant, it is essential that they are able to process information and draw conclusions, recognise the external opportunities and challenges the business faces and finally assess the business's internal condition.

Identify what information is available and what is needed

Information gathering will involve background research and reviews of published information. It will demand effective questioning of those with experience of the business and its situation to get them to share the information they have (and which they may not even know they have!). This process involves both problem definition and questioning skills. Problem definition is reviewed in Chapter 5. Questioning skills are critical to communication and are considered in Section 7.4.

Often in a decision-making situation it is not a lack of information that presents a problem, it is that too much is available. The consultant always walks a tightrope between not gaining enough information and so making uninformed decisions and having so much that focused decision making is impaired. Having identified what information is available in a situation, a consultant must decide which information is pertinent to the decision in hand. The information that is needed to make the decision an effective one must be distinguished from that which is merely a distraction. The balance will lie in the nature of the decision, its significance to the consulting project and the business and the type of information available.

Process information and draw conclusions

Information must be processed in order to identify the important relationships within it. For example, it is not just the fact that the market is growing but *why* it is that is critical. Drawing conclusions from information demands an understanding of patterns of relationships and causal linkages that connect businesses, their customers and their environments. Creative approaches to analysis and developing solutions are discussed in Chapter 9.

Once connections have been made and conclusions drawn, it is necessary to identify their impact on the courses of action open to the client business and their significance to the consulting project.

Recognise the business's strengths, weaknesses and opportunities and challenges

All businesses are different. They develop strengths that allow them to deliver certain sorts of value to particular customers in a special and valuable way. They have weaknesses that leave them open to attack by competitors. A business's environment presents a constantly shifting kaleidoscope of possibilities. Some offer new opportunities to serve customers better and so grow and develop the business. Others expose weaknesses that at best leave the business in a position where it will fail to reach its potential and at worst will cause its decline.

Assess the business's financial situation

Financial performance is fundamental to a business's success. It is only through a sound financial performance that a business can survive. An analysis of a company's financial situation offers a route to understanding its performance in its marketplace, the risks to which it is exposed and the resources it has available to invest in the future. Methods of financial analysis will be considered in detail in Chapter 6.

Evaluate the business's markets and how they are developing

If the market is growing, new business opportunities may present themselves but new competitors may be attracted to them as well. If the market is in decline, business pressures may be building. If the market is fragmenting, new niches may be opening up and innovation may be rewarded. An analysis of trends in the business's markets, combined with a consideration of the firm's capabilities, can be used to define consulting project outcomes that make a real contribution to the business's development. The techniques that can be used to explore market conditions and the opportunities they present will be considered in Chapter 6.

Assess the business's internal conditions

The business must have internal conditions that are flexible and responsive to new possibilities and have the resources needed to innovate in an appropriate way. The business must have the capacity to grow in response to those possibilities or be able to get hold of the resources it will need to invest in growth. These resources include human skills as well as productive capacity.

Analyse the way in which decision making occurs within the business

Understanding the possibilities open to a business and devising ways in which those possibilities can be exploited is only the first half of the consultant's responsibilities. If the consultant is to offer real value to a business, he or she must also help the business make those possibilities a reality. Usually a consultant must convince the client business that what he or she is suggesting is a real opportunity. To do this an effective consultant must understand decision making in the business. They need to know who is involved in the decision-making process and the roles different individuals play. It also means they should be sensitive to who will gain (and who might lose) if particular ideas are put into practice. The consultant must be aware that not all objections are purely rational. Analysing the decision-making processes in the client business is a first stage in building relationships with individuals in the business. Models that assist in this analysis are discussed in Chapters 6 and 9.

3.4 Relationship-building skills

Analysis skills offer an insight into where the client business might go. Project management skills offer an ability to deliver the project necessary to move the business forward. However, these skills are of only very limited use if the client firm's management and influential outsiders cannot be convinced that this is the right way to go. They have to give their support to the project and the direction it offers. Gaining this support demands relationship-building skills.

> The essential relationship-building skills are building rapport and trust, communicating ideas effectively and negotiating objectives and outcomes.

Build rapport and trust with the client

Two people have a rapport when they communicate with ease and work together effectively and from this comes trust. Rapport can be built not only through face-to-face meetings but also through written and verbal communications as well. Rapport and trust are very important in ensuring that the consulting project goes well and meets its objectives. Guidance and some hints on how to build rapport are given in Chapter 7.

Question effectively

Questioning is not only a way to get information (though this is important), it is also a way to build rapport and to control the direction of a conversation. Questioning is discussed in Section 7.4.

Communicate ideas succinctly and precisely

Ideas must be related in a way that is succinct and precise and uses no more technical jargon than the client is comfortable with. Ideas are used to encourage the business's managers to implement plans and its backers to make supportive investment decisions. Ideas must be communicated in a way that convinces people that they are good and are worth implementing. This conviction comes as much from the 'how' of communication as from the 'what', that is, from the form of the communication as well as its content.

Negotiate objectives and outcomes

A consulting project must have definite objectives and outcomes and these must be defined and agreed by consultant and client. This is a process of negotiation that results in the formal project brief. The need to negotiate is not an admission that there is necessarily a conflict between the client and the consultant. Rather, it is a recognition that the consultancy exercise will work best when both client and consultant have clear expectations as to what will result from the consulting exercise and what the responsibility of both parties will be in achieving them. The consultant must be aware that disappointment in consultancy (for both client and consultant team) results more from unclear expectations than from poor outcomes. Ways to approach negotiating the outcomes of the project are considered in Chapter 5.

Work effectively as a member of a team

Many consulting tasks will involve an extended management team in the client business as the consulting task will have significant resource implications and will be complex to deliver. Chapter 7 considers the issues involved in and the skills needed for team working.

Demonstrate leadership

Leadership draws together a variety of relationship skills – not least articulation of vision, motivation and communication – into a coherent behavioural strategy. However unlike the formal hierarchical structure that is often found in business, in a consulting team, a 'leader' may not be necessarily apparent. Although a senior member of the consulting firm has 'sold' the project and in the proposal is described as 'leading' the team, in reality, it is the senior consultant on the ground working with the client who may be the true leader. Or someone from the client may have been given responsibility to 'manage' this project instead of their normal job and thus they could be regarded as the leader. This is a rather tricky and fluid situation for the consultant, and the leadership skills required are discussed in Chapter 7.

> The project management, analysis and relationship skill areas do not work in isolation. They must operate in conjunction and in balance with each other. Relationship building must be based on a proficient analysis of the business and the people in it. Project management must be aimed at delivering negotiated outcomes. Good project management skills offer a base on which can be built a trust that outcomes will be delivered.

3.5   The consulting selling process

There are many consultants, often with similar skills. So how does a firm choose to use one consultant over another? Personal experience is a very strong motivator: people feel more comfortable with those they have worked with before or are recommended by someone they trust. Below is a list of factors leading clients to select a particular consulting firm from Czerniawska and May (2006):

1 ability to deliver;
2 experienced consulting team;
3 specialist expertise;
4 originality of approach;
5 experience of client sector/market;
6 reputation;
7 existing relationship with individual.

Clearly it is about getting a good job done, and if the consultant is known to the client and has the capabilities then it is a win–win situation. However, there are times when the potential buyer of consulting does not personally know who they can turn to: then they must look for information on who might help them. As with buying any service, the potential buyer of consulting has some common criteria, which would fulfil the above factors:

- Have I heard of this company (i.e. a 'brand' that I trust)?
- Do they offer the service I require?
- Are their rates competitive?
- Do they have testimonials from other satisfied customers?
- Are they efficient at handling my initial enquiry?
- Do I trust and empathise with the representative(s) of the company who I meet, i.e. do they speak the same language and understand my issues?

From a consultant's point of view, they need to ensure that any potential clients are not only aware of them and their capabilities but also have a good (if second-hand) opinion of them.

> Consultants have to effectively market themselves, just like any business. This demands a marketing strategy and an action plan, detailing the activities that they will undertake.

Figure 3.1 overleaf shows the process that an effective consultant goes through to achieve a sale.

Step 1: Identify potential targets

Depending on the size of the consulting firm, i.e. the number of consultants they have and the skills of those people, the targets could be defined as follows:

- All those from one type of industry, e.g. food and drink, or a sector within an industry, e.g. frozen food.
- Firms of a certain size (turnover between £50 and £100 million or those with profits in excess of £50 million, for example).
- In geographical terms by region (Europe, for example), country or even area within a country, e.g. north-west England.

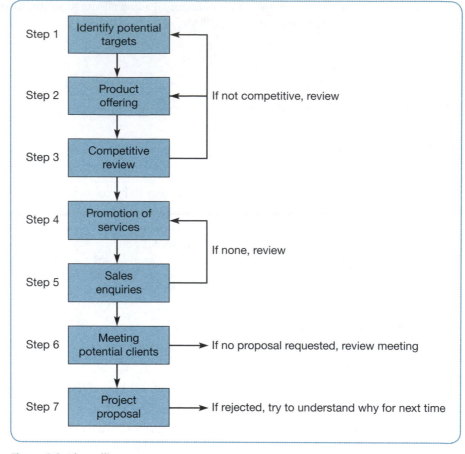

Figure 3.1 The selling process

- With personal contacts of consulting firm's members: these could be former colleagues or those that they have worked with in a consulting capacity.
- All those requiring a particular product or service; for example, cost reduction in factories.

In these more difficult times, some consultancies may form 'strategic alliances' with other firms who have complementary skill sets. For instance, those firms with a good client base but limited functional skills may team up with a practice that is expert in delivering a particular product or service, such as the application of customer relationship management systems. Consulting firms may also link up with other professional service providers, such as accountants and lawyers, to provide new client opportunities.

It may be counter-intuitive but a consultant also needs to think about who they *do not* want to work with. This could be a particular industry that they have a moral objection to; for instance, firms involved in gambling, or those that require additional regulation, such as the finance industry. It could be that a certain firm has standards of ethics that the consultant may feel uncomfortable with, particularly those located in another culture (see Chapter 4 for a further discussion of consulting across borders). In the Institute of Consulting's Code of Practice, it says that a consultant should:

- Put client interests first, doing whatever it takes to serve them to the highest possible standards at all times.

- Consider for each potential new engagement the possibility of it creating a conflict of interest.

- Act independently and objectively, and exercise professional care to establish the facts of a situation and bring to bear an informed and experienced judgement.

If the type of client would prevent you from fulfilling these obligations, then clearly you should not work for them.

When the consultant has identified the firms they wish to target, they need to think about the key people within their target companies. It might be assumed that this is obvious but, in selling consultancy, there are complex relationships that must be understood to identify who will ensure a consulting project goes ahead. Heiman, Miller and Tuleja (2011), in their book *The New Strategic Selling*, have identified four types of 'buyers' who are all-important when consultants are considering selling their services:

- *Economic buyer* – this is the person who ultimately approves the funds for the project to go ahead. They could be the chief executive or the finance director or, in more complex organisations, the head of a department that will benefit from the consulting project. They have the right to veto a project when everyone else has agreed. They can also be a strong ally in accepting an unpopular consulting assignment; for example, large-scale change programmes. While many consulting projects have been sold just with the approval of the economic buyer, they are never as well implemented unless the other buyers are considered.

- *User buyer* – these will be the ones who are directly affected by the consulting project. They may have to devote time to the project in addition to their 'day' job. The outcome of the project may influence their future job or career. Critically, their input can 'make or break' a project and determine whether a consulting firm is able to get repeat business. In the sale process, they can be valuable sources of information for the proposal to make it as 'sellable' as possible. They do not, however, sign the cheque, so while concentrating solely on this group can yield a creditable proposal, it will not get the funds approved.

- *Technical buyer* – these are specialists within the firm who will 'vet' any consulting proposals; for example, the head of IT will be the technical buyer for a new customer relationship management system. They can judge whether the proposal is feasible given the company's current position. So while they cannot give a final 'yes' (like the economic buyer), they are in a position to reject a proposal on technical grounds. Again they may be a good source of information for the proposal but consultants need to maintain their impartiality, especially if they are advocating a radical solution.

- *Coach* – this is your 'friendly face' in the target company (occasionally they may be outside the target firm but would have a close professional relationship with it). They can find you the other buyers within the organisation and make introductions. They can also help you if you are having problems getting the information you need from user and technical buyers. What they cannot do is complete the sale for you. However, not having a coach makes the process much harder and the success rate lower.

> Targeting the right business and individuals within it determines the success of a sale.

Step 2: Product offering

The next stage is to understand what will be offered to potential clients. These could range from very specific products; for example, offering commercial due diligence to private equity houses interested in investing in new technology firms, to more general ones which rely on the skills of the consultants themselves; for example, organisational development. David Maister's chapter on 'The Anatomy of a Consulting Firm' in Fombrun and Nevins (2004) argues that the structure and management of consulting firms is determined by two key factors: the degree of customisation in the firm's work activities and the extent of face-to-face interaction with the client. So a consulting firm has to think about whether it is going to offer mainly a standardised process, where all potential clients get an 'off the peg' solution or a customised one which is bespoke. Both have their advantages: the first is easy to administer and less highly skilled staff are needed. The latter attracts higher fee rates and the work is more intellectually rewarding for the consultant. The reality is that few firms can offer both with credibility, just as designer labels struggle to be aspirational and mass market. The other variable is the extent to which a consultant is involved with the client, and this is explored further in Chapter 8.

Step 3: Competitive review

The key is for the consultant to be able to offer something that differentiates themselves as far as possible from their competitors. As with any good marketing strategy, they need to understand their competitors' services. They can then compare themselves and ensure that what they offer is competitive. Given that personal relationships are often important in selling a consultancy, you may want to look for 'gaps' where your competitors are not operating. This may be because they think those customers are too small for them or that they are not natural buyers of consulting; for example, other professional services such as lawyers or accountants.

Step 4: Promotion of services

Consultants must then tell their potential customers what they have to offer. All the standard promotional techniques can be used: face-to-face meetings, mailings, advertisements, use of social networking sites, such as LinkedIn, and links to the website. However, as consultants' key benefit is their personal skills, public relation events, such as speaking at business conferences and other meetings where potential clients may attend, also offer a useful tool.

Perhaps the most powerful promotional tool a consultant has is their previous work for a client. This 'repeat business' is highly sought after, as it is relatively cheap to acquire and the likelihood of success should be greater as the consultant knows the buyers better. However, just working for one client has its risks. In any business, putting all your resources in one area makes you highly vulnerable if your customer moves away from you. In this situation you could also start to lose one of your main functions: that of an independent voice.

Step 5: Sales enquiries

This should elicit sales enquiries, if the steps above are correctly carried out, i.e. the correct target audience has been identified, with the right product offering and correctly promoted.

There are broadly two types of sales enquiries. The first is where the client has worked with the consultant before and the consultant has had an active role in getting the enquiry. For example, at the end of a business strategy project, there may be new opportunities for the consultant to help the firm implement it. This could include developing a marketing strategy or new product development. Obviously the consultant has to have the right skills to be able to offer these additional services but provided the first project went well, they have a good chance of succeeding.

The second type of sales enquiry is where the client has not worked with the consulting firm. This can either be as a result of a formal competitive tender process (often used by the public sector as a way of achieving best value) or an invitation to make a proposal following an informal meeting (business presentation, for example, discussed above). The former will be a definite brief and a consultant can decide whether they wish to join the competitive bidding process, where chances of success are lower than the latter type of invitation to make a proposal. Turning down the latter would only be done in extreme circumstances when there were no resources available or the consultant felt the proposal was beyond their scope of expertise.

> The consultant will know if their promotional activities are working if they receive appropriate invitations to make a proposal.

Step 6: Meeting potential clients

The next stage – meeting with the client to discuss the project – is sometimes the hardest as it relies on listening carefully to the potential client's issues and the reason for their sales call.

> An effective consultant will *not* go into a sales meeting with the aim to sell a specific project, even if it is a formal tender.

If the consultant tries to sell a specific project, it will be at their peril! This is one of the biggest mistakes a consultant can make and the most disastrous. It could lead either to the project proposal being rejected by the client or if in the event the project does go ahead, it does not deliver what the client wants. It may take quite a few meetings and a lot of preparation before the consultant is clear about what exactly the client needs to address their issue. Here the consultant should not be afraid to ask, even simple, questions. Trying to look clever but not understanding what the client is saying can be fatal! A client should not expect that the consultant knows everything about their business.

Neil Rackham, in his book *Spin-Selling®* (1995), identifies four stages in a sales meeting:

- preliminaries,
- investigating,
- demonstrating capability,
- obtaining commitment.

Preliminaries are critical because many potential clients will make up their mind in the first few minutes of meeting as to their opinion of the consultant. For any business meeting, you should be punctual and dress appropriately. The latter is not as straightforward as it used to be when a business suit was the universal uniform. Many IT and creative firms have an official (or unofficial) casual dress policy and turning up to such an organisation in a three-piece-suit and tie for men (and the equivalent for women) might give the impression that you are not used to working in such an environment. However there are no hard and fast rules. The key is to do your homework and ideally find a 'coach' (see section above on types of buyers) as quickly as possible within the firm, who can help you with such matters.

The next stage involves uncovering the client's needs through investigation, i.e. asking the right questions. In a complex sale such as a consultancy project, this may involve two stages. The first elicits 'implied needs' that need to be gently tested. For example, the client may believe that the reason for their low sales is that they are targeting the wrong sort of customers. Questions such as, 'How are your competitors doing?' or 'Who are your *right* customers?' may show that in fact their products are in a poor competitive position. So the 'explicit need' has been identified. The next stage in a successful call is demonstrating your capability. This does not mean that you come up with a solution there and then, but show the potential client that you have worked in this area before. Finally, you need to obtain commitment. This is usually in the form of agreeing with the client that you will prepare a proposal.

Step 7: Project proposal

The final step in the selling process is the project proposal, which is discussed in more detail in the sections below.

> **A good proposal will be the result of a consultant really understanding the client's needs and having gone through the selling process properly.**

A poor proposal can be the result of the selling process going wrong, particularly the last stage when the consultant meets with the potential client.

3.6 The function of the project proposal

> **The project proposal is a short, straightforward document. It has two simple aims: to state what the consulting exercise aims to achieve and to get the client to commit to it.**

Despite its brevity the project proposal is very important. It is the pivot about which the whole project revolves. A good proposal gets the project off to a good start. A weak one will hinder the project from the outset. The proposal is what the client is *buying* from the consultant. It should make a compelling case as to why the client should employ you as a consultant. To do this it must demonstrate that you understand the client's requirements and have a creative and innovative solution (see the factors that a client is looking for in Section 3.5).

A further and equally important function of the proposal is to manage the client's *expectations*. If expectations are met or exceeded with the project, then the client will be satisfied. If expectations are not met, disappointment will inevitably result, even if the consultant thinks that the project has gone well. If the client recognises the proposal as what he or she is buying then it is against this that the final project delivery will be compared. Some managers have an unrealistic idea of what a consultant is capable of. If a business is failing because it is producing products or services that customers see as out of date no amount of clever consulting techniques can rescue that situation. That is apart from the blunt truth that the firm has to look for new products or exit the market!

The project proposal demands a balanced approach from the consultant. The temptation to 'get a sale' by offering a lot must be tempered by a care not to raise the client's expectations so high that they cannot be met. There are a few simple rules that will allow this balance to be struck. First, understand what the client would *really* like for his or her business. Do not fall into the trap of assuming that he or she will want what the 'textbooks' suggest they *should* have, or that they must take what you think is best for them. Managers often reject the obvious answers for very good reasons. Second, enquire into, and gain a thorough understanding of, the extent to which the client expects the consulting exercise to contribute to the overall goals for the business. It is particularly important to ensure that the client makes the distinction between the consulting project offering a means to achieve the business's goals and actually implementing them. This is an issue about which the consultant and client can easily develop different expectations.

Developing this understanding of the client's needs and expectations must take place at the preliminary analysis stage of the project. It is best done through a personal meeting between the manager and the consulting team or a representative of it. At this stage the objective of the meeting should be to gather information about the business and what might be done for it. It is not a time to start negotiating on outcomes. It is better to wait until the written proposal has been presented before starting negotiating on precisely what can and cannot be achieved. The proposal helps here. It provides something tangible around which discussions can centre. The initial proposal can always be modified in light of further discussion. How to approach these negotiations will be dealt with fully in Chapter 5. If the proposal is modified, however, do produce a final written version so that finalised aims, objectives and outcomes are clear to all and can be referred back to.

3.7 What to include in the proposal and an example

The proposal needs to be succinct and must make an impact.

The proposal must speak for itself; you cannot rely on having an opportunity to explain it in person. Typically it will be one to two pages long. If it is longer than this it will risk losing its impact. If the proper groundwork has been done, then it will really be the confirmation of a project. There are some key elements which, when included in the proposal, add to its impact and help it communicate effectively within the constraints described above. These will now be described in detail.

A title and executive summary

All that is necessary is a short title for the project, perhaps the client company's name and a brief descriptive phrase. This provides a reference for the project in the future and helps locate it in the minds of all involved. An executive summary is a paragraph giving a statement of what the project aims to achieve, in broad terms. It should have detailed objectives for the project.

It should also have outcomes, which are subtly different from objectives. They are a statement of what the business *will be able to do* as a result of receiving the consulting exercise and the delivery of its objectives. Both objectives and outcomes are best summarised in the form of a bullet-point list. They should be complete in themselves. Do not be tempted to expand on them or qualify them with subsidiary paragraphs. If the consulting exercise is long and complex it may be proper to develop interim objectives and outcomes for the intermediate stages of the project. The development and articulation of good objectives and outcomes are discussed in Chapter 5.

Client's requirements

This should be a brief statement about the company, the opportunities or issues it faces and the scope of the project. The scope may be drawn from the types of consulting projects described in Chapter 2. The background statement should aim to convey the fact that the consultant understands the key issue or issues and is committed to addressing them. It should not be a complete description of the business and its situation. This would be far too long and as the client possesses this information they would not be interested.

Our approach

This section provides an opportunity for the consulting group to describe how it will address the exercise. It should first highlight the overall approach in broad terms. Then it might detail specific activities such as workshops, market research, analysis and guidance with implementation. It should not give a detailed exposition of the methodologies that might be adopted. This section is an opportunity for the consulting team to indicate what it has to offer and that it is different or special. It is a further opportunity to manage the client's expectations and in particular to emphasise the distinction between developing a plan for the business and actually implementing it.

Activity and time plan

The time plan is an indication of when the activities and outcomes of the exercise will be delivered and identifies important milestones en route. Milestones are key events along the way to the final delivery and might include things like meetings with the client and information providers, interim reports and presentations. The amounts of detail in the time plan will reflect the length and complexity of the project.

Key personnel in the consulting team

This is perhaps the most important section after detailing your approach. Consulting is about paying for people's skills and knowledge. It is also useful to describe, briefly, what will be the individual roles of the consultants in the team. The client may not meet all of these people but it adds weight to the proposal if you can demonstrate the breadth of experience you have in your organisation. The information you give about each person should be relevant to the project and ideally list similar projects that they have worked on. Be realistic and honest – putting down lots of names may impress but if you know that they will have little or no contact with the project, then the client may feel you are deceiving them.

Brief summary of relevant experience

This is an optional section but may be useful to add 'weight' to your proposal, particularly if this is a new client. It can take the form of brief case histories that your firm has undertaken, although not necessarily with the consultants that will be involved in this particular project. Consultants in large firms often share knowledge and can draw on the resources of their colleagues. It may be placed outside the main proposal in an appendix.

Costings

Costings are statements of how much the project will cost the client. Important elements are the consultant's fees, the consultant's expenses (often just a pro rata cost on top of fees) and any direct expenditure needed. Direct expenditure might be needed for buying market research or undertaking surveys.

What not to include in the proposal

It is as important to know what *not* to include in the project proposal as knowing what to include.

A lot of background on the business does not usually help. It 'pads out' the proposal, making it longer than it need be. It tells the client things he or she already knows and runs the risk of losing his or her interest before the important aspects of the proposal are reached. The temptation to discuss the methodology that will be adopted should also be avoided. The formal business analysis techniques used by the consultant in developing an understanding of the business and how it might be moved forward is the consultant's concern – not the client's! A simple analogy with the repairing of your car makes the point. If you take your car to the garage for repair, you are not particularly interested in what tools the mechanic will use. Management consulting is the same. The consultant is an expert who is brought in because he or she knows how to call upon a range of tools to deal with business issues. There is no reason to reveal those tools to the client before the project starts. Exhibit 3.1 presents an example of a project proposal along the lines discussed in this chapter.

Exhibit 3.1 Consulting proposal

A New Strategic Direction for W&G Cracking Pie Company

Executive Summary

We welcome this opportunity to work with you on a new strategic direction for your business. Our extensive knowledge and expertise not only of the market you operate in but also of the issues medium-sized companies such as yourselves face, means we can ensure that we can offer you the best practice in this area, leading to a successful outcome.

The consulting project aims to:

- Identify the strategic options available for W&G Cracking Pie Company (W&G CPC) for the next five years
- Develop a new strategic planning process that works for W&G CPC
- Create a framework to develop specific internal project teams to deliver the strategy

As a result of this consulting exercise W&G CPC will be able to:

- Deliver the required sales and profits for the key stakeholders
- Run an annual strategic planning process
- Have an ongoing five-year strategic plan
- Measure progress against a defined set of objectives

Your requirements

Since its establishment in 2010 by its two founders, W&G CPC has grown rapidly from its initial base in the north of England and now covers the whole of the UK. Its main product, W's Self-Heat Superpie, which accounts for 75 per cent of its sales, is now stocked in all branches of the leading supermarkets. However, over the last year sales growth has slowed and profitability has reduced. Your private equity backer has expressed concern over your forward plans and whether they will continue to invest in your business. You therefore need to develop a strategy for the next five years which will increase your market share in the UK with new products as well as look for overseas opportunities either directly or with a partner organisation. This has to be achieved both in terms of increased sales and profits to satisfy the continued support of your financial backers.

Our approach

We will build your new strategic planning capability using our unique and tried and tested tool, the *Strategy App*®. In Stage 1, working with senior members of your management team, we will build a number of initial strategic options through in-depth interviews, workshops and a review of the available marketing research. These options will then be presented to your board, together with the recommendation of a favoured option. In Stage 2, the project team, comprising of our consultants and selected members of your team, will build your new strategic planning process and prepare a new strategic plan. In Stage 3, the joint team will identify the areas and the personnel involved for the internal project teams required to carry out the new strategy.

Time plan

Key events in the project will be as follows:

Stage	Activity	Timing
1	Background research and interviews	April 2016
	Workshop 1 – 'Where we are now?'	May 2016
	Workshop 2 – 'Where do we want to be?'	June 2016
	Presentation of strategic options	July 2016
2	Workshop 3 – 'Building a new strategic process'	September 2016
	Presentation of new process	October 2016
3	Workshop 4 – 'Building the project teams'	November 2016

Key personnel

There will be three consultants involved in this project. Mr A will lead the project and ensure that the work is completed to your satisfaction. He has 20 years' experience in this field and has worked on similar projects, using the *Strategy App®* for many medium-sized consumer goods companies. He will be assisted by Mrs B, an experienced consultant in the area of strategic planning. She will be responsible for the majority of the work outlined above and be your main point of contact on a day-to-day basis. Finally, Miss C, an analyst in our specialist Consumer Goods practice, will carry out the required research. She is a recent MBA graduate and has worked with Mr A on a project for Doc M's Pasty Ltd.

Costings

There are two elements to this proposal. The first is the fees charged based on the estimated time spent by our consultants:

Mr A	5 days @ £2,000	£10,000
Mrs B	30 days @ £1,000	£30,000
Miss C	20 days @ £500	£10,000
Total		£50,000

The second is our expenses. These will be charged at cost; however, we estimate that they will be around 10 per cent of our fees. If this figure is likely to be significantly higher, then we will inform you in advance.

Team discussion points

1 Compare the essential skills listed in this chapter for a consultant and those that are required for an effective manager. What are the similarities and what are the differences?

2 You have decided to set up a company with some of your fellow students that will offer consulting services to local businesses who rely on the student trade. Go through the selling process described above to identify your targets, products you will offer and your promotional ideas to get sales enquiries.

Summary of key ideas

Figure 3.2 The consultant must always convince the client that the service on offer is of real value!

Source: Copyright © Scott Adams, Inc./Dist by UFS, Inc. Reproduced by permission.

The effective consultant offers the client firm a way to add value that it cannot do on its own. To do this the consultant must call on three areas of management skill:

- *analysis skills* – an ability to know where to go and how to get there;
- *relationship-building skills* – an ability to take people along with you;
- *project management skills* – an ability to make it happen!

The sales process of a consulting project has to be structured to be effective. Potential target companies, their buyers and product offerings should be looked at first. Then a check for competitiveness is required, followed by a promotional plan. This should lead to sales enquiries, sales meetings and the invitation to write a proposal.

The project proposal is a critical part of the consulting project. It does two things:

- It sells what the consultant has to offer.
- It can be used to manage the client's expectations about the outcomes of the consulting exercise.

The proposal should be a short, impactful document. The key elements to include are:

1 a title;
2 executive summary – overall aim for the consulting project and what the business will be able to do as a result of the project;
3 a brief statement of the client's requirements;
4 a statement about your approach to the project – how you intend to tackle the project and why this will be effective;
5 a time plan detailing key events;
6 details of key personnel;
7 costing for the project, detailing fees and expenditure.

Key reading

Fombrun, C.J. and Nevins, M.D. (2004) *The Advice Business: Essential Tools and Models for Management Consulting*. Upper Saddle River, NJ: Pearson Prentice Hall (Chapters 2 and 9).

Markham, C. (2004) *The Top Consultant: Developing Your Skills for Greater Effectiveness* (4th edn). London: Kogan Page (Chapters 4 and 5).

Further reading

Cheverton, P. (2015) *Key Account Management* (6th edn). London: Kogan Page.

Czerniawska, F. and May, P. (2006) *Management Consulting in Practice*. London: Kogan Page (Chapters 1 and 2).

Gray, D. (2004) *Start & Run a Profitable Consulting Business* (2nd edn). London: Kogan Page (Chapters 14 to 17).

Greiner, L. and Ennsfellner, I. (2010) 'Management Consultants as Professionals, or Are They?' *Organizational Dynamics*, 39 (1), 72–83.

Heiman, S.E., Miller, R. and Tuleja, T. (2011) *The New Strategic Selling* (revised 3rd edn). London: Kogan Page.

Heiman, S.E., Miller, R. and Tuleja, T. (2011) *The New Successful Large Account Management* (3rd edn). London: Kogan Page.

Maister, D.H., Galford, R.M. and Green, C.H. (2002) *The Trusted Advisor*. London: Simon & Schuster UK.

Mintzberg et al. (2013) *The Strategy Process* (5th edn). Harlow, Essex: FT Prentice Hall (Chapter 6).

Newton, R. (2010) *The Management Consultant: Mastering the Art of Consultancy*. Harlow, Essex: FT Prentice Hall (Chapters 5, 9 and 10).

Rackham, N. (1995) *Spin-Selling*®. Aldershot, Hampshire: Gower.

Weiss, A. (2009) *Getting Started in Consulting* (3rd edn). Hoboken, NJ: John Wiley & Sons (Chapters 6 and 7).

Weiss, A. (2012) *Million Dollar Consulting Proposals: How to Write a Proposal That's Accepted Every Time*. Hoboken, NJ: John Wiley & Sons.

Case exercise

SM Scanning

SM Scanning (SMS) was set up in 2014 by two brothers, Jake and Sam, both with INSEAD MBAs. They had spotted an opportunity in the market place for small and medium-sized companies to use social media data analytics to help with all kinds of market research and to give strategic insights.

Unlike traditional marketing research, this type of data analytics helps organisations capture, measure and analyse social media data. This enables a closer understanding of social conversations and trends, for example. Using this data, models can be built to help predict behaviour and so give insights into possible courses of action. The speed and responsiveness of this approach is one of its greatest assets though one of the perceived downsides is the inability to know what might be the exact outcomes of the analyses given that it is totally dictated by the users of social media. The concept behind SM Scanning was to offer not only 'data mining' but also a consultancy service suggesting exactly what to do with the data extracted – a service not often provided by the large data analytics organisations.

The brothers knew that the biggest companies could afford to buy the software needed both for data mining and the associated analysis but smaller operations could not. Without doubt, the two felt that smaller organisations could make better-informed and more up-to-the-minute decisions if they were helped by an organisation that had access to the software and, without the need to acquire it, offer insights based on that data.

The plan was to lease and then possibly buy the rather expensive software, depending upon the economics, as the company grew. They would then carry out specific, tailored research and build a consulting company designed to use the outcomes to help develop, build and refine strategies and develop specific responses to key developments in the marketplace. Examples included tracking brand reputations and providing almost instant market feedback on specific events like product recalls. The key difference to the larger, existing competition was to be the strategic analysis of the markets and the consulting offering built on this.

The brothers had the benefit, between them, of having lived and worked on four continents. They were multilingual, young and able to devote their time to their embryonic business. They had complementary skills too: Jake was an adept salesman and Sam an excellent and broad technologist and project manager. Between them, they had previously worked in a wide variety of industries including data analytics. Coupled with the skills honed on their MBA courses, they felt they were well equipped to spearhead this concept.

From the start they had clear ideas on market analysis and segmentation but soon the issue of addressable markets (those that might be interested in the offering) and what they might actually win over arose. The key question was which companies and which departments within those companies would be most likely to buy their services? The markets for their services were very diverse. So after trying the more traditional approaches, by sector, for example, they looked at the more modern segmentation methods such as those used in the US by futurists with their 'trendbanks' and created their own versions to help identify potential seams for their work.

Initially, they succeeded in getting in front of some bigger companies still not penetrated by the larger data analytics outfits as these seemed good first targets with money. However, once introduced to the concept, these companies were indeed keen to buy the software for themselves. They recognised the strategic nature of such a purchase and were loath to outsource this.

At the smaller and medium end of the market they were similarly successful in securing quality meetings. Jake, the salesman, rarely failed in getting in front of the right people and Sam, the technical guru, produced excellent, up-to-the-minute, relevant insights. But here too, despite all their efforts, over and over again they met with only modest success – not in keeping with their expectations.

But undeterred and ever proactive, they called upon a group of friends whose backgrounds might help them to challenge their thinking and suggest how they might improve their success rate.

Some of the feedback included identifying that:

● There were a couple of large players in the market (for whom this business was small) and a few very small players suggesting that the overall market was not (yet) large. This raised the question what actually was the size of the current market for the products? Were SMS actually creating a market that didn't exist?

- Target industries still included a large number of very big companies. Was it wise to be 'distracted' by them given their longer-term intentions? As a small start-up, would SMS have credibility with them? Was this just a market entry tactic?
- One view of the market suggested that it existed because the software products did not do their jobs properly – selling 'basic' software was not enough. The products needed to be more customer-oriented. Once rectified, the supposed niche would no longer exist.
- Clients were not using the power of the software as they might – buying the software but not analysing it. What if SMS focused on just data analysis, was this an opportunity?
- Who were the buyers within the organisation? How were they responding to the product concept? Were they threatened by it? Would they do better in other countries?
- SMS pricing looked high compared to the cost of the basic software. It seemed very unlikely that clients would pay as much for the 'data analysis plus' as for the product.
- Was it a technical issue? With increased focus on full data integration was data analysis being squeezed out from the middle?
- Were the advertising agencies the problem? They provided reports as part of other contracts and were known to control the market, but had set low expectations of what was possible using cheap tools this meant clients were not interested.
- What problem was SMS actually resolving? Perhaps social media was just not a priority.

SMS's few successes had come where there was a personal, strong connection with an individual – an introduction to a business known to 'feed' off positive feedback from social media:

- nights clubs trying out new formats or menus
- views on mobile and phone banking services
- restaurant chains with topical or seasonal offerings
- new product releases: fast feedback
- useful for Corporate Social Responsibility work and reputation analysis

One of the key outcomes of the individual discussions asked: were SMS *creating* a market rather than just finding one. Were they 'crossing the chasm' rather than, as they had believed at the outset, in 'the bowling alley'?

Jake and Sam, still determined but now confused, wanted to grow the business. Their key backer decided some objective assessment of where they were going was required so called you in.

1 How else might SM Scanning have gone about finding markets for their services?

2 Based on the evidence above, what other issues do you think SMS faces and what other help/type of consulting project might you suggest?

3 Prepare a proposal on how you might help them as a consultant.

Chapter 4

Consulting across borders and cultures

Respecting and understanding the fundamental value of diversity is vital to who we are and the way we do business.

Douglas N. Daft (Chairman/CEO of the Coca-Cola Co., 2005)

> ## Learning outcomes
>
> The learning outcomes from this chapter are to:
>
> - appreciate the additional challenges and complexities implied by operating internationally both for the client and the consultant;
>
> - have an awareness of the specific areas where consultant input will benefit the company;
>
> - understand how consultant expertise can add value;
>
> - understand how the consultant–client relationship can best be managed.

Given the increasing international aspect of business today, it is important that, as a consultant, you are aware of the issues that face your client. This can be in terms of either their export plans or the wider international marketing strategies that they wish to adopt. Further, many firms now routinely operate multinational teams where potentially sensitive cultural issues may arise in the course of a consulting project. Looking first at exporting, 'Whoever said "exporting is fun" had obviously never actually done any. There are many words that might describe exporting, but "fun" would not be the most obvious one. "Frustrating" would be in there somewhere, as would "complicated", "confusing", "unpredictable", and even "infuriating".' (Sherlock, 2006).

The sheer number of companies either exporting or marketing their brands on a global basis testifies to the appeal of operating outside the home market. Successful brands such as Chanel, Gucci, BMW, Nescafé, Colgate, Heineken, Dettol and Nike, to name but a few would never have developed to the extent they have if their owners had opted for the safety and security of the domestic market alone. The attraction of 'going abroad' is obvious:

access to larger markets, seeking opportunities for growth if the home market is mature or in economic recession, enjoying economies of scale through increased production volumes, or gaining first-mover advantage over a competitor by launching ahead of them in unexploited markets.

In the twenty-first century, firms compete in a truly global market. Advances in technology, the Internet, improvements in transportation, the greater freedom to move capital across frontiers, the lessening of international political enmity (though by no means complete) and the growing integration of common markets and liberalized trade pacts mean that the company may need rather than simply wish to operate outside its home country.

Yet for the unwary there are more pitfalls than prizes, and a manager contemplating overseas activity will require a far wider range of knowledge than if the company were simply to remain domestic. Which country to enter? What are the political, economic, social, technological, environmental and legal issues? How will culture impact on the marketing programme? Can the domestic brand name be used, or does the trademark belong to someone else? Is the brand name offensive or comic in the local language? What level of presence should be established? Would a local partner be more appropriate, and if so – who? Does the product need to be modified or reformulated? How will the products reach the end-user? How can planning and forecasting be conducted with any degree of confidence? Most important – how will payment be made?

None of these issues need deter the company. Rather, they need to ensure their managers are fully equipped and prepared so that decisions can be taken confidently as the result of good information.

No manager, however competent, will be able to deal successfully with these issues without expert assistance.

> **The role of the consultant is to help the firms with their international strategies and the issues involved in selling products and services abroad.**

4.1   Factors encouraging international operation

> **When helping a client with their overall strategy, a consultant needs to consider the firm's desire to expand internationally.**

The principal economic factors behind international trade by firms fall under three main headings.

Fulfilling an unmet need

First, because of the non-availability or difficulty of producing an item in one country, the need will be met by importing from elsewhere. The first exports from the British Isles some two thousand years ago are said to have been Cornish tin ore exploited by the Phoenicians and transported to their Mediterranean homeland. Similarly, nowadays commodities such as citrus fruit, coffee, tobacco and oil are imported by countries unable to source them in their home market.

Comparative advantage

Second, there is the argument mooted by David Ricardo's theory of the law of comparative advantage, also known as his comparative cost theory. This postulates that countries will gain from international trade if each country focuses its resources solely in industries where they are most internationally competitive, and trades with others to obtain products no longer made locally. In other words, the country exports commodities in which it has maximum comparative cost advantage or minimum comparative disadvantage (Robert L Formani).

Differentiated products

Third, and most appropriate to the overall thrust of this chapter, there is the opportunity for differentiated products. There are sound commercial reasons for seeking to develop a presence outside the domestic market. The most compelling of these will clearly be the potential for significantly increased turnover and profit through offering goods and services to a substantially greater number of customers. Yet who will be these customers? To date, they have managed quite happily without the company's offering. They may have different tastes and requirements, and may live in countries that are difficult to access. They may not respond as readily to the company's promotional message as do its domestic consumers. Nor may they have the same levels of affluence or discretionary spending. Consequently, while the prospect may be very simple, the reality may prove more challenging. Together with increased volume would come other benefits – the achievement of economies of scale, increased plant throughput, or better utilisation of company resources such as procurement, R&D, packaging development and graphic design, the cost of all of which would be spread over a significantly larger output. Similarly, the company's leverage with its suppliers and agencies would be enhanced because of its greater buying and negotiating power.

Hedging against risk

A company operating internationally should also be able to spread any risk by virtue of the fact that it is not confined simply to one country, where the economy may go into recession or the market and product lifecycles may have matured. Potential peaks and troughs of seasonal demand may also be offset due to the company being in a wider number of markets. Further, increased and more efficient factory utilisation should be able to deliver greater security of employment, enhanced workforce morale and new training and skilling opportunities. Operating internationally will also boost the company's image and increase its exposure. It will develop global brands, market more competitive products, which reflect overseas market requirements and legal issues, and potentially improve the rate of its technological development through the need to respond to world market opportunities. In theory, a higher calibre of management may be able to be recruited, because of the greater challenges presented, the prospect of increased job satisfaction and the sheer appeal and excitement of working in an international environment with customers of differing cultures.

Challenges

What may be an opportunity for one company, however, may be a threat for another. In this context, it is intriguing to consider a North American perspective. Smaller nations such as the UK, the Netherlands or France, which have a long history of maritime trading and interaction with differing cultures through their colonial history, have for years viewed the wider world as an opportunity and have successfully established global brands. Yet the North American attitude may be more sceptical. In his book *Marketing Management* (2015) Professor Philip Kotler writes, 'most companies would prefer to remain domestic if their domestic market were large enough. Managers would not need to learn other languages and laws, deal with volatile currencies, face political and legal uncertainties or redesign their products to suit different customer needs and expectations. Business would be easier and safer'.

Kotler then goes on to cite what he considers to be the key challenges in marketing internationally:

- huge foreign debts accumulated by countries such as Indonesia and Mexico;
- unstable regimes which expose foreign firms to the risks of expropriation, nationalisation and limits on profit repatriation;
- foreign exchange problems which may decrease the value of a country's currency;
- host country government regulations which may include the requirement for majority ownership by a local partner; tariffs and 'invisible' trade barriers;
- corruption and the expectation of bribes (prohibited under US law);
- technological pirating and copying, an example being the production of low-cost generic pharmaceuticals once the patent has expired;
- the potentially high cost of product and communication adaptation;
- the 'moving target' threat implied by changes to the country's national boundaries.

Taken together, these might represent a powerful argument for isolationism, yet the skill will lie in appreciating that certainly there are likely risks, but that the company is properly informed about the nature of such risks, and can therefore plan how to address them, including developing contingency plans. A consultant will have a key role in facilitating such thinking.

Credit

Even the seasoned international operator will be contending with these risks and concerns on a daily basis. While cash with order might be a desirable prospect, payment tends often to involve a longer period of credit, possibly 90 or even 180 days. An extreme case would be Syria in the 1970s, when an import licence would not be issued unless the exporter granted 365 days' credit. Clearly, the need for extended credit poses cash flow problems, especially at times of high interest rates in the supplier country, and it may be necessary to engage a factoring company to carry the credit risk at a discounted price.

Exchange rates

As identified by Kotler, interest and exchange rates pose further threats, as do economic 'boom and bust' cycles. Hedging against exchange rate movement, keeping abreast of expert financial opinion, and maintaining close awareness of the eco-political environment in the country of destination will be important disciplines for the company to follow in such circumstances. Buyers may default, import duties may be increased without warning, price controls may be introduced, new packaging and labelling laws may be announced – all of these have to be taken in the company's stride as the realities of operating across frontiers. The challenge is to manage them so that the potential gains can be achieved despite the obvious risks.

4.2   Researching and selecting overseas markets

Country selection

Deciding which countries to enter will be a critical decision for the company.

If it makes the wrong choice it will be confronted with two sets of costs: the expense, distraction and complexity of failure, as well as the opportunity cost of missing the chance to enter a market where its offerings might have proved more successful (Bradley, 2002). Consequently, accurate information, the systematic screening of several countries according to clearly defined criteria, and the ability to take a dispassionate and objective decision as to which to enter and in what sequence will be important considerations. It is here that an independent consultant can add significant value. But these will merely identify what are *prima facie* the best opportunities: the next step will be to conduct market research inside the countries themselves to ascertain whether the company's offerings will be attractive to potential customers, and whether an appropriate revenue and profit flow can be enjoyed as a result.

Government agencies can also be of assistance. The UK Trade and Investment export services, for instance, include bespoke support packages for first time exporters and businesses looking to grow their exporting capabilities; tailored support for medium-sized businesses and a wide range of additional services including digital and online support suitable for all types of business.

Containing risk

For small and medium enterprises, overseas market entry may simply be reactive, such as receiving an unexpected order or enquiry. Alternatively, they may plan to venture abroad, but in a low-risk manner. Johanson and Vahlne (1977) suggest three sets of criteria for such an approach:

(i)   low 'psychic' distance, or low uncertainty about the country and the difficulty of obtaining information about it (psychic distance is taken to mean differences in language, culture, political system, level of education or level of industrial development);

(ii) low 'cultural' distance; in other words, low perceived differences between the home and country of destination cultures;

(iii) low 'geographic' distance, namely the relative ease of supplying the country concerned.

Market segmentation

Larger, more ambitious organisations will be able to identify overseas market opportunities through a more systematic process. First, countries can be segmented according to what Hollensen (2004) describes as their 'general' and 'specific' characteristics. The first set of criteria will include the geographic location, language, political factors, demographic trends, economic development, industrial and retail structure, degree of technological advancement, social organisation, religious customs and standards of education and literacy. Their specific characteristics will include cultural peculiarities and behaviour that drive consumer behaviour, lifestyle and consumption habits, personality traits and general attitudes, tastes and predispositions. From such criteria an overall profile can be developed for the country or countries under consideration and their relative attractiveness defined. It goes without saying that for such a process to be effective, it will need to be conducted from a fully informed standpoint.

Political risk

Another form of screening addresses the political risk of entering a particular country. The Business Environment Risk Index (BERI), developed by Frederick Haner of the University of Delaware in 1972, conducts periodic assessments of countries on various political, economic and financial factors. These include political stability, economic growth, currency convertibility, labour costs and productivity, short-term credit, long-term loans/venture capital, attitudes towards the foreign investor and profits, risk of nationalisation, inflation, balance of payments, enforceability of contracts, bureaucratic procedures and delays, quality of communications, local management and partners and professional services and contractors. Each of these has a weighting, and scoring is on a 1–4 scale, with a maximum overall score of 100. This process will give a clear indication of the relative appeal of different countries, but a more in-depth analysis will be needed before an entry decision can be taken with confidence.

Leveraging the firm's competences

Hollensen proposes a broader approach which will also take into account the firm's particular competences as well as its existing presence in various countries. He advocates a market attractiveness/competitive strength matrix. Criteria determining market or country attractiveness are market size, market growth, customer buying power, market seasons and fluctuations, average industry margin, competitive conditions (concentration, intensity, entry barriers, etc.), market prohibitive conditions (tariff/non-tariff barriers, import restrictions, etc.), infrastructure, economic and political stability and 'psychic' distance. A view of competitive strength will be developed via market share, marketing ability and capacity (i.e. country-specific know-how), the products' 'fit' to the market demands, price, contribution margin, image, technology position, product quality, market support, quality of distributors and service and access to distribution channels. Both sets of criteria can be scored, and the resultant coordinates plotted on a two-dimensional matrix. This will then allow the firm to identify the clusters or sets of countries in which to invest to grow, those in which to have a more selective strategy, and those where the best option may be to harvest, exit or licence out.

While there are several means of conducting desk research on potential markets, the key consideration is the need for factually correct information to underpin it. Some of it may be obtainable from published sources, but the company is unlikely to have the resource or the ability to provide it themselves. Consequently, the services of knowledgeable consultants with in-depth market knowledge will prove invaluable, even indispensable. So too will the next stage of the exercise – conducting market research. The principle remains the same: selecting the appropriate methodology to identify the appeal of the company's offerings and likely demand among potential customers. Again, the sophisticated process this implies can only be conducted by experts with substantial local knowledge.

4.3 Market entry options

Having identified the country or countries offering best potential, the company has to decide on how it will develop a marketplace presence.

This is the most critical phase, as it amounts in effect to the launch of a new product line. Here local knowledge is indispensable and a consultant can provide this. This, in essence, will require a cost/benefit analysis determined by the level of commitment and investment the company is intending to make, the level of marketplace control to which it aspires, and the level of risk it is prepared to take. As in many business contexts, the greater the investment, the greater the control, and the higher the risk, the higher the potential reward (see Figure 4.1).

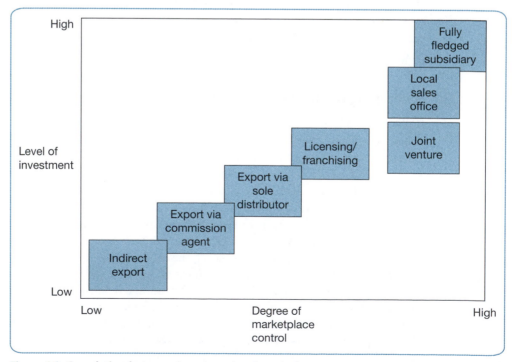

Figure 4.1 Correlation between investment and control

Indirect export

The safest approach is indirect export, whereby the company sells to a third-party export merchant based in the same country. This trading company (sometimes known as a confirming house) will then deliver the goods to the overseas customer and obtain payment. While such an arrangement allows the company quick and secure payment and will free them from the risk of servicing politically volatile markets, and while it spares them the cost of setting up an export organisation, it has many downsides. First, the company has no control over the ultimate destination of its products and has no say over how they are sold and promoted in the marketplace. It has no contact with the customer and is entirely dependent on the exporting company. The latter is only likely to be interested in products with a ready demand, and may negotiate a low price in return for the volume it is ordering. This may well bring the additional risk of re-import into the domestic market at prices below the established market norm.

Agents and distributors

At the next level, the company may opt for traditional, direct export to a third party located in the country. In broad terms, this may be to a sole distributor with the capability to serve the level of market demand, or it may be on an 'open market' basis, whereby a commission agent solicits orders for direct delivery to sundry third parties who pay the exporting company direct. Of the two approaches, the sole distributor has several advantages: they are the direct link between end customers and the exporter, they control selling prices, they carry stock to ensure continuous replenishment, they are familiar with customs, banking and clearance procedures, and they will input to the local marketing programme. But title to the goods is passed to the distributor once payment has been made, pricing will need to be such that the distributor can supply the local market at an acceptable margin, the distributor's marketing and promotional skills may be limited and the company's fortunes are dependent on the distributor's strength and competence in the marketplace.

It will be necessary to ensure adequate share of the distributor's mind, as they will carry other lines from other companies, all of whom are eager to ensure that the distributor is performing well on their behalf. Conversely, a commission agent carries little financial risk, does not hold stock, and being dependent on a percentage of the orders secured will be motivated to seek orders in large volume from reliable customers – but this carries a further risk of market saturation not necessarily related to demand, and makes forecasting particularly difficult. In both cases, though, the company will have to set up an export department, have the ability to ship its goods and process the necessary paperwork, enter into legal agreements, ensure it receives payment and undertake market visits, all of which carry further cost.

Licensing and franchising

A third mode of entry is via licensing or franchising. Rather than export finished products, the licensor grants the right for a determined period of time to an overseas company to use its manufacturing process, trademark, patents and other proprietary know-how in return for an agreed royalty based on sales. It may also make additional profit through exporting particular raw materials and components. The licensor will need to undertake quality control assessments, and will have the right to receive full sales data in order to calculate their royalty entitlement. A clear understanding has to be reached over responsibility for the local marketing campaign, and the licensor will have to accept that in return for licensing out its brand it will lose marketplace control. Further, if the licensee is particularly successful, the licensor will need to appreciate that the benefit in terms of revenue and profit has accrued to the licensee rather than themselves.

Joint ventures

A joint venture with another party may provide a further means of establishing a local presence at a reduced level of investment. In essence, the exporting company joins with a local trader or investor to establish a joint company where both share ownership and control. It will permit quick access to the market, share the investment risk, share research and development costs, possibly enjoy fiscal benefits from governments eager to encourage inward investment and potentially have access to free circulation of goods within the economic bloc or customs union to which the country belongs.

Such a move may be necessary for economic or political reasons, the overseas company may lack the financial or managerial resources to 'go it alone' or it may be the only way to enter a country whose government prohibits direct import of finished goods. Further, a skilled local partner may prove invaluable through its knowledge and connections in negotiating the labyrinth of bureaucracy in a new and challenging market. Yet the venture has to be a meeting of minds rather than a marriage of convenience. The partners will need to adapt to and respect each other's culture. There may be disagreements over strategy, marketing or investment policy. The host country government may stipulate a majority local (possibly even government) shareholding. Further, a global organisation will be unable to impose its corporate marketing or manufacturing strategy on a reluctant partner. Identification and selection of the right partner will require particular skill and clear agreement on the details of the future *modus operandi* and indeed *modus vivendi.*

Subsidiaries

Finally, the company may decide to invest directly in establishing a wholly owned subsidiary in the country. This may vary from a local or regional sales office supervising sales through distributors and coordinating the local marketing programmes to a fully fledged manufacturing, selling, distributing and marketing organisation. There may be local country government incentives to take such a step, so as to provide job opportunities, or it may simply be a calculated risk by the company which considers the benefits of closeness to the market, customers, banks, government agencies and suppliers to outweigh the scale of its investment. There should be savings in the cost of freight and the cost of manufacture, and the ability to customise products to local market needs will be facilitated. Once established, the local subsidiary (sometimes known as a branch company) may also identify potential local acquisition opportunities to strengthen their leverage with the distribution chain. Locally recruited staff may prove to be of a higher calibre than those working for a distributor, since the kudos of being employed by a multinational company may prove a powerful incentive. Nevertheless, there are potential drawbacks, namely the risk of devalued currency, foreign exchange shortages, restrictions on profit remittance, protective local laws and political–social upheaval, deteriorating markets, nationalisation or expropriation. Further, in order to entice expatriate management to what might be considered a hardship appointment the company may need to offer a high salary, more luxurious accommodation standards, regular home visits, and a finite period of appointment with a guarantee of re-entry to the home country. This level of investment decision is clearly one that will not be taken lightly, as the ability to reduce or close down the operation if circumstances so require may prove especially costly.

4.4   Export management issues

The export manager with responsibility for a country or series of countries will need to have a wide awareness and good knowledge, though not necessarily expertise, of a plethora of subjects specific to the daily reality of exporting. Exotic new terms such as drawback, incoterms, demurrage, groupage, letters of hypothecation, general average and *del credere* risk will enter the exporter's lexicon.

> **The ability to contend with these export terms, in addition to skills in negotiation, distributor motivation, marketing planning and sales forecasting will be crucial to a successful performance.**

It is not the intention in this section to give a comprehensive exposition of all aspects of export practice so much as to highlight the more important areas and to indicate how consultants can help.

Quotations

The exporter needs to decide on what basis a price quotation will be given to the importer. First, there is the price itself, that upon which the exporting company will realise its profit. Will it be based on the published wholesale price in the home country, will it be expressed in a standard export price list, will it relate to an increase (or not) over the price previously used, will it be established from an in-market price to the customer worked backwards down the price structure, will it have to take account of price controls in the overseas country, or will it be negotiated or offered as a tender bid? Having determined this price, it will be necessary to agree what element of freight, insurance, duty or other factors to include in the quotation. Prices can be quoted at any stage of the journey from the factory gate to the importer's premises, depending on the point at which title and risk are to be transferred. The Incoterms 2010 rules or International Commercial Terms are a series of predefined commercial terms published by the International Chamber of Commerce intended to communicate the obligations, costs and risks associated with transportation and delivery and are incorporated into export sales contracts across the world. Consultants can provide valuable assistance in this process – for example, in identifying the most competitive insurance and freight rates.

Payment

The means whereby the exporting company will be paid have an obvious importance. Some companies with an established system of trading may have an open account arrangement, but it is generally the case that each order will have to be paid via an individual transaction. The most common forms of transaction are by Letter of Credit or drawing a Bill of Exchange. Either method has advantages and disadvantages. Commercial banks will provide guidance on method of payment issues, but a consultant may also have specialist knowledge.

Shipping

Another area where expertise will be needed concerns shipping – identifying the most appropriate carrier, deciding the preferred routing, negotiating the particular freight rates, booking the order for shipment, assembling the necessary paperwork and appreciating the particular issues of hazardous or inflammable goods, those requiring special stowage, etc.

In this particular area, a shipping and forwarding agent can be of considerable assistance, especially to a small or medium enterprise or those new to exporting. Such agents are experts in their field, and will have an up-to-date and thorough knowledge of transport methods and the relevant carriage rates. They will be aware of port conditions and specific customs requirements, and they may be able to consolidate small shipments from different exporting companies into a single 'groupage' consignment, thereby enjoying more favourable freight rates (Walker, 1970).

Law

Additionally, the exporter should have a good awareness of aspects of mercantile law. This will include the law of contract, laws governing agency, the sale of goods, negotiable instruments, marine insurance and the carriage of goods by land, sea and air. Access to expert legal knowledge will be indispensable in cases of dispute. Further, the importing country may have additional laws of their own regarding the legal status of agents, the payment of commission, corporate liability, trademark protection, trade with countries with whom they disagree politically and other commercial practices.

Product modification

Products may need to be modified or given special packaging not for any particular consumer benefit but rather because of specific local laws or by virtue of the rigours of the physical distribution process. Consider the food industry: innocuous products such as prepared mustard bound for Sweden have in the past needed to have the tartrazine colouring agent removed. The same country had more stringent rules on the level of permitted impurities in peanut butter than did the UK. The unfortunate story of Scottish skier Alain Baxter should be heeded: he was stripped of his Olympic bronze medal after failing a routine drug test. He had inadvertently used a US version of a nasal inhalant which, unlike its UK equivalent, happened to include levoamphetamine, a mild form of methamphetamine. Differences in formulation can therefore have serious consequences.

Labelling

Consumer products intended for sale in Israel quite understandably require labelling in Hebrew. Foodstuffs destined for the same country need a kosher certificate, which might require the visit of a rabbi to the manufacturing plant. Labelling laws, expiry dates, distributors' addresses, safety warnings, etc. all need to be accommodated. Clear honey shipped at times of severe cold can set, and soft drinks stored in containers at high temperatures on vessels plying the Arab Gulf can boil and flocculate. Cereals may be prone to infestation by weevils and therefore require additional protection. All of these are the facts of life of exporting, and all will add cost and complexity to the manufacturing operation. Yet again, without specialist knowledge of such requirements, the exporter will be at a considerable risk.

Regulatory matters

Pharmaceutical products attract further regulatory issues. Most countries will require registration even though the item in question is freely on sale in its country of origin. A certified Free Sale Certificate may be sufficient, but it may be necessary also to provide raw material specifications, the method of manufacture, the product ingredients and a certified statement of the consumer price in the country of origin. The documentation will need to be processed, and it may take two years or more before approval is given. Access to informed regulatory affairs knowledge will be crucial.

4.5   Culture

> **One of the biggest issues facing a consultant with a multinational assignment is the different cultures involved.**

Good consultants recognise these early on in the consulting process and ensure they adapt their way of working without compromising the project. Cultural differences may be national cultural differences in a largely homogeneous society, or there may be important subcultures – such as Latinos in the USA, Turkish immigrants in Germany, or the differing ethnic communities in South Africa. These differences will manifest themselves both in consumer and business behaviour. Managers and consultants should develop a keen awareness of these cultural differences, and respect them, for they will be the rules by which they will need to play if they intend to compete successfully.

Diversity

One example of cultural diversity is the strong influence of Islam on daily life in the Arab world, the emphasis on observing prayer times, modesty of dress and the avoidance of alcohol and pig meat. A Westerner who is not a Muslim will still need to observe the Ramadan fast if he is in an Arab country at the time. But he will also enjoy a greater degree of hospitality and personal attention than may be the norm in his home country. Another particular feature of doing business in the Arab world is the concept of *wasta*, loosely defined as connections, influence, clout or favouritism – in other words, the 'who you know' that can help smooth the way through opaque bureaucracy. The fastidious Westerner may find this distasteful, but it is a way of life that has to be accommodated. In Chinese culture, 5,000 years of Confucianism, which seeks harmony and equilibrium, place great importance on connections (*guanxi*), interpersonal relationships (*renqing*), courteous and refined behaviour (*keqi*) and the need to preserve face (*mianxi*).

In Latin societies, attitudes to time (the *hora latina*) are often more casual than in 'low-context' cultures such as Germany or Switzerland. Haggling and bargaining are part of the way of life in Turkey, India and the Middle East. German companies are especially formal in conduct, and colleagues within the same organisation are likely to be known by their titles and surnames: people may spend ten years working together without knowing one another's first name. Israelis pride themselves on straight, blunt talking almost to the point of rudeness, and expect the same in return: they will have little patience with subtlety and understatement. In Holland and Scandinavia, the concept of companionship is more greatly refined than in the UK or USA: the Dutch concept of *gezellig* implies sharing one's personal feelings in a very personal way while being together in a small group (Arnould, Price and Zinkhan, 2004). National spirit is implied in untranslatable words such as *sisu* (Finland), *hwyl* (Wales) or *lagom* (Sweden). Finally, there is the facilitating role of *bakhsheesh* in Turkey and the Levant, *dash* in West Africa or *coffee money* in Malaysia and Singapore: what Western attitudes might consider to be bribery.

Cultural determinants

Much has been written on the determinants, characteristics and elements of culture. In 1983 Geert Hofstede identified four dimensions determining national culture, adding a fifth in a further piece of research with Bond in 1988 (in Hollensen, 2004). The five elements are:

- power distance – the degree of inequality between people in physical and educational terms;
- uncertainty avoidance – the degree to which people prefer formal rules and fixed patterns of life;
- individualism – the degree to which people in a country learn to act as individuals rather than members of groups;
- masculinity – the degree to which 'masculine' values such as achievement, performance, competition and success outweigh 'feminine' values such as quality of life, warmth of relationships, care and concern and the environment;
- time perspective – whether the tendency is for pragmatic long-term thinking as opposed to a conventional, short-term time horizon.

Hampden-Turner and Trompenaars' 1994 model identifies eight 'value dilemmas' driving national cultural features (in Morden, 2007). These are (at either end of the spectrum) strict adherence to rules as opposed to flexibility and exceptions; analysis of concepts or events versus their integration into wholes (deconstructionism and constructionism); communal as opposed to individual focus; internal focus on the society in contrast to an external orientation of people to their environment; the perspective of time as a linear rather than a cyclical concept; status based on age, education, class or race as opposed to status on the basis of achievement or merit; emphasis on hierarchy versus equality within the community and affective, expressive and emotional behaviour rather than neutral, subdued and controlled emotion.

Business etiquette

Finally, and of particular value to the international manager, Mead (1990, in Brassington and Pettitt, 2006) groups eight behavioural factors influencing business conduct. These are:

- time – attitudes to punctuality, the sanctity of deadlines, discussion time and acquaintance time;
- business cards – when to offer them, whether to have them translated, who gives first and how much attention to give them when received;
- gifts – whether they should be given, their size and value and whether they should be opened in front of the donor;
- dress – dress codes and levels of formality;
- entertainment – the type and formality of social occasions, table manners and etiquette, cuisine, cultural and religious taboos and venues (e.g. restaurant or private house);
- space – the meaning of office size and location and the selection, quality and arrangement of furniture;
- body language – greeting conventions, facial and hand gestures, physical proximity, touching and posture;
- material possessions – whether or not it is polite to comment on them or admire them. Managers intending to spend time in different business cultures would do well to seek expert advice on such issues.

4.6 International marketing

Adaptation or standardisation

> For many large companies, such as Unilever, international marketing is firmly established and the consultant needs to understand the key processes that are operated.

It could be argued that the ideal prospect for a company intending to market its brands internationally would be that it will be able to sell the same product as in the home market, without any form of adaptation, using the same brand name, the same graphic design and the same advertising message – although the more enlightened company may concede that it will be necessary to communicate in a language the consumer will understand! In a celebrated article in the *Harvard Business Review* in 1983, Theodore Levitt challenged the accepted marketing wisdom of providing products and marketing programmes specific to particular consumer requirements when he wrote, 'The world is becoming a common marketplace in which people – no matter where they live – desire the same products and lifestyles. Global companies must forget the idiosyncratic differences between countries and cultures and instead concentrate on satisfying universal drives.' He foresaw a convergence of lifestyles and a homogeneous, American-influenced global market. Joseph Quinlan, a senior economist at Dean Witter Reynolds, called the emerging consumers in this new world the 'global MTV generation' who 'prefer Coke to tea, Nikes to sandals, and Chicken McNuggets to rice, credit cards to cash' (Kotler, 2015).

Consumer behaviour

In today's demassified, individualistic global marketplace, such views now seem simplistic, even flawed. No company sets out deliberately to make life difficult for themselves, but they would ignore at their peril real differences and factors that militate against total standardisation. First, consumer habits and spending power do vary; for example, less affluent consumers in the developing world may seek shampoo in sachets rather than more expensive larger sizes, hand-held items such as cups or razors may need to be made smaller for Japanese hands, ketchup may need to be spicier in a country such as Mexico, taste in confectionery will vary considerably between the USA, France and the UK, and a powdered chocolate drink to which boiling water is added in the UK may need to be repositioned quite differently in France, where ownership of kettles is lower and the product is a milk-based breakfast drink for children. It will therefore be imperative to research consumer attitudes both to avoid expensive blunders and to identify genuine differences in habit.

Branding

Brand names may also prove a challenge. Just as English-speakers may snigger at brands such as Bum snack foods (Spain), Sor-Bits chewing gum (Denmark), Aseol toilet cleaner (Spain), Plopsies chocolate cereals (France), Pschitt carbonated drinks (France) or Kuk & Fuk pasta (Slovakia), so seemingly innocuous brands such as the Vauxhall Nova ('won't go' in Spanish), Mist (dung in German), Zip, Nike and Aero (all of which have obscene meanings in Arabic) and the direct Spanish translation of Airwick's Magic Mushroom (Seta Mágica) will cause amusement, even offence, in some countries. Again, careful research or simply reference to a linguist with a good knowledge of colloquialisms and slang will help to prevent embarrassment.

Advertising

Similar considerations apply to the advertising and promotional message. Clever, subtle taglines in one language or culture may not transfer to another. A rational scientific approach may be preferred in one society, a humorous one in another. There may be laws forbidding the use of white-coated laboratory 'experts' promoting a personal care product, children may not be used in advertising in some countries, beer may be advertised but may not be shown actually being drunk in some parts of the world, superlative statements may be disallowed, comparative advertising may be illegal, nudity may be appropriate to one culture but gratuitously offensive to another and in some Islamic countries it is forbidden to feature women in advertising. The company therefore faces a dilemma: on the one hand it will not wish to produce an advertisement so bland that it lacks any cut-through, yet on the other it will need to avoid wasting money unnecessarily on too many different creative executions for the same brand. To quote Kotler (2000) on Levitt, therefore, 'so perhaps Levitt's globalization dictum should be re-phrased. Global marketing, yes. Global standardization, not necessarily'. Keegan (1995) has identified five possible strategies that may be appropriate for products and promotion in overseas markets, as shown in Figure 4.2.

Ethics

A feature of today's world is the spectre of consumer retaliation against global brands and their owners if they believe they are acting unethically. This was most apparent in the Seattle riots in 1999, when symbols of globalisation were attacked. A further example was the action by French sheep farmer José Bové, who in 1999 dismantled his local branch

	Do Not Change Product	Adapt Product	Develop New Product
Do Not Change Promotion	Straight Extension	Product Adaptation	Product Invention
Adapt Promotion	Communication Adaptation	Dual Adaptation	

Figure 4.2 Keegan's five international product and promotion strategies

Source: Kotler, Philip, *Marketing Management*, 11th ed., Prentice Hall © 2003, p. 395. Reprinted and electronically produced by permission of Pearson Education, Inc., Upper Saddle River, New Jersey.

of McDonald's in protest against a US hike in the tariff on Roquefort cheese. Similarly, 'anti-brand' websites have been spawned against brands/companies accused of unethical practices such as animal testing, animal cruelty, use of child labour, heavy-handed 'brain-washing' marketing campaigns, damage to the environment, paying low prices to farmers and growers in the developing world or association with dictatorial political regimes. In her seminal polemic *No Logo* (2010), Naomi Klein castigates many well-known brands and companies for what she considers inappropriate global marketing behaviour.

By the same token, in the conclusion to his searing indictment of the American fast-food industry *Fast Food Nation* (2002) Eric Schlosser writes, 'Future historians, I hope, will consider the American fast-food industry a relic of the twentieth century – a set of attitudes, systems and beliefs that emerged from post-war southern California, that embodied its limitless faith in technology, that quickly spread across the globe, flourished briefly, and then receded, once its true costs became clear and its thinking became obsolete'. He goes on to say, 'This new century may bring an impatience with conformity, a refusal to be kept in the dark, less greed, more compassion, less speed, more common sense, a sense of humour about brand essences and loyalties, a view of food as more than just fuel'. In other words, the global marketing company should remember to respect basic human values and not to ride roughshod over ethical concerns in its pursuit of profit. Companies should be prepared to be challenged on this issue by the consultant.

4.7   Global marketing planning

Strategic planning

> **For successful international marketing, planning processes are important and should be understood by the consultant.**

A company whose business success depends on the ability to coordinate and manage its key product categories across a number of regions faces a considerable challenge in the strategic planning process. It may be that the company is underperforming through undisciplined planning and inadequate or inconsistent processes – still worse, a wish to placate the various power bases within the organisation without taking tough, dispassionate decisions. Yet the organisation need not be overwhelmed if the process is clear and logical, roles and responsibilities are understood, there is constructive iteration between the centre and the operating units and 'sign-off' authority is clearly demarcated.

Let us consider the situation of a global organisation whose brands are in first and second position in most of its key categories. They will be at differing stages of the lifecycle, be contending with different competitors and will not carry the same product range in each country. Some may seek growth through a market penetration strategy; others may call for a product development strategy. The task of those responsible will be to allocate global resources in order to deliver the best result. In addition to the global product categories there may well be strong pockets of business in non-global categories in particular countries. This may be due to past entrepreneurialism or acquisition. The appropriate growth and investment support for these businesses will need to be integrated with the global categories.

Resource allocation

Figure 4.3 shows a resource allocation process developed by a consultant in collaboration with a multinational company's key country and category managers. The process should start with the corporate HQ defining the overall growth and profit objectives for the business that will satisfy the investor and analyst community. Thereafter, they should review and challenge interim proposals, and they will set the final targets and budgets. The executive directors should normally include global directors responsible for operations (sales) and marketing. The global operations director should be able to propose to their various regional directors the initial targets necessary to deliver the overall objectives. They will review their proposals, decide on prioritisation between regions and major countries, arbitrate and resolve issues of conflict, and ensure the delivery of the targets, including making necessary changes to the investment plans in order to achieve the profit commitment. Their marketing counterpart, responsible for global categories, will need to outline the broad category growth and profit targets, review and challenge their global category directors' proposals, prioritise between categories, validate the quality of the proposed marketing programme and closely monitor its implementation.

Global category directors responsible for specific categories will respond to the global marketing director's initial growth targets, and will discuss individual category growth and investment plans with the various regional directors. They will establish outline category priorities in the larger countries, coordinate new product launch programmes, develop global advertising campaigns and ensure a healthy programme of research and development activity. Thereafter they will monitor progress in their respective categories, identify such 'course correction' measures as may be necessary to deliver the target and support and encourage regional and country implementation of the marketing mix.

Implementation

The regional director should prioritise his target across the various countries reporting to him, assign an overall strategic role to each country, ensure there are appropriate plans to deliver the necessary results from the important non-global category businesses, monitor

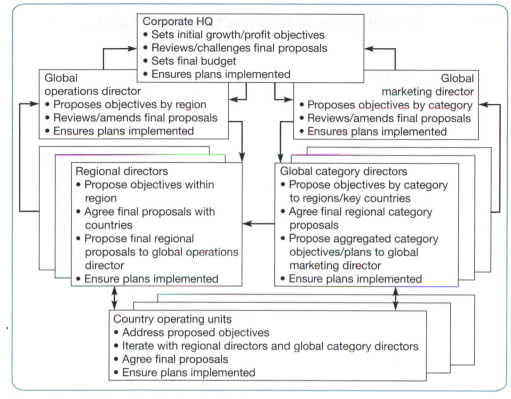

Figure 4.3 A global marketing planning 'loop'

and deliver implementation of the plans and address and resolve operational, fixed cost and other organisational issues. But only the operating units in the respective countries and regions will deliver the results needed. Corporate HQ, executive directors, regional and category directors do not sell anything to anyone. It is therefore vital that the countries are able to respond purposefully to the broad targets that cascade down to them from corporate HQ. It is equally vital that their responses are given a fair hearing, and that they can in due course agree local sales targets, investment needs and marketing programmes which will enable them to deliver a satisfactory result. This may take more iteration, but it is a critical phase. Once these plans have been finalised and are owned by the operating units, the latter will need to apply themselves to the specific tasks required to implement the local sales and marketing programme. In addition, they will be able to identify new opportunities and to develop contingency plans.

For such a process to run smoothly, it is imperative that the approach should not change from year to year, that each participant recognises and values others' roles, discussions are open and honest and that there is a strict timetable for completion. As well as designing and championing the process, an important role that can be played by a consultant is to act as a challenging partner, questioning constructively the various assumptions behind the sundry growth plans and investment needs advocated.

4.8   Managing the client–consultant relationship

Expertise

As this chapter has illustrated, there is no shortage of subjects in the international business world that need to be known and understood by the effective consultant. Clients will need help and advice on a number of topics. Whether it is understanding if general average can be declared over a jettisoned cargo or whether the act will in fact be construed as barratry, whether it is to appreciate that a two-litre bottle will not fit easily inside the average Spanish refrigerator, whether it is to realise that the English advertising slogan will have an unfortunate double entendre in another language, whether it is to learn the ways of conducting business with an Indian counterpart, whether it is to be taught the key principles of key account management in the USA or whether it is the need for a second pair of eyes to assess the intended business plan, there are very many opportunities for consultant advice.

Adding value

The challenge, though, must be whether the consultant will add value. If they are no more than discussion facilitators, or if they merely provide the information and opinions the company could have found out for themselves had they taken the trouble to ask (and indeed believe) their own staff, the investment will have been costly and unnecessary. What is sought from the consultant is genuine expertise, particular subject knowledge, the application of best practice and rigorous, high standards – in short, the provision of superior knowledge and skill not generally available within the company.

Collaboration

To succeed, the relationship must be professional, based on mutual respect. The consultant is neither a hired hand nor a white knight coming to an ailing company's rescue. A company capable of utilising this expertise has appointed them because of their perceived ability. But the personal chemistry must be good. An arrogant, overbearing and inflexible consultant will not endear themselves to the company with whom they are working. Nor will one who trades on their international reputation and assigns inexperienced staff to the project. Nor will one who sets out to make themselves indispensable to the company and who draws out the time and scope of the project, still less will one who feels it appropriate to involve themselves in the internal politics of the organisation. For they will only be as good as the way in which they deliver the brief they have been given. Consultants play a pivotal role in guiding and assisting companies in aspects of their international operation, but in the final event it is the job of the company to ensure that they derive the maximum value from their investment.

> ### Team discussion points
>
> 1 What value can the right consultant deliver to an international firm that the company's own management could not provide for themselves?
>
> 2 What do you think would be additional challenges in managing a multinational team for a consulting project?

Summary of key ideas

- The role of the consultant in helping firms with their international strategies can be a major area of work; however, this brings with it additional complexities.
- Operating internationally has great appeal, but implies considerable additional complexity and risk for the company.
- The company needs to be fully informed in order to take overseas investment decisions with confidence.
- Specialist agencies and consultants play a key role in providing information and expertise.
- A company operating internationally needs to understand and to defer to the differing cultures in the countries where it is present, and should behave as a responsible global citizen.
- Clear rules and defined responsibilities are vital for an efficient performance.

Key reading

Hollensen, S. (2013) *Global Marketing* (6th edn). Harlow: Pearson.

Noonan, C. (1999) *The CIM Handbook of Export Marketing.* London: Butterworth-Heinemann.

Reuvid, J. and Sherlock, J. (2011) *International Trade: An Essential Guide to the Principles and Practice of Export.* London: Kogan Page.

Further reading

Albaum, G., Duerr, E. and Strandskov, J. (2011) *International Marketing and Export Management* (7th edn). Harlow, Essex: FT Prentice Hall.

Arnould, E., Price L. and Zinkhan G.M. (2004) *Consumers.* New York: McGraw-Hill.

Bradley, F. (2002) *International Marketing Strategy* (5th edn). Harlow, Essex: Pearson Education.

Branch, A.E. (2006) *Export Practice and Management.* London: Thomson Learning.

Brassington, F. and Pettitt, S. (2006) *Principles of Marketing.* Harlow, Essex: FT Prentice Hall.

Browaeys, M.-J. and Price, R. (2011) *Understanding Cross-Cultural Management.* Harlow, Essex: FT Prentice Hall.

Deresky, H. (2010) *International Management – Managing Across Borders and Cultures* (7th edn). Harlow, Essex: Pearson Education.

Formani, Robert L. 'David Ricardo, Theory of Free International Trade' in *Economic Insights*, Federal Reserve Bank of Dallas, Vol 9, No 2.

Johanson, J. and Vahlne, J.E. (1977) 'The internationalization process of the firm: a model of knowledge development and increasing foreign market commitment', *Journal of International Business Studies*, 8 (1), 23–32.

Keegan, W.J. (1995) *Multinational Marketing Management* (5th edn). Upper Saddle River, NJ: Prentice Hall, pp. 378–381.

Klein, N. (2010) *No Logo.* London: Fourth Estate.

Kotler, P. (2015) *Marketing Management* (15th edn). Harlow, Essex: Pearson Education.

Levitt, T. (1983) 'The globalization of markets', *Harvard Business Review*, May–June, 92–102.

Morden, A. (2007) *Principles of Strategic Management*. London: Ashgate Publishing.

Morrison, J. (2011) *The Global Business Environment* (3rd edn). Palgrave Macmillan.

Schlosser, E. (2002) *Fast Food Nation*. London: Penguin Books.

Sherlock, J. (2006) 'Be prepared – it's a jungle out there', *Exporting World,* Sept/Oct, pp. 30–31.

Usunier, J.-C. and Lee, J. (2009) *Marketing Across Cultures* (5th edn). Harlow, Essex: FT Prentice Hall.

Walker, A. (1970) *Export Practice and Documentation*. London: Butterworth-Heinemann.

Case exercise

Bill Chieftain

The Bill Chieftain brand of clothing originated in the 1960s and was best known for its buttoned-down, narrow-collared shirts that were beloved of the 'Mods'. Throughout the 1970s and 1980s, they became part of the 'uniform' of the skinheads and other groups of young men seeking to define their identity. By the 1990s, however, the company that made them in Ireland was suffering, like many of its competitors, from cheap, foreign competition and was struggling to survive. A white knight arrived in 1995 in the shape of 2B venture capitalists, which saw an opportunity to make the Bill Chieftain brand popular once more, and they bought the company. 2B employed a dynamic new management team who brought with them extensive experience of the fashion industry.

Over the following five years, sales and profits rose fivefold as the brand was extended into menswear, womenswear, shoes and other accessories. This was on the back of a successful campaign that highlighted the heritage of the brand. Practically all the sales came from the UK as the management team concentrated on developing the brand there. There always had been a small amount of sales abroad, particularly in Germany and the US, through small specialist retailers, catering to young men who followed the 'skinhead' fashions.

In 2000 2B were reviewing their investments and asked the management team to put together a three-year plan. In order to continue with their investment in the company, 2B required that sales and profits be doubled to £200 million and £40 million respectively. The management team's response was to expand internationally, building on the business that they already had in their two main export markets of Germany and the US. Their reasoning was that these were two of the biggest markets in the world and they would only need to get a 1 per cent market share in both countries to achieve their targets. They also felt that they did not need to change their strategy, which was to exploit the 'Britishness' of the brand and in particular to use the advertising that highlighted Bill Chieftain's appeal among young men of a certain type. They argued that as it had worked so well in the UK, it was bound to work elsewhere.

2B are not entirely convinced by the management team's arguments and decide to employ some external consultants to look at the strategy and advise whether 2B should continue their investment or sell up now.

1 You are the consultant employed by 2B. What information would you ask the management team to consider evaluating their international marketing strategy?

2 The management team are advocating setting up sales offices in these two countries. What other alternatives should they look at and why?

3 The majority of their production is moving to the Far East, principally China, for the clothes and Vietnam for the leather goods; what impact do you think this may have on their strategy?

APOLLO TECH SOLUTIONS CASE STUDY

Part One

Apollo Tech Solutions (ATS) were an established player in the information and communication technologies (ICT) market. The business was started in the early 1970s by two brothers, John and Robert Southwell, to sell phone equipment (handsets and exchanges) to small- to medium-sized enterprises (SMEs) in their local area of the Midlands in the UK. By the end of that decade they had increased their coverage and were supplying equipment to larger firms across England. Their big opportunity for expansion came with the deregulation of the telecom market in the late 1980s as they started to sell additional products and services, such as infrastructure and maintenance service contracts, to clients. They built a solid reputation for reliability and as a result had excellent customer relationships. This was to be critical as many of these customers remained loyal when new technologies and competitors came on the scene.

During the 1990s, they further diversified by offering their clients the ability to outsource communications with the building of a network of call centres. However, it was the early 2000s when they began to grow rapidly thanks to the opportunities made possible by high-speed Internet (broadband) connections. This revolutionised communication and also the way that information could be used in the business environment. ATS capitalised on these new markets by acquiring businesses and also developing new opportunities internally.

In 2005 the two brothers decided that they wanted to float the business, having largely stepped away from the day-to-day running of the business (although John was still Chairman and Robert sat on the Board). The City was eager for the flotation and the shares were over-subscribed leading to a high initial price. The Southwells resigned their positions and a new Board was put in place to reflect the changed status of the company. Stephen Irvine, the Chief Executive Officer (CEO), also restructured his team with a new Chief Financial Officer (CFO), Tom McPherson, and the appointment of a new position of Strategy Director. The latter post was filled by Samuel Arnott, who had previously worked for a rival ICT supplier in a similar role and before that had been a management consultant at one of the leading consultancy firms.

One of the first actions by Irvine was to restructure the business into two divisions: 'Apollo Comms', which comprised of the original business of supplying telecom-related services to businesses and 'Apollo Advance', which brought together all the units offering Internet Protocol (IP) – based solutions to communications and information sourcing. The company thrived until the downturn of 2008, when its inherent weaknesses began to show, and by 2011 the share price was half that of the initial flotation six years previously. While initial investors had seen growth opportunities in the new businesses, the sentiment in City was now quite negative and ATS was seen as a 'laggard', because of the large proportion of its business (and profits) in 'old' technologies.

In early 2012 Irvine asked Arnott to put forward recommendations on how they might address the fundamental issues the business faced.

- Apollo Comms (AC) provided 60% of the revenue but contributed 90% of the profits; however, the profit growth rate was only 2% a year in what was a mature market with growth at a similar rate.

- Apollo Advance's (AA) profits were growing at 5% a year but only contributed 10% of the profits and AA was in a market that was growing 20% a year.

A strategy going forward would not be easy, not least because Arnott was faced with two opposing views from Irvine (CEO) and the equally powerful McPherson (CFO). The former thought that there were limited growth prospects for AC and it was the opportunities offered by AA that should be pursued. However, the strategy had to be one of organic growth as there were no funds available for more mergers and acquisitions. McPherson had different ideas; he believed the way forward was to increase profits by making cost savings in both divisions. Both men, however, agreed that a new strategy needed to be in place, not least because it would give them ammunition at the next Annual Results presentation to show the investors that they were actively looking to improve the bottom line. This they hoped would encourage positive sentiment and drive up the share price, leading to their incentive share options improving.

While the 'safe' option advocated by McPherson was not without its merits, Arnott also agreed with

Apollo Tech Solutions Case Study (continued)

Irvine that AA was underperforming but the question was by how much and perhaps more fundamentally why. What was it about the business that was not working? Arnott had his own theories stemming from the fact that AA was in reality a string of smaller businesses bolted together with no central function or coherence. Was it therefore the business model that was being used that was the problem or the processes or the people in the business or a combination of all or some of these?

Arnott had been a reluctant user of consultancy in the past, having been a consultant himself and was therefore a bit sceptical of the grand promises that consulting firms make. However, in this case, he decided he wanted to use outside expertise to try and quantify what the upside could be in terms of growth of the AA division. On a personal level, he was curious to see what the current leading global consultancies could offer by ways of solutions and set his sights high. He negotiated a budget equating to 1% of the company's profits, so that he could get bids from these leading players.

Having prepared a brief (that did not include his budget), he approached three firms.

- ITL, the largest non-accountancy-based management consultancy worldwide with a strong record in strategy development and implementation across a wide range of business sectors.

- Ferguson & Co, a much smaller operation than ITL but known particularly for its strategy work and with a dedicated division for the ICT market.

- EuroComms Solutions, the acknowledged expert in the ICT market that worked across many functional areas including strategy and change management.

The brief Arnott gave them was to identify the best growth route for Apollo Advance and to offer a degree of quantification of their findings. The target would be a plan to double revenue in five years, while maintaining gross margin, leading to a quadrupling of profits within the AA division. It needed to be achieved on a sustainable basis and give Apollo a long-term competitive advantage. It was made clear that the main division (AC) was not included in the brief and the consultants would only be employed for the first stage (strategy development) not implementation.

Questions

1   Was Arnott right to bring in consultants for this project, what else might he have considered?

2   Thinking about the brief to the three consultancies, discuss what other options Arnott could have pursued.

3   Prepare an initial proposal – what questions would you ask Arnott?

PART TWO

Project evaluation and analysis

Chapter 5

Defining the destination, developing a strategy and understanding change

Small opportunities are often the beginning of great enterprises.

Demosthenes

Learning outcomes

The learning outcomes from this chapter are to:

- recognise the *rational*, *cognitive* and *political* dimensions of a business problem;
- understand how a problem may be *defined* to make it amenable to resolution;
- understand the distinction between the *aim*, *objectives* and *outcomes* of the consulting project;
- be able to *define* an effective aim, objectives and outcomes for the project;
- be able to *articulate* the aim, objectives and outcomes in a convincing and influential way;
- be able to identify the *core competences*, *strategic resources* and *intrinsic culture* of the organisation
- develop and write a *Project Charter*;
- use the principles from the Six Sigma DMAIC and/or DMADV processes;
- understand the levels of client–consultant interaction depending on the type of consulting project undertaken;
- recognise the *drivers* of organisational change.

Consultants are usually called in to the client business in order to address some 'problem' the business has identified. The problem will be defined as something that prevents the business reaching its potential. The word 'problem' has a negative connotation.

> To a consultant and the client business, a problem may actually be *positive*.

A problem might well be an opportunity the business could potentially exploit as much as an issue that restricts the business. Problems do not present themselves. The firm's managers identify them.

For students working perhaps on their first consulting project it is important to understand that the nature of the work is not an academic exercise. It is a task addressing a business problem which requires a satisfactory resolution. It most certainly is not a research dissertation. The latter is intended to enable the student to demonstrate academic ability, research skills and critical thinking. It can be *deductive*, testing a theoretical proposition by employing a research strategy specifically designed for the purpose of its testing, or *inductive*, developing a theoretical conclusion as the result of observing empirical data. It may be *exploratory*, aiming to seek new insights, ask new questions or assess topics in a new light; *descriptive*, designed to produce an accurate representation of persons, events and situations; or *explanatory*, focusing on studying a situation or a problem in order to explain the relationships between variables.

The author will need to have an understanding of recondite, esoteric subjects such as ontology, epistemology, positivism, phenomenology, taxonomy and ethnography. The output will be a lengthy document upwards of 15,000 words with a substantial review of academic literature and a scholarly validation of the preferred research method. Such a work may indeed have great academic value but it will be of no immediate use to a client seeking a more down to earth answer to their problem.

5.1 Identification of opportunities and issues with the client organisation

Evaluating the problem

> A problem has three facets that determine the way in which it will be understood and acted upon by managers: the *rational*, the *cognitive* and the *political* (see Figure 5.1).

The *rational* facet refers to the way in which the problem is seen in a logical manner. It reflects a formal or semi-formal evaluation of the way in which resolution of the problem might affect the business. It will be based on a dispassionate consideration of the economic 'value' or cost of the problem and the business's ability to address it. The *cognitive* facet refers to the way in which individual managers see a problem. It reflects the way in which the problem is processed by a manager's mental faculties. Cognitive style and strategy determine the way in which managers see the world, process information about it and deal with challenges. The manager's cognitive style and strategy will influence the way in which the problem appears in the manager's mental landscape and will determine the priority the manager will give it.

Ultimately, the problems that a firm faces must be dealt with by the business as a whole. The *political* facet reflects the way in which a problem is received and processed by

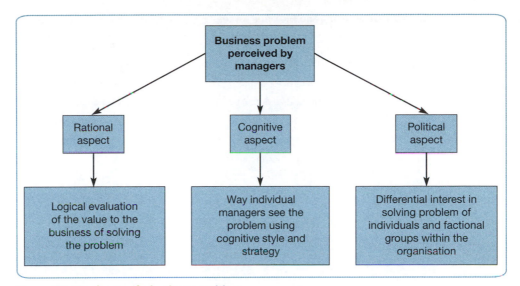

Figure 5.1 The facets of a business problem

the individuals who make up the organisation. Not all managers have the same objectives. Different individuals and groups have different interests. A particular problem will affect different managers in different ways, and some more than others. Some issues may be problems for some managers and opportunities for others. These differences will affect the way in which the managers work together as a team to address the problem. Ultimately, if the organisation's politics become pernicious, managers may actually work against each other.

The astute consultant recognises each of these facets. The rational is important because it determines the value the consultant can create by resolving the problem. The cognitive is relevant because it affects the way in which the consultant communicates with the client and can positively influence him or her. The political is significant because the success of a project will depend on persuading the whole organisation to see the benefits of a particular course of action and to unite behind it. Four dimensions of a problem will be relevant to its definition. These are the *current situation* of the business, the *goals* of the business (that is, the state it aspires to achieve), the *supporting forces* (factors which assist the business to achieve its goals) and the *blocking forces* (those factors which impede the firm and prevent it from achieving its goals). Supporting and blocking forces may be internal to the firm (under the direct control of the firm's managers) or external to it (*not* directly under the control of the firm's managers). Some important supporting and blocking forces are listed in Table 5.1. The challenge for the consultant is to define the business problem in the following terms.

How can supporting forces be used and developed to achieve the set objectives?

The key issues are how the business can capitalise on internal supporting forces and how the firm's managers can exploit external supporting forces, possibly bringing these external supporting forces into the organisation. An example is taking control of customer demand through an effective marketing campaign. Here the external supporting force of customer goodwill is converted into an internal supporting force of marketing capability.

Table 5.1 Supporting and blocking forces

	Internal	External
Supporting forces	Cost advantages (scale/experience)	Relationships with customers
	Unique resources	Investors' goodwill
	Innovative products	Location in business network
	Product knowledge	Expanding market potential
	Market knowledge	High profit margins
	Business location (especially for distributors)	
Blocking forces	Lack of management experience	Limited market potential (market decline)
	Lack of capital	Competitor activity
	Lack of product knowledge	Changes in customer interest (particularly for fashion-sensitive products)
	Limited knowledge about the environment	High entry costs

How can blocking forces be overcome or avoided so that the business can move forward?

Blocking forces by definition limit the business. Overcoming an internal blocking force is the responsibility of the firm's managers. It is they who must take the initiative and address the problem. The priority given to this will depend on the business's plans and the significance of the blocking force. An external blocking force is outside the control of the firm's managers. The firm must develop strategies that take account of the external blocking forces in the business environment and mitigate their impact. For example, a lack of knowledge must be addressed through organisational learning. Sectors in which competitors (especially stronger competitors) are active should be given lower priority than those in which absence of competitors creates an opportunity.

A problem is best defined in relation to these four facets. They can be used to guide investigation of the problem and to specify the information that is required in order to define it. This framework works well as the basis of a brainstorming session. This is best undertaken with members of the consulting team and with key information providers from the client business.

Reinterpreting problems as opportunities

Problems, by their very nature, are negative. They demand to be solved, but they are unlikely to inspire. Opportunities are positive and call to be exploited. Problems, especially when their resolution is difficult, may be divisive. Managers may work at devising solutions but some energy may also be diverted into avoiding recrimination. If a problem is 'internal' to the business, it follows that someone somewhere must have caused it. A problem is someone's *fault*. Rather than solve the problem, a manager prefers to ensure that someone else is blamed for it. This is a self-defence mechanism, but it does not help the firm. Problems may become embroiled in the internal politics of the organisation and can exacerbate them.

An opportunity is external to the firm. It is there to be exploited. While managers may resist identification of problems, minimising them or even denying their existence, they will readily seek to take credit for identifying an opportunity. Managers should collaborate willingly to exploit an opportunity. Human nature is such that people are constrained to deal with problems but motivated to capitalise on opportunities. For the consultant, therefore, it is likely to be more productive to refer to taking advantage of opportunities rather than addressing problems.

To an extent problems and opportunities may be two sides of the same coin. Translating one to the other may be a matter of rhetorical approach or learning from mistakes. For example, a new product launch has not gone as well as expected. This is a problem: the return on the investment is not as good as expected. However, it represents an opportunity to understand customer demand better and develop an improved product or marketing mix. A competitor moves into a market. *Prima facie* this is a problem, as it will increase competition, but it confirms that the sector is an attractive one for the player who can best exploit it. Further, an additional competitor investing in the market will increase market size, heighten consumer awareness and put other firms on their mettle to improve the competitive appeal of their offerings.

A word of caution is appropriate: although it is preferable to refer to opportunities rather than problems, it is important to be realistic. Too much emphasis on the positives can make the proponent appear glib and unable to come to terms with the real world. Others may doubt the person's decision-making ability. If they cannot see the problem, how can their decisions address it? Further, individuals who tend to see problems rather than opportunities (and this is to some extent a part of the cognitive perspective discussed above) may feel that those who emphasise the positive are ignoring their concerns. Turning problems into opportunities – negatives into positives – should not be a mantra; it should be a tool used as part of an overall communication strategy. It should be used not to deny problems but to put them into context. Revealing the opportunity makes the problem seem tractable and tackling it worthwhile

5.2   Problem analysis, specification and quantification

The consultant needs to fully understand the nature of the problem.

The consultant is presented with a 'problem' by the client. Before they can start to solve this problem, they need to analyse it and discover whether the client has correctly identified the problem and its root cause. This should be done before any formal proposal is given to the client.

Stage 1: Brainstorm the causes

Using members of the consulting team and the client, some of the causes of the problem need to be explored. The chosen problem should be clearly stated and the rules

Table 5.2 Possible causes of a poor response rate

Not sent to a named person
Survey is too long
The language used is too complicated
The incentives are inadequate
It is not clear how the interviewee should respond
The person to whom the completed questionnaire should be sent is not obvious
It has not been sent to enough people
The mailing list details are out of date
The information requested is confidential or too personal
The target is too busy
The respondent is suspicious of the survey's motives
Our organisation has failed to process the completed questionnaire

Table 5.3 Suggested categories for grouping causes

Service industries	Manufacturing industries	Process steps
Policies	Machines	Determine customers
Procedures	Methods	Advertise product
People	Materials	Incentivise purchase
Plant/technology	Measurements	Sell product
	Mother nature (environment)	Ship product
	Manpower (people)	Provide upgrade

Source: www.isixsigma.com (Tools and Templates>Cause and effect>The Cause and Effect a.k.a. Fishbone diagram).

of *brainstorming* (see Section 9.3) should be followed so as to answer the question. The question could be: *Why is the response to my questionnaire too low*? See Table 5.2 for some responses to the question.

Stage 2: Group the causes into major categories

This is often a helpful way to sort a lot of ideas that have come from the brainstorming session. The Six Sigma website has suggested three sets of categories which may prove a useful guide (see Table 5.3).

So, using the example above, the responses could be grouped as described in Table 5.4.

Stage 3: Construct a 'cause and effect' diagram

This useful tool (often called a 'fishbone diagram') was developed by Kaoru Ishikawa, a Japanese management expert who was particularly concerned with the achievement of total quality within the workplace. For this and other problem-solving techniques, students are referred to Ishikawa's book *What is Total Quality Control? The Japanese Way*.

Table 5.4 Major causes of poor response

Not reaching the right person (policies)	Not going to a named person
	It has not been sent to enough people
	The mailing list details are out of date
Target not completing the survey (people)	Survey is too long
	The language used is too complicated
	The incentives are inadequate
	The information requested is confidential or too personal
	The target is too busy
	The respondent is suspicious of the survey's motives
Survey completed but not processed (procedures)	It is not clear on how the interviewee should respond
	The person to whom the completed questionnaire should be sent is not obvious
	Our organisation has failed to process the completed questionnaire

Here it provides a picture of the problem ('effect') and the likely causes. By using this, the groupings can be challenged further and *major* causes identified. The minor causes should be those that may easily be resolved or do not have a significant impact on the problem. Figure 5.2 takes the example and uses the cause and effect tool.

Stage 4: Getting to the root cause of the major problems

Having established the major causes of the problem, it is important to determine the *root* causes. The '5 Whys' is a useful tool to challenge thinking and uncover the true root of the problem. It keeps asking 'why' until a meaningful answer to the root cause is uncovered. Sometimes it takes fewer than five whys and sometimes more to reach an answer. An example of this process follows, based on the analysis of an unsuccessful sales call.

Problem statement: The last sales call was not successful.

1 *Why?* Because the customer did not buy.
2 *Why did the customer not buy?* Because the product did not seem right for her.
3 *Why was the product not right for her?* Because it did not address any needs she had.
4 *Why did the product not address any needs she had?* Because it was too complex for her business.
5 *Why did you not know this before the call?* Because I did not know about the business she was running.
6 *Why did you not know about the business she was running?* Because no research had been done in advance.

The solution to this problem is clear. A competent salesperson does his or her homework!

In the above example, if it is decided that the mailing list being out of date is a major cause of the problem, the root cause can be explored (Table 5.5). In this example, it is the

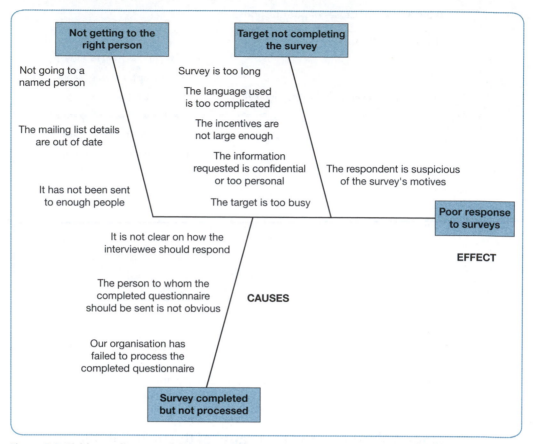

Figure 5.2 Fishbone diagram of the causes of low response to surveys

last answer that identifies the means of resolution, for including an update of the mailing list *is* within the firm's control and therefore can be undertaken. In comparison, if the analysis had stopped at answer 4, the identified solution would have been to try to change the budget that had been given, which is harder or perhaps impossible to achieve.

Table 5.5 Root cause of why the mailing list is out of date

1 **Why** is the mailing list out of date?
   ● Because we haven't updated it

2 **Why** did you not update it?
   ● Because we cannot afford it

3 **Why** can you not afford it?
   ● Because we did not put it in our budget for the year

4 **Why** did you not put it in your budget for the year?
   ● Because we had no room in the budget we were given

5 **Why** did you have no room in the budget you were given?
   ● Because we thought it was not necessary

5.3   Objective setting: defining the desired end-state

Aims, objectives, outcomes and actions

An activity is normally undertaken with a clear understanding of its intended result.

Whether it is in sport, war or business, plans will be developed with a view to delivering a precise outcome, to deliver a desired future state. An investor is not just interested in the current profitability of a company; they are just as interested in what the company's *future* profitability will be. Good managers do not simply accept what future conditions might be: they should try to control them and to *shape* the future. Managers operate with a conscious picture of the state they wish to create: where they want their organisation to be, what they want the organisation to do, what they want it to be like. This is described as the business's vision. Managers should articulate in explicit terms what they and their organisation wish to achieve. They will talk about their *goals, aims, objectives, missions* and *outcomes*.

Sometimes these words are taken to be synonymous. At other times, users imply subtle distinctions between them. While each has a distinct definition in management theory, it may not necessarily follow that such precision of meaning applies within the client organisation. The consultant should recognise differences in meaning between such terms and how the client interprets them. This aids thinking about the rationale for the consulting project and makes communication more effective and meaningful. Appropriate and well-defined aims, objectives and outcomes are the cornerstone of successful project management. They provide a business case and form the solid platform on which a successful project can be built. The consultant develops aims, objectives and outcomes in the preliminary analysis phase. They are communicated to the client through the proposal. They function to keep the project on track and help the consulting team maintain focus and monitor progress during the process of delivery. They can then be used to assess what the project has actually achieved at delivery. The following discussion highlights the differences between aims, objectives and outcomes. Knowledge of these differences will aid the consultant in analysis and communication with the client at the different stages of the project.

Aims

The aim of the project is its *overall goal*. It is the *broad* scope of what that project aspires to achieve. An aim is the starting point of a project. It is first articulated as a desire: a sense that things might be different and better. Most businesses share a set of common desires – for example, to grow, to be more profitable, to be more secure or to compete more effectively. It is from these general desires that the aim of a consulting project can be distilled. In defining an aim, a consultant is refining the desires of the firm's managers. The way in which this will be done will depend on a number of factors. Some of those the consultant needs to take into account include the following.

- **The extent to which managers have already articulated their desires for the business.** Unless the client has a clear view of what is expected of the project the consultant must first help them to clarify, understand and define their aims, playing a facilitation role rather than imposing objectives of their own.

- **The level of detail in that articulation.** As a business moves forward to pursue its aims, it changes. It may choose to modify its internal processes. It may reorganise itself. It develops its relationships with external stakeholders. At the commencement of the project the extent of these changes may not be known. Consideration must be given to the *detailed* implications of pursuing and achieving particular goals for the firm as a whole. If this will necessitate radical change, the consultant must support the client and encourage them to appreciate these changes.

- **How appropriate the aims are for the business.** Not all its desired aims are necessarily appropriate for a business. The outcomes may, for example, move the business into an area where competitive pressures are unsustainable. They may expose the business to too high a level of risk. In short, they may reduce rather than increase its ability to reward its stakeholders. In this case, the consultant is obliged to inform the client that the aim is not in the business's best interests. This should result in a reconsideration of the aims.

- **The extent to which aims are realistic, given the firm and its situation.** Even if the aims are *appropriate* for the business, consideration must be given to how *realistic* they are. Can the business *really* deliver them? Two factors are important to this consideration. First: can the aims realistically be achieved given the situation in the market in which the firm operates? It is pointless having an aim of achieving sales of £10 million with a product whose total market is worth only £5 million. Second: are the aims reasonable, given the resources the firm has available to pursue them? It is not usually realistic for a small firm to aspire to market leadership using just its own cash flow. It might do so were sufficient new investment capital able to be found. If this is the course decided upon, acquiring additional capital will need to be incorporated in the project.

- **The way in which the desires are particular to the firm and are distinguished from the general desires all firms have.** All firms have ambitions of some sort. Generic aims might include a desire to grow, to increase profits or to make cash flow more stable. These are common to most businesses. The consultant must be careful to distinguish between those aims the firm will share with all other firms in its sector and those that can properly be said to be exclusive to the business. The distinction is important because businesses pursuing shared aims tend to meet each other in direct competition. Aims that are exclusive may be a way of differentiating the firm, focusing its mind on how it can deliver sustained competitive advantage.

- **The scope of the consulting project relative to the business as a whole.** Some aims are general. They relate to what the business as a whole wishes to achieve. Other aims may be more localised and will relate to a limited part of the firm only. There are three dimensions along which aims usually become specific to a part of the business. They may relate to one particular part of the business or business unit within the firm. They may refer to the development of a particular product range from within the firm's entire product scope. Third, they may refer to a particular functional activity within the firm, such as marketing, production or human resource management.

A project should be summarised by a *single* aim, not a list. The important thing is that the aim summarises the project in a succinct way so that all involved can recognise it and subscribe to it. It might even be thought of as the *mission* for the project. It is not necessary that the aim quantifies the project or gives away all the details. That is the purpose of objectives and outcomes, discussed below.

A good way to start the aim is with a phrase such as

It is the aim of this project to . . .

or

This project aims to . . .

For example:

This consulting project aims to give New Firm Ltd an analysis of its main competitors to aid decision making about competitive positioning.

or

It is the aim of this consulting project to develop a promotional plan for the effective launch of the Ideal product range.

Mission

In many ways, a business may be thought of as a permanent and ongoing project. Certainly, an entrepreneur will see the development of their venture as a project of great importance. In the case of the business as a whole its overall aim is defined by the business's *mission*. A mission statement clarifies to employees and other stakeholders the overriding reason for the firm's existence. It should be a distinctive and compelling statement of *what* it will achieve and *how*. A mission can include a statement of what the firm offers, to whom it is offering it, the source of its advantages in the marketplace, its aspirations and the ethical values it will uphold (see Wickham (1997) for a review of business missions).The aims of a consulting project should resonate with the firm's mission and enable it be accomplished.

Objectives

An aim is a *broad* statement. It is a *wish*. *Objectives* provide the details of how this wish will be made into reality. A single aim may be split into a number of objectives. These may be listed. One way to start the objective list is with the phrase:

The objectives of the consulting project are to . . .

The specific objectives may be put into a bullet-point list after this statement. A number of tests should be applied to an objective list to ensure that the objectives provide the basis for a good project. Good objectives must be able to answer questions such as the following:

- Are the objectives consistent with the agreed aim? If not, they must be revised.
- Is the objective well defined? To prevent misunderstandings it should not be ambiguous.
- Will achieving the objectives actually be good for the firm? If the aim is appropriate and the objectives are consistent, then logically they should also be desirable.
- Are the objectives likely to be achieved given the environmental conditions the firm faces? Can new business be delivered in the face of competitor responses?

- Does the firm have the necessary resources to deliver the objective? If so, is this project the best available use for them? If the firm does not have the resources to hand, can it obtain them? Is obtaining these additional resources part of the consulting project or is it a separate project? Is there a clear 'milestone plan' with precise deliverables and individual responsibilities?

- Can the objectives be quantified? Objectives should be quantified numerically. It is not just *what* will be achieved, but *when* it will be achieved and, critically, *what it will be worth when it is*.

This definition of objectives is often referred to as having SMART targets: objectives which are Specific, Measurable, Achievable, Realistic and Timebound. If objectives are vague and unquantified it is particularly important that the client's expectations are carefully managed and not allowed to become unrealistic. Some understanding of what these objectives mean for the firm must be found. It is important that what the project can achieve is communicated in an unambiguous way.

Actions

Good objectives inspire managers to follow them through. They are a *call to action*. Actions are what managers actually do in order to achieve objectives. A collection of coordinated actions is a *plan*. It is implementing a plan of actions that actually consumes resources. Plans organise actions in two dimensions. The first is linear, as a *sequence in time*. Actions follow one another. Some actions can be undertaken only after others have been completed. Actions must be properly sequenced. The stages of the consulting project reviewed in Chapter 2 are an example. The second dimension is *coordination*, the ordering of actions between individuals. The advantage of team working is that it allows individuals to distinguish and differentiate the contribution they make. If the value this potentially offers is to be realised then individual contributions must be properly integrated. Planning will be dealt with in more detail in Chapter 11.

Outcomes

Outcomes are what will be *made possible* if the objectives are achieved. Outcomes are the difference that is made by achieving the objectives. An outcome is something that takes the business along the road to achieving its organisational mission. It is the outcomes of a project that really sell it to the client. The outcomes define the value of the project to the client. A good way to start an outcome statement is:

As a result of this project the business will be able to . . .

Defining outcomes gives the consultant a chance to check the value of what is being offered to the client. Three important aspects to question are as follows:

- **Are outcomes consistent with aims?** Are the outcomes of the project in line with the aims agreed for the project? Is the outcome the fulfilment of an aim? Will the outcomes take the business along the road that it wants to go? Critically, will the outcomes help the business deliver its mission?

- **Are outcomes attractive?** Will the client business and the decision-making unit involved in bringing in the consultant recognise the outcomes as ones which are right for the business and which they desire to see happen? Managers are not always rational. They do not always do what the consultant might see as being in the best interests of the firm. Consultants drive change and change is usually political. Different managers see the benefits of change in different ways. If there is an issue, question how different individuals and groups might see the project outcomes. One approach is to consider the different types of client involved in the project (see Section 1.5).

- **Will the client recognise the value created by the consultant?** If managers find the outcomes attractive, do they recognise the contribution the consultant is making to their delivery? Do they feel that they can achieve them unaided? If not, why not? The process consulting mode (see Section 1.6) can be particularly prone to leaving managers feeling that the consultant has not made a contribution, especially when process consulting is at its most effective!

5.4   Understanding and reconciling consultant and client objectives

Understanding your own objectives

The consultant will have objectives that are distinct from those of the client.

People work together because this allows greater value to be created. In working together, they agree to the aims and objectives of a project. However, individuals will have their own personal objectives that may differ from those of others involved in the project. Managers pursue their own interests as well as the interests of their organisations. The consulting project is no different. This does not detract from the potential for working together – far from it. It is the fact that the client and consultant have distinct objectives that allows them to work together and create value for each other.

- **Gaining a valuable managerial experience.** A consulting project is an opportunity to engage in a high-profile, senior-level managerial experience. If it is to be a valuable part of an overall management education, it needs to be an experience of a particular sort. It should involve contact with senior managers. It should demand that a strategic perspective be taken. It should require that initiative and innovation be brought to bear. Formal managerial skills should be used and developed. If any of these things are missing, the value of the consulting experience will be reduced. Ensuring that the project will have these elements should be an objective for any student undertaking a consulting project.

- **Practising particular skills.** The consulting project provides an opportunity to apply in a real business situation the ideas and skills developed throughout a formal business education. It calls in equal measure on all of the skill areas that mark the effective manager: *analysis skills*, which enable opportunities to be spotted; *project management skills*, which can be used to exploit those opportunities; and the *relationship-building skills*, which enable the value of those opportunities to be communicated and used to motivate others. The consulting project is a chance to see that these skills are of value and to refine their use. It is a proper personal objective that the project be pursued in such a way that these skills are called on in a meaningful and balanced way.

- **Gaining evidence of achievement.** The consulting experience also provides an opportunity to demonstrate managerial ability. The skills used in consulting are transferable to a variety of managerial roles. Successfully completed, the consulting project is something that can be used to enhance the curriculum vitae when applying for positions in the future. It is a very reasonable objective to view the consulting exercise as a way of gaining real and visible evidence of managerial competence. How this can be done is discussed fully in Chapter 13.

Understanding the client's objectives

Clearly, the main objective of the client is to develop the business in a particular direction. However, this is not the client's only objective. They may also have a number of subsidiary objectives that will colour the way the project is approached. Whereas the formal objectives of the project will be explicit, discussed and documented, the client's subsidiary objectives will usually be implicit. It is worthwhile to develop an understanding of them. Recognising the client's subsidiary objectives gives the consultant an insight into how a good working relationship can be developed. Some important subsidiary objectives for the client might be as follows.

- **An opportunity to develop general understanding.** Consultants are experts. Experts have interesting things to say. The manager may regard working with consultants as an opportunity to explore and develop their understanding of management in general and the specific management tasks they face. This general understanding will develop in areas that go well beyond the bounds of the particular project.

- **An opportunity to explore the business in general terms.** Managers must be close to their businesses. Their success depends on an intimate knowledge of and sensitivity to the details of the business they are managing and the specific features of the sector in which it is operating. However, by being so close the manager may not find it easy to stand back and form a holistic view of the business. It is, as the saying goes, easy to lose sight of the wood for the trees. Working with a consultant is an opportunity to redress this situation.

- **An opportunity to talk about the business.** Managers often are proud of the businesses for which they have chosen to work and certainly will have strong views about it. An entrepreneur will be very pleased with what they have achieved. The interest the consultant shows is flattering. The consulting project gives the manager a chance to talk about the business in which they are involved. This is something most will relish. It is something the consultant can use. Asking the manager to talk about the business will be the first step in building a positive relationship and engendering rapport. It will give the manager the confidence to be open and provide the consultant with the information needed to do the project well. Rapport can be built and openness encouraged through an effective questioning technique.

Reconciling your own objectives with those of the client

In a good consulting exercise, the client and the consulting group work together as part of a team. This does not mean that the client and consultant necessarily share every objective. As discussed above, the client and consultant bring their own distinct objectives to the project.

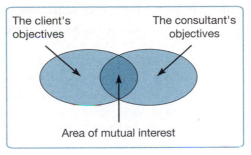

Figure 5.3 Negotiating objectives

Usually these will be compatible: the client and the consultant team can agree on a set of coordinated actions and common outcomes which will deliver the objectives desired by both parties. Occasionally there may be a misalignment and the consultant and client must negotiate the objectives of the project so that they are reconciled. This process is illustrated in Figure 5.3.

Misalignments occur for a number of reasons. Some of the most common are as follows.

- **The client expects too much of the consulting team.** The client may harbour unrealistic expectations about what the consulting team can achieve. The kind of problem that is highlighted may be of a highly technical nature. The project may require specific industry knowledge to be applied. Often, the client will expect the consulting team to build relationships with outside agencies (particularly customers and investors) in a way that the team simply does not have the experience or time to manage properly. Projects which demand that the consulting team go out and act as a sales force selling products to customers (rather than just develop and advise on a marketing or selling strategy) are examples of this kind of demand.

- **The client expects too much of the project.** The outcomes expected may be unrealistic given the resources the client is willing to put into the project. Unfortunately, whereas most managers recognise their own resource limitations, some may think that consultants have access to an unlimited supply. Typical are market research projects. The client may be quite clear about the market information wanted but may not recognise the cost involved in gaining that information.

- **The project does not have sufficient scope.** It is easy for the client manager to look upon the consulting team as an additional, low-cost resource rather than as partners in the development of the business. It is tempting for client managers to assign tasks that are important, but of low level. Such items may be repetitive. They will not demand that interpretive skills be brought to bear on information obtained. They will not challenge at a sufficiently intellectual level. Such tasks are of such limited scope that they do not demand the full range of skills and insights that would be expected of a consulting challenge. These jobs should really be undertaken by the business itself. An example would be a project that involves simply creating a list of potential customers rather than developing an understanding of a new customer segment.

- **The client is not willing to define specific outcomes.** Not everybody works to objectives. Some managers may simply not take the trouble. Others make a policy of not setting them. They prefer to deal with things on a contingency basis as they arise. They may present this as 'flexibility'. Problems will arise if the client resists setting objectives for the project. Without clear objectives, the consulting team has no idea of what to aim for. Expectations cannot be managed properly.

It will be tempting for the client to simply see the consultant team as an extra resource. If objectives are not set, the quality of the consulting exercise as a learning experience must be in doubt. With a little thought, it should be relatively simple to deal with these situations. Some useful rules of thumb are as follows.

- **Agree on aims before discussing objectives.** As noted above, aims are broad in scope, and therefore tend to be less contentious than detailed objectives. It is better to agree on the overall aim of the project before moving on to specifics. If there is any debate about objectives, either within the consulting team or with the client, then the agreed aim can be used as a reference point.

- **Break down projects into sub-projects.** If the client is too ambitious about the project, or expects too much from it, then expectations must be managed. The idea for the project should not be rejected out of hand. Rather, the manager should be encouraged to explore the project they are proposing. The project may be broken down into relevant sub-projects. It may be that one of these will present a more realistic project.

- **Have the client prioritise outcomes.** Having broken the project down, objectives should be assigned to each sub-project, and the client asked to prioritise. If they must choose, which is most important to them? The argument to use is that it will be better for a realistic project to be done well rather than risk disappointment at the outcomes of one that is too ambitious.

- **Use the proposal.** The proposal documents the project's aims, objectives and outcomes (see Section 3.7). If these are written and communicated, the client must recognise them. The aims and objectives of the project must reflect the interests of the manager. However, it is the consultancy team that will actually articulate and document them. This is an advantage which might be used positively. In the preliminary discussions with the manager it is likely that many ideas will emerge. In distilling these into the proposal, the consultant has an opportunity to emphasise and prioritise. The consultant should, however, avoid the temptation to impose ideas on the client. The latitude available here should not be used simply as an opportunity for the team to present the project they believe to be appropriate. The best projects are those to which the client has a genuine commitment.

- **Understand the client's desired outcomes.** Ultimately, it is the project's *outcomes* – the things that the business will be able to do as a result of the project – that are important. This is the difference that the project will make to the business. It is these that the client ultimately 'buys'. The importance of this must be emphasised. The consultant must understand what it is that the client wants the business to do. Once this understanding is in place the project can be designed to achieve the outcomes.

- **Focus on win–win outcomes.** Ultimately, the client and consulting team must work together. The manager will be gaining insights of value to their business. The consulting team will be gaining a valuable learning experience. There is mutual benefit, not conflict. The consulting team should not hesitate to explain that they are seeking a project that will add to their experience in a meaningful way. The team should make it plain that the manager's knowledge and experience will be an important part of this. Most managers will be flattered that their insights are valuable in this way. It will certainly encourage them to shape the project so that it will provide a good learning experience. A general point: focusing on win–win scenarios like this is the essence of good negotiating practice. Negotiating objectives is about aligning the project so that the outcomes desired by the client and those desired by the consulting team are achieved.

5.5   Developing a strategy for the destination

> The consultant needs to understand what they are trying to improve or change and when the aim has been achieved. An important starting point is 'project charter'.

As previously stated, clarifying the causes of the problem is vital. This is also true for the end point or destination. An example is given in Table 5.6.

Project information

This provides a quick summary, the name of the leader in case they need to be contacted, the timing of the product and a brief description.

Team members

As well as a team leader, it is invaluable to have a sponsor for the project. This person usually is someone senior within the organisation who will own the project and who can help if there are issues in delivering the project, resistance within the organisation or problems of slippage and scope creep and who will exercise his or her authority and influence to ensure implementation. Team size should be as restricted as possible (no more than six) but it may be necessary to involve others on an ad hoc basis, particularly if expert guidance is required.

Scope of the project

Sometimes an issue may be part of a larger problem within the organisation. For example, poor sales may be due to ineffective sales technique (which a project could address) but it may also

Table 5.6 Outline of a project charter

Project information	Business case
Leader:	(Why are we doing this?)
Project start:	
Project end:	
Brief description:	
Team members:	**Problem to be solved**
Sponsor:	(What will be the benefit to us?)
Leader:	
Core team:	
Ad hoc members:	
Scope of the project:	**Project goals**
(What should and should not be included)	(What are the objectives?)
Project timeframe:	Project measurements
(Key milestones and dates)	(What tools will be used to establish whether the project is successful?)

be due to the wrong type of salespeople being recruited, which may be beyond the control of the team. It is therefore important that it is clearly stated what is part of the project and what is not. However, at the end recommendations could be made if such wider issues were highlighted.

Project timeframe

This should detail the date of the final delivery of the project outputs together with key events along the way. Attention should be paid to events that will entail significant involvement with the client managers so that they can timetable this into their schedules. Any points at which the client managers will be expected to make expenditure should also be detailed so that they can manage their budgets. Finally, any events, such as interim reports and presentations, which will reassure the client managers that the project is on track, should be considered.

The business case

It is rare that a consulting project is done for its own sake. It normally has wider implications. For example, a project to improve advertising effectiveness will have the ultimate aim of increasing sales and profits through a cost-effective improvement in market share.

Problem to be solved

This is a detailed description of the problem and the root causes that are to be investigated. By solving this problem, the project will bring benefits to the organisation that should be articulated.

Project goals

This is a clear statement of what is intended to be achieved that is measurable.

Project measurements

In general all objectives should be measurable but it is sometimes difficult to put hard numbers on everything from the outset. Nonetheless, there needs to be some control measure or yardstick against which success can be determined. This also links back to the business case.

5.6 Understanding the client's defining characteristics

'The consultant needs to understand the individual peculiarities of the client business.

No two organisations are the same. All are what they are, where they are as the result of the strategies, decisions and changes in their particular history. Each has a set of defining characteristics which shape the way in which they operate – what might be considered their personal DNA profile. These may be strengths that can be leveraged or weaknesses which need resolution or correction. By acquainting themselves with these characteristics the consultant can more readily appreciate the challenge presented and form a dispassionate, informed view of the scale of the task facing them and the issues which will impact upon the likelihood of the project succeeding. The consultant can 'get inside the head' of the client organisation by understanding elements such as its business model, its core competences and capabilities, the quality of its resources, the relationship between its strategy and its processes and its culture.

Business model

The business model describes how the product, information and service functions are structured and the flow between the various participating parties and departments. Having an overview of the firm's business model will be invaluable for a consultant embarking on a project. There is a simple technique for mapping this flow. The process requires capturing a series of succinct statements that best describe:

- What are the relevant customer needs or behaviours?
- What the basic offer looks like, in response to these needs or behaviours.
- What the 'entrepreneurial invention' element of the business looks like. Even in an established business there should be some uniqueness in the response.
- What the source of competitive advantage might be for the business.
- And thus the added value or potential for added value for the customers and indeed for the business itself.

The model has some links to the Value Chain, as outlined in Chapter 6. Drawn as an interrelated group in a circle, the technique can best be illustrated with the example in Figure 5.4.

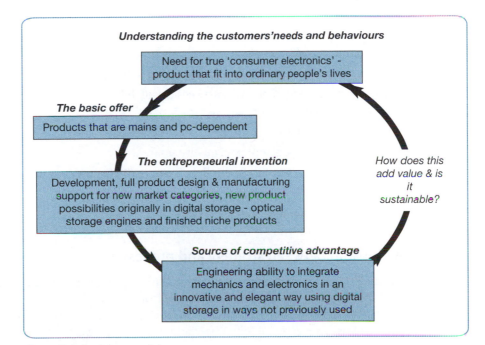

Figure 5.4 Business model

The challenge is to capture these statements simply and to seek to identify the added value if there is any. In this example, the source of added value is not clear.

Core competences

A firm will need to have threshold capabilities – those capabilities which are essential for it to be able to compete. These alone will not create competitive advantage. The firm needs distinctive, ideally unique capabilities of its own which its competitors cannot easily match. Such unique resources will critically underpin competitive advantage, but what will more likely enable the organisation to achieve this advantage will be what Gary Hamel and C.K. Prahalad term *core competences*. These are the activities and processes through which resources are deployed in such a way as to achieve competitive advantage in ways that others cannot imitate or obtain (Johnson, Scholes and Whittington, 2014) – or, put more simply, 'what do we do well?'. Challenging an organisation to identify its core competences will enlighten the consultant as to the firm's view of itself. If the answer to 'what *should* we do well?' differs from 'what *do* we do well?' the consultant will be able to identify part of the way forward.

Resource quality

Part of the answer may be provided by conducting a Resource Audit. This will enable both client and consultant to identify the organisation's human, financial and material resources and how they are deployed. It will be a systematic review of the entirety of the resources consumed by the organisation. The Ms model (BPP Learning Media, 2010) categorises them as follows:

- Machinery: age, condition, value, cost of replacement.
- Make-up: culture, structure, patents, brands, goodwill.
- Management: size, skills, loyalty, career progression.
- Management information: ability to generate and disseminate ideas, innovation, information systems.
- Markets: products, customers, specialised or general, regional, national and international.
- Materials: source, suppliers, wastage, cost, availability, future provision.
- Manpower: number, skill levels, efficiency, industrial relations, flexibility, innovatory capacity, wages, churn.
- Methods: processes, outsourcing, quality assurance.
- Money: credit, cash surpluses or deficits, sources of finance, gearing, debts.

Such a list is by no means exhaustive, but conducting such an audit will enable the consultant to draw a rich picture of the organisation.

Relationship between strategy and processes

While the firm's resources and capabilities are finite and tangible, the consultant needs also to establish whether the firm needs to do some of the things it does, or whether they are better outsourced. Activities and processes require people to manage them and will incur cost. Thus it is quite acceptable to ask whether they may be conducted more cheaply and

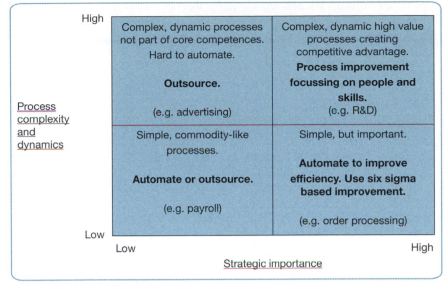

Figure 5.5 Harmon's process-strategy matrix

Source: Harmon, P. (2007) *Business Process Change: A Guide for Business Managers and BPM and Six Sigma Professionals*, 2nd ed., p. 171.

efficiently, and with greater expertise, outside the organisation. Harmon's process-strategy matrix (see Figure 5.5) analyses processes in terms of their complexity and their strategic importance (i.e. the value they add). The analysis creates four types of process, each of which may be amenable to an improvement strategy.

Organisational culture

A further critical factor to enable the consultant to understand the client organisation is to appreciate its particular culture – how its members behave and how strategy is developed. The cultural web (Johnson, Scholes and Whittington, 2014) identifies six physical manifestations of culture which coalesce to form the firm's paradigm, its beliefs, values, basic assumptions and collective experience (see Figure 5.6). These are expressed as:

- **Stories** – past events and personalities who are talked about. This can illustrate the behaviour the firm encourages and the things it values.
- **Symbols** – a firm's logo, premises and dress code; the titles it gives its people and the form of language it uses can indicate the nature of the firm.
- **Power structures** – where does the real power reside, and who has the greatest influence on the firm's strategies and operations.
- **Organisational structure** – both the formal organisational hierarchy and the 'unwritten' lines of power that indicate whose contribution is most valued.
- **Control systems** – financial systems, quality systems and rewards. Knowing which areas are most closely monitored will reveal what the firm considers to be most important.
- **Rituals and routines** – people's daily behaviour and routine actions. These signal what is considered acceptable and what is valued by management.

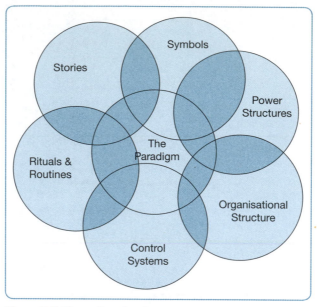

Figure 5.6 The cultural web

Source: from *Exploring Public Sector Strategy*, Pearson Education, Ltd. (Johnson, G. and Scholes, K. 2001) p. 301, © Pearson Education, Ltd. Used by permission.

5.7 Developing the strategy for the journey

Projects may differ but analytical approaches can be standard.

No two consulting projects are alike, but there are some common processes which consultants can adopt to form the basis of a framework. One that is popular at the time of writing is the 'Six Sigma' methodology.

Six Sigma

This was originated by Bill Smith at Motorola. Smith developed a means of increasing profitability by reducing defects in manufacturing and services. His objective was to eliminate defects altogether – defects being anything outside customer specifications. Six Sigma purports to reduce the probability of defects to the level defined by the area more than six standard deviations (σ) from the mean, i.e. 3.4 items in one million. The Six Sigma methodology is a measurement-based strategy that looks at process improvement through defined projects. Bill Smith's ideas were first adopted by Allied Signal (now Honeywell) and General Electric. The latter has estimated benefits of $10 billion in the first five years of operation (http://www.isixsigma.com/new-to-six-sigma/getting-started/what-six-sigma/, consulted 30 November 2015). For more information, the student is referred to *Six Sigma Way* by Peter S. Pande, R.P. Neuman and R.R. Cavanagh (2014) and *The New Six Sigma* by Matt Barney and Tom McCarty (2003). At the heart of these two methodologies is the DMAIC (define, measure, analyse, improve and control) process and the DMADV (define, measure, analyse, design and verify) process. The first (which is discussed below) is for existing processes and is the most widely used. The latter is for new processes or products.

DMAIC process

Figure 5.7 shows the outline process.

Define

The requirements for this phase include understanding the real problem and its causes and the objectives of the consulting exercise. Any current processes may be mapped out to get a common view of the 'way things are done now'. Consultants often refer to this as the 'As Is' paradigm. The project charter outlined in Section 5.4 is the document issued after the 'define' phase has been completed.

Measure

Having defined in your project charter what measurements are to be used, it will be necessary to start collecting some historical data to use as a benchmark. When doing this, the challenge needs to be made as to whether the data:

- continues to be key to the project;
- is reliable and not liable to interpretation;
- is cost effective to collect;
- is able to be collected in the future.

Is the measure sensitive enough to answer whether proper progress is being made? The question may also be asked how the measure will change if the project goes off schedule. Will it change a lot or only a little for minor delays, moderate delays or major delays?

Analyse

This is the critical phase as you assess what is wrong with the current process and what you need to do in order to improve things. Consultants often call the resulting improved process the 'To Be' process. Key questions that you need to ask are:

- Who do we need to involve to make the changes happen?
- What other resources do we need?

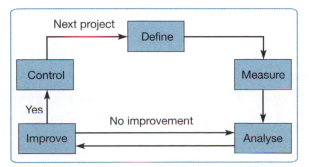

Figure 5.7 The Six Sigma DMAIC process

- What are the potential pitfalls we may face?
- What are the downsides if we fail to implement?
- What are the risks to the other parts of the business in implementation?

Improve

Here an implementation plan is drawn up of how the improved processes will be introduced. This plan would include the breakdown of work required by sub-project if necessary. The implementation plan would then be carried out and the results of the improved process monitored using the measurement tools described in the 'measure' phase. If the initial results were not as expected, it may be necessary to go back to the 'analyse' phase to ensure that the correct problems with the current process and solutions have been identified.

Control

This is the final phase where the consultant will usually hand control back to the process owner within the client company. In order for this to be done, the consultant (and their team) needs to ensure that the changes in the process are well embedded in the client organisation and all relevant personnel are trained in the new process. Any auditing of the process will now be the responsibility of the client process owner and this is critical to ensure that the improvements are maintained.

It can be that at this stage the next project is defined, which relates to further improvements in this process or related processes. In this case much of the learning in the original project should be used, so as to avoid the cost and time of repetition.

DMADV process

Known also as DFSS (Design for Six Sigma) the DMADV project methodology features five phases:

Define

Design goals that are consistent with customer demands and the enterprise strategy.

Measure

Identify characteristics that are critical to quality, measure product capabilities, production process capability and measure risks.

Analyse

To develop and design alternatives.

Design

Elaborate an improved alternative best suited as a result of the analysis in the previous step

Verify

Finalise the design, commission pilot runs, implement the production process and transfer it to the process owner.

5.8   The need for change in the client organisation

As change can be problematic, consultants can help to facilitate.

Organisations undergo continual change. For most of the time this change is incremental. It takes place in a gradual way with small steps. Managers may not recognise that change is taking place unless they specifically reflect upon it. At intervals, though, the change is more radical and is manifest as a specific management project. Given that change is often difficult, both in terms of the best direction for change and the implementation of that change, consultants are often called in to support the project. John P. Kotter, in his book *Leading Change* (2012), has a useful discussion as to why organisations need to change and how to succeed in bringing about such change.

Change is often forced upon an organisation by factors such as:

- being loss-making, or facing other financial difficulties;
- large new competitors successfully entering the marketplace;
- new regulations or other restrictions on trade;
- changes in purchasing habits by major customers;
- new technology that changes the way the business operates;
- growth driven through delivering new products or serving new markets;
- new managerial approaches (often associated with political manoeuvring).

When an organisation is in such a crisis, the first stage of change is usually a turn-around effort that aims primarily to stabilise the organisation. The objectives and the projects involved are very clear. Although this phase often involves recrimination – individuals look for someone to blame for the crisis – eventually all involved are motivated to meet this challenge.

This may be followed by an attempt to implement a radically new strategic approach that aims to put the organisation back on a growth track. This is usually harder to implement, as it demands major structural or cultural change. Here there are multiple objectives and projects, resulting in a complex and dynamic situation that is more difficult for participants to follow. In this case, Kotter emphasises the importance of leadership, as opposed to management of change. Leadership establishes direction, aligns people, motivates and inspires to create change. Good management in a period of change should focus on planning, organising and problem solving to produce some degree of order and coherence during the change episode.

Team discussion points

Discuss the following statements. Argue as to whether they might be true or not:

- Only an outsider can really see the problems an organisation faces.
- Change is always good for an organisation.
- A consultant and client's objectives can always be reconciled.
- Always turning problems into opportunities can sometimes be seen as unrealistically optimistic or naive.

Summary of key ideas

- The problem a consultant has been called in to address has three facets: the *rational,* the *cognitive* and the *political*.
- The consultant must be aware of each of these facets.
- When defining the problem it is useful to consider four dimensions: the *current state* of the business; the *desired goals* of the business; *supporting forces*: those things which will help the business achieve its goals; *blocking forces*: those things which will restrict the business and stop it from achieving its goals.
- Supporting and blocking forces can both be further divided into *internal* and *external* dimensions.
- It is important to go through a process to get to the root causes of a problem. This involves challenging the reasons why there is a problem, uncovering the *major* causes and then asking 'why' until the answer is able to be 'solved' by the consulting team.
- A consulting project is defined in terms of its *aims, objectives* and *outcomes*.
- The aim of the project is a single statement of the project's broad goal, what it aims to achieve.
- The objectives of the project are a detailed list of the things the project aims to achieve. Good objectives are SMART. They are a call to action and to initiate a plan.
- The outcomes of a project are what the business will be able to do if the objectives are delivered.
- A consulting project has both a destination and a journey.
- The destination can be defined through the use of a project charter.
- The prospect of reaching the destination can more readily be established by understanding the defining characteristics of the organisation.
- The project journey can be mapped out using the Six Sigma DMAIC process.
- Change is essential for organisations if they are to maintain their competitive position in a dynamic marketplace. Leaders deliver change.

Key reading

Johnson, G., Scholes, K. and Whittington, R. (2014) *Exploring Corporate Strategy*. Harlow, Essex: Prentice Hall.

Glückler, J. and Armbrüster, T. (2003) 'Bridging uncertainty in management consulting: the mechanisms of trust and networked reputation', *Organization Studies*, 24 (2), 787–794.

Further reading

Andreas, S. and Andreas, C. (1987) *Change Your Mind – And Keep the Change*. Moad, UT: Real People Press.

Barney, M. and McCarty, T. (2003) *The New Six Sigma*. Harlow, Essex: Prentice Hall.

French, W.L. and Bell, C.H. Jr (1999) *Organization Development* (6th edn). Upper Saddle River, NJ: Prentice-Hall.

Goldsby, T.J. and Martichenko, R. (2005) *Lean Six Sigma Logistics*. Boca Raton, FL: J Ross Publishing.

Hamel, G. and Prahalad, C.K. (1990) 'The core competence of the organisation', *Harvard Business Review*, 68(3), 79–91.

Harmon, P. (2014) *Business Process Change: A Guide for Business Managers and BPM and Six Sigma Professionals* (3rd edn). Waltham, MA: Morgan Kaufmann Publishers, imprint of Elsevier.

Hayes, J. (2014) *The Theory and Practice of Change Management* (4th edn). Basingstoke, Hampshire: Palgrave.

Ishikawa, K. (1985) *What Is Total Quality Control? The Japanese Way*. Harlow, Essex: Prentice Hall.

Johnson, G. and Scholes, K. (2001) *Exploring Public Sector Strategy*. Harlow, Essex: Pearson Education Ltd.

Kotter, J.P. (2012) *Leading Change*. Boston, MA: Harvard Business School Press.

Pande, P.S., Neuman, R.P. and Cavanagh, R.R. (2014) *Six Sigma Way* (2nd edn). New York: McGraw-Hill Education.

Pyzdek, T. and Keller, P.A. (2014) *The Six Sigma Project Handbook* (4th edn). New York: McGraw-Hill Education.

Silberman, M. (ed.) (2001) *Consultant's Tool Kit: 50 High-impact Questionnaires, Activities and How-to Guides for Diagnosing and Solving Client Problems*. (2nd edn) New York: McGraw-Hill Education.

Silberman, M. (ed.) (2003) *Consultant's Big Book of Organizational Development Tools*. New York: McGraw-Hill Education.

Wickham, P.A. (1997) 'Developing a mission for an entrepreneurial venture', *Management Decision*, 35(5), 373–381.

Case exercise

Delphi Fashions

Delphi was started 5 years ago by the two owners: Samantha Godfrey and Yvonne Hazelwood. Prior to starting this business, they both had extensive experience in the garment industry. Samantha's experience had been predominantly in underwear, outerwear and workwear and Yvonne's in ladieswear and fashion. When they first started working together, they concentrated on workwear and fashion. The former gave them good (if somewhat dull) steady business and the latter more interesting if variable work. In all cases, they were producing garments for others to sell on: either designers who would sell to retailers or wholesalers selling workwear.

The workwear market became increasingly competitive and as more of their potential business went abroad, they decided to concentrate on the fashion side. They established good relationships with a number of designers who produced high quality garments that sold at the mid to upper end of the market. Business remained good until autumn last year when one of their major customers (60% of turnover) decided to cease trading and their other customers reduced their orders.

Last year, they had made a decision to try and sell direct by setting up a website and doing a fashion show in their home town. This concentrated on fashion for the larger lady as they felt that there was a gap in the market here. Their latest diversification was into cloth handbags that they designed and produced. These were low cost as they could be made to order. Again they hope to sell these direct to the consumers via the website.

Since the end of last year they have had no firm orders of work from their usual customers. The attempts to find new customers have been unsuccessful, as it appears that either the designers are sourcing all their garments abroad or the new designers are no longer working for themselves but joining large fashion houses. They are also concerned that the few enquiries to date have been small and also the prices have been so low that the margin is paper-thin after they have taken their costs into account. They realised that a garment that they sell on for £30 retails at over £100 once the wholesaler and retailer have taken a cut. In order to remain in business they needed to drastically improve the margin they make.

The obvious solution would be to design and sell to the consumers direct but with their limited resources, this would be difficult as they have found as no sales have come from the fashion show or the website. Another option would be to sell to retailers that would have a lower profit margin but would have the advantage of more reliable sales. As the above is risky, they would also like to continue their 'CMT' (cut, make, trim) business i.e. making clothes to order for customers using their designs. Their problem is finding suitable customers.

In the short term, Samantha and Yvonne need to find some more 'CMT' customers to keep the business afloat while they build their 'design and produce' range of clothes for the larger woman and the bespoke handbags. They feel that their long experience in clothes production would work well with new fashion designers who are very creative but perhaps short on practical experience! In the longer term, they want to take more control of their business by selling their own designs (under their label) to consumers either direct or via selected retailers. They believe that in this cost conscious world, it is the only way to compete.

Delphi have brought in a consultant to help them with their marketing plan for the business. The consultant has identified the key objectives as follows:

CMT Business

1 Understand the current market for CMT in the UK by reviewing market reports and other published literature and conduct interviews with former customers and other contacts in the garments industry.

2 Identify sources for new CMT customers

3 Understand Delphi's competitive advantage in relation to these new customers

4 Build a business proposition to take to the new customers and identify the correct approach

5 Outline financials to ensure the survival of the business

Design and produce business

1 Understand the current market for high quality (?bespoke) ladies fashion in the UK by reviewing market reports and other published literature and conduct interviews with former customers and other contacts in the garments industry.

2 Review range of products and determine which will be used in this business

3 Identify routes to market and decide on the strategy for each one

4 Look at pricing strategy to ensure maximum competitiveness and profitability

5 Refine website and other promotional tools to reflect the positioning of the products

1 Are these the right objectives to build the marketing plan? What would you do differently?

2 Does Delphi Fashions need more than help on building a marketing plan? What other areas of the business need looking at?

3 What tools would you use to try and analyse the problems the business is facing? What is your rationale?

Chapter 6

Evaluating client capabilities and business opportunities

However beautiful the strategy, you should occasionally check the results.

Winston Churchill

Learning outcomes

The learning outcomes from this chapter are to:

- introduce a range of analysis techniques to review the business and its environment;
- understand what is meant by and what is the basis for building a business's success (competitive advantage);
- illustrate how to use a range of techniques in order to identify strategic options for the business.

One of the key skills that a consultant can bring to a client is the ability to look at the business in a different way.

Each client will have their own set of tools and processes which relate to their business. Consultants should have their own distinct toolkit which assists them in analysing the client's current and future position and in bringing insight into these. The tools and techniques outlined below provide a basic toolkit in a progression through the lifecycle of a project as follows:

- understanding the context in which the client operates, including external factors and competition;
- reviewing the current position of the client;
- identifying potential future options for the client;

● assessing these options in the light of external factors;

● defining the way forward for the client.

Many of the tools use graphical representations to convey the concept and analysis to the client so these are emphasised in this chapter. Within each section, the methods are described in ascending order of difficulty of use except where one is a precursor to another. There is a huge range of techniques available. For examples see Key Reading and www .valuebasedmanagement.net. The key is to choose the right tool for the project and this comes with experience.

Using the toolkit

The range of tools introduced in this chapter varies considerably both in their ease of use and in the functional coverage that they provide (see Figure 6.1).

The tools in the top left-hand quadrant are powerful but are for specific purposes, dealing with a narrow aspect of the business. Those in the bottom right are 'general purpose' and are normally the first options considered for any project. A junior consultant would be expected to be able to use the tools in the bottom half of the grid, whereas those in the upper half are best left to more experienced consultants.

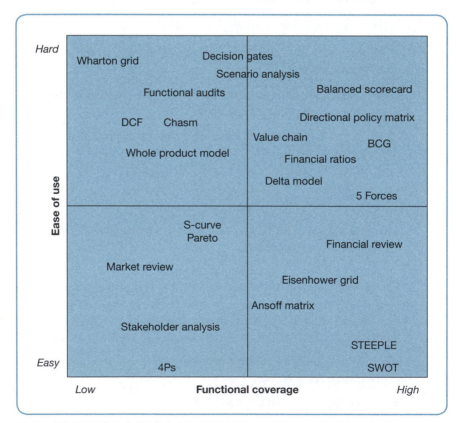

Figure 6.1 Use of analytical tools

6.1   Preliminary analysis techniques

> **Consultants need to start by asking why the business organisation or system exists, what is its mission or purpose and what are its objectives?**

Consultants also need to establish how this business system fits externally – not just in comparison with competitors but in the 'bigger picture'. Three useful techniques to help set the scene are the SWOT, STEEPLE and stakeholder models.

SWOT and STEEPLE

The *SWOT analysis* is a good basic technique for getting the analysis started. SWOT is an acronym standing for 'strengths, weaknesses, opportunities and threats'. The SWOT analysis provides the consultant with a concise and comprehensive summary of a business. It offers an immediate and accessible insight into the capabilities of the business. However, it is descriptive and other tools are needed to analyse the ways in which it might use them. Normally presented as a four-box matrix, typically, a SWOT analysis will identify a broad-based group of strengths and weaknesses coupled with a number of opportunities and threats. The SWOT analysis can be generated through a brainstorming session. It can also be used to keep a summary of features identified by other analysis techniques. However, it should be recognised that the 'opportunities and threats' side of the SWOT analysis represents an external view. This side of the equation should be kept realistic (see Figure 6.2).

The usefulness of the SWOT analysis has been questioned both by managers and academics, despite its popularity (see Hill 1997, for example). Instead of abandoning it, attempts have been made to 'improve' it as a planning tool. One of the latest is the 'meta-SWOT' (Agarwal et al., 2012) that uses a wider range of weighted factors to assess the company.

Strengths Things under the control of managers which will help the business achieve its goals.	**Weaknesses** Things under the control of managers which will hinder the business and prevent it from achieving its goals.
Opportunities Things outside the control of managers which will offer the business a means of achieving its goals.	**Threats** Things outside the control of managers which will hinder the business and prevent it achieving its goals.

Figure 6.2 SWOT analysis

In order to take a closer look at the business system and 'bigger picture' factors in which the business operates, it is useful to use a technique like the *STEEPLE analysis*. STEEPLE, like SWOT, is an acronym. It stands for 'social, technological, economic, environmental, political, legal and ethical' factors. It was originally called the PEST analysis (political, economic, social and technological factors). When environmental and legal factors are included it is known as PESTEL.

- *Social* factors are those that relate to the societal development of buying groups. Look for changes in social trends and attitudes that will affect consumption.

- *Technological* factors are those that relate to the knowledge used in the design, production and delivery of outputs. Technology is changing continually. New products are constantly being developed and existing ones are redesigned. There are broad technological trends which will have an impact on every business. Each industry and sector has its own proprietary technological base where the effects of technological developments are localised. Look out particularly for paradigm shifts: step-wise changes in technology that can pose enormous threats to some business or represent huge opportunities for others.

- *Economic* factors are those that relate to the overall economy. Look for growth in economic wealth (GDP) and its distribution in relation to customer groups. Consider the effects of economic booms and recessions. Other important factors include the impact of interest rates (which make borrowing more expensive) and exchange rates. A strengthening of a currency makes imports cheaper and exports more expensive. Exporters are hit when a currency strengthens, importers benefit. A weakening of the currency has the reverse effect.

- *Environmental* factors refer to 'green' issues. These tend to have more importance in some industry sectors than in others, such as chemicals or packaging, but are always worth considering. A good example is the disposal of toxic waste.

- *Political and legal* factors are those that relate to governance and the attitudes of government agencies. Look for political favour and disfavour, influence with government, lobbying and potential new laws that may give or take away legislative monopolies or change the conditions under which trading will take place.

- *Ethical* factors, such as environmental concerns, play more of a part in medical and food-related businesses, for example, but again should be considered as a matter of course even when their influence is not believed to be strong. An example is the use of human genome data.

Stakeholder analysis

Management decisions affect many parties including the management themselves, shareholders, employees, customers, suppliers, authorities, communities in which the company operates and the environment from local to global. Stakeholder analysis suggests that all of these must be considered as fairly and justly as possible. Some stakeholders are far more significant and influential than others and it can be very important to recognise who the key players are. Figure 6.3 shows one way of mapping stakeholders so that the stakeholders can be managed optimally.

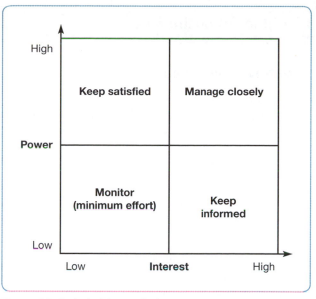

Figure 6.3 Stakeholder analysis

Audits

Audits are powerful tools for preliminary analysis. There are a range of different types which may be appropriate depending upon the nature of the client and the type of project. These include:

- Organisational audit
- Operations audit
- Patent and copyright review
- Design and innovation audit

An organisational audit reviews the split of functions and responsibilities across the whole organisation and often includes comparison with similar organisations. The operations audit is focused on the processes and procedures that are used by the organisation to fulfil its function.

> Organisational and operations audits can give important insights into what makes the organisation behave the way it does.

The last two audits are more specialised and are particularly relevant in creative or knowledge-rich organisations. The patent and copyright review assesses the current status of intellectual property (IP) within the organisation and identifies areas of strength and weakness across the organisation's IP portfolio. It is important to note that any attempt to assess the strength of individual patents should be left to qualified patent attorneys. The design and innovation audit reviews the processes used to develop new concepts and designs and is focused on identifying how these can be improved. Many consultants have their own specific approaches to each of these audits and these are well covered in the literature.

6.2 Capabilities of businesses

Competitive advantage

There are a number of ways in which business strategy can be defined. At one level, a strategy is simply the consistency of the actions the business takes, the fact that it sells a particular range of products to a definite customer group. In this respect all businesses have a strategy of sorts. At another level, a strategy is the way in which the business will compete and beat its competitors. It is the way in which it develops an edge in the marketplace.

> Ultimately a strategy must dictate the way the business behaves; it must become a plan – a 'recipe for action' to succeed in the marketplace.

A firm's competitive advantage is the basis on which the performance of the business is built. Note that competitive advantage is usually a combination of elements rather than a single one. A competitive advantage is derived from something that:

- the firm *possesses*;
- creates *value* for its customers;
- in a way is *unique*;
- competitors find difficult *to imitate*.

A firm can be said to have competitive advantage when it is able to sustain profits that exceed the average for the industry.

A good place to start the process of identifying the source of competitive advantage (if any) is by asking a few key questions about the reason for the business's existence or the *business idea*. It is valuable to distil the responses to these questions to a key sentence or maximum two for each question:

- What is the need or behaviour in the market that the type of product or service the firm is providing satisfies?
- What is the basic (existing) offer out there in the market place that satisfies this need?
- How does the firm's offering differ or how is it special in a way that the customer values?

Analysing the answers to these questions should provide a clear insight into what the source of competitive advantage is or might be: remember it must meet the criteria listed above.

Market segmentation

Market segmentation is the process of dividing a market into distinct subsets (segments) that behave in the same way or have similar needs and can be targeted. Because each segment is fairly homogeneous in their needs and attitudes, it is likely to respond similarly to a given *marketing mix* (also known as *the 4 Ps*: **P**roduct or service, **P**lace – including demographics as well as geography, **P**romotion, and **P**rice). Broadly, markets can be divided according to a number of general criteria, such as by industry, geography or profession. Small segments are often termed niche markets or speciality markets.

However, all segments fall into either business-to-consumer (B2C) or business-to-business (B2B) markets. Although it has similar objectives and it overlaps with B2C markets in many ways, the process of B2B market segmentation is quite different. The overall intent is to:

- identify groups of similar customers and potential customers;
- prioritise the groups to target;
- understand their behaviour and to respond with appropriate marketing strategies that satisfy the different preferences of each chosen segment.

Successful segmentation requires that segments are:

- substantial – large and profitable enough;
- accessible – can be reached efficiently;
- different – will respond to a different marketing mix;
- actionable – the firm must have a product for this segment;
- measureable – the size and purchasing power of the segment can be measured.

There is another way of looking at segmentation – called defining by *centre points*. This technique looks at segments in a different way taking an ideal customer as the centre of the hypothesised segment and envisaging segments like a swarm of bees or school of fish with an identifiable centre. The market strategy is then focused on that centre with communications and a range of products/services dedicated to addressing that ideal customer's needs and wants, known as the *whole product* (see Figure 6.4).

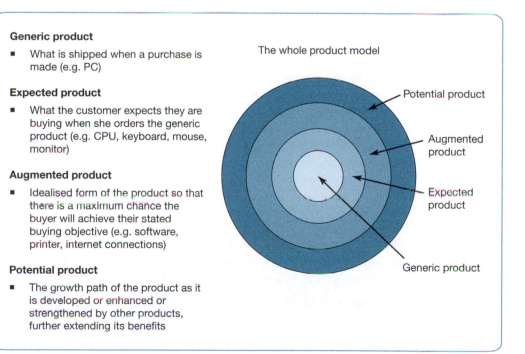

Generic product

- What is shipped when a purchase is made (e.g. PC)

Expected product

- What the customer expects they are buying when she orders the generic product (e.g. CPU, keyboard, mouse, monitor)

Augmented product

- Idealised form of the product so that there is a maximum chance the buyer will achieve their stated buying objective (e.g. software, printer, internet connections)

Potential product

- The growth path of the product as it is developed or enhanced or strengthened by other products, further extending its benefits

The whole product model

Potential product

Augmented product

Expected product

Generic product

Figure 6.4 Whole product model

Financial analysis

Finance and accounting are disciplines in their own right. All that is necessary here is to outline the principles of financial analysis and give a flavour of the approach that is important to the consultant. Businesses are required by law to keep accurate records of their income and expenditure and to produce accounts. Most of this information is publicly available on the web either free or at nominal cost. The complexity of the accounts will depend on the business and its legal status. Whilst accounting practices vary between countries, the principles behind all company accounts are the same.

The financial situation of a firm is fundamental. The health of a firm's finances is not just an indication of how successful it has been in the past; it is also an indication of the resources it has available to reward its stakeholders and to invest in new projects.

> **When evaluating a business, its performance and its potential for the future, the consultant must have an appreciation of its financial situation.**

There are three key financial statements that outline the financial position of an organisation:

- the *profit and loss account*,
- the *balance sheet*, and
- the *cash flow forecast*.

The *profit and loss account* is a basic statement of the trading activity of the business over a period, usually one year. It relates to the balance between the income and outgoings of the business. The different levels of expenditure included in the profit and loss account give an indication of the *cost structure* of the business.

The *balance sheet* is a statement of what the firm owns (its *assets*) and what it owes (its *liabilities*). It is a statement of what is owned and owed at the time the balance sheet is produced. Accounts usually have two balance sheets (or the balance sheet quotes two columns of figures), an *opening set* and a *closing set*. The closing set is for the date of the balance sheet, the opening set for an earlier point in time (usually one year before). Comparison between the two gives an indication of the changes in the firm's assets and liabilities over the period.

The *cash flow statement* is normally used as an internal forecasting tool. The forecast takes into account not only the elements of income, outgoings and assets that appear in the profit and loss statement and balance sheet but also their timing. These factors are used to develop a model of when cash flows into and out of the business and hence determine the ongoing cash position of the firm. Many profitable businesses fail because they do not manage their cash resources properly hence the dictum 'cash is king'.

The figures in the balance sheet and profit and loss account do not, by themselves, offer a complete picture of the firm. It is only when they are related to each other through *financial ratios* that they provide additional insight. There are three types:

- *Performance* (or operating) ratios measure how well the firm is using the resources it has to hand.
- *Financial status* ratios measure the stability of the business and indicate how well it could weather a financial storm affecting income or expenditure.
- *Investor* ratios give an indication of its performance as an investment vehicle.

Care should be taken when using ratios. They give absolute indications of a business performance and can be revealing, yet they provide a full picture only when they are compared with other ratios. This comparison may be historical, as a trend in the ratios of a particular firm over time, or cross-sectional, as a comparison at a particular time of the ratios of a number of firms in the same or related sectors.

Performance ratios	● ROS (return on sales) = profit/sales
	● ROCE (return on capital employed) = operating profit/capital employed
	● ROE (return on equity) = profit after tax/shareholder funds
Financial status ratios	● Debt ratio = (long-term debt + short-term debt)/capital employed
	● Interest cover = operating profit/interest owed
	● Current ratio = current assets/current liabilities
	● Quick ratio = liquid assets/current liabilities
Investment ratios	● Earnings per share (EPS) = profit after tax/number of shares issued
	● Price/earnings ratio (P/E) = market price of share/EPS
	● Market capitalisation = market value of shares × number of shares
	● Dividend cover = EPS/dividend per share
	● Dividend yield = dividend per share/market price per share

Pareto analysis

Every business is different. However, the contribution to sales and profits of different lines in a multi-product firm follows quite a consistent pattern: a (relatively) small number of leading lines will make a large contribution while a (relatively) large number of low-volume lines will make a small contribution. This is called the Pareto rule. It is sometimes called the '80–20' rule because often the top 20 per cent of lines make a contribution of 80 per cent to sales and profits.

A Pareto curve can be drawn by listing the product lines in order of sales or profits, with those that make the highest contribution being first. A graph can then be drawn with the cumulative contribution on the vertical axis and the percentage of total product lines on the horizontal axis. The curve will look something like that in Figure 6.5.

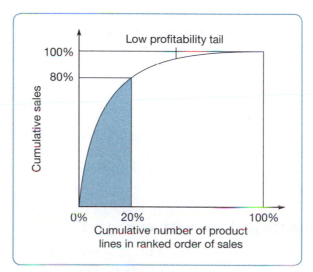

Figure 6.5 Pareto analysis

> A Pareto analysis is useful if a firm is considering rationalisation of its products or services.

Whereas different product lines make different levels of contribution, each line typically accounts for a fairly similar level of costs, particularly fixed costs. In general, profitability will be increased by divesting of product lines in the 'tail' of the curve. As with any general recommendation, though, this should be judged in light of the business, its situation and the product concerned.

S-curve analysis

Most products exhibit a characteristic growth curve with an early stage with increasing growth, a middle stage with high growth and a final stage where growth drops to zero. This pattern is depicted in graphical from and appears as an S-curve (see Figure 6.6).

The life of most products can be depicted as a graph of total sales against time. The early stage has high risk. The middle stage consumes a lot of resources to expand production and the sales platform. Mature products are usually the profitable 'cash cows' but with a finite life.

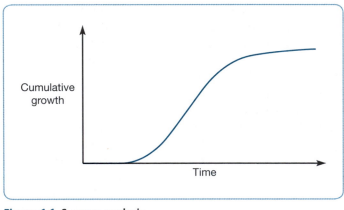

Figure 6.6 S-curve analysis

> A balanced product portfolio should contain a range of products at different stages in their lifecycle.

S-curve analysis reviews the sales profile of each product to identify their stage in the lifecycle. This allows the product portfolio to be adjusted to achieve a balance between risk, resource requirements and profits that is consistent with the firm's strategic objectives.

Wharton grid – uncertainty and risk

S-curve analysis introduced the idea of assessing the firm's product portfolio. The Wharton grid reviews the portfolio in a different way by looking at both the market for

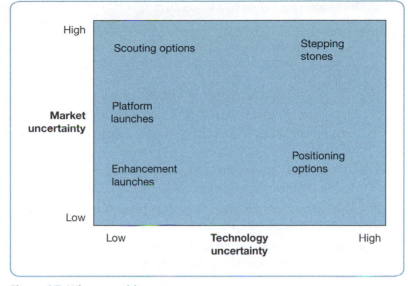

Figure 6.7 Wharton grid

products and the technologies they use (see Figure 6.7). The grid shows an assessment of the degree of uncertainty and hence risk in these two factors for each product type. The balance of risk, both along each axis and between the two axes, and the acceptable degree of uncertainty depends on the nature and maturity of the firm and reflects its strategic vision.

Whilst the Wharton grid is normally used to assess the current product range and planned developments, it also provides a useful framework for looking at future options and how they fit into the overall product portfolio.

Porter's Five Forces

Michael Porter originally identified three basic types of competitive advantage, namely *cost* (lower cost advantage), *differentiation* (delivery of benefits that exceed those of competing products) and *focus* (focusing on a particular buying group, segment or product line – servicing a market particularly well). These are known as *positional advantages*. There is also a *resource-based view* which emphasises that a firm utilises its resources and capabilities to create an advantage that results in superior *value chain* creation. This view suggests that a firm must have resources and capabilities that are collectively superior to those of its competitors. Examples of the sources of such resource-based advantages include: patents and trademarks, proprietary know-how, installed customer base, reputation of the firm and brand equity. Together these resources and capabilities form the firm's *core competencies*.

> *Porter's five forces* offers a useful means for understanding the industry context in which a company operates and may help suggest how to develop an edge over rivals.

141

This model (see Figure 6.8) offers an insight into the drivers of competition:

- *Intensity of rivalry among players* – influenced by the number of firms, their market share and cost bases, switching costs (when a customer can freely move from one product to another), levels of product differentiation and exit barriers (the cost of abandoning a product).
- *Threat of substitutes* – price changes in products in other industries affecting the industry under scrutiny, substitution of one product by another in a different industry (one example is the advent of smart phones supplanting cameras, diaries and digital music players).
- *Buyer power* – the impact customers have on an industry. For example, where there is one buyer and many suppliers, the buyer has the real power.
- *Supplier power* – the impact suppliers have on an industry. Where a supplier holds a company to ransom over a critical resource, the supplier exerts real control.
- *Barriers to entry* – the possibility that new firms may enter the industry also affects competition. There may be high barriers to entry if there are considerable costs associated with entering a market or where the prices are too low to attract new entrants (a deterrent) or where there are patents in place. The government can also create such barriers through regulation.

For a useful set of templates to use Porter's Five Forces, see Dobbs (2014).

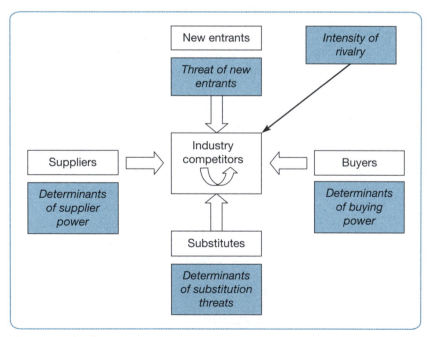

Figure 6.8 Five forces

The Delta Model (and sixth force)

Hax and Wilde, in *The Delta Project* (2001), argue that their model provides a means of unifying the Porter's framework (five forces as above and value chain – see below) with the resource-based view to developing strategy. They identify three distinctive strategic positions offering very different approaches to achieve customer bonding. These go beyond the 'best product' (i.e. low-cost/differentiated option mentioned earlier) and further develop the 'focus' option to give 'total customer solutions' and 'system lock-in'(see Figure 6.9).

The Delta Model also offers a 'sixth force' to add to Porter's five forces, namely, *complementors*. A complementor is a firm engaged in the delivery of products and services that enhance the firm's product and service portfolio. These are typically, though not necessarily, external and are easily overlooked. A classic example of this is the Microsoft Windows operating system and software companies. To get the best coverage and market penetration, a software company needs to be compatible with Windows.

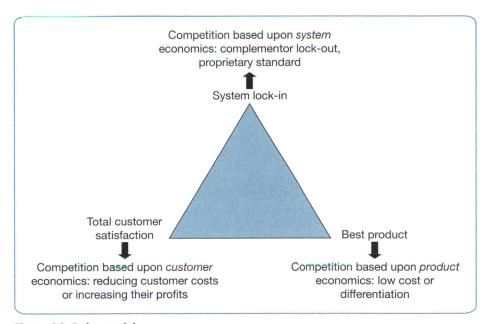

Figure 6.9 Delta model

Source: Hax, A.C. and Wilde, D.L., *The Delta Project: Discovering New Sources of Profitability in a Networked Economy*, 2001, Palgrave Macmillan. Figure 1.1, page 10. Republished with permission of Palgrave Macmillan.

Value Chain

Value chain analysis describes the activities within and around an organisation and relates them to an analysis of the competitive strength of the organisation.

It evaluates which value each particular activity adds to the organisation's products or services (see Figure 6.10). This idea was built upon the insight that an organisation is more than a random compilation of machinery, equipment, people and money. Only if these

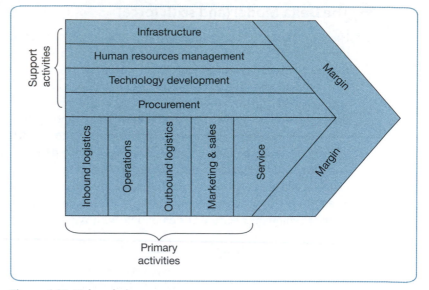

Figure 6.10 Value chain

Source: Reprinted with the permission of Free Press, a Division of Simon and Schuster Inc. from *Competitive Advantage: Creating and Sustaining Superior Performance* by Michael E. Porter. Copyright © 1985, 1998 by Michael E. Porter. All rights reserved.

things are arranged into systems will it become possible to produce something for which customers are willing to pay a price.

> **Porter argues that the ability to perform particular activities and to manage and optimise the linkages between them is a source of competitive advantage.**

Porter distinguishes between primary activities and support activities. Primary activities are directly concerned with the creation or delivery of a product or service. They can be grouped into five main areas: inbound logistics, operations, outbound logistics, marketing and sales and service. Each of these primary activities is linked to support activities that help to improve their effectiveness or efficiency. There are four main areas of support activities: procurement, technology development (including R&D), human resource management and infrastructure (systems for planning, finance, quality, information management, etc.).

In most industries, it is rather unusual that a single company performs all activities from product design, production of components and final assembly to delivery to the final user by itself. Most often, organisations are elements of a value system or supply chain. Hence, value chain analysis should cover the whole value system in which the organisation operates. A typical value chain analysis can be performed in the following steps:

- analysis of own value chain – which costs are related to every single activity;
- analysis of customers' value chains – how does the product fit into the bigger value chain;
- identification of potential cost advantages in comparison with competitors;
- identification of potential value added for the customer – how can a product add value to the customer's value chain (e.g. lower costs or higher performance) – where does the customer see such potential?

Ideally there should be some linkage between the cost within the organisation of a particular function and the value it (ultimately) delivers relatively to the firm's goods.

The Balanced Scorecard

Traditionally, approaches to performance measurement have relied heavily on financial accounting measures. Motivated by the belief that this approach was obsolete, a study sponsored in the early 1990s by the Nolan Norton Institute (part of KPMG) revealed that reliance on summary financial measures was hindering organisations' ability to create future economic value. The outcome of this and subsequent work is captured in the *Balanced Scorecard*.

> The Balanced Scorecard is a set of measures and a management system that emphasises that both financial and non-financial measures must be part of the information system for employees at all levels in the organisation (see Figure 6.11).

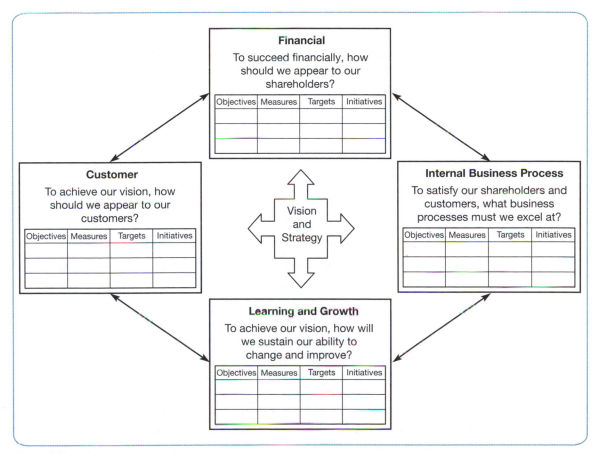

Figure 6.11 Balanced scorecard

Source: Reprinted by permission of *Harvard Business Review*. Adapted from Figure 1.1: Translating Vision and Strategy – Four Perspectives from *'Using the balanced scorecard as a strategic management system'* by Kaplan, R.S. and Norton, D.P. (Jan–Feb 1996). Copyright © 1996 by the Harvard Business School Publishing Corporation. All rights reserved.

Frontline employees must understand the financial consequences of their actions, for example, it argues. The scorecard is designed to translate a company or business unit's mission into tangible objectives and measures. The 'balance' is between outcome or lagging measures (financial) and the drive for future performance or leading measures (driven by the internal activities that give rise to the financial results). Most scorecards have four 'perspectives' with typical generic measures like:

- *financial* – return on investment and economic value-added;
- *customer* – satisfaction, retention, market and account share;
- *internal* – quality, response time, cost new product introductions;
- *learning and growth* – employee satisfaction and information system availability (see Figure 6.11).

The trick with the scorecard is to find and use the most appropriate measures for a firm or organisation for its specific objectives and with its mission in mind. When looking at a firm, it is worth considering what metrics are used and why. Bearing in mind the old adage 'you get what you measure', ask: are the factors that are being measured the right ones for the organisation and are they right at this time?

6.3 Identification and evaluation of strategic options

A number of techniques are available that are designed to help with the identification and evaluation of options for development. First of all, consider the strategic Ansoff matrix.

The Ansoff Matrix

The Ansoff matrix offers strategic choices for achieving the company's objectives.

There are four main categories for selection:

- *Market penetration* – here the firm markets its existing products to its existing customers. This means increasing revenue by, for example, promoting the product, repositioning the brand, and so on. However, the product is not altered and no new customers are sought.
- *Market development* – here the firm markets our existing product range in a new market. This means that the product remains the same, but it is marketed to a new audience. Exporting the product, or marketing it in a new region are examples of market development.
- *Product development* – this is a new product to be marketed to our existing customers. Here the firm develops and innovates new product offerings to replace existing ones. Such products are then marketed to our existing customers.
- *Diversification* – this is where the firm markets completely new products to new customers. There are two types of diversification, namely, *related* and *unrelated* diversification. Related diversification means remain in a market or industry with which the organisation is familiar. Unrelated diversification is where the firm has neither previous industry nor market experience. Clearly the risks are higher in the top right-hand box of Figure 6.12.

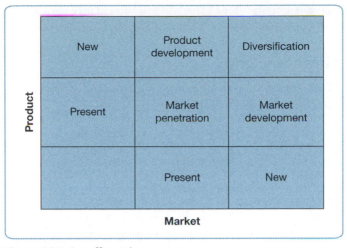

Figure 6.12 Ansoff matrix

It is important to recognise that any matrix can be expanded from a 2×2 grid to a N×N grid
or to a graph with continuous axes. When using continuous axes, it is useful to adjust the
size of each entry, for example a circle, according to another dimension such as the sales
revenue for that item. An example of an extended version of the Ansoff matrix using a 3×3
grid is shown in Figure 6.13 as used to review a consultancy business. This splits both axes

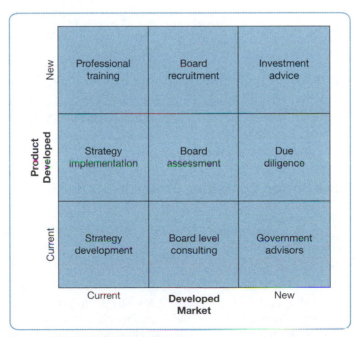

Figure 6.13 Extended Ansoff matrix

into current, developed (i.e. an evolution of an existing product or market) and new. This split can give a better reflection of how product expansion actually works.

Eisenhower grid

The Eisenhower grid addresses the important issue of setting priorities in strategy implementation (see Figure 6.14).

> The model reviews the relative importance of tasks to achieving a successful strategic outcome and when they impact on the business.

In a straightforward situation where the tasks are independent, they should be undertaken in the order: top right, bottom right, top left, bottom left. When, as is usually the case, there is some degree of interdependence between the tasks, the Eisenhower grid can be used to highlight and review the relative significance and hence priority of each task to help ensure a successful implementation.

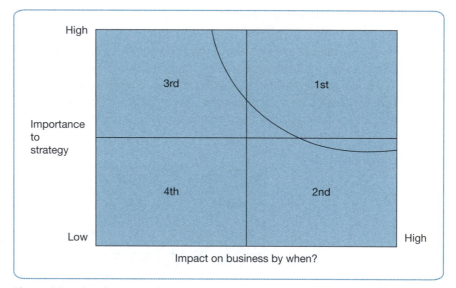

Figure 6.14 Eisenhower grid

The Boston Consulting Group matrix (BCG)

> The BCG matrix aims to show the cash-generating and cash-absorbing parts of the product portfolio.

The matrix compares the growth rate of the sector in which the product range lies (plotted vertically) and the competitive index – the ratio between the market share of the range in its sector divided by that of the most important competitor (plotted horizontally). The BCG matrix assumes that market share relates to profitability, an assumption that has validity but must be challenged for specific businesses (see Figure 6.15).

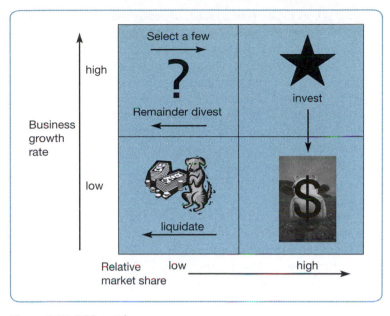

Figure 6.15 BCG matrix

Source: Boston Consulting Group. Adapted from *The Product Portfolio Matrix* (1970). The Star, the Dog, the Cow and the Question Mark – The Growth Share Matrix.

The four quadrants are given evocative labels and the BCG makes recommendations about the product range based on its position in the matrix. Products in the low-growth, high-competitive index quadrant are called *cash cows*. These can be milked for cash. Above these, in the quadrant for high-growth, high-competitive index products are the *stars* – the company's success stories. Stars may generate some cash but they are equally likely to need investment in order to protect them from competitive attack. In the high-market-growth, low-competitive-index quadrant are the *question marks* (sometimes called *problem children*). These are products about which a decision must be made – to invest in improving the competitive position (to make them stars) or to divest (to drop the product). The final quadrant contains the low-market-growth, low-competitive-index products. The products here – called *dogs* – are said to be cash sinks. They take up more cash than they generate and have poor prospects. The recommendation is to divest these.

The dividing lines between the quadrants are to some extent dependent on industry conditions. Often a 10 per cent growth rate is used to separate high from low growth. A competitive index of one (i.e. a market share equal to competitors) is used to separate a good from a bad competitive position. More information can be obtained by means of the BCG matrix if circles of different sizes, reflecting the sales or profit contribution that they make, represent products. The BCG matrix offers broad recommendations. However, like any analytical method, its recommendations should not be followed blindly but interpreted in light of the particular features of the company's situation.

Evaluating future plans

The evaluation of future investments; for example, new product developments or capital investments, requires financial analysis to review the expected risk and returns. The core

149

issue is how to compare a real cash outlay today with a potential return in the future. The common method for addressing this problem is to apply a discount rate to the future returns using a discounted cash flow (DCF) model.

DCF models are commonly summarised in one of two forms. The first, net present value (NPV), uses an agreed discount rate. It gives the total of the discounted cash values throughout the life of the investment, as per the gain and loss example given above. The discount rate is chosen to reflect the level of risk in the project. A low rate would be appropriate for buying equipment to build a standard product but a high rate would be appropriate for developing a product using new technology. NPV gives an absolute indication of the potential return on an investment.

The second type of DCF summary, internal rate of return (IRR), works in a slightly different way. The discount rate is varied to achieve a NPV of zero. The rate that achieves this is the IRR. IRR is a relative indication of the potential return. It can be compared with the perceived level of risk in the investment to decide whether the investment is justified. DCF analysis is a generic tool that can be applied to all levels of investment from buying a piece of production equipment to evaluating the potential of a new product and on to buying a complete business. All DCF models carry a high level of risk and their results should be interpreted with caution. The more complex the business case, the greater the uncertainty and hence the greater skill required to use the tool effectively.

6.4   Planning for the future

Decision gates and the Product Creation Process

Many firms suffer from having far too many projects in their product development pipelines for the limited resources available.

> *Decision* or *stage gates* define major control points that are used to decide which projects are ready to move to the next phase.

A control gate is used to determine if the products for the current phase of work are completed based on the criteria set out at the beginning of the project and that the project is ready to move forward to the next phase. Controls are used to get formal sign off of that phase of work by the system's owner and management. They are particularly valuable when developing new products and are widely used.

Stages are where the action occurs. The players on the project team undertake key tasks to gather the information needed to advance the project to the next gate or decision point. Stages are cross-functional (there is no R&D or marketing stage) and each activity is undertaken in parallel to enhance speed to market. To manage risk, the parallel activities in a certain stage must be designed to gather vital information – technical, market, financial, operations – in order to drive down the technical and business risks. Each stage costs more than the preceding one, so that the game plan is based on incremental commitments. As uncertainties decrease, expenditures are allowed to rise and risk is managed.

Stage1 – Scoping	A quick and inexpensive assessment of the technical merits of the project and its market prospects.
Stage 2 – Building the Business Case	This is the critical homework stage – the one that makes or breaks the project. The business case has three main components; product and project definition, project justification and project plan.
Stage 3 – Development	Business case plans are translated into concrete deliverables. The manufacturing or operations plan is mapped out, the marketing launch and operating plans are developed and the test plans for the next stage are defined.
Stage 4 – Testing and Validation	The purpose of this stage is to provide final and total validation of the entire project: the product itself, the production process, customer acceptance and the economics of the project.
Stage 5 – Launch	Full commercialisation of the product – the beginning of full production and commercial launch

Preceding each stage is a decision point or gate which serves as a go/kill and prioritisation decision point (see Figure 6.16). Gates deal with three quality issues: quality of execution, business rationale and the quality of the action plan. The structure of each gate is similar:

- *Deliverables* – inputs into the gate review – what the project leader and team deliver to the meeting. These are defined in advance and are the results of actions from the preceding stage. A standard menu of deliverables is specified for each gate.

- *Criteria* – what the project is judged against in order to make the go/kill and prioritisation decisions. These criteria are usually organised into a standard list containing both financial and qualitative criteria but change somewhat from gate to gate.

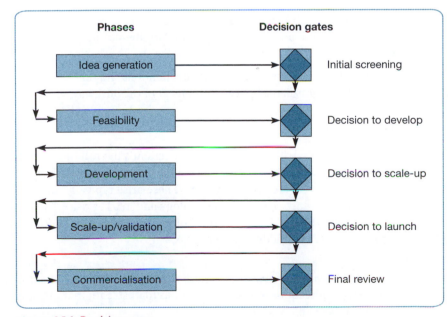

Figure 6.16 Decision gates

● *Outputs* – results of the gate review. Gates must have clearly articulated outputs including: a decision (go/kill/hold/recycle) and a path forward (approved project plan, date and deliverables for the next gate agreed upon).

Gates are not merely project review points, status reports or information updates. They are tough decision meetings. Many leading companies have overhauled their product innovation processes, incorporating the critical success factors discovered through best practice research, in the form of a decision or stage-gate new product development process. According to several independent research studies (such as Booz-Allen Hamilton and AMR Research) between 70 and 85 per cent of leading US companies use decision or stage gates to drive new products to market.

Rapid change, new technology and increased competition are some of the factors generating unprecedented uncertainty in today's markets. Planning for the future has never been so difficult. Two well-documented and well-established approaches to planning for the future are the *directional policy matrix* and *scenario planning*.

The directional policy matrix

The directional policy matrix (DPM) is similar to the BCG matrix but it uses more general factors to determine market attractiveness (plotted vertically) and competitive position (plotted horizontally) to look at future options. Important factors in determining market attractiveness are market growth rate, profitability, stability of profits, customer strengths and environmental conditions (defined by means of the STEEPLE analysis – see earlier). Important factors in determining competitive position are market share, production and technical expertise and relationships with distributors and buyers. Different factors can be weighted if they differ in significance. Each axis is divided into three levels – labelled high, medium and low – giving nine sectors in total.

> The DPM enables recommendations to be made on investment and divestment on the basis of the position of the product in the matrix.

As with the BCG matrix the recommendations should not be followed blindly but used to provide insights in the light of the context of the business.

The Chasm

A sound strategy will have reviewed the client's overall operating environment, which necessitates taking a 'big picture' view of the firm. There are risk areas that the strategy can miss because there are discontinuities. These arise typically for innovative product areas which can introduce significant technology and market risks. The former can be managed by thorough processes but the latter is often more difficult. Geoffrey Moore's seminal work 'Crossing the Chasm' addresses this issue.

> The *Chasm* arises because a small part of the market may like the new product, giving early indications of success, whereas mainstream markets might be unwilling to adopt it (see Figure 6.17).

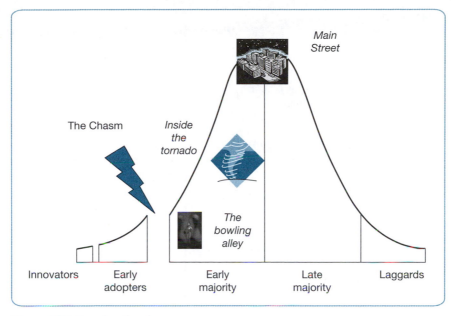

Figure 6.17 Crossing the chasm

Source: Geoffrey A. Moore, *Crossing the Chasm*

This problem can be planned for and overcome by understanding where customers lie in the spectrum of adopting new ideas and identifying key customers across the chasm. A bridgehead can then be established before major investment is incurred. This whole product analysis involves working with the sales and marketing team to understand the market structure and then approaching suitable candidates to test the concept at an early stage. Innovative clients maintain a database of customer characteristics for particular types of product to support future projects.

Scenario Analysis

A scenario describes a possible future business environment but is not a prediction. It explores the extremes that challenge the existing business model. It is a useful tool for elevating business thinking to a different plane. A scenario should be engaging, interesting, challenging and credible, as well as logically consistent with the known facts. It is useful to create a set of scenarios describing a range of possible futures that are ideally mutually exclusive and collectively exhaustive – no more than four scenarios is the norm. Scenarios can be presented in many different forms, such as in a script or a timeline or within a discussion. The descriptive scenarios need to be supported by some numerical analysis, which should test the credibility of each scenario, explore the magnitude of changes in the environment and evaluate the impact of those changes.

An example of the four worlds developed for one project is shown in Figure 6.18. The two most important, independent factors that affected the future of the firm were developed as axes in discussion with the client. Then four worlds were defined which reflected the combination of the two sides of each axis. Teams from the client then developed the forward view for each world to assess its impact on the firm and these were shared and discussed.

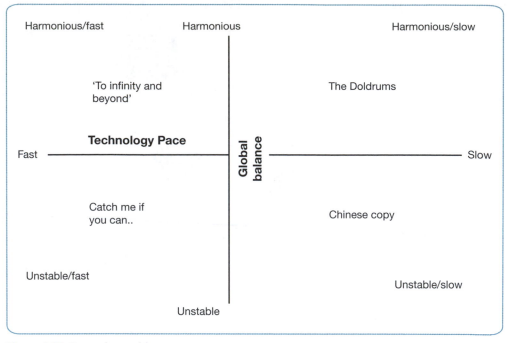

Figure 6.18 Scenario worlds

The scenarios are then used to challenge existing business models and stimulate new ideas. Knowing the impact of the other worlds enables clients to develop the most resilient strategy. They form the basis of a strategic debate that is radically different to the traditional business planning cycle. Scenario planning creates a flexible plan for the business that is composed of a variety of options. The business moves forward by shifting its weight between these options. This enables the business to adapt its plans to the evolving environment.

Team discussion points

1 How might the choice of analysis tools affect the outcome of the project and the client's expectations?

2 What scenarios might be relevant to the future of business schools?

3 How important is market segmentation in understanding the opportunities available to a client?

Summary of key ideas

A number of techniques are available to the consultant to aid analysis of a business and its environment. An evaluation might include the following:

- a simple summary of the business's capabilities and the environment in which it operates;

- a review of the business's source of competitive advantage and the environment in which it operates;
- an evaluation of the firm's performance and product performance;
- identification and evaluation of strategic options;
- planning for the future;
- an assessment of markets and their segmentation;

Key reading

Cadle, J., Paul, D. and Yeates, D. eds (2010) *Business Analysis* (2nd edn). Swindon, British Infomatics Society Limited.

Evans, V. (2013) *Key Strategy Tools: The 80+ Tools for Every Manager to Build a Winning Strategy*. Harlow, Essex: Pearson Education.

Further reading

Agarwal, R., Grassl, W. and Pahl, J. (2012), 'Meta-SWOT: introducing a new strategic planning tool', *Journal of Business Strategy*, Vol. 33 Iss 2 pp. 12–21.

Dobbs, M. E. (2014) 'Guidelines for applying Porter's five forces framework: a set of industry analysis templates' *Competitiveness Review*, 24, 1, 32–45.

Gertner, M. I. (2013), 'The Value Chain and Value Creation', *Advances In Management*, 6, 10, 1–4.

Harvard Business Review (2001) *Harvard Business Review on Innovation*. Boston, MA: Harvard Business School Publishing.

Hax, A.C. and Wilde, D.L. (2001) *The Delta Project: Discovering New Sources of Profitability in a Networked Economy*. Basingstoke, Hampshire: Palgrave Macmillan.

Hax, A. (2010) *The Delta Model: Reinventing Your Business Strategy*. New York: Springer.

Heijden, K. van der (2005) *Scenarios: The Art of Strategic Conversation* (2nd edn). Chichester, West Sussex: John Wiley & Sons.

Hill, T. (1997) 'SWOT analysis: It's time for a product recall', *Long Range Planning*, 30, 1, 46–52.

Kaplan, R.S. and Norton, D.P. (1996) *The Balanced Scorecard: Translating Strategy into Action*. Boston, MA: Harvard Business School Press.

McKenzie, W. (2010) *FT Guide to Using and Interpreting Company Accounts* (4th edn). Harlow, Essex: FT Prentice Hall.

Moore, G.A. (2014) *Crossing the Chasm: Marketing and Selling Disruptive Products to Mainstream Customers* (3rd edn). New York: HarperCollins.

Porter, M.E. (2004) *Competitive Strategy – Techniques for Analyzing Industries and Competitors* (New ed). New York: Free Press.

Porter, M.E. (2004) *Competitive Advantage – Creating and Sustaining Superior Performance* (New ed). New York: Free Press.

Ramirez, R., Selsky, J.W. and Heijden, K. van der eds (2010) *Business Planning for Turbulent Times: New Methods for Applying Scenarios*. Abingdon, Oxon: Earthscan.

Case exercise

Dance-a-Boogie

Dance-a-Boogie (DaB) was set up ten years ago by three former graduates of leisure management and recreation. They had, as a team, cut their teeth in big sports and leisure companies but had decided to strike out and set up for themselves. The three had complimentary skills: Danny was a marketer and salesman through and through, Ray was the project manager – keeping everything on spreadsheets, whilst Stu had catering in his blood. The three had the support of a small group of non-execs, including a retired accountant and a solicitor.

Over the years, their business, Dance-a-Boogie had allowed the three friends to become highly successful in their chosen markets – events and parties for groups large and small, ranging from birthday parties to corporate events. Though largely female, their target audiences spanned groups in their mid-twenties to those who had been teenagers in the 80s.

But they had reached a crossroad. The team realised that, though totally self-financed to date, to expand further from their current sites would require external investment – and the plan was to open operations in other suitable cities. Although respectably profitable to date, they needed to impress would-be investors. They felt that one way to improve the steady performance and attract financial support was to sweat their assets.

The six venues they leased around the UK were filled well most weekend evenings, and especially around the major seasonal times like Christmas and peak wedding season (July to September). However, during the day they were largely unused and they were underused during normal weeknights too. Location was a factor too: the centres of cities with universities were particular targets.

Dance-a-Boogie's particular successes included hen parties and tailor-made private corporate events. The corporate offerings had the potential to make more money to being paid for centrally and usually to celebrate some particular success. The venues all had a real club feel, being not too big or too small – any one venue housed no more than 250 people, and were a safe place for women alone or in groups.

The individual night's formulae were tried and tested: either disco suited to a particular night out ('70s, for example, or with the focus on a particular music genre – Motown, garage etc.) or live bands with guests dressing up in the style of the performing band. Dance-a-Boogie prided itself on the quality of food that was provided in the all-inclusive, pre-paid price. The only additional costs on any particular night were drinks on which DaB made good margins. Only pre-booked parties were admitted.

Danny led the way and decided to take some outside advice.

1 What analysis techniques would you use and why?

2 What would a SWOT analysis and a close look at segmentation of Dance-a-Boogie's target market tell the team?

3 What market research material and social media techniques would be required to help the decision making with respect to 'sweating the assets'?

Chapter 7

Working with clients and teams: the 'soft' skills

Between stimulus and response, man has the freedom to choose

Victor Frankl

Learning outcomes

The key learning outcomes of this chapter are to understand:

- how to work with clients to both satisfy organisational needs and to influence them in order to ensure a successful project;

- how to communicate effectively, work with and challenge the client where needed;

- what makes a team work, team dynamics and how to successfully lead a team;

- a key member of the team, namely, yourself.

Often the hardest part of being a consultant is learning to effectively use the 'soft' skills of setting up a project, influencing and working with teams. This is a vast subject underpinned by a lot of research. The aim of this chapter is merely to give an overview and highlight some tools and approaches that might help the consultant.

Establishing and maintaining a good relationship with the client is key to an effective project.

In order to understand why, here are a couple of scenarios. The first scenario is that the consultant has been asked to help manage a taskforce charged with designing some new procedures as part of some organisational change. The organisation has never had a taskforce, but the consultant has been told that their role is simply to 'sit in from time to time and make comments' as needed. The consultant does not think that this would provide enough support to ensure success in this important aspect of the change process. The second scenario is that the consultant has been asked to provide some 'skills training' to a work group with a history of conflict and dissent. The consultant suspects that training at this point may not be well received by the group and that the causes of the problem are deeper than skill deficits. Both these situations illustrate a dilemma.

> If the consultant's initial view of the relationship, and the intervention that will be required, differs from what the client thinks is needed or wanted, then such situations are likely to end with disappointment and lead to a no-win situation.

Much advice is available to new and practising consultants on how to be effective practitioners, but little is focused on the special problem of agreeing with the client on the best role to adopt. Champion, Kiel and McLendon, in an article called 'Choosing a consulting role' (1990), provide clear guidance for the consultant (and client) on the most appropriate role. In order to undertake this kind of practical assessment and to facilitate collaborative agreements between client and consultant, three things are needed:

- a clear understanding of the purposes of a consulting relationship;
- a language for talking about consulting roles;
- the criteria for determining which role might be most appropriate in a given situation.

7.1   Client needs, consultant's response

In any consultation, the clients will have two types of need:

- The need for results requiring concrete outcomes associated with a project. These might include changes to the bottom line or organisational structure, information shared, skills learnt or changes to behaviour and attitudes.
- The need for organisational growth necessitating increased capacity to perform new functions or exhibit improved behaviours on a sustainable basis. If a high level of growth is achieved as a result of the consultation, then the client should be able to do the job the next time with less or no outside help.

The need for one or the other – concrete results or organisational growth – will vary depending on the nature of the consulting project. For example, in performing a one-time service with which the client is unfamiliar, the consultant's major focus is likely to be 'getting the job done' for the client. However, in helping the client perform an important and recurring task, the appropriate emphasis is on helping the client to learn how to perform that task over time rather than merely producing an immediate result. When project outcomes are specified in this way, it is easier to determine what services are needed from the consultant and what contributions are needed from the client system to bring about the desired changes. Champion et al. proposed that by constructing a grid model of consulting, using as the two axes 'consultant responsibility for growth' and 'consultant responsibility for results', one could specify the consulting roles appropriate for the mix of services. Champion et al. developed a nine-box grid, but for simplicity, a four-box grid is shown here (see Figure 7.1).

Figure 7.1 Consultants' responsibility for growth and results model

Source: After Champion, D.P., Kiel, D.H. and McLendon, J.A. (1990) 'Choosing a consulting role', *Training and Development Journal*, 1 February.

- **In the partner role** – the consultant has a great deal of responsibility for results and growth. This assumes that both the client and the consultant have the capacity to successfully perform aspects of the task and that both will share the responsibility for the results. It also assumes that a big improvement in the client's capacity to perform the task is an important goal. Here, the client is ready to learn in a hands-on way and the consultant can teach, effectively, as well as guide the task to successful completion.

- **In the coach role** – the consultant's concern is almost entirely for the capacity of the client to perform the task. The coach tries constantly to help the client clarify and set goals, maintain positive motivation and develop and implement effective plans. The coach is often removed from the performance of the situation. He or she may have to rely on the client's data about what is happening in the project. Hence much of the skill is in helping the client to gather, analyse and develop conclusions from his or her own experience.

- **In the reflective observer role** – the client is most responsible for results and capacity building; the consultant is least responsible. The consultant's task is limited to feeding back observations and impressions. In spite of the low activity level of the consultant, this role can have a dynamic effect on a client system that is skilled in using such assistance. The reflective observer can help clients monitor themselves on such ambiguous but crucial indicators as trust, teamwork and openness.

- The consultant who takes on **the hands-on expert role** actually undertakes the task on behalf of the client. In this role the consultant has most, if not all, of the responsibility for producing good results. The client is not expected to grow in capacity very much. He or she will need the consultant again next time in order to perform the task equally well.

159

> A consultant may play multiple roles simultaneously within a client system but with different clients.

He or she might be a coach to one manager, a reflective observer for the team the manager leads and a partner for a taskforce of other managers. Errors can arise from the consultant's attempt to play more than one role simultaneously with the same client without clear agreement to do so. Choosing the right role for the right situation is key.

7.2 Key skills: influencing

> In any business, effectively influencing others makes tasks easier, but this is particularly true for consulting projects.

There is no right way, nor is there only one way to influence others. Everything is a factor when influencing people. People, places, events and situations influence everyone constantly. Sometimes people are affected more or less, but they are continually being influenced by what happens around them. So also in the workplace, any task requires people to influence others much of the time. This may take the form of gaining support, inspiring others, persuading people to become their champions, engaging someone's imagination or creating relationships. Whatever form it takes, being an excellent influencer makes a job easier.

People like being around those who use their influencing skills well. There is a buzz, or sense that things are happening when they are about. Truly excellent influencing skills require a healthy combination of interpersonal, communication, presentation and assertiveness techniques. Good influencing is about adapting and modifying one's personal style whilst being conscious of the effect it is having on others and yet remaining true to oneself. Behaviour and attitude change are what is important.

Influence can be exerted through coercion and manipulation. This may even produce results but this is not influencing – it is forcing others to do things against their will. This approach will not win support. Clients are far more willing to 'come halfway' (or more) if they feel acknowledged, understood and appreciated. They may even do, or agree to, something they would not previously have done because they feel good about making the choice. The cliché 'perception is reality' rings true in the context of influencing. It does not matter what is going on internally for someone – if it is not perceived by the other person, then it does not exist, other than in the former's mind.

A vital skill

Influencing can sometimes be seen as the ability to 'finesse' – almost a sleight of hand. The other party is not prodded into seeing the influencer's view of the world but is persuaded, often unconsciously, into understanding it. Sometimes a person is so used to his or her own personal style, or way of being or pattern of communicating, that they do not think of how it is being received and do not think of behaving in any other way.

Influencing is about being able to move things forward, without pushing, forcing or telling others what to do.

One of the most powerful forces that affect people's behaviour is the avoidance of humiliation. No one wants to embarrass themselves if they can help it, so changing their own behaviour entails a certain risk. If that behaviour change is deliberate, and they have made an effort to see the world from the other person's point of view, then humiliation can be avoided on both sides. Whatever the arena a consultant works in, influencing others is about having the confidence and willingness to use one's own behaviour to make things happen.

Push and pull of influencing

There are two main sets of skills for influencing, and they are classified as push and pull skills. Push skills involve being a better advocate or promoter of a point of view. They are about being precise, stating views clearly and being prepared to specifically request what is wanted. Pull skills are essentially about trying to understand the other person's agenda through questioning and listening so that one can understand the other person's point of view and, as a result, position the proposal appropriately to meet their needs. The other benefit of listening first is that being listened to makes a person feel very positive towards the listener.

As Figure 7.2 shows, there are effective and ineffective push and pull skills. Starting initially down the push route, when someone is not successful in persuading the other person,

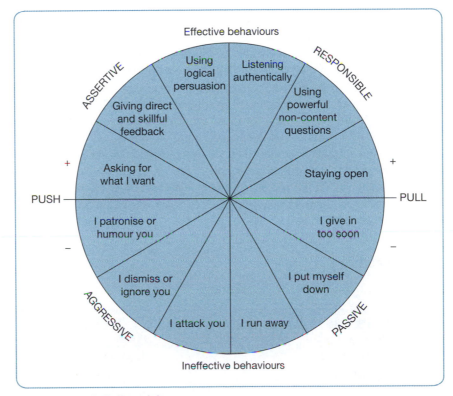

Figure 7.2 Push–Pull model

the tendency is to 'push' harder and as a result start moving into the ineffective area. Similarly, with pull skills, the tendency can be to become so aware and empathetic towards the other person's point of view that the consultant is reluctant to assert their own views.

> The key lesson from this is if 'pushing' is not successful, then switch to 'pulling' and vice versa.

7.3   Key skills: communications and rapport

Communicating effectively is the main skill the consultant needs to get by in the world (see Chapter 12). Interestingly, the spoken word actually counts for very little in terms of the total message; voice tone and body language count for far more. Key to success is getting the message across quickly and effectively and in a way that the audience relates to and wants to act on positively.

> Rapport is the skill of building cooperative relationships. It is the 'dance' that people do naturally.

Rapport skills enable the consultant to quickly put others at ease and create trust. Mastering the skill of building physical rapport requires being able to sense what is going on, quickly and accurately, and demonstrate behavioural flexibility.

There are the two obvious measures of a person's ability to produce results through rapport: the degree to which they can perceive the other person's postures, gestures and speech patterns; and the elegance with which these can be matched through rapport. Physical matching is only one aspect of this; being aware of the other person's inner self is another. Establishing rapport creates an environment of trust, confidence and participation. Mastery of rapport skills allows the consultant to get on with anyone anywhere, greatly increases the consultant's confidence and effectiveness and makes it easier for others to communicate with the consultant. Rapport needs flexibility of thought and behaviour. Liking the other person is not necessary for rapport. But having confidence in a person's competence for the task in hand is. If credibility for the task cannot be established, consider changing the task or person.

Matching

The building blocks of matching are:

Body language	
Posture	Orientation
Weight distribution	Gestures – arms and hands
Legs and feet	Facial expression
Eye contact	Breathing rate

Voice quality	
Tone	Volume
Tempo	Pitch
Sounds	

Leading

This changes the other person's behaviour by getting them to follow a lead (for example, from slumping to a more upright posture, or from speaking quietly to speaking more loudly). This is one way to test that the other person does indeed have rapport. Having rapport, and hence being able to lead others, makes it easier to achieve mutually desired outcomes, like reaching agreement. It is, however, a *choice*. There may be some people with whom a consultant would choose not to have rapport. In this case, it is possible to deliberately 'mismatch'.

Mismatching

This allows a person to break rapport, to interrupt or to avoid communicating. To mismatch, the consultant, for example, needs to alter their body and/or voice to make them deliberately different from the other person's. This will subtly and unconsciously interrupt the flow of communication, giving them the opportunity to redirect the interaction. However, mismatching can seriously damage relationships and it should be used only when direct requests fail.

7.4 Key skills: listening and questioning

The art of listening and of asking questions enables the consultant to gain a much deeper insight into the client's issues.

To be listened to is a striking experience – partly because it is so rare; when one person listens to another the former feels known and understood, not only that, listening intently to someone else provides him or her with a great win–win. If someone feels they have been listened to, they are more inclined to return the compliment. Listening is a talent that is given to everyone and, while some are more natural with it than others, it is certainly a skill that can be learned and developed. Most people do not listen at a very deep level. Their day-to-day preoccupations do not require more than a minimum of listening. As with physical fitness, so too with listening; to be a good listener, 'listening muscles' need to be exercised and developed.

Attention and impact

There are two aspects to listening. One is attention or awareness. This is the receiving of information through not only what is heard but also listening with all the senses.

The attention is on all the information and signals being received: the words, the energy and the impressions. The second aspect is what the listener does with what is heard. The impact of the choices that are made as a result of what is heard is also important. To understand the process of attention and impact, imagine a crowded room. Smoke is detected by someone – it could be a fire. Attention is drawn to the smoke. It is seen and then a decision is made. Someone might yell fire, or mention it casually to the host, or grab a fire extinguisher. Each of these choices will have a different impact.

Levels of listening

There are three levels of listening. At level 1 the attention is all internal. People listen to the words of the other but focus only on what it means to them. The spotlight is on the individual: their thoughts, judgements, feelings and conclusions about themselves and others. At level 1 there is only one question: what does this mean to the listener? There are many times when this is appropriate – for example, when information is needed when travelling. Answers, explanations, details and data are needed. The flight is late – how does this affect the person concerned? People who are led are often at level 1. That is their job, to look at themselves, but it is definitely not the place for a coach or leader.

Coaching happens at level 2, where there is a sharp focus on the other person. It can be seen in a person's posture when they are listening at this level – for example, leaning towards the speaker. There is a great deal of attention on the other person and little on the outside world. All listening at level 2 is directed at the speaker; the listener's awareness is totally on the other person. They listen for their words, their expression and their emotion, everything they communicate. At this level people are unattached to their own agenda. They are no longer trying to work out what to say next; it will come spontaneously from the absolute curiosity about what the other person is saying.

At level 3 a person listens at '360 degrees'. They listen and are aware of everything that is going on around them. If level 2 is like being 'hard-wired' to the other person, level 3 is like a radio field. The radio waves are completely invisible, yet the listener knows they are there because they can hear music coming from the radio. It takes a special receiver to pick up level 3 signals and practice to learn how to tune it properly. For many people this is a new realm of listening.

Powerful questions

Questions focus another person's attention in a way that a statement or presentation would find much harder to achieve. This is because of the way the brain works. People make decisions and take actions based on their own logical and intuitive reasoning.

> A presentation or statement *may* engage someone's thinking but a question *always* does.

Consider this question: what is the weather like right now? Even though it is a pretty routine question, your mind goes straight away to consider it. So even though you knew you were unlikely to have to come up with an answer you still did this. People love answering questions. The consultant is not often concerned with simple questions or ones that test general knowledge. His or her questions challenge a person's thinking. The consultant may be asking the respondent to think about something differently, that increases self-awareness or that builds responsibility. Most people are taught, from an early age, to pursue the right answer. Interviewees hope to answer interviewers' questions correctly. At work, requests for problem solving are the norm. An answer's value derives from its ability to solve a problem. A useful answer is more likely if the problem is properly defined, and a well-defined problem is usually stated in the form of a question.

To understand the effectiveness of questions, begin evaluating the quality of the questions asked. Successful people not only ask a lot of questions but they also learn to ask *powerful* questions. The most effective leaders are the ones that ask the best questions. The way in which questions are asked and the type of questions will determine the response received. The way in which a question is framed sets the direction for the conversation. The intent of a powerful question is to reveal more, to learn more and to see new possibilities and solutions. So, powerful questions lead to greater creativity. Powerful questions gain their power from their simplicity. A powerful question is usually short and seemingly even 'dumb'. For example, 'What outcome do you want?' or 'What's the next step?' or 'What did you learn?' appear simple on the surface, but these questions cause people to become introspective and more reflective. They are able to get to the heart of the matter. Notice that powerful questions are open-ended and 'what' questions. They move a conversation forward because they require reflection and more than a 'yes' or 'no' answer. Their intent is to go beyond getting information – it is to provide focus and to help gain both insight and clarity.

So questions are the means used to excavate new information, to compare someone's perspective with reality and to learn more about what others are thinking and perceiving. When someone does not ask questions, the assumption is that everything there is to know is known about the subject or the person. This is rarely the case.

7.5	**Working with teams**

Many studies have shown the importance of teamwork. In one such study carried out by the former UK Department of Trade and Industry on some of the UK's top-performing companies, it was established that teams were *the* principal building blocks for business success.

> **Teams play such an important role in moving organisations forward because a group of minds working together is smarter than a group of individuals working independently.**

Whether or not this always holds true depends on the team in question and, more importantly, at what stage of development the team is. The key to the success of the above-mentioned organisations is not just that they used teams but that they were able to form and develop high-performing teams in a relatively short period of time. By studying the common factors within high-performing teams, some of the vital ingredients necessary for improving the performance of any team can be established.

Common vision

Fundamental to any group of people working together effectively is a common vision. Victor Frankl, in his account of how people survived the terror of concentration camps, asserted that people will tolerate almost any 'what' or 'how' if they have a big enough 'why'. With effective teams, it is the 'why' that makes them overcome obstacles and do whatever it takes to succeed. In defining the team's purpose, two basic criteria need to be met. First of all, the vision has to be exciting enough to make people want to give their absolute best. Second, it needs to be sufficiently clear to align the team's actions towards its achievement.

Setting up a team to win

It is vital, when setting up a team, to ensure that it is given the best possible chance of success from day one. Besides getting commitment through a compelling purpose, it is necessary to:

- Select the right people and for the right reasons. This should include a balance between technical expertise and other skills like communication, leadership and creativity. The real genius of a great team is often in the diversity of the people it brings together.

- Explore the current situation and any circumstances associated with it, clarify the desired outcome and what it will mean to the success of the business and, finally, examine all plausible paths between the two before coming up with a clear strategic plan.

- Clarify what autonomy the team has in making decisions. One secret to empowering people within teams is to give them a clear boundary of responsibility with which no one will interfere. This symbol of trust, no matter how small, is what makes people feel as if they really make a difference.

- Wherever possible, guarantee commitment from significant people who have an indirect influence on the success of the team. One of several ways to achieve this is to set up a 'steering' team to clear the path for the actions of the main 'project' team.

- To increase the commitment from people within the team, begin by defining what will be required from each person in terms of time, resources, and so on. The benefit of this is that it will counter any fears people may have of over-committing themselves.

Finally, and above all, ensure that people begin with an expectation of success, even if the 'how to' is not yet evident. The only way to discover what is possible is to go beyond it into the impossible. Consider how it is possible that a talented group of managers with individual IQs well in excess of 120 might have a collective IQ of 55. The key to overcoming the above paradox is to accelerate team performance by giving each team member the necessary skills and encouragement to learn from experience, allow internal conflicts to surface and deal with them, play to each person's relative strengths and use advanced thinking strategies for developing innovation, problem solving, scenario planning, etc. The same attributes that define a successful individual (a willingness to take responsibility for the results they produce, flexibility and a thirst for constant improvement) apply to high-performing teams. The only addition to this is open communication, the essential glue that brings the component parts of a team together. When the intelligence of the team exceeds the intelligence of the individual members, there is an extraordinary capacity for coordinated action.

Stages of team or group development

There is a classical model of team or group development captured in the four words: *'forming, storming, norming and performing'*:

- 'Forming' best describes the immature group. It is about awareness.
- 'Storming' captures a team in conflict.
- 'Norming' refers to a team who are now sharing.
- 'Performing' refers to a highly productive team, effective in its activities.

The model assumes that every group will go through some part of each stage. The more the group members know each other and have worked together before, the less the time spent in the first three stages. Forming is about team building, ground rules, role clarification, task understanding and gaining of individual member commitment. Though each stage is critical to the development of a high-performing team, without the first three stages, the model argues, there may not be high performance. The stages often play out simultaneously or in different order. A team may start out by storming if the forming stage is not given attention and time. A team may norm and then storm about another issue or part of the team's responsibility. The key is to work through the storming stage by developing methods for handling conflict: dialogue and consensus decision making are the strongest methodologies.

This scheme, first proposed in the mid-1960s, was updated latterly to incorporate 'adjourning' to represent the closure of the team. At the turn of the century, Timothy Biggs suggested that an additional stage be added of norming after forming and renaming the traditional norming stage 're-norming'. This addition is designed to reflect that there is a period after forming where the performance of a team gradually improves and the interference of a leader, content with that level of performance, will prevent a team progressing through the storming stage to true performance. This puts the emphasis back on the team and its leader as the storming stage must be actively engaged in to succeed.

Belbin

Meredith Belbin published *Management Teams* back in the 1980s. This work remains highly respected and widely used to this day. Belbin studied how members of teams interacted during business games run at the Henley Management College. The key conclusions from his work describe what an effective team looks like. Belbin identified eight key roles for a successful team, expanding this later to nine. These are often separate from the role each team member has formally in the organisation.

- The **Coordinator** (formerly known as the 'Chairman') ensures that all members of the team are able to contribute to discussions and decisions of the team. Their concern is for fairness and equity among team members. Those who want to make decisions quickly, or unilaterally, may feel frustrated by their insistence on consulting with all members, but this can often improve the quality of decisions made by the team.
- The **Monitor-Evaluator** is a sober, strategic and discerning member who tries to see all options and judge accurately. This member contributes a measured and dispassionate analysis and, through objectivity, stops the team committing itself to a misguided task.

- The **Implementer** is the practical thinker who can create systems and processes that will produce what the team wants. Taking a problem and working out how it can be practically addressed is their strength. Being strongly rooted in the real world, they may frustrate other team members by their perceived lack of enthusiasm for inspiring visions and radical thinking but their ability to turn those radical ideas into workable solutions is important.

- The **Plant** is a creative, imaginative, unorthodox team member who solves difficult problems. Although they sometimes position themselves far from the other team members, they always like to present their brilliant idea.

- The **Resource Investigator** is the networker for the group. Whatever the team needs, the Resource Investigator is likely to have someone in his or her address book that can either provide it or knows someone else who can. This may be physical, financial or human resources, political support, information or ideas. Being highly driven to make connections with people, the Resource Investigator may appear to be flighty and inconstant, but the ability to call on their connections is highly useful to the team.

- The **Shaper** is a dynamic team member who loves a challenge and thrives on pressure. Winning is the name of the game for this team member. Committed to achieving the end required, they will challenge, argue or disagree and will display aggression in the pursuit of goal achievement. Two or three in a team, according to Belbin, can lead to conflict, aggravation and in-fighting.

- The **Team Worker** is concerned to ensure that interpersonal relationships within the team are maintained. They are sensitive to atmospheres and may be the first to approach another team member who feels slighted, excluded or otherwise attacked but has not expressed their discomfort. The Team Worker's concern with people factors can frustrate those who are keen to move quickly but their skills ensure long-term cohesion within the team.

- The **Completer Finisher** is the details person within the team. They have a great eye for spotting flaws and gaps and for knowing exactly where the team is in relation to its schedule. Team members who have less preference for detail work may be frustrated by their analytical and meticulous approach, but the work of the Completer Finisher ensures the quality and timeliness of the output of the team.

- The **Specialist**, the ninth role, was added by Belbin later. The Specialist brings particular knowledge to the team. They are passionate about learning in their own particular field and are likely to be a fountain of knowledge, enjoying imparting this to others. They also strive to improve and build upon their expertise. If there is anything they do not know, they will happily go and find out. Specialists bring a high level of concentration, ability, and skill in their discipline to the team, but can only contribute on that specialism and will tend to be uninterested in anything else.

> **Each team member may exhibit varying mixes of the above roles – none is 'pure'.**

Managers or organisations building working teams should ensure that each of the roles can be performed by a team member. Some roles are compatible and can be more easily fulfilled by the same person, whilst others may not. A team need not be as many as nine people, but should be at least three or four. Also the roles played may and will be different at different times and in different teams. Simple self-assessment forms are available online to help analyse team members. This technique provides a very useful 'handle' to the consultant when starting to work with a new group or team.

Learning styles

Another useful tool in the armoury of the consultant is an assessment of so-called 'Learning Styles'. The learning styles terms still widely recognisable today – **Activist**, **Reflector**, **Theorist** and **Pragmatist** – were identified and coined by Honey and Mumford. The tool, used for middle and senior managers in an organisation, assumes that these styles are acquired preferences that are adaptable either at will or through changed circumstances rather than being fixed personality characteristics. The Honey and Mumford *Learning Styles Questionnaire* is a self-development tool and differs from the original Kolb's Learning Style on which it is based in that it invites managers to complete a checklist of work-related behaviours without directly asking managers how they learn. Having completed the self-assessment, managers are encouraged to focus on strengthening under-utilised styles in order to become better equipped to learn from a wide range of everyday experiences. This questionnaire has been widely used for assessing preferred learning styles in the local government sector in the UK.

7.6   Leading a team

Consultants may well be called upon to lead a team. This can be daunting at first but research clearly demonstrates that a consultant can lead a team in a way that creates a positive so-called 'climate'. Furthermore, a positive climate is not just desirable; it has a direct link with better performance.

Climate: the 'weather' in an organisation

People in organisations frequently describe what might be called a 'weather system' that directly affects how they behave. Real, physical climate may be changeable or steady, stormy or sunny, hot or cold. This affects physical comfort and may also affect feelings of well-being. The metaphorical climate of the work unit may be almost as tangible, with the same powerful impact on day-to-day behaviour.

> **Climate is relatively long-lasting. It reflects perceptions of the atmosphere in a work unit and may affect behaviour.**

If someone believes that their boss will punish them if they make a mistake, the usual effect will be that they start behaving defensively and cover up their mistakes.

Symptoms that something is wrong

If there are problems with climate, some or all of the following might be seen:

- a high level of grievance and/or complaint;
- low performance standards;
- conflict and hostility between team members;
- people avoiding talking to or listening to each other;
- people being afraid to speak up;
- managers being perceived as unapproachable;
- lack of effective communication with other teams;
- confusion about the overall goals of the team;
- widespread confusion about individual tasks and roles;
- apathy and lack of involvement about where the team is heading;
- people failing to acknowledge each other's good work;
- confusion about working procedures as a group;
- relationships with other teams being fraught with hostility and mistrust;
- poor performance compared with other teams doing similar tasks.

Climate is one of the best-researched areas of organisational behaviour and one of the few where it is possible to demonstrate a direct relationship between cause and effect. Kurt Lewin was a German Jew who fled Germany in the 1930s. His experience of Nazism led to a lifelong interest in what made people behave the way they did. How, for instance, could a whole country have submitted to a dictator like Hitler? He did some interesting experiments in the 1940s and 1950s with boys' clubs where the only variable was the way the boys were led. Three leadership styles were identified:

Authoritarian: A stern I-know-best style: the boys were told what to do and got little praise

Laissez-faire: A pleasant leadership style but one that gave little direction

Democratic: A style that involved the boys and took their wishes into account

The results were startling. The *authoritarian* leader achieved early good results, but the moment the leader left the room, chaos broke out and the group members often destroyed their work. Achievements also diminished over time. The *laissez-faire* leader created a pleasant atmosphere but little was achieved in the way of output. The *democratic* style nearly always started with a degree of apparent excitement and perhaps confusion but always outperformed the others over time. George Litwin and Robert Stringer continued this work at Harvard. They hired groups of students who did not know the purpose of the study and who were put into three groups. They were asked to build models using Meccano. Each group had identical goals. Again, the only variable was leadership style. The names are different but essentially the styles were variants on Lewin's work and the results were similar.

The power-led group suppressed contributions from the group and created strict rules and regulations. The results were:

- high initial productivity;
- subversive behaviour breaking out among the group with covert or overt struggles for power with the leader;

- inability to innovate or flex production;
- inability to keep costs competitive;
- lower overall productivity;
- a conservative, formal and cold climate.

The affiliative group (cf. Lewin's laissez-faire group) stressed cooperative behaviour and participative decision making rather than product excellence or productivity. It resulted in:

- flexibility and creativity;
- workers who enjoyed the climate and felt loyalty towards the group;
- lower output;
- frustration and struggles for leadership developing inside the group which often took attention away from production.

The achievement-led group (cf. Lewin's democratic group) stressed participative goal setting, competitive feedback, pride and teamwork. It resulted in:

- the highest productivity and biggest profit margins;
- loyalty to the team; a feeling of satisfaction in the work;
- high-quality products;
- people reporting a much greater feeling of individual responsibility for their work;
- a high level of innovation and creativity.

The cause and effect relationship

What both these pieces of work show is that there is a direct cause and effect relationship:

LEADERSHIP
↓
CLIMATE
↓
MOTIVATION
↓
PERFORMANCE

> **Varying the leadership style affects the climate; the climate in turn affects motivation and motivation affects performance.**

The lessons

For the team leader the lessons are clear. The achievement style is the one that makes people both happy and productive. So what are the key pieces of behaviour that are needed? Further research with companies has shown that the 'climate' research holds true in the 'real' world. For instance, teams whose performance was rated highly on measures such as customer satisfaction and net profit also showed that they had a positive climate along the lines of Litwin and Stringer's 'achievement' focus. There is a consistent pattern in these four areas.

Clarity	• Make it clear where people fit into the organisation and the team. If there is confusion, talk it through and make it clear. • Clarify the boundaries of people's roles. If they are unclear, make them clear. • Set clear objectives and expectations. • Make it crystal clear who has what authority to make decisions.
Standards	• Establish high standards through discussion. • Communicate these high standards. • Challenge complacency – keep on looking for increased quality and quantity. • Involve customers in standard setting.
Recognition	• Give people very frequent positive feedback and do it immediately. • Balance this with negative feedback when necessary but keep the emphasis on the positive. • See mistakes as opportunities to learn for the whole team.
Team working	• Talk positively about the team so that people feel proud to belong to it. • Create an atmosphere of trust by dealing with conflict openly so that there are no hidden agendas. • Support, encourage and reward innovation. • Devote time to team communication – looking at feelings as well as facts.

The other good news about climate is that it can be changed quickly and that change is within any leader's control.

7.7 Challenging constructively

Many consultants stumble mid-project as client team members behave as though it is 'business as usual'. It is easy, at this stage, to assume that major change is not possible. Using a technique such as 'outcome-frame thinking' can help improve the process. Much of what humans do, the decisions they make and how they respond to challenges, is based more on an automatic response to the circumstances at hand than on conscious choice. These responses are preconditioned by past experience or they may be based on personality – but they are not the only option. Victor Frankl, a Jewish psychiatrist who was imprisoned in a concentration camp during the Second World War, wrote of his discovery of what he called the 'ultimate human freedom'. One day, naked and all alone in a small room and having just been tortured, he began to realise that while his captors could control his entire environment and could do what they wanted to his body, ultimately it was up to him to decide within himself how all of this was going to affect him. Between what happened to him, or the stimulus, and his response to it, was his freedom or power to choose his outcome.

The proactive model

$$E \quad + \quad R \quad = \quad O$$
$$(Events + Response = Outcome)$$

People often talk of being like victims or feel that it is 'others' that are difficult. This model is deceptively simple but very powerful. Take this example. Imagine agreeing with a partner or a friend that you were going to cook them dinner at 8 p.m. one evening. They do not appear till 10 p.m., with no excuse and no phone call, and the dinner is ruined. That is the event – it cannot be changed. What reaction might there be to this situation? You might say 'Your dinner is in the dog' or have a row. Now with that kind of response, the outcome is a miserable evening and potential loss of friendship. In this situation events have been allowed to drive the outcome.

Now consider what would have happened if you had thought about the outcome you wanted before making the response. For example, if the desired outcome were still to have a pleasant evening and remain friends with that person, then you would think about a better response. You can still let the other know you are unhappy but in a controlled way, and perhaps ask the other person to go and get a takeaway and wine. Here you are far more in control of a more desirable outcome.

> **Thinking about the outcome has resulted in a suitably tailored response.**

So this simple formula is very powerful. Starting to think in terms of the desired outcome gives a much better chance of achieving it. As Victor Frankl showed, an individual is always in charge of his or her response and there are many ways to alter it.

Outcome-frame thinking

Building on the earlier discussion about questioning, this technique is useful for making people reframe their apparent problems so that they see them in a new light. The very word 'problem' creates a sense of weight, worry and difficulty. If the consultant goes down the 'problem' route, they run the risk of increasing the size, scope and depth of the problem for the person they are trying to help.

Here are some examples of problem-frame thinking:

- Whose fault is it?
- Why have you not done anything about it yet?
- What is stopping you doing something?
- What does having this problem say about you as a person?
- What does having this problem say about you as a professional?
- What forces outside your control are contributing to this?
- What are the negative consequences?
- What further problems is this leading to?

The general effect of questions like these is to rob the person concerned of power. They increase the chances of feeling helpless and a victim.

This approach of outcome-frame thinking is very different. It empowers a person.

> **When asked outcome-frame questions, the consultant can often see a visible difference in the way the other person responds.**

Here are some examples of powerful outcome-frame questions using the same themes as the problem-frame questions above:

- What do you want?
- What else will that do for you?

- What will it look, sound and feel like when you have what you want?
- What resources outside of you do you have to get what you want?
- Who else can help you?
- What will getting what you want confirm about you as a person/professional?
- What further benefits could there be?
- What is the first step to getting what you want?

Identifying shared interests

This is about putting yourself in the other person's shoes: what could explain their present behaviour? What, in their minds, is standing in the way of their seeing things like you do? What range of interests do they represent? What other players are involved? What other human needs is this session going to meet, e.g. for recognition, security, affection, prestige or a sense of having control over their lives?

Being assertive

Assertiveness means believing in the right to be heard as well as respecting the rights of others. The consultant has the right to be there, be treated respectfully, ask for information, disagree, change their mind, be listened to, think before reacting and ask for time to consider or reconsider.

Making your own thinking visible

As a consultant, it is important to state any assumptions; for example, 'Here is what I think and this is how I got there.' Make the reasoning explicit: 'I have come to this conclusion because . . .' Give examples of what would happen if the proposal were implemented; for instance, 'If we were to do this, you would see something like this . . .' Actively encourage others to test any hypotheses, e.g. 'How does this strike you so far?' 'What flaws suggest themselves?' 'Do you have any worries about it?' Ask for the other person's view.

Resolving conflict: one-to-one

> **Conflict arises in teams or between individuals primarily because of lack of understanding of each other's position or unwillingness to explore the other person's point of view and search for areas of agreement.**

One of the best ways to deal with conflict is to impose, as a facilitator, a somewhat artificial structure on the dialogue between the parties in conflict. Nancy Kline, in her superb book *Time to Think*, proposes the following structure for resolving issues. First, get the individuals involved to agree to the structure below.

Explain that each person takes it in turn to speak for three minutes on the issues they wish to discuss. During this time the other party can only listen. They may not ask questions or show agreement or disagreement. They must simply pay attention. Each person has those minutes and that space totally to themselves. They do not need to build on or pay attention to anything the other party has said. After each party has had their three minutes the drill is continued until the facilitator believes that they have reached a better understanding. The process should not be stopped too soon, even if one party has gone silent. It is their space. Usually this simple process alone is enough to resolve many issues. If, however, there is insufficient common ground, then the facilitator may allow each party to question the other party for three minutes at a time. In this case, the rule is that all questions should be designed to check and test understanding and the facilitator should oversee this. This process, although deceptively simple, has enormous power.

Resolving conflict: groups

There are various techniques for diagnosing and fixing dysfunctional teams. The perfect team does not exist, but if a team's shortcomings start to generate problems or derail the tasks in hand, something needs to be done quickly. According to Anne Field (*HBR*, April 2009), dysfunctional teams can take many forms. These are all too familiar:

- **The team of individualists:** everyone is out for themselves, their department or their function. Jockeying for power and passive resistance are common.
- **Factional teams:** individual team members are loyal to their faction, not to the team itself.
- **Conflict-avoiding teams:** everyone goes along to get along. Creativity and innovation suffer; mediocrity prevails.
- **Indecisive teams:** discussions are circular. For every two steps forward, the team takes one-and-a-half back.

Trust, cohesiveness and purpose

According to Field, the source of most team dysfunctions most commonly lies in a lack of trust, the inability to engage in productive conflict or insufficient clarity of purpose. Since one of these problems tends to trigger another, most dysfunctional teams suffer more than one of these. Once diagnosed, these issues can be addressed. Simple techniques like creating opportunities for team members to get to know each other better can help build trust, for example. Cohesiveness can be improved by strengthening the bonds between individual members. The use of personality tests, such as Myers Briggs (see later in this chapter), and sharing the results can be very helpful. Of course, it is always important to be sure that a clear goal is set for any team. Communicated well, this can generate energy and excitement.

Six Thinking Hats

Another technique that is useful to help resolve issues within a group or team is Dr Edward de Bono's 'Six Thinking Hats'. The use of this technique gives team members permission to speak in a 'different voice' or from a different perspective. Though the 'six hats' is a thinking tool for both group discussion and individual thinking, it does also provide a means for groups to think together more effectively and can be used to resolve otherwise thorny issues. It is a means to plan thinking processes in a detailed and cohesive way.

The premise of the method is that the human brain thinks in a number of distinct ways that can be identified, deliberately accessed and hence used in a structured way. De Bono identifies six distinct states in which the brain can be 'sensitised'. In each of these states the brain will identify and bring into conscious thought certain aspects of the issues being considered; for example, gut instinct, pessimistic judgement and neutral facts. Dr de Bono believes that these states are associated with distinct chemical states of the brain. The approach allows the development of strategies for thinking about particular issues.

De Bono describes the six states, to each of which a colour is assigned, as follows:

- **Information (white)** – considering purely what information is available, asking what the facts are.
- **Emotions (red)** – instinctive gut reaction or statements of emotion and feelings (but without any justification).
- **Bad points (black)** – logic applied to identifying flaws or barriers, seeking mismatch.
- **Good points (yellow)** – logic applied to identifying benefits, seeking harmony.
- **Creativity (green)** – statements of provocation and investigation, seeing where a thought goes.
- **Thinking (blue)** – 'thinking about thinking'.

The coloured hats are used as metaphors for each state. Switching to a state is symbolised by the act of putting on a coloured hat, either literally or metaphorically. In practice, coloured balls can also be used or, more commonly, just a reference to a hat.

7.8 Knowing yourself: psychometric tests

> Whether the consultant finds themselves working largely alone, with colleagues or with a client team, it is invaluable to have a degree of self-awareness when embarking on any project or consulting activity.

Indeed, applying certain tools to oneself may be a salutary lesson for a consultant. There are various psychometric tests on the market that may help in this process.

Myers–Briggs Type Indicator

Use of assessment tools like the Myers–Briggs Type Indicator (MBTI) (Figure 7.3) may be worth the investment. This tool is widely used and recognised. Indeed, the publisher of the MBTI instrument describes it as 'the world's most widely used personality assessment', with as many as two million administered annually. The MBTI assessment is a psychometric questionnaire designed to measure psychological preferences about how people perceive the world and make decisions. The MBTI focuses on normal populations and emphasises the value of naturally occurring differences. None of the types is better or worse.

Fundamental to the Myers–Briggs Type Indicator is the theory of psychological type as originally developed by Jung. Jung proposed the existence of two dichotomous pairs of cognitive functions:

- the 'rational' (judging) functions: *thinking* and *feeling*;
- the 'irrational' (perceiving) functions: *sensing* and *intuition*.

Jung went on to suggest that these functions are expressed in either an introverted or extroverted form. From Jung's original concepts, Briggs and Myers developed their own theory of psychological type, on which the MBTI is based.

Jung's model regards psychological type as similar to left- or right-handedness: individuals are either born with, or develop, certain preferred ways of thinking and acting. The MBTI sorts some of these psychological differences into four opposite pairs, or *dichotomies*, with a resulting 16 possible psychological types. However, Briggs and Myers theorised that individuals naturally *prefer* one overall combination of type differences. The 16 types are typically referred to by an abbreviation of four letters – the initial letters of each of their four type preferences (except in the case of *intuition*, which uses the abbreviation *N* to distinguish it from Introversion).

The four pairs of preferences or dichotomies are:

- Extroversion vs Introversion;
- Sensing vs Intuition;
- Thinking vs Feeling;
- Judgement vs Perception

ISTJ 'Doing what should be done'	ISFJ 'A real sense of duty'	INFJ 'An inspiration to others'	INTJ 'Sees room for improvement in everything'
ISTP 'Will try anything once'	ISFP 'Sees much - shares little'	INFP 'Noble service to help society'	INTP 'A love of problem solving'
ESTP 'The ultimate realists'	ESFP 'You only live once'	ENFP 'Giving life an extra squeeze'	ENTP 'One exciting challenge after another'
ESTJ 'Life's administrators'	ESFJ 'Hosts and hostesses of the world'	ENFJ 'Smooth talking persuaders'	ENTJ 'Natural leaders'

Figure 7.3 MBTI and the types in a nutshell

Source: Modified and reproduced by special permission of the Publisher, CPP, Inc., Mountain View, CA 94043 from *Introduction to Type* ®, Sixth Edition by Isabel Briggs Myers. Copyright 1998, 2012 by CPP, Inc. All rights reserved. Further reproduction is prohibited without the Publisher's written consent.

These terms have specific technical meanings relating to the MBTI that differ from their everyday usage. For example, people who 'prefer' judgement over perception are not necessarily more *judgemental* or less *perceptive*. Extroversion means 'outward-turning' and introversion means 'inward-turning'. Someone reporting a high score for extroversion over introversion cannot be correctly described as *more* extroverted: they simply have a clear *preference*.

Point scores on each of the dichotomies can vary considerably from person to person, even among those with the same type. However, Myers considered the *direction* of the preference to be more important than the *degree* of the preference. The expression of a person's psychological type is more than the sum of the four individual preferences. The preferences interact through type dynamics and type development. The preferences for extroversion and introversion are often called 'attitudes'. Briggs and Myers recognised that each of the cognitive functions can operate in the external world of behaviour, action, people and things (*extroverted attitude*) or the internal world of ideas and reflection (*introverted attitude*). The MBTI assessment sorts for an overall preference for one or the other.

Five Factor Model

In contemporary psychology, the **'Big Five' factors** (or **Five Factor Model**, **FFM**) of personality are five broad domains or dimensions of personality that are used to describe human personality. The Big Five factors are: *openness, conscientiousness, extraversion, agreeableness and neuroticism*. The neuroticism factor is sometimes referred to as 'emotional stability'. Some disagreement remains about how to interpret the openness factor, which is sometimes called 'intellect' rather than openness to experience. Beneath each factor, a cluster of correlated specific traits are found. For example, extraversion includes such related qualities as gregariousness, assertiveness, excitement seeking, warmth, activity and positive emotions.

The Five Factor Model is a descriptive model of personality, commonly known by the acronym OCEAN:

- **Openness** – (inventive/curious vs consistent/cautious). An appreciation for art, emotion, adventure, unusual ideas, curiosity and variety of experience.
- **Conscientiousness** – (efficient/organised vs easy-going/careless). A tendency to show self-discipline, act dutifully and aim for achievement; planned rather than spontaneous behaviour.
- **Extroversion** – (outgoing/energetic vs solitary/reserved). Energy, positive emotions and with the tendency to seek stimulation in the company of others.
- **Agreeableness** – (friendly/compassionate vs cold/unkind). A tendency to be compassionate and cooperative rather than suspicious and antagonistic towards others.
- **Neuroticism** – (sensitive/nervous vs secure/confident). A tendency to experience unpleasant emotions easily, such as anger, anxiety, depression or vulnerability.

Identifying the traits and structure of human personality has been one of the most fundamental goals in all of psychology. The five broad factors were discovered and defined by several independent sets of researchers (including Digman and later Matthews, Deary and Whiteman). These researchers began by studying known personality traits and then factor analysing hundreds of measures of these traits in order to find the underlying factors of personality. At least four sets of researchers have worked independently for decades on this problem and have identified generally the same Big Five factors. However, because the Big Five traits are broad and comprehensive, they are not nearly as powerful in predicting and explaining actual behaviour as are the more numerous lower-level traits.

16PF

The 16 personality factors were derived by psychologist Raymond Cattell and are measured using the 16PF questionnaire. Figure 7.4 shows the list of 16 factors together with a typical set of results.

Cattell referred to the 16 factors as *primary factors*. They were developed in the 1940s and 1950s by scientifically sampling the widest possible range of behaviours, including using ratings by observers, questionnaires and objective measurements of actual behaviour. This took more than a decade and was later validated in a range of international cultures over time. Thus, these factors were seen to represent a fairly comprehensive listing of the basic dimensions of human personality. He then factored these primary traits (performed a second-order factor analysis) and discovered a smaller number of overarching personality factors or domains that provided the overall structure and meaning for the primary traits. He labelled these Second-Order or *Global Factors*. For example, Extroversion was found to be a Global Factor that contained primary factors Warmth/Reserve (A), Social Boldness/Shyness (H), Liveliness/Seriousness (F), Group-Orientation/Self-Sufficiency (Q2), and Forthrightness/Privateness (N).

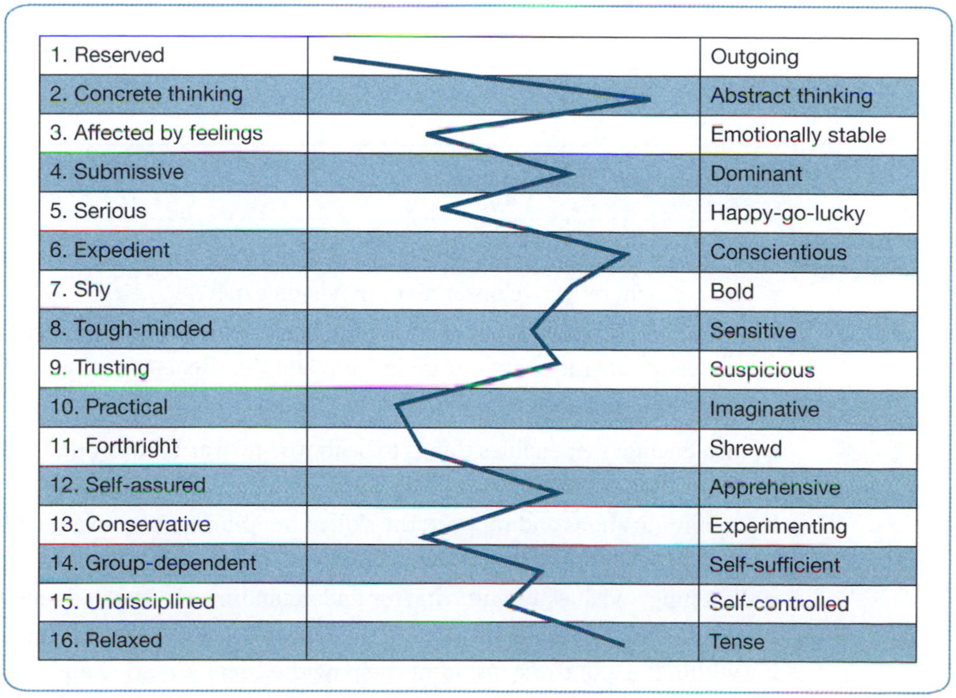

1. Reserved		Outgoing
2. Concrete thinking		Abstract thinking
3. Affected by feelings		Emotionally stable
4. Submissive		Dominant
5. Serious		Happy-go-lucky
6. Expedient		Conscientious
7. Shy		Bold
8. Tough-minded		Sensitive
9. Trusting		Suspicious
10. Practical		Imaginative
11. Forthright		Shrewd
12. Self-assured		Apprehensive
13. Conservative		Experimenting
14. Group-dependent		Self-sufficient
15. Undisciplined		Self-controlled
16. Relaxed		Tense

Figure 7.4 16PF Plot Example

In the original fourth and fifth editions of the 16PF, there were five global factors that correspond fairly closely to the later 'Big Five'.

- BF Openness => 16PF Openness/Tough-mindedness;
- BF Conscientiousness => 16PF Self-Control;
- BF Extraversion => 16PF Extroversion;
- BF Agreeableness/Disagreeableness => 16PF Independence/Accommodation;
- BF Neuroticism => 16PF Anxiety.

In fact, the development of the Big Five factors began by factor analysing the original items of the 16PF. The above tools offer a range of ways of improving self-awareness – invaluable to any consultant.

Team discussion points

1 Belbin Team Roles measure behaviour rather than personality. So whilst an individual's personality traits are acknowledged to be fairly stable and unchangeable, behaviour can and should change to enable working in new environments and with fresh challenges. Each member of the team should complete a Belbin questionnaire (basic ones are available online), then for your team:

   - draw up a table of the scores and identify areas of potential weakness explaining why you have chosen these;
   - suggest how they might be filled or minimised in the current team.

2 Actively consider your individual team members' rapport skills. At the next available opportunity, make a note of examples of good and bad rapport.

Summary of key ideas

- Consultants need to identify which role to adopt on a particular assignment: that of partner, coach, reflective observer or hands-on expert.
- The right role to adopt depends on the situation; consider the organisational situation, characteristics of the client and consultant and the client–consultant relationship.
- Key 'soft skills' for a consultant are:
  - Influencing, as it enables things to be moved forward. Rarely does a consultant have any authority, so this is key to success;
  - Communications and rapport, the skill of building cooperative relationships. This 'oils the wheels' of any successful project;
  - Listening and questioning: vital for understanding and engagement with the client.
- Projects are always made up of different teams – within the client company and possibly within the group of consultants helping the client. Creating and working well with teams is vital.

- Projects are beset with challenges: it is in their nature. Knowing how to challenge constructively enables obstacles to be overcome in the best and most effective manner.
- The consultant is a key member of the project team. Knowing yourself – your strengths and weaknesses – and keeping up to date with how these change will prove invaluable.

Key reading

Belbin, R.M. (2010) *Management Teams: Why They Succeed or Fail* (3rd edn). Oxford: Butterworth-Heinemann.

Champion, D.P., Kiel D.H. and McLendon, J.A. (1990) 'Choosing a consulting role', *Training and Development Journal*, 1 February.

Further reading

Blanchard, K. and Miller, M.R. (2014) *The Secret: What Great Leaders Know and Do*. San Francisco: Berrett-Koehler Publishers.

Bono, E. de (2000) *Six Thinking Hats*. London: Penguin Books.

Cattell, H.E.P. and Schuerger, J.M. (2003) *Essentials of 16PF Assessment*. New York: John Wiley & Sons.

Covey, S.R. (2004) *7 Habits of Highly Effective People*. London: Simon & Schuster.

Covey, S.R. (2006) *The 8th Habit: From Effectiveness To Greatness*. London: Simon & Schuster.

Digman, J.M. (1990) 'Personality structure: emergence of the five-factor model', *Annual Review of Psychology*. 41: 417–440.

Field, A. (2009) 'Diagnosing and fixing dysfunctional teams', *Harvard Business Publishing Newsletters*, 12 March.

Frankl, V. (2004) *Man's Search for Meaning*. London: Rider.

Gallwey, W.T. (2003) *The Inner Game of Work: Overcoming Mental Obstacles for Maximum Performance*. Mason, OH: Texere Publishing.

Goleman, D. (2005) *Emotional Intelligence: Why It Can Matter More Than IQ*. New York: Bantam Books.

Honey, P. and Mumford, A. (2006) *Learning Styles Questionnaire 2006: 80 Item Version*. Coventry: Peter Honey Books.

Johnson, S. (1999) *Who Moved My Cheese? An Amazing Way to Deal With Change in Your Work and in Your Life*. London: Vermilion.

Kline, N. (2015) *More Time to Think: The Power of Independent Thinking*. London: Cassell.

Knight, S. (2009) *NLP at Work: The Essence of Excellence* (3rd edn). London: Nicholas Brealey.

Lewin, K. (1997) *Resolving Social Conflicts*. Washington, DC: American Psychological Association.

Litwin, G. (1990) *Motivation and Organizational Climate*. Boston, MA: Harvard University Press.

Matthews, G., Deary, I.J., and Whiteman, M.C. (2009). *Personality Traits* (3rd edn). Cambridge: Cambridge University Press.

Myers, I.B. and Myers, P.B. (1995) *Gifts Differing: Understanding Personality Type*. Mountain View, CA: Davies-Black Publishers.

Tannenbaum, R. and Schmidt, W.H. (1973) 'How to choose a leadership pattern'. *Harvard Business Review*, 1 May.

Whitmore, Sir J. (2002) *Coaching for Performance: Growing People, Performance and Purpose*. London: Nicholas Brealey.

Wiseman, R. (2004) *The Luck Factor: The Scientific Study of the Lucky Mind*. London: Arrow.

Case exercise

Queenswick Adult Social Care

Queenswick is a city in northern England that has suffered from industrial decline and a lack of investment in the later years of the twentieth century. Its population numbers 250,000, nearly 20,000 of who are over 75. The population declined by 7.5% between 1991 and 2001. Almost half of its inhabitants live in rented accommodation, compared with the national figure of 30%. Nearly 7% of the adult population are out of work. Of the 376 local authorities in England and Wales, only 22 have a worse level of unemployment. Some families on its estates were experiencing second generation unemployment. Its schools were often near the bottom of the GCSE league tables and the city suffered from above-average teenage pregnancies, drug use and antisocial crime. In recent years there had been an influx of Kurdish refugees together with workers from Poland and the Baltic States. For several years its city council was labelled the worst performing in the country, though in recent years substantial progress had been made.

As perhaps could be expected for a city experiencing such deprivation, there was a high degree of dependency on the city council for providing adult social care. Although the city council website provided substantial, easily accessed and well-explained information, with links to the various adult social care departments, this was of little obvious use to people without computers or the technological literacy to use them. Consequently, a high proportion of service users preferred to make contact by telephone, in the expectation of discussing their problems with a sympathetic respondent.

The council's Initial Contact Centre was staffed by five people, normally handling around 200 calls a week. They categorised the calls into different levels of priority and they were then forwarded to the department they believed to be most appropriate. However, they were not trained experts and cases could therefore be routed to the wrong department and risk being handled incorrectly. This could cause delays, duplication of information with different departments often asking the same initial questions and customers never seeing or speaking to the same person more than once. There was also a lack of communication between the various departments. Apart from the frustration, distress and irritation caused to vulnerable customers with a high degree of dependency who sought to build a trusting relationship, this was a costly and inefficient service which did not engender confidence and risked giving the council a bad name.

Queenswick City Council therefore engaged a student management consulting team from the local university to address three objectives:

- To review the customer pathway through the adult social care system
- To highlight the problem areas and recommend solutions to make the system more efficient
- To improve the overall experience for the service users

The brief for the team therefore was to meet with different members of the social care team and the Initial Contact Centre staff, review the workflow analysis, measure the volume of calls and the different departments to which they were routed and examine the council's website.

They also needed to address the system from an outside perspective as if they were service users, identifying issues that would affect these individuals directly. The consulting team's intention was to streamline the process so that it would run more smoothly and efficiently with a system that would be easier to understand, quicker and better working both for the service user and the council.

The consulting team also drew on an example of best practice from the neighbouring Coverley County Council's 'See and Solve' team. This consisted of a front team of about twenty personnel, all of whom have been trained to a high standard. Using a solution-based questioning method, it was possible for some 60% of calls received to be re-routed to staff outside the adult social care system. The 'See and Solve' team could therefore field the calls and assess them and also draw directly on a small team of Subject Matter Experts (SMEs).

This was not quite the easy experience the consulting team anticipated. The Initial Contact Centre staff members were hostile and uncooperative and did not appreciate what they saw as unwarranted intrusion. They were busy enough as it was, without a group of students telling them how they should be working. What experience, if any, did these 'kids' have? As a result, this part of the process took much longer than expected. Despite this, the student consultants arrived at some precise recommendations:

- Create a group of Subject Matter Experts consisting of an occupational therapist, a social worker, a benefits expert, a health care worker, a community liaison worker and a housing officer.
- Ensure that the Initial Contact Centre is expanded and that they are well trained, knowing what are the right questions to ask.
- Allocate each service user a case officer who acts as the main point of contact for the individual who deals with them from beginning to end.
- Create review teams to conduct regular audits to determine the efficiency and overall performance of the new system.

Some KPIs were also proposed – for example, all cases should have an assessment completed within four weeks, ideally two, with a care plan set up and in place within eight weeks of first contact.

These proposals would imply some degree of cost due to training needs, redeployment and possible recruitment but they would lead to an improved service and, crucially, more satisfied customers with much more confidence in the council. However, when they were presented the team did not enjoy the reaction they expected. The client felt the proposals were far too costly to implement. With the council already having to make significant savings in its budget, how could they seriously propose spending time and money training people and moving others around? The client said they needed a properly quantified business plan with costs and benefits clearly identified. Then there was the issue of the trade union: industrial action had already been threatened over possible redundancies, so redeployment would not be achieved without argument. The client also wondered aloud if some of the current staff would be able to be trained successfully as they plainly weren't up to the job. What was he supposed to do with them? Surely it would be easier to leave things as they are?

1 If you were the consultant, how would you have dealt with the attitude of the Initial Contact Centre staff?

2 What needs to be done to get the project back on track?

3 How would you resolve the client's anxiety over budget cutbacks and the anticipated trade union reaction?

APOLLO TECH SOLUTIONS CASE STUDY

Part Two

The deadline for submitting proposals was 8 April 2012 and Arnott was looking forward to receiving three submissions from the consulting firms. He cleared his diary and arranged the meetings for the following two weeks. Ferguson & Co and EuroComms Solutions came back immediately with dates to present their initial proposals to him; however, ITL seemed very reluctant to agree to time. Finally, Arnott was contacted by the Senior Partner in their Strategy Division with some unwelcome news. ITL had decided not to bid for the project. Even though Arnott had negotiated what to him seemed like a large budget, ITL were not prepared just to do the first stage. They would only be interested in the project if it included implementation, and thus a budget of about three to four times larger. Although disappointed, Arnott understood their decision and appreciated their honesty. So he was left with two to choose from.

Arnott wanted the two consultancies to have credibility in the ICT sector, including detailed market knowledge and evidence of effective strategy development programmes, which were critically evidence based. First up was EuroComms Solutions that brought an impressive list of former and current clients in the ICT sector around Europe across a broad range of functional areas. They continually emphasised that their market knowledge was second to none but said very little about the impact that their projects had had on their client businesses. This made Arnott a bit suspicious about their ability to deliver the competitive advantage sought from this project.

Ferguson & Co, on the other hand, were well prepared. They offered key insights into the ICT market and the use of their dedicated 'Knowledge Centre' to provide quick and detailed market analysis. They also clearly demonstrated how they had helped companies define and implement new strategies. Arnott was impressed with them, particularly when they appeared to offer a 'success fee' in the form of a payment based on profit growth. They also came in on budget for the project, which was to last six to eight weeks based on a core team of six from their side and an internal team of four from Apollo. There was just one slight niggle in the back of Arnott's mind. Ferguson & Co had presented this as the first stage in a process with the clear implication that they would continue on with the implementation. He also later learnt that their apparent appealing offer of a 'success fee' was dependent on Ferguson & Co doing

the whole project. Like ITL, they said this would be in the order of three to four times the original estimate.

The deciding factor in favour of Ferguson & Co was the lead Partner, Carl Klingner, who was very experienced and assured Arnott that he would personally lead the consultant team. Thus satisfied, Arnott gave his recommendation to the Apollo Tech Solutions Board and after some deliberation, Ferguson & Co was engaged to start the project on the 1 July, with the aim of presenting the strategy the first week of September. The timing was not ideal given this was the summer holiday period but the consultants felt confident that they could complete the project on time. In order to hit the ground running, Arnott asked Klingner for a detailed work plan so he could ensure that the key managers and directors within Apollo were available.

The plan for 'Project Moon' was as follows:

Week 0 (Set-up)

- Establish 'Project Office' to be based at Apollo's headquarters in Solihull, ensuring equipment available.
- Appoint members of the project team from Apollo – one full-time and three part-time – and Arnott to brief them.
- Collate all relevant internal data that the team would need.
- Initial meeting with team from Ferguson & Co – project leader (Klingner), a senior manager on site (Samantha Allen), a consultant and three analysts so that they could 'hit the ground running' the following week.
- Arnott's PA to set up interviews.

Weeks 1-3

- One-day workshop with all new members of Project Moon team to decide on priorities and work out a detailed plan of action.
- Internal and external market research analysis.
- Interviews with senior managers at Apollo Advance as well as ATS main board.
- Confirm attendees for the workshops.

Apollo Tech Solutions Case Study (continued)

Weeks 4-5

- Workshop 1 – 'Where are we now?' An agreement of the current status.

- Workshop 2 – 'Where do we want to be?' A discussion of the options presented by the Project Moon team and decision on those to pursue.

Weeks 6-7

- Presentation to review strategic options available to core team of Project Moon plus Arnott, Irvine and McPherson, and select those which offer the highest potential.

- Workshop 3 – 'Building a new strategy for Apollo Advance in terms of products, skills and capabilities'.

- Workshop 4 – 'Identifying implementation requirements'.

Week 8

- Present to the Board of Apollo Tech Solutions.

- Present to the senior managers of Apollo Advance.

Arnott was determined that he should keep an eye on proceedings even though he had a two-week holiday booked in mid-July. So the appointment of the team members from within Apollo was critical. His obvious candidate for the full-time role was the senior manager in his department who was responsible for the AA division. He was eminently suitable being another former management consultant, but Arnott worried that he did not fully understand the business and so felt he would be better suited to one of the part-time roles. There was also another factor. The CFO (McPherson) had been openly critical of this project, concerned about its 'value for money'. So Arnott decided to appoint one of McPherson's Finance Managers, Jill Davy, who was a commercial accountant. Davy readily accepted seeing it as a potential career-enhancing move.

On 1 July, the Project Moon team assembled in their temporary 'office' and the consultants from Ferguson & Co outlined their plans to their Apollo counterparts and Sam Arnott. Carl Klingner explained that they would be using Ferguson & Co's key tool 'The Strategic Flight Deck' to work through the process. There were five key inputs:

1 What are our products and services that we deliver to our customers?

2 Who are our competitors by product range and service and how do we rate against them?

3 What are the largest opportunities for us to pursue in the marketplace now and in the future?

4 Who are our customers and how do they rate us?

5 What are our main implementation challenges in terms of processes and people?

There would be both a top-down and a bottom-up approach. The former would be gained through one-to-one interviews with between 8 and 12 of the senior managers and conducted by Samantha Allen, the lead consultant. These would be complemented with the weekly workshops involving between 6 and 8 second-tier managers, Arnott and Davy, run by Allen. All the background work ('bottom-up' side) was to be carried out by the consultant and analysts from Ferguson & Co and aided by the part-time members from the Apollo side.

All the team members were excited to get started, none more so than the analysts, two of whom had only just joined Ferguson & Co after completing their degrees. All felt positive that this project was going to be a success, including Sam Arnott.

Questions

1 If you were ITL, would you have refused the business and why?

2 How would you have structured the team for 'Project Moon'?

3 What do you think might be the potential pitfalls in the plan?

PART THREE

Undertaking the project

Chapter 8

Working with the client

In war as in life, it is often necessary when some cherished scheme has failed, to take up the best alternative open, and if so, it is folly not to work for it with all your might.

Winston Churchill

Learning outcomes

The learning outcomes from this chapter are to:

- understand the levels of client–consultant interaction depending on the type of consulting project undertaken;
- demonstrate how benchmarking can help the smooth running of a project;
- show the different roles that members of the client organisation can play;
- understand why organisations resist change;
- appreciate the types of consultant interaction that facilitate change;
- identify resistance by the client and learn ways to overcome it;
- recognise the types of *problem* that might challenge the progression of the project;
- learn the most effective *response* to make in the face of such challenges.

You are ready to start working on the consulting assignment. You have a well-prepared proposal that the client is happy with. You have done all the preparations and your team is in place. So everything is going to go perfectly from now on. Well, yes and no. It's a good start – as experience shows, if you start badly, you never recover. However, that is not to say that problems cannot occur during the project. They can be minor things like key people not being available on the client side at the time you need them, leading to the project taking longer than anticipated.

> **The most damaging to a final successful outcome is a greater degree of resistance by members of the client company to the changes you are proposing.**

This may include those individuals who were originally supportive, but now are concerned about their position and, for political reasons, switch allegiance. In that situation, you could spend a disproportionate amount of time trying to get the individual back on board. When something goes wrong, you need to be dispassionate and concentrate on what is best for the project. This means remaining confident about your ideas, as showing any weakness in this area would strengthen the hand of your opposition. Remember, you did not come in to do this project to be liked, but to be an effective consultant.

8.1   Consultant–client engagement for project implementation

As no two consulting projects are alike, nor is the level of engagement that a consultant has with a client. Figure 8.1 looks at the spectrum of consultant–client relationships, depending on the level of intimacy the consultant has with the client. Type A is when the consultant is briefed and delivers a report at the end, but the level of intimacy with the client is low. An example of this would be a market research brief. In this case the client would tell the consultant what information they require, agree the questions, and the next interaction would be the findings from the research.

A more traditional view of a consulting project would be where the external consultants do most of the work but they have regular contact with the client, as in Type B. An example of this type of project would be a commercial due diligence. This is a review of a business that is for sale and a prospective purchaser wants to ensure that they are making a good investment. The brief is clear and the view from the consultant has to be independent, but a buyer wants to be kept informed of progress in case the consultant uncovers any major issues that would prevent the sale.

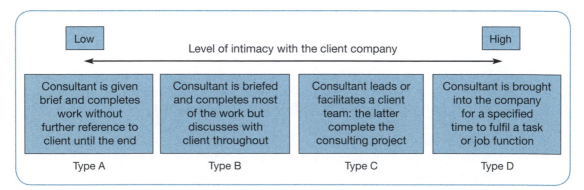

Figure 8.1 Consultant–client interaction

The bulk of the work that many professional management consultants undertake would fall into the third category (Type C), where the consultant would lead or facilitate a client team.

The reasons for this are:

- cost – external management consultants do not come cheap;
- a better knowledge of the issues that the client company faces;
- any solutions are likely to be better embedded and therefore implemented;
- it is a good training for the members of the client team;
- the client has more control over the project.

The last category (Type D), where effectively the consultant becomes a full-time member of the client organisation, is often called interim management (see Chapter 2 for a more detailed discussion). There may be a role or specific project for a limited time that the client needs someone to fulfil but at the same time wants him or her to be part of the organisation. In cases where the client company is in dire straits, specialists called 'company doctors' are brought in to try to rescue the company.

As was discussed in Section 3.5 on the selling process, there is also the issue of whether a standardised or customised process is being offered. While standardised processes are often associated with a lower level of intimacy with the client company, as in the example above with regard to a market research project, this is not always the case. IT consultants often implement standardised computer systems in client companies where they are engaged almost as an interim manager. Having a customised process does usually mean a higher level of intimacy with the client, as the consultant needs to have a greater understanding of the client. However, there are exceptions where a customised approach is needed but little client contact is needed. This is because the client is expecting the consultant to come up with an 'answer'. The consultant in this case would probably be a leading thinker or 'guru', who would be applying their considerable skills and knowledge to provide a solution.

So where do you position yourself? There are no hard and fast rules but where you start on the spectrum, you generally should stay for the duration of the project. Otherwise it leads to confusion both for you and the client.

You need to ask yourself the following questions to try to determine your position:

- Does the client not have any of the required specialist skills and understanding to undertake this task (Type A)?
- Does the client understand the task required but lacks all the required skills to undertake it and may also want an independent view (Type B)?
- Does the client understand the task and have some of the skills internally but not all the required resources and want to gain best practice from an outsider (Type C)?
- Does the client usually have both the knowledge and the skills for the project but is lacking them at this time (Type D) or has other reasons to use a consultant, e.g. an investor requests it?

As the use of management consultants has become more widespread and many managers have direct experience of using them, a degree of cynicism has crept in as to the consultant's worth to the business. This has also engendered increasing uncertainty amongst clients, and a consultant should be aware of the type of client they are working with. Pemer and Werr (2013) have identified four types: 'controlling', 'instrumental', 'trustful' and 'ambivalent'. Each has a different attitude to the use of consultants and this reflects how they behave during the consulting project – see Table 8.1 below.

Pemer and Werr (ibid) have further identified which types of projects 'fit' best with each type of client and the mutual relationship (Figure 8.2). It is important therefore to think about this before embarking on the project, as a mismatch may have serious consequences.

Table 8.1 Summary of the four different conceptions of uncertainties in the client-consultant relationship

Their view on	Controlling client	Instrumental client	Trustful client	Ambivalent client
Consultants	'Parasites' Disloyal, inexperienced, too dependent on theoretical models, not taking responsibility for their ideas or work	'Tools' Competent in their area of expertise but acting for their own good	'Colleagues' Very competent and experienced, loyal and taking responsibility for their ideas and work	'Saviours' More competent and experienced than the client and the client organisation. Good at handling complex problems.
The client organisation	Skilled, knows more than the consultants but relies sometimes too much on them	Skilled, but sometimes in need of extra resources or competence	Not very skilled, needs help with complex issues. Does not always understand the importance of the consulting projects	Not very skilled, knows less than the consultants. In need of extra help and expertise when difficult and complex situations arise
The client manager	Strong, controlling, dominating	'Natural' leader	Identifies with the consultants	Low self-esteem
Appropriate use of consultants	Limited tasks, analysis, data mining, secretaries	Any kind of task as long as it is well defined	Strategic issues, change projects	Complex problems, important projects
Consultant–client relationship	*Unequal and distrustful* The client must monitor and control the consultants to stop them from stealing information or expanding their projects	*Equal but distrustful* As long as clear divisions of labour and responsibilities are in place, the relationship can be friendly	*Equal and trusting* Friendly relationship. Close consultant-client collaboration needed to learn from the consultants	*Unequal and trusting* The client looks up to the consultants and expects them to solve the problem for him/her

Source: Pemer, F. and Werr, A. (2013) 'The Uncertain Management Consulting Services Client', *International Studies of Management & Organization* 43 (3), 33.

	Low ← Relational uncertainty → High	
High ↑ Performance uncertainty ↓ **Low**	**Ambivalent client** **Type of projects:** Complex problems **Type of relationship:** Subordinating teacher–pupil relationship	**Controlling client** **Type of projects:** Delimited tasks, analysis **Type of relationship:** Control, dominating the consultants
	Trustful client **Type of projects:** Change and strategy **Type of relationship:** Co-operation, partnership	**Instrumental client** **Type of projects:** Any project as long as it is well defined **Type of relationship:** Control, clear division of roles

Figure 8.2 How perceived performance and relational uncertainties relate to legitimate uses of consulting services and consultant–client relationships

From Pemer, F. and Werr, A. (2013) 'The Uncertain Management Consulting Services Client', *International Studies of Management & Organization* 43 (3), 35.

8.2 Relationship with the client during the project

In Chapter 7, we discussed the key interpersonal skills required to be a successful consultant, and these are key to maintaining a good relationship with the client during the project. As David Maister points out in his chapter 'The Consultant's Role' in Fombrun and Nevins (2004), *The Advice Business*, a consultant has to be seen to be *helping* a client to be successful. Just providing the right answer is not enough. You have to deal with the client's emotions (and also the politics within the client company). Maister gives the common emotions your client might feel when using consultants:

1 *Insecure* – the employment of an outside person to address some of the issues the firm faces may be an indication of failure on the part of the client.

2 *Threatened* – a consultant is looking at my area of expertise; will this highlight my weaknesses?

3 *Personal risk* – the client could feel that they are losing control giving an outside person responsibility for looking at their business.

4 *Impatient* – a consultant is often called as a last resort when the corporate ship is sinking, so the client may be more impatient for success.

5 *Worried* – what will these consultants discover and will it be to my detriment?

6 *Exposed* – outsiders will be able to look at the inner workings of the company and this can pose a risk if, for example, the company is subsequently up for sale.

7 *Ignorant* – the client does not fully understand what the consultant is proposing but finds it hard to articulate this without appearing incompetent.

8 *Sceptical* – often when clients have had unsatisfactory outcomes with previous consultants, they are naturally wary of others.

9 *Concerned* – clients worry that they often get a 'standard' package instead of a customised one for their business, as this is easier for the consultant.

10 *Suspicious* – consultants' (unfairly) poor reputation may precede them and for many clients they are worried that they are not being sold 'snake oil'!

Given this, the consultant has to tread very carefully. They have to maintain a professional distance to remain objective but must be sensitive to the client's needs.

> **Trust is the key to building and maintaining a good relationship between client and consultant.**

Mick Cope in his book *The Seven Cs of Consulting* (2010) has developed the mnemonic TRUST to reinforce this idea of trust:

- *Truthful* – the consultant and the client must be truthful to one another. It would be very easy to tell the other person what you think they want to hear but this is a short-term gain. While the truth may be painful, it is a prerequisite for a sound business relationship.

- *Responsive* – this is about the consultant engaging totally in the client's world and being responsive to the client's needs.

- *Uniform* – a consultant must be consistent in their ideas and attitudes towards the project. If they continually change their mind, the client will become confused and begin to doubt the abilities of the consultant to complete the task.

- *Safe* – given some of the emotions a client may feel, as described above, it is important that the client can feel safe working with the consultant. This may be done formally through secrecy agreements or informally through constant dialogue and reassurance.

- *Trained* – it may sound obvious, but it is important that the client believes the consultant is competent in the area of expertise that they are being consulted about. This could come in the form of previous work experience for the individual or through the consulting firm's reputation.

8.3   Client relationships and business ethics

Underlying this sense of trust is the application by the consultants of sound business ethics. This is something that should be done not only when selling the project and putting together the proposal (see Section 3.6) but also *during* the project. Once engaged in a project, a consultant may inadvertently be drawn into the client business and so the client becomes over-dependent on the consultant. While from a personal point of view, you may be flattered by this but you lose your independence and risk making inappropriate decisions to 'please' your client. At the other end of the scale, once in, a consultant may feel that they have 'carte blanche' to do whatever they want and undertake tasks that are not relevant to the agreed project. As long as you stick to the brief and keep your distance, such problems should not arise.

Consultants, unlike other business professionals such as accountants or lawyers, are rarely members of a professional body. The main body in the UK representing smaller consulting firms, the Institute for Consulting (IC), for example, lists just over 500 accredited consultants, which is a fraction of the tens of thousands known to be operating. Furthermore, the IC and the Management Consultancies Association (MCA), that claim to represent the larger organisations, only have a voluntary code with regard to ethics (see Section 3.5), albeit having a sanction of expulsion if members are found in breach of the code. However, even if this penalty is applied it does not stop the consulting firm from continuing in business.

Some have argued (O'Mahoney, 2011) that this has led to pressure on the individual consultant, whether operating on their own or as part of a larger organisation to accept personal responsibility for their interactions with the client. This 'individualism', however, brings its own issues, namely insecurity on the part of the individual, which may affect their performance and institutional conflicts, where the pressure to work in a certain way to complete the project is at odds with business ethics. In these situations, the individual consultant should try to stay true to the project's aims and objectives. While this may cause some friction both within the consultant's own company and possibly that of the client as well, it will ultimately ensure less stress and sleepless nights! Above all, if a course of action feels wrong and unethical do not do it, whatever the consequences.

8.4 The desire for change by the client organisation

A consultant's work within an organisation invariably leads to change within it. If it does not, then the consultant's role was a waste of time and resources!

> **The consultant needs to understand what *type* of change is required, based on the impact it will have.**

Balogun and Hope Hailey (2008) have identified four types of strategic changes:

- *Adaptation* – the most common type which occurs incrementally within the current operating model resulting in small tweaks in the processes.
- *Reconstruction* – essentially a rebuilding of the organisation done over a short period of time within the existing way of working, resulting in a change of structure.
- *Evolution* – a long-term project to incrementally change how the company fundamentally operates.
- *Revolution* – a radical change both to the processes and the structure of the organisation.

While a consultant may believe that a business should embark on more radical change (that is evolution or revolution), actually implementing it is much harder than a more simple 'adaptation' approach.

> **Businesses are made up of individuals and they normally resist change unless the need for that change is clearly recognised and accepted.**

Change brings with it uncertainty and individuals are normally averse to uncertainty. So a consultant has to 'sell' not only the project but the changes that it will bring.

Individuals may not always see the need for change, particularly when it is radical. The management team may be locked into groupthink, as discussed in Section 1.11, for example. Recognising the need for change often represents what psychologists refer to as a *Gestalt* shift: the sudden dawning of a whole, and integrated, new way of seeing things.

> **Once the need for change has been recognised and becomes a desire for change by the organisation, it usually takes place with a predictable pattern of events.**

Kotter (2012) has developed an eight-stage process on successful change within organisations.

Stage 1: Establishing a sense of urgency

The old motto 'if it ain't broke, don't fix it' often pervades businesses, which delay change because of complacency. These sources of complacency are:

- the absence of a major and visible crisis;
- too many visible resources, e.g. expensive corporate headquarters;
- low overall performance standards;
- organisational structure that focuses employees on narrow performance goals;
- internal measurement systems that focus on the wrong performance indices;
- lack of sufficient performance feedback from external sources;
- a kill the messenger, low-candour, low-confrontation culture;
- human nature with its capacity for denial, especially if already busy;
- too much 'happy talk' from senior management.

These are part and parcel of the 'groupthink' mentality considered in Section 1.11. You will have succeeded if enough of the management feel that the status quo has to change.

Stage 2: Creating a powerful coalition

Only with the right kind of team will you be successful with change, as this sends out powerful messages about the importance of this project. The key characteristics you should look for are:

- position – are enough key players on board, especially the main line managers, so that those left out cannot easily block progress?

- expertise – are the various points of view, disciplines, experience, nationality, etc., adequately represented?
- credibility – does the group have enough people with good reputations?

Stage 3: Developing a vision

As with any strategic planning, it is critical to have an effective vision. Kotter describes an effective vision as having the following characteristics:

- imaginable – conveys a picture of what the future will look like;
- desirable – appeals to the long-term interests of all those who have a stake in the enterprise;
- feasible – comprises realistic, attainable goals;
- focused – is clear enough to provide guidance in decision making;
- flexible – is general enough to allow individual initiative and alternative responses in the light of changing conditions;
- communicable – is easy to communicate; can be successfully explained within five minutes.

Stage 4: Communicating the change vision

Never underestimate how much you need to communicate in business, and when you are going through a programme of change this is vital. Kotter has shown that businesses *under*-communicate by a factor of ten! Some simple rules to bear in mind are:

- simplicity – all jargon and technobabble must be eliminated;
- metaphor, analogy and example – a verbal picture is worth a thousand words;
- multiple forums – big meetings and small meetings, memos and newspapers, formal and informal action are all effective for spreading the word;
- repetition – ideas sink in deeply only after they have been heard many times;
- leadership by example – behaviour from important people that is inconsistent with the vision overwhelms other forms of communication;
- explanation of seeming inconsistencies – unaddressed inconsistencies undermine the credibility of all communication;
- give and take – two-way communication is always more powerful than one-way communication.

Stage 5: Empowering employees to act on the vision

After communicating the vision to employees, you need to make structures compatible with it, as unaligned structures block needed action. For example, more customer-focused visions often fail unless customer-unfocused organisational structures are adapted. Second, you need to provide the training employees need, as without the right skills and attitudes people feel disempowered. You need to consider what new behaviours, skills and attitudes will be needed when major changes are initiated, and decide how to deliver these in a cost-effective, meaningful way. Finally, you need to address managers who stifle needed change – there is no greater disincentive to an employee.

Stage 6: Generating short-term wins

A change process can take a long time, so it is important to have some short-term wins that are visible, unambiguous and related to the change effort. Although targeting short-term wins does increase the pressure on people, it can be a useful way of keeping up the urgency, especially when the end is a long way off in a major programme.

Stage 7: Consolidating improvements and producing more change

While celebrating early wins is important, these should add to the momentum rather than slowing it down by making people think that the job is nearly done. As the project progresses, additional people should be brought in to project manage and developed to cope with all the changes. The senior people should focus on keeping clarity of shared purpose for the overall project and maintaining urgency levels. Finally, unnecessary interdependencies should be eliminated.

Stage 8: Anchoring new approaches in the culture

The most critical part of the process is to ensure that the new ways of working are embedded in the culture of the organisation. However, new approaches sink into a culture only after it is very clear that they work for individuals and are better than the old way. Communication continues to be vital, as without verbal instruction and support people are often reluctant to admit the validity of new processes. Perhaps the hardest part of all is that it may involve changing personnel to achieve a cultural change. Going forward, decisions on human resources will be critical. If HR processes are not changed to be compatible with the new practices, the old culture will re-emerge.

Why do firms fail with change programmes?

It is perhaps obvious to say, but they fail because they do not follow the eight-stage process described above. It is not always a lack of enthusiasm. Sometimes it is over-enthusiasm that trips them up in wanting to get the job done as quickly as possible. Getting the balance right between being thorough and ponderous is also difficult.

> The consultant can help by being a dispassionate observer and guide the client change team when he or she thinks they are off track.

Key warning signs for the consultant that this is happening when the client team do the following:

1 There is too much complacency and they are forging ahead without establishing a high enough sense of urgency in employees.

2 They have failed to create a sufficiently powerful guiding coalition.

3 Their vision is weak.

4 They have under-communicated the vision.

5 They permit obstacles to block the vision. Whenever people avoid confronting obstacles, they disempower employees and undermine change.

6 They fail to create short-term wins: without these, too many employees give up or join the resistance.

7 They declare victory too soon: until changes sink deeply into a culture, which can take between three and ten years, new approaches are fragile and subject to erosion.

8 They neglect to anchor changes firmly in the corporate culture: change sticks only when it becomes 'the way we do things around here'.

There has been a lot of debate around the apparent low success rate of change programmes with the figure of 70% failing often quoted. Hughes (2011) has challenged this, arguing that the inherent measurement of success is not clear cut. The true extent of organisational change is often ambiguous and results are not noticed immediately but over a long period of time especially if the culture of the business had to change. Also, there is the human element, with those affected having a range of emotions from ecstatic at the prospect of change to those who are fearful of the consequences. Finally, there is the tricky issue about *what exactly is measured*. Original aims and objectives may be changed as the project progresses, because of unforeseen events. Clearly, consultants involved in major change programmes have to be sensitive to such issues and ensure the client has realistic ideas of what the change programme *can actually deliver*.

8.5 Change-enhancing interactions by the consultant

The consultant can facilitate change at a variety of levels and by engaging in each of the stages described above. Important interventions include:

- providing information that highlights the need for change, i.e. information that rationalises one or more of the issues discussed in Section 5.8;
- ensuring that this information is integrated into the managers' decision-making roles, with special attention to the cognitive and political dimensions of the decision as well as its rational dimension;
- challenging groupthink by inviting the managerial team to share a new perspective, not least through challenging assumptions and the set of options under consideration;
- providing new options for consideration;
- evaluating and reconciling the different political positions of management factions;
- exploring the change process and taking away fear of it, not least through exploring, evaluating and reducing uncertainty about the future.

These different types of intervention are not separate. Rather, they are elements that might be combined to produce a strategy for a particular intervention. At any one time one element may be more important than others. Cope (2010) has identified seven themes that a consultant should consider when trying to understand and address what he terms the 'human elements of change':

1 **System dynamics** – what are the deep systemic issues that will cause the change stage to hit problems?

2 **Organisation and disorganisation** – what factors related to the organisation of the system will impact the success of the change?

3 **Understand the resistance** – how can people be encouraged to be involved in the transformation?

4 **Change spectrum** – what type of change interventions can be effected to help people through the change?

5 **Consumer segmentation** – how can the consumers be segmented into groups based on their desire for change?

6 **Methodology** – determine from the outset what methodology will be used to drive the engagement.

7 **Energy mapping** – understand where the forces are who can impact the change.

Overlaying this are 'unwritten rules' of the organisation that Peter Scott-Morgan has described in his books *The Unwritten Rules of the Game* (1994) and *The End of Change* (2001).

> **Unwritten rules within organisations can often cause a change programme to fail if they are ignored.**

Unwritten rules are caused by the written rules of a company, the behaviour or actions of its leaders and the external environment. So, for example, a consulting programme that can determine the optimal spend for marketing would be seen as a 'good thing' by the chief executive and finance director but a 'bad thing' by all in the marketing department. This is because there is an 'unwritten rule' that the more the marketing department can spend on promotional activities, the more they can demonstrate their capabilities and thus further their careers. So the consulting project aimed at cutting marketing spending would be quietly 'killed off' by the marketers by them claiming it to be unworkable.

Another factor potentially influencing the success of a change programme is the firm's structure. Today's fast moving business world demands that large corporations are as flexible as their smaller rivals as market conditions change. Old formal hierarchical structures often have to sit beside more responsible ways of working that Kotter (2014) has described as 'dual operating system' that have to adhere to the following principles:

- Many people driving important change, and from everywhere, not just the usual few appointees.
- A 'get-to' mindset, not a 'have-to' one.

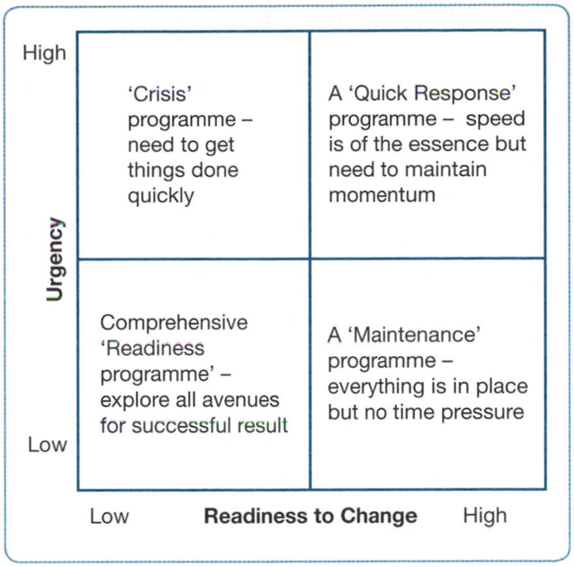

Figure 8.3 Readiness to change

- Action that is head- and heart-driven, not just head-driven.
- Much more leadership, not just more management.
- An inseparable partnership between the hierarchy and the network, not just an enhanced hierarchy.

Ensuring 'readiness' to change

Consultants can play a critical role in ensuring that the client is 'ready to change'. This 'readiness' concept was first developed by Armenakis et al. (1993) to allow proactive managers (and consultants) to use before resistance sets in. Their concept focuses on the message for change and addresses two issues:

(a) the need for change, that is, the discrepancy between the desired end-state (which must be appropriate for the organisation) and the present state;

(b) the individual and collective efficacy (i.e. the perceived ability to change) of parties affected by the change effort.

By combining with the urgency of the change required, strategies can be modified to deal with these, see Figure 8.3.

8.6   Overcoming resistance

While it would be nice if everyone in the client team (and your team!) agreed with all the changes proposed, it rarely happens.

Understanding resistance

According to Ryan and Oestreich (1998), resistance occurs because people fear:

- loss of reputation or credibility;
- embarrassment/loss of self-esteem;
- possible damage to their career (and therefore financial prospects);
- potential damage to their relationship to their superiors;
- an implicit rejection of them and their abilities;
- an unwelcome change in their role, job transfer or demotion;
- loss of their job itself.

> **Indirect expressions of concerns or visible resistance mask real or underlying concerns, so they should not be ignored.**

It is rarely voiced explicitly and Peter Block (2011) has detailed some of the forms resistance can take:

Give me more detail	You keep being asked for more information as a way of stalling
Flood you with detail	This is where the client turns the table and constantly gives you more information, so analysis becomes harder
Time	That is the client does not have the time right now to deal with you . . .
Impracticality	Here you are continually reminded that we must live in the 'real world', i.e. your suggestions are unrealistic
I'm not surprised	In other words, what you have told the client is not new, as in 'I'm glad you spotted that deliberate mistake . . .'
Attack	Unfortunately one of the most common responses if there are no other options to resist
Confusion	Or, 'I don't understand what you are telling me' despite having done so on numerous occasions
Silence	The hardest to deal with as you have literally nothing to go on!
Intellectualising	Theories that take you to dead ends
Moralising	What people *should* do rather than what they ought to
Compliance	Although this is what you want, some form of (constructive) resistance is natural . . .
Methodology	You hope that the client is not an ex-consultant or done this before . . .
Flight into health	Actually things were not as bad as we first thought, having looked closely at it . . .
Pressing for solutions	Demanding answers from day one is not uncommon but can be very disruptive

Steps to deal with resistance

You need to allow people to voice genuine concerns and not to get irritated when you think you are encountering resistance. The first thing is to identify the form of resistance (see above). To do this, pay particular attention to the person's body language. Are they generally open and friendly but speaking negatively? Is something being continually repeated as this is probably the heart of the problem? Second, you need to 'acknowledge' the resistance.

Do not ignore it! Tell the person in a non-aggressive way what you think is their issue and how that impacts the project (and indirectly you). Then let them respond. Allow them to talk and open up to you: resist the temptation to provide solutions there and then. There may be other forms of resistance surfacing. Keep in mind that this is not a reflection on you and your abilities as a consultant. So do not seek to defend your actions. You need to find a solution that works for both parties.

> **One of the most effective ways of dealing with resistance is engagement: people find it harder to resist something if they are part of it and 'own' it.**

Perhaps you do not necessarily *need* the input of this person per se to complete the consulting task, but getting them involved could make or break the final outcome.

8.7 Benchmarking project progression

Benchmarking, defined as evaluating or checking (something) by comparison with a standard, is a process through which specific achievements are predicted, defined and evidenced. A consulting project will have an overall set of objectives (see Section 5.3). However, these may be broken down into a series of intermediate and subsidiary objectives, based on the objectives and outcomes specified in the project charter. This is particularly useful if the project is a long or complex one.

Benchmarking involves:

1 identifying the relevant intermediate stages of the project;
2 defining specific objectives for each intermediate stage;
3 anticipating what will be appropriate evidence that each subsidiary objective has been achieved (this will be related to the means of measurement specified in the project charter);
4 delivering on the objective and producing the evidence.

What constitutes evidence will vary depending on the project and the nature of the subsidiary objective. It may be of a quantitative, numerical nature that is formally measured. It may take the form of the production of a particular document or obtaining some evidence. It may be that a particular meeting has taken place, in which case notes from the meeting will constitute the evidence.

> **The production of the evidence is a good discipline in that it substantiates progression of the project.**

Building on the project charter that was discussed in Section 5.5, overleaf is an example of a benchmarking document.

From Table 8.2, we can see that the large project of completing and executing a marketing plan has been split into ten subsections, each with its own goal, measurements, the date

Table 8.2 Example of a benchmarking document

Project information		Team members	
Leader: Mr Y (Excel Consultants)		Sponsor: Mrs G (AB Company – 'ABC')	
Project start: October 2015		Leader: Mr Y	
Project end: June 2016		Core team: Mr Y, Miss H and Mrs J from Excel and Mr D, Mr U and Ms X from ABC	
Brief description: Marketing plan for ABC		Ad hoc members: Mrs P, Mr K and Miss L from ABC	
Project goals	**Measurements**	**Date for completion**	**Responsibility**
1 Market assessment	Audit data	Nov. 2015	Ms X
2 Consumer assessment	Market research	Dec. 2015	Mrs P
3 Product assessment	Competitive review	Nov. 2015	Mr U
4 NPD review	Pipeline	Dec. 2015	Mr D
5 Marketing strategy	Strategic statement	Jan. 2016	Mr Y
6 Product strategy	NPD plan	Feb. 2016	Mr K
7 Promotional strategy	Promotional brief	Mar. 2016	Mrs J
8 Sales strategy	Sales plan	Mar. 2016	Miss H
9 Pricing strategy	Pricing plan	Mar. 2016	Miss L
10 Review	Sales and profits	Jun. 2016	Mr Y

for completion and, most critically, who is ultimately responsible for delivery. The project leader, Mr Y, can ensure that the project is running smoothly by ensuring that key dates are adhered to. More critically, he can ensure that projects are completed in the correct order, as it would be impossible to complete a product strategy without doing an NPD review, for example. This can also flag up any potential problems to completing the whole project on time. This is discussed further in Chapter 11.

8.8   Understanding the roles of client team members

In the example above of a benchmarking document, there are three outside consultants but seven members of the client team directly involved in the project. There would also be many others in the client's organisation that would be involved to some extent. In addition to the benchmarking document, it might also be useful to think about the roles that these people play. A tool, called a responsibility assignment matrix (or 'RAM'), may be used to list the activities. It has four main categories under which one or more members of the client organisation are listed. These categories are:

● **Responsible** – typically this is the person or group of people who will be performing the task. It may be useful to identify one person who is ultimately responsible.

● **Accountable** – here there can only be one person and the buck stops with him or her!

Table 8.3 Example of a responsibility assignment matrix

Project goals	R	A	C	I	S
1 Market assessment	Ms X	Mr Y	Mrs P, Mr K, Miss L	Mrs G	Mr D, Mr U
2 Consumer assessment	Mrs P	Mr Y	Mrs J, Mr K, Miss L	Mrs G	Mr D, Mr U
3 Product assessment	Mr U	Mr Y	Mrs J, Mr K	Mrs G	Miss L
4 NPD review	Mr D	Mr Y	Mrs P, Mr K, Miss L	Mrs G	Mr U
5 Marketing strategy	Mr Y	Mrs G	Mrs P, Mr K, Miss L	Mr A	Mr D, Mr U
6 Product strategy	Mr K	Mr Y	Mrs P, Miss L	Mrs G	Mr D, Mr U
7 Promotional strategy	Mrs J	Mr Y	Mrs P, Mr K, Miss L	Mrs G	Mr D, Mr U
8 Sales strategy	Miss H	Mr Y	Mrs P, Mr K, Miss L	Mrs G	Mr D, Mr U
9 Pricing strategy	Miss L	Mr Y	Mrs P, Mr K	Mrs G	Mr D, Mr U
10 Review	Mr Y	Mrs G	Mrs P, Mr K, Miss L	Mr A	Mr D, Mr U

- Consulted – this may be for political reasons but, more critically, their advice will ensure that the activity is done properly.
- Informed – these have no direct impact on the project but need to be kept in touch because of the wider implications of a consulting project within a company.

  You may also want to have an additional category:

- Supports – these can provide further resources to conduct the work or have a supportive role in the implementation of the project.

  So, taking the benchmarking document in Table 8.2, we can construct a responsibility assignment matrix for the project (Table 8.3).

8.9 Types of project shock

Things go wrong. No matter how good the planning, there will always be things outside the consultant's control. No matter how good the anticipation, some events will be unpredicted.

> **Planning is about building in the flexibility to respond to the unexpected.**

Some of the more common reasons why the project is knocked off course are as follows.

Changes in client's interests

One of the most common challenges to the project is that the client's interests suddenly change. This may be because he or she suddenly sees a new project more positively or as having higher priority than the one discussed initially. This can easily happen with a small, fast-growing business that faces constantly changing priorities.

Changes in the client's business situation

A consulting project is relevant only in that it helps the business achieve its goals. If a major change in the business's situation takes place and causes it to change its overall goals, the relevance of the consulting project will change as well. The project may suddenly not be relevant at all! If the business faces particular difficulties, the priority of the managers may be to address immediate concerns. Short-term interests will come to the fore. Interest in longer-term goals and the consulting project's contribution to them may seem to evaporate.

Cuts in expenditure

Even if the consulting exercise is offered on a no-fee or success basis, resources may have to be dedicated to supporting activities such as market research. Budget cuts are a fact of managerial life. If resources are tight, the project may be targeted as having low priority. Clearly, a cut in the money available will limit the activities for which it was planned.

Loss of key people

This can either be in the client team or indeed the consulting team. Particularly with long-term projects, people move jobs both within and between organisations. While no one is indispensable, the loss of them may leave a serious gap in skills and expertise. This should be filled quickly, ideally by another member of the project team, so that they can get to work straight away. A more difficult issue would be to replace a key supporter in the client's senior management team, as a replacement would take more time to get on board. It must be done though to ensure the project continues to run smoothly.

Misinterpretation of information

If the interpretation of information about the business and its environment by the project is wrong, it may lead the business in the wrong direction. Typical areas of misinterpretation are overestimating the resource capabilities of the business, underestimating, or missing altogether, a competitor in the marketplace and over-optimism about the potential of a market or a product within it. The impact on the project will depend on the information concerned and the nature of the misinterpretation. The potential consequences can be minimised by recognising the limitations of the information available, modelling the scenarios that result from changing that information and building appropriate flexibility into the plan adopted. Always ask: what will happen if this information is wrong? If the consequences are significant, the first step is to check the information. Second, be aware of contingency plans that can be implemented if it is incorrect.

8.10   Responding to project shocks

An effective response to a project shock is the sign of a good consultant.

Each shock must be tackled on its own terms. It is important here to be prepared and avoid panic. Although the details of a crisis may come as a surprise, crises themselves should not. Consider likely scenarios and sketch out contingency plans. Think about what is necessary to get the project back on track. When a crisis occurs, team relationships are stretched. Recriminations take place and blame is apportioned. Such a response should be avoided. Once the nature of the shock has been appreciated, effective crisis management demands that the following steps be taken.

Refer back to aims and objectives

The first response should be to refer back to the aims and objectives of the project. Ask whether the tasks for the project can be modified so that the original aims and objectives can still be achieved. If resources are cut, can a lower-resource approach offer the same, or at least satisfactory, results? If the objectives are affected, can they be renegotiated within the framework of the original aims? If resources are limited, can some objectives be given priority over others?

Evaluate resource implication

If the resources available for the project are affected, the impact of this change needs to be considered. Activities must be modified or dropped in a way that either least affects the original aims or fits best with new ones. If the resource is a person's skills within the team, the possibility of using other people to cover must be considered. If time and resources allow, an attempt may be made to replace that person. If the person is part of the client organisation, the loss of that relationship must be considered. Ask how that person fitted into the overall profile of relationships with the client. What information was he or she providing? Can new relationships be built with others in the client organisation to replace the person?

Modify plans

Consider the implications for the project plans. Ask what tasks will be affected. How will their undertaking be affected? What about the timescale of their delivery? What knock-on effects will there be on tasks further downstream? If the aims and/or objectives are altered, will new tasks be needed? Will planned tasks have to be dropped?

Communicate

Don't be tempted to hide problems. Draw people in and make them party to resolution of the problem. Consider who will be affected and how. Ask what ideas they might bring to bear on the problem and what resources they can offer towards its solution. Avoid both understating and overstating problems and ensure that others are informed of all the issues, but avoid panicking them. When communicating a problem try to communicate its solution as well, or at least open up the possibility of a solution to which others might contribute.

Team discussion points

1 Consider the way in which your team is working. On an individual basis, consider how team working might be improved and develop a change strategy using the ideas in this chapter. Each presents a one-page summary of the strategy to the other team members. Where are areas of agreement and disagreement? How might these be reconciled?

2 Thinking about your project highlight the issues that you *may* face in terms of project shocks. What contingency plans can you put in place to deal with them if they arise?

Summary of key ideas

- Understanding the relationship the consultant has with the client is important as it determines how a project is conducted.

- All those in the client company that the consultant interacts with should have a clearly defined role.

- Individuals within an organisation often resist change, especially if it is seen as 'change for change's sake'.

- Kotter has developed a generic eight-stage model for effective organisation change management.

- This model specifies a number of interactions that the consultant can call upon to effect successful organisational change dynamics.

- Key to a successful project is understanding and overcoming resistance by client employees.

- Consulting projects can be knocked off course for a variety of reasons. Usually shocks result from changes in client interest, external events or changes in resource availability.

- An ability to respond effectively to a project shock is the sign of a good consultant. Key elements in a response strategy are preparedness for what might happen, a focus on the implications for the aims of the project, analysis of the resource implications and how this affects plans and communication of the issues.

- Good leadership in a crisis situation is characterised by a measured response, control of panic in others and an emphasis on solutions rather than problems.

- Benchmarking involves anticipating and generating evidence that the journey is progressing to plan.

Key reading

Cope, M. (2010) *The Seven Cs of Consulting: The Definitive Guide to the Consulting Process* (3rd edn). Harlow, Essex: FT Prentice Hall (Chapters 4 and 7).

Fombrun, C.J. and Nevins, M.D. (2004) *The Advice Business: Essential Tools and Models for Management Consulting*. Upper Saddle River, NJ: Pearson Prentice Hall (Chapters 12, 13, 17 and 23).

Further reading

Armbrüster, T. (2010) *The Economics and Sociology of Management Consulting*. Cambridge: Cambridge University Press (Chapter 4).

Armenakis, A. A, Harris, S. G and Mossholder, K. W. (1993) 'Creating readiness for organizational change' *Human Relations* 46, 6, 1–23.

Balogun, J. and Hope Hailey, V. (2008) *Exploring Strategic Change* (3rd edn). Harlow, Essex: FT Prentice Hall.

Block, P. (2011) *Flawless Consulting* (3rd edn). San Francisco, CA: Jossey Bass.

Burnes, B. (2014) *Managing Change* (6th edn). Harlow, Essex: Pearson.

Carnall, C.A., and R.T. By (2014) *Managing Change in Organizations*. (6th edn). Harlow, Essex: Pearson.

Hughes, M. (2011), 'Do 70 per cent of all organisational change initiatives really fail?' *Journal of Change Management*. 11 (4), 451–464.

Johnson, G., Scholes, K. and Whittington, R. (2014) *Exploring Corporate Strategy* (10th edn). Harlow, Essex: FT Prentice Hall (Chapter 14)

Kotter, J.P. (2012) *Leading Change*. Boston, MA: Harvard Business School Press.

Kotter, J.P. (2014) 'Capturing the Opportunities and Avoiding the Threats of Rapid Change', *Leader to Leader*, Fall, 32–37.

Newton, R. (2010) *The Management Consultant: Mastering the Art of Consultancy*. Harlow, Essex: FT Prentice Hall (Chapter 10).

O'Mahoney, J. (2011) 'Advisory Anxieties: Ethical Individualisation in the UK Consulting Industry', *Journal of Business Ethics* 104, 101–113.

Pemer, F. and Werr, A. (2013) 'The Uncertain Management Consulting Services Client', *International Studies of Management & Organization* 43 (3), 22–40.

Ryan, K.D. and Oestreich, D. K. (1998) *Driving fear out of the Workplace* (2nd edn). San Francisco, CA: Jossey Bass.

Scott-Morgan, P. (1994) *The Unwritten Rules of the Game*. New York: McGraw-Hill.

Schaffer, R. (2002) *High-Impact Consulting: How Clients and Consultants Can Work Together to Achieve Extraordinary Results* (2nd edn). Chichester, West Sussex: Jossey Bass Wiley.

Sturdy, A. and Wright, C. (2011) 'The active client: The boundary-spanning roles of internal consultants as gatekeepers, brokers and partners of their external counterparts', *Management Learning* 42(5), 485–503.

Case exercise

Anglia Vending Services

Anglia Vending Services (AVS) is part of Anglia Food Services, a large company specialising in providing contract catering services to large organisations both in the private and public sector in the UK. The board of Anglia Food Services have conducted a strategic review and decided that AVS is no longer core to their future strategy and they are seeking a buyer for it. One of the potential buyers is AVS's own management team, who are being backed by private equity company Martins. Sales and profits have been declining for the last five years but the management are confident that as an independent entity, they can turn this around. Martins Private Equity (MPE) believes that this is a good investment for the medium term but the manager in charge wants an independent review of the proposed acquisition.

You have been called in by MPE as an expert in this industry to look at the AVS management team's business plan. Senior staff at AVS is naturally wary of you and reluctant for you to talk to their customers. This is a business based on customer relationships. They think that you may inadvertently jeopardise these relationships, as the customers will want to know why you are talking to them. So they give you a very limited number of customers to contact. These you find have been 'briefed' by the AVS team and so you are mainly getting a very positive message about AVS.

However, there is a more major problem you need to address when trying to evaluate the long-term prospects for AVS. Unlike the contracts of the main parent company, which tend to be fixed for at least five years, those that AVS deal with are 'rolling' ones renewable every year over a three- to five-year period. The management team optimistically believe that this means they can pick up a lot of new business. You, though, realise the downside of this 'flexibility' in the marketplace. In a worst-case scenario, AVS could *lose* all its existing contracts within three to five years. While they may be able to replace them with new business, it will probably be at a higher cost, thus impacting profits.

You are therefore very concerned about this project, as you feel you have one hand tied behind your back in the execution. You also do not believe that the business model the management team at AVS is using is a viable investment opportunity. You meet with the manager at MPE to discuss your concerns. However, he is under pressure from his bosses to complete the deal and instead asks you to work with the management team to prepare a more robust plan. This would involve changing the way AVS operates to ensure longer, more sustainable contracts.

1 You have two 'project shocks' here: one relating to the consulting process and one impacting on the outcome. How do you address these?

2 The scope of the consulting project has changed. How will you deal with this?

3 Assuming that you are happy to work with the management team at AVS, how would you get them to change their way of thinking about their business?

Chapter 9

Creative approaches for developing solutions

One never notices what has been done; one can only see what remains to be done.

Marie Curie

Learning outcomes

The key learning outcomes from this chapter are to:

- recognise the importance of a *creative approach* to developing a solution;

- learn the techniques of brainstorming and mind mapping to generate ideas;

- understand how to use the seven basic tools for simple analysis;

- have an awareness of the seven new management tools for more sophisticated analysis.

Solutions today must be data-driven.

One of the most fundamental changes in the way managers approach their tasks has been the growth in the information available to them. At the touch of a button a manager can now call up an amount of information it would have taken a manager just one generation ago weeks, if not months, to collect. This information can take a variety of forms: it may be numerical information, facts, commentary, opinions or items in a list. Despite the growth in the availability of information, managers' jobs do not seem any easier. If anything, they are harder. Managers must learn not only to make decisions but also to collect, manipulate and store ever more data upon which effective decision making must be based.

Ultimately, most managers have access to the same information about the competitive world they work in. 'Secrets' are less important in business than many think. Information technology makes data on the business and its environment readily available. Numerous commercial and government organisations offer information and analysis on business sectors.

Modern market research techniques can quickly identify new potential business opportunities. The Internet provides a stream of information on customers, suppliers and competitors.

Competitiveness is built not so much on *access* to data but on ability to *use it effectively*. Underpinning this is the ability to identify and adopt an appropriate analysis strategy so that data become information and information becomes the knowledge that leads to effective decision making. Analysis may call upon straightforward and familiar techniques. The simplest may be so trivial that they may not be recognised as analysis at all – the addition of sales from different product lines to produce an overall sales figure, for example. At the other end of the scale there are techniques that are extremely sophisticated and demand an intimate knowledge of their manipulation if they are to be used properly. Many statistical methodologies used in market research fall into this category.

Whatever the analysis technique adopted, analysis is an area where the consultant can add value. The consultant creates value by identifying the client's decision-making requirements, directing the client towards the right technique, assisting them in using it and helping to identify the insights it offers.

9.1 How to use analysis to develop solutions

Fundamentally, analysis is about identifying the patterns and relationships that exist in data.

An analysis strategy is a specific way of manipulating data so that such patterns and relationships can be revealed. Data in their raw form are not very informative. Our minds are the product of evolutionary pressure. Humans are primarily visual animals. Our evolution has not equipped us to make sense of rows and tables of figures. What it has done is make us good at making decisions when faced with clear verbal or visual codes. A good analysis strategy orders and organises data so that they are converted into verbal or visual codes that can inform decision making. Most of the analysis strategies used by management consultants make use of one or a combination of the following basic approaches.

Categorisation

Categorisation is a process whereby data, facts or items are sorted into different groups by virtue of their features. This allows the significance of the information to be identified. Categorisation is different from classification. Categorisation uses internal criteria. Classification uses externally imposed criteria. Categorisation makes no demands on theoretical insights, whereas classification does. Important examples of categorisation used in management include the strengths–weaknesses–opportunities–threats ('SWOT') model and the political–economic–sociological–technological ('PEST' also known as 'STEEPLE') model used to analyse a business and its situation (as discussed in Section 6.1). Here factors that make an impact on the business are sorted on the basis of their type, making their implications clearer.

Classification

Classification is also a process whereby items are sorted into different groups. This time, the groups are defined by external criteria rather than by arbitrary features. An example of the use of classification is Porter's generic strategy model (1980). Here, a business's basic choice of strategy is defined as cost leadership, differentiation or focus ('niche'). These criteria are theoretically *a priori*. They are derived from theoretical insights as to how businesses compete. These strategies do not have simply an arbitrary relationship to each other (as do the categorisation examples). Rather, they are defined by the external criteria of competitive approach and business scope.

Porter's generic strategies are a specific example of *strategic group analysis*. This is a powerful technique which can provide an insight into the structure of an industry and the competitive environment of an individual firm. The method involves identifying the factors that characterise players in an industry and determine how they compete. These factors are then used to classify the players into different strategic groups. This technique has been used extensively to help managers understand their competitive environments and position their firms within them. Peteraf and Shanley (1997) offer a good review of the technique. Strategic groups are explored from a cognitive perspective by Reger and Huff (1993).

Similarly, Weirich's TOWS matrix (Johnson, Whittington and Scholes, 2014) is a useful tool for building broad strategic intentions from the issues identified in a SWOT analysis. It is another four-box matrix which identifies options that address different combinations of the internal and external factors. If the firm has mainly Strengths and Opportunities, it should adopt an *aggressive* strategy using its strengths to maximize the opportunities. If it has Strengths yet faces Threats, it should adopt a *diversification* strategy leveraging its strengths to minimise the threats. If it has mainly Weaknesses yet has identifiable Opportunities, it needs to *reconfigure*, to re-engineer its processes and to put itself in good shape to capitalise on these opportunities. But if the firm is in the unenviable position of having mainly Weaknesses and Threats, it will need to adopt a *turnaround* strategy, emphasising speed of change, rapid cost reduction or revenue generation, restructuring or downsizing.

Numerical analysis

Numerical analysis is any technique where numbers are combined in order to understand how they relate to each other. An *equation* or *function* is a 'recipe' which describes in definite terms how the numbers should be combined. Generalised instances of data are represented by symbols – called *variables* – in these equations. Another way of thinking about a function is that it is a *map* that relates one set of data to another.

The simplest form of equation is the *ratio*. In a ratio one number is divided by another so that the relative magnitudes of the numbers, rather than their absolute magnitudes, are revealed. Financial analysis uses a variety of profitability and liquidity ratios to assess the performance and stability of a firm. This is discussed further in Section 6.2. Statistical analysis uses more complex numerical relationships. It is used in a wide variety of business situations, including market research. Management science is a technical discipline that offers a highly sophisticated mathematical approach to support managerial decision making. It is concerned with using mathematical techniques to model managerial decision-making situations and to calculate optimal solutions and strategies for management problems. It is not normally called upon by managers, but does have important applications in a number of areas; for example, determining production capacity requirements and modelling the effect of advertising on sales. Given its mathematical nature, such consulting is usually undertaken by specialist consultants.

Association

Association is the recognition that two things are in some way connected. If two things are associated this suggests that the consideration of one thing might be made easier, or more revealing, if the other thing is considered at the same time. An example of association might be the fact that managers usually notice competitors within their own strategic group more than those in other strategic groups. Here the association is made between an organisation's presence in a strategic group and the cognitive picture of competition held by a manager from that organisation. Another example arises from qualitative market research where buyers associate different products and the degree to which they might be substituted with each other. Association might be noticed as a result of using the analysis techniques described. It may be emphasised and enhanced by the use of the visualisation techniques described in Sections 9.4 and 9.5.

Correlation

Correlation is more precise than association. It is the recognition that the *variation* in one variable occurs in step with that of another. A correlation may be identified statistically by the measure of a correlation coefficient. A correlation of $+1$ indicates that the two variables follow each other perfectly and in the same direction. A correlation coefficient of 0 indicates that the two variables are totally independent. A correlation coefficient of -1 indicates that the two variables follow each other perfectly but in opposite directions. An example of correlation might be the fact that in many industry sectors costs are seen to be positively correlated to market share. This suggests that increasing market share might in turn increase profitability. This suggests that a strategy to increase market share will increase not only sales but also underlying profitability (see the review by Bourantis and Mandes, 1987, for discussion of this issue). Correlation suggests that there *might* be a causal link between the two variables but it does not *prove* it. A good correlation is suggestive, though. It is an invitation to explore further for possible causal relationships.

Causation

Causation *explains* correlation. Causation suggests that two variables are correlated because there is a cause-and-effect link between them. It provides an important insight for management because, if a causal link exists, control of the cause will automatically lead to control of the effect. Care should be taken in assuming the order of causation, though. Suppose that factor A is found to be correlated to factor B. It is true that A might cause B. But it is also true that B could be causing A. It might also be true that both A and B might be caused by a third factor, C. C may or may not be known. If necessary, another concept may have to be introduced in addition to the two known correlates to provide a full picture of what is going on.

The relationship between 'planning' and 'performance' provides a very good example of the problem of assigning cause and effect in management. This is particularly pertinent to us as so many consultancy exercises advocate and involve planning activity. It is a theme discussed critically by Henry Mintzberg in his book *The Rise and Fall of Strategic Planning* (2000). In some sectors it has been observed that there is a link between planning activity and financial performance. This is an *association*. Further, if planning is quantified as the investment of time and effort in creating, documenting and communicating long-range strategies and plans, and performance is measured as return on capital employed, then planning activity and performance vary together in a positive way. This is a *correlation*. From this it is tempting to assume that *planning* results in *performance*. This would certainly be a justification for engaging in it.

However, this is only one possible interpretation of the correlation (which is of the 'A leads to B' type). It is also possible that good performance leads managers to plan (the 'B leads to A' type) or that planning and performance are the result of a third factor (the 'C leads to both A and B' type). Thus further variables must be postulated to understand the full causal picture. Plausible arguments for all three scenarios can be developed.

- *Causal link A leads to B.* An example is 'planning is an aid to decision making'. The argument might run as follows. Performance is improved if resource-allocation decisions are made better. Planning guides decisions about the allocation of scarce and valuable resources. Because these decisions are more effective when planned, the business's performance is enhanced. On this basis planning should be encouraged.

- *Causal link B leads to A.* An example is 'planning activity is a way of using "spare" resources'. The argument might run as follows. A good performance by the firm brings in resources. Managers want to use those resources. They may see planning as a way of doing so. Planning adds nothing to performance. In fact, it may be positively wasteful; it may, for example, be just a way for managers to show their ability and importance to colleagues. Planning is, in effect, an *agency cost* expended when the firm's managers can afford it. On this basis planning should be discouraged. Reducing planning may even enhance performance further.

- *Causal link C leads to A and B.* An example is 'planning and performance are both the result of information being available'. The argument might run as follows: if managers have access to a great deal of information, their decision making will be better, so the firm's performance will be enhanced; they may also feel that because the information is obviously valuable they should make maximum use of it. A good way to use it is in planning. Planning not only demands that the information be used; it is a very visible way of using it. Both performance and planning result from the availability of information.

In this case care should be taken about advocating planning activity. Planning itself does not enhance performance (information does). But this is only a 'first order' interpretation of cause and effect. A deeper analysis might reveal that planning activity does in fact influence the type of information managers seek. It might also influence the way information is used to support decision making. The caveat really shows that simple causal links are difficult to isolate in systems as complex as business organisations. McGuire (1997) considers creativity in relation to hypothesis explanation (broadly, explanations as to why things happen). The context is psychology, but the ideas are widely applicable. He suggests that there are five basic heuristics involved in being creative about hypotheses.

- *Attention to odd occurrences:* the unusual calls attention to itself. It is easy to dismiss the odd as just that – unrepresentative of the normal. But in being dismissed, the opportunity to build richer hypotheses within which the odd becomes normal might be missed.

- *Simple conceptual analysis:* attempts to reclassify and re-categorise observations and experiences in new ways so that new patterns and ideas emerge.

- *Complex conceptual analysis:* builds on the simple by using more formal deductive, diversifying and meta-theoretic ideas (theories that relate theories together).

- *Reinterpreting the past:* re-examining old experiences using single and multiple, cross-sectional and longitudinal case studies. ·

- *Collecting new data:* formal collection of new data and its analysis by quantitative and qualitative techniques.

These approaches range from simply thinking about things in fresh ways to using formal, and perhaps, technical techniques. Different consulting demands, and the approach and skills of different consultants, will lead to different levels. What matters to the client though is the original idea – not how it was generated!

9.2   Mind mapping

> **The first and most important person the consultant must communicate with is themselves.**

The idea of communicating with oneself may seem a rather strange one. After all, it might be argued, we know what's inside our own head. In fact, the complete contents of our minds are not immediately or transparently available. We do not have instant access to our subconscious. In order to access our thoughts, memories and ideas we must constantly communicate with ourselves. We mentally (or even actually) talk to ourselves. We are engaged in a constant personal dialogue. Recognising this personal dialogue and making use of it can improve analysis. We become more effective when we learn actively to bring up ideas from our subconscious and communicate with ourselves about them. One of the most powerful techniques for doing this is *mind mapping*.

If we write down ideas in an essay form we are constrained to a linear format. Because of the nature of writing (like speaking), one idea must follow another. Ideas are, at best, connected to two others: the one in front and the one behind. At a fundamental level, our minds do not work like this. Mentally, one idea is connected to a host of others in the form of a *semantic network*. Mind mapping is a technique that explores this network. It does not constrain concepts to be arranged in linear fashion. Tony Buzan in his book *Use Your Head* (2010) describes mind mapping very well, along with other creative techniques.

Mind mapping is a straightforward personal creativity technique. An initial concept is written down in the middle of a blank sheet. This sheet can be as large as is practical. Using lines and/or arrows, the concept is then connected to the next one that comes to mind. The process is repeated. As the map builds, webs and branches of ideas form. Different colours or line styles may be used to relate ideas in different ways. The only rule is that there are no

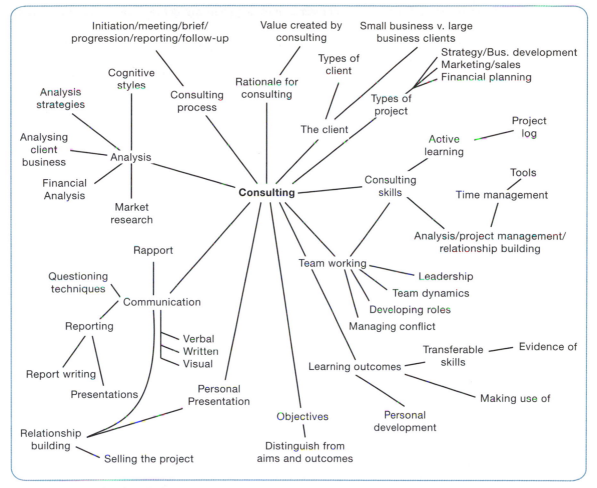

Figure 9.1 Example of a mind map

rules! Let the mind run away with itself. Connect ideas even if the connection does not, at first, seem sensible. Innovation comes from creating new relationships. If no new insight is obtained, it does not matter. It should not be forgotten that a mind map is a *personal* communication. There is no need to show it to anyone else if you do not want to. Once a map has been created, further mind maps can be used to rationalise and organise the ideas that develop. By way of an example of the technique, Figure 9.1 illustrates the mind map used by Philip Wickham to lay the foundations for the first edition of this book.

9.3 Brainstorming

Harnessing a group's collective creativity will deliver more enlightened results.

Brainstorming is a technique that facilitates group creativity. The creativity of a group is, potentially, more than the sum total of the creativity of the individuals in it. By acting in concert to enhance each other's creativity, a group can achieve more than individuals working alone.

To be effective, brainstorming must be organised properly. A facilitator should lead the brainstorming session. Perhaps, but not essentially, the facilitator will be the group leader. The person in the group who has responsibility for analysis also makes a good facilitator. Find a room where the session can be held. There should be no disturbances. The room should have presentation facilities such as a laptop and projector or a flipchart. Seating should be comfortable and informal. Everyone should be able to see the screen or flipchart. Ideally, five to seven people will be involved. Larger groups may be used, as more people mean more ideas, but there is also the risk that the returns can diminish. The task of the facilitator becomes more difficult as the group becomes larger. If a large number of people can be involved it may be better to split the group into a series of subgroups that can address particular aspects of the issue under study. Ideas may be brought together at the end using a plenary session.

The facilitator should then announce the objective of the session. This might be a statement of the concept, idea or product that is to be explored and what the session aims to achieve. Stimulus material, such as illustrations and examples of products, can be introduced at this stage. The facilitator then invites comments, making it clear that only *positive* comments are allowed. Criticism of others' ideas is not accepted. *All* ideas are transferred to the overhead or flipchart. The facilitator must resist the temptation to select ideas at this stage. It is up to the facilitator to control debate, ensure that comments are positive and that the debate is relevant to the objectives. The facilitator should encourage all present to make a contribution.

When the ideas begin to dry up (usually after 20 to 30 minutes) the facilitator should start to draw the debate together. Key ideas are summarised. At this point evaluation can be invited. Even at this stage it should be positive. Simple 'rubbishing' of ideas must be discouraged. When this constructive criticism has been completed (some 15–30 minutes) the facilitator can draw the session to a close with a summary of what has been achieved. It is always good practice to produce a written summary of what has been found at the session. This can be distributed to those present. It is a record of the session and may encourage the submission of further ideas.

9.4 Seven basic tools

Various well-established tools exist to order and present data.

Flowcharts

A flowchart is a symbolic representation of a *process*. The stages in the process are represented by stages in the flowchart. The relationships between different stages can then be illustrated. For an example of this see Figure 2.3, used to represent the consulting process.

Checklists

A systematic list used to ensure consistency and completeness when performing a task. Checklists help to reduce the risk of failure or oversight. Examples would be the Apollo mission checklists, clinical practice guidelines or methods of manufacture in industry. For the consultant they can be useful when examining processes. A simple one used widely in consulting is a benchmarking document, see example in Table 8.2.

Pareto analysis

See Section 6.2

Cause and effect

This is concerned with causality, the relationship between a set of factors (cause) and a phenomenon (effect). Ishikawa's fishbone diagram (see Section 5.2 and Figure 5.2) is a good illustration of such an analysis.

Histograms

First introduced by Karl Pearson in 1895, they are the most well-known graphs used. Essentially, they are a form of graphical representation giving a visual impression of the distribution of data. More commonly known as bar charts, they assess the probability distribution of a given variable by depicting the frequencies of observation occurring in certain ranges of values. Figure 14.1 showing the key industry sectors in the European management consultancy market is an example.

Scatter diagrams

Developed by Francis Galton these are a form of mathematical diagrams using Cartesian coordinates to display values for two variables for a set of data so as to establish the degree of correlation or relationship (should there be any) between them. The independent variable is plotted on the horizontal axis and the dependent on the vertical axis. Figure 9.2 is an example.

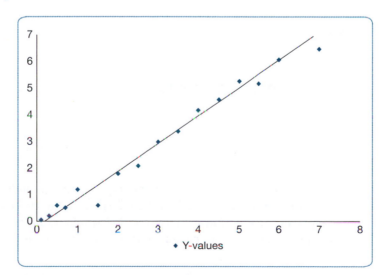

Figure 9.2 Example of a scatter diagram

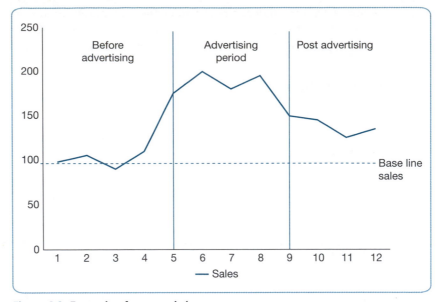

Figure 9.3 Example of a control chart

Control charts

Also known as Shewhart charts or process-behaviour charts, these are used to study how a process changes over time. They can show if a manufacturing or business process is operating in the way that is expected. If it is not, then a case can be made to undergo a formal examination of it for improvement. It can also challenge whether the original parameters set as 'normal' or 'expected' were in fact the correct ones. A simple example might be how a product's sales and market share develop following a particular promotional campaign, as demonstrated in Figure 9.3. The sales are measured in a four-week period prior to the advertising to give a baseline level. The test has shown that the advertising has increased sales not only while the advertising was running but also afterwards, showing that the promotional campaign had the desired effect.

It is important to note that these tools can be applied to both simple and more complex problems.

9.5 Seven new management tools

More recent analytical tools have been developed for addressing more complex issues.

For more complex analyses the following tools, first propounded by Mizuno (1988) and refined in the *Memory Jogger 2* (Brassard, 2010), should prove useful. The first four are relatively simple to use. However, the last three would be for the more experienced consultant, as the type of information required is quite complex to record.

Affinity diagrams

Devised by Jiro Kawakita in the 1960s (hence also known as the KJ diagram), these are used for organising ideas and data. They can enable a large number of ideas developed from brainstorming (see Section 9.3) to be sorted into groups for review and analysis. The methodology is low-technology: each idea is recorded on a separate note or card (Post-Its are especially useful for this), apparently related ideas are then sought and finally are sorted into groups. Table 5.4, the major causes of a poor response to a questionnaire, is an example of this.

Interrelationship digraph

This tool takes the affinity diagrams a stage further. It shows all the interrelated cause-and-effect relationships involved in a complex problem or series of problems and helps to clarify the desired outcomes. By creating this network of related events, it helps consultants analyse the clear links between the different aspects of a complex situation. Often businesses struggle to make such connections as they are too 'close' to the problem, and it can take an outsider such as a consultant to help them make these connections in a dispassionate way.

Tree diagram

In a consulting exercise, we not only need to see the 'big picture' and make connections but we also need to break down problems into more manageable pieces (see Section 11.5 on breaking down tasks). This tool is therefore useful to break down broad categories into ever finer levels of detail. It can show any level of detail of tasks that are required to accomplish an objective but at the same time preserve the interrelationships. It aids the consultant to look at specific, concrete solutions for the business to implement, rather than generalities. The Pyramid Principle for organising your thoughts as discussed in Section 12.4 and shown in Figure 12.3 is a good example.

Matrix diagram

This is a very popular tool amongst consultants, as evidenced by the numerous examples in this book! Matrix diagrams show the relationship between key criteria. A very simple one as an example is the Ansoff matrix (Figures 6.12 and 6.13). Other very well-known ones include the *generic strategy model* of Michael Porter, the Boston Consulting Group's (BCG) *cash-flow matrix* (see Hedley, 1977 and Figure 6.15) and the *directional policy matrix* (DPM) developed by Robinson, Hitchens and Wade (1978) and discussed in Section 6.4. It provides not only information about the relationship but also possible courses of action. There are more complex versions than the standard N × N version, depending on the number of variables. Figure 9.4 shows a 'Y-shaped' matrix giving the primary and secondary relationships based on the global marketing planning loop discussed in Section 4.7.

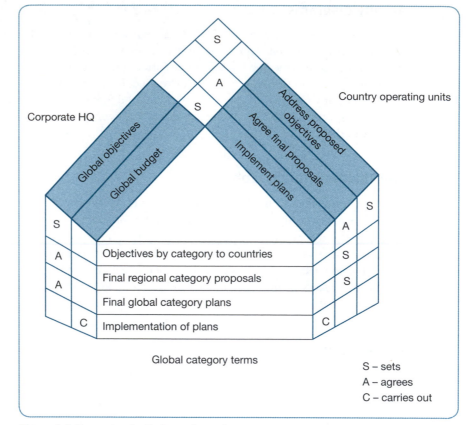

Figure 9.4 Example of a Y-shaped matrix

Prioritisation matrices

This tool is used to prioritise items and describe them in terms of weighted criteria. Sometimes called an impact/urgency matrix, it is used to narrow down options either based on those that are most desired or those that will be most effective. Although the visual is relatively straightforward, it can sometimes be very hard to agree the 'scores' that are used. Developed from factory production analysis, where the details were measurable, it is now used in wider management consulting where it is less clear cut. While clearly a useful tool, care has to be taken that the results do not come to be seen as statements of *fact*, rather the well-judged *opinion* of those who put them together. A way to do this is to clearly show the

Issue	Impact	Urgency
Improve the marketing processes	High	High
Improve the competences within marketing	Medium	High
Improve the learning within the organisation	Medium	Low
Have better organisational fit to requirements	Low	Medium
Make better use of the tools available	Medium	Medium
Reset the culture and mindset to a new way of working	High	Low

thinking behind the decision. The table below is an example using information from the case study in Chapter 12.

Process Decision Programme Chart

A useful way of planning is to break down tasks into a hierarchy, using first a tree diagram. Then taking the Process Design Programme Chart, you can extend the tree diagram down to further levels to identify areas to work on and particular risks. Different coloured boxes in the example shown in Figure 9.5 are used to highlight the status of each stage in the process. Possible concerns are shown in the 'clouds', used to indicate their uncertain nature.

Activity network diagram

Sometimes referred to as 'the arrow diagram', this tool is used to plan the appropriate sequence or schedule for a set of tasks and related sub-tasks. It also comes from quality improvement processes for production but is now also used to map any process. It is essentially a more complex flow diagram that allows for parallel tasks and loop mechanisms. Figure 4.3 is an example of this.

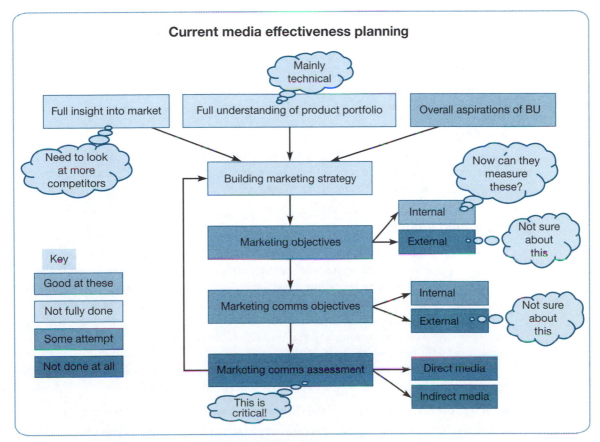

Figure 9.5 Example of a Process Decision Programme Chart

> ### 9.6 Other analysis methods

> **Further methods exist to promote creative solutions.**

Features analysis

Features analysis is a method for encouraging innovation specifically about products and services. It can be built on both mind mapping and brainstorming methods. The first stage is to identify a product or service or a product or service category. The product or service is then stripped down into a list of features that define it in the eyes of its users. The next stage is to manipulate this list so that insights can be gained. Some ways of manipulating features include the following.

Prioritising

Ask the following questions:

- Which features are most important to the user?
- What are users willing to pay for?
- How does this differ between different user groups?
- To what extent are users willing to play off one feature against another?

Modifying

Ask what happens when features are removed, made larger, made smaller, made more obvious or less obvious, are made variable and so on.

Blending

Ask what happens if features of one product are combined with those of another. How attractive would the hybrid product look to a potential buyer? Figure 9.6 provides an example of features analysis in the form of a mind map.

Forcefield analysis

Lewin's forcefield analysis (Figure 9.7) consists of the identification of forces that promote and hinder change. Promoting forces should be exploited and the effect of hindering forces reduced. It is traditional to represent these forces by arrows whose individual dimensions correspond to their perceived strengths. Promoting and hindering forces are then shown pointing from opposite sides to a vertical linear datum line. This representation is useful for purposes such as brainstorming and staff briefings, but two lists in order of magnitude are just as useful for purposes of analysis.

Senior (drawing on the advice of Carnall and Huczynski and Buchanan) suggests a practical route to apply the forcefield analysis concept (ACCA, 2010):

- Define the problem in terms of the current situation and the desired future state.
- List the forces supporting and opposing the desired change and assess both the strength and the importance of each one.

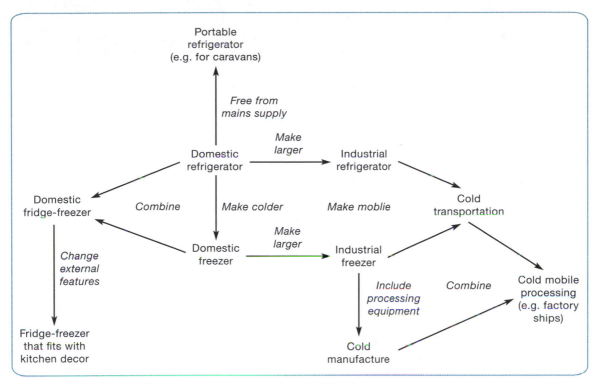

Figure 9.6 A mind map of features analysis on uses for a 'cold box'

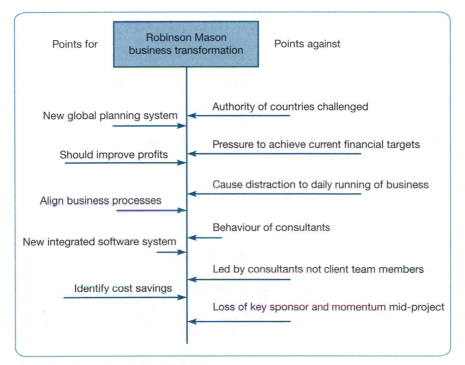

Figure 9.7 Example of a forcefield diagram

- Draw the forcefield diagram.
- Decide how to strengthen or weaken the more important forces as appropriate and agree with those concerned. Weakening might be achieved by persuasion, participation and coercion or bargaining, while strengthening might be achieved by a marketing or education campaign, including the use of personal advocacy.
- Identify the resources needed.
- Construct an action plan including event timing, milestones and responsibilities.

Team discussion points

1 Each member of the team should take one of the seven basic tools and apply the technique to their project. Then they should present it to the rest of the team.

2 Discuss which of the seven new management tools you think will be most appropriate for your project and say why.

Summary of key ideas

- Business success is not dependent only on having access to information. It is also based on using it to create new insights and spot new opportunities.
- An analysis strategy is a means of manipulating data so that patterns and relationships can be revealed. Important elements of an analysis strategy include using categorisation, classification and numerical analysis followed by identifying associations, correlations and causal linkages.
- A good way to reveal patterns and relationships in data is to visualise them. Important visualisation techniques include diagrams, flow charts, graphs and matrices (grids).
- Various proven tools are available to visualise the information that has been gathered and to allow structured analysis of more complex management and planning issues.
- A number of techniques can facilitate individual and group creativity. Particularly useful to the consultant are mind mapping, brainstorming and features analysis.

Key reading

LeBlanc, J. (1998) *Thinking Clearly: A Guide to Critical Reasoning*. New York: Norton (Introduction).

Tague, N.R. (2005) *The Quality Toolbox* (2nd edn). Milwaukee, WI: ASQ Quality Press.

Further reading

ACCA – P3 Business Analysis. (2010) London: BPP Learning Media.

Bourantis, D. and Mandes, Y. (1987) 'Does market share lead to profitability?' *Long Range Planning*, 20 (5), 102–108.

Brassard, M. (2010) *The Memory Jogger Plus 2* (2nd edn). Salem, NH: Goal/QPC.

Buzan, T. (2010) *Use Your Head*. London: BBC Active.

Hedley, B. (1977) 'Strategy and the business portfolio', *Long Range Planning*, 10 (2), 9–15.

Johnson, G. Whittington, R., and Scholes, K. (2014) *Exploring Strategy* (10th edn). Harlow, Essex: Pearson Education.

McCann, A. (1995) 'The rule of 2×2', *Long Range Planning*, 28 (1), 112–115.

McGuire, W.J. (1997) 'Creative hypothesis generating in psychology', *Annual Review of Psychology*, 48, 1–30.

Mintzberg, H. (2000) *The Rise and Fall of Strategic Planning*. Harlow, Essex: Pearson Education.

Mizuno, S. (1988) *Management for Quality Improvement: The Seven New QC Tools*. Cambridge: Productivity Press.

Peteraf, M. and Shanley, M. (1997) 'Getting to know you: a theory of strategic group identity', *Strategic Management Journal*, 18 (SI), 165–186.

Porter, M.E. (2004) *Competitive Strategy: Techniques for Analysing Industries and Competitors* (New edn). New York: Free Press.

Reger, R.K. and Huff, A.S. (1993) 'Strategic groups: a cognitive perspective', *Strategic Management Journal*, 14, 103–104.

Robinson, S.J.Q., Hitchens, R.E. and Wade, D.P. (1978) 'The directional policy matrix – a tool for strategic planning', *Long Range Planning*, 11 (3), 8–15.

Thompson, A.A. et al. (2013) *Crafting and Executing Strategy: The Quest for Competitive Advantage*. Maidenhead, Berkshire: McGraw-Hill Education.

Case exercise

Youth Travel Agency

Youth Travel Agency (YTA) is one of the two largest travel organisations for students and young people in the world. It was founded in the 1970s initially with bases in Australia and the UK and today it operates from more than 100 countries. Originally set up to provide discounted airline tickets and basic accommodation for young people, it now offers a whole range of holidays, arranges work and volunteering abroad and sells insurance. After an unsuccessful attempt to appeal to a wider audience (i.e. non-youth) in the 1990s, the policy now has been to stick to their particular segment of the market. As their target audience usually only makes one significant trip, their plan was to grow sales by offering them additional services, both at the start of the trip and during it. This has largely proved a successful model as their clients have usually come to YTA if they required extra services whilst abroad. However as access to information on alternative suppliers has become much easier, their clients have become less 'brand loyal'.

The growth and extent of electronic communication and the desire to have a closer and longer relationship with their existing customers has led the directors to review their customer relationship management (CRM) strategy. Their target market is particularly tech-savvy and they need to ensure that they are using the right means of communication both for them to contact the client and vice versa. This has to be balanced by the potential costs that could be incurred in the set-up of information systems versus the added value that they may bring.

As the consultant that they have brought in to help with their CRM strategy, you have conducted a series of workshops with senior members of the management team. In these you have identified the current state of play (As Is) and also confirmed what the future should look like (To Be). From this, it is clear that the broad strategy that the YTA needs involves a system that could personalise the service they offer, to increase customer loyalty but at a minimal cost. Like much of the travel industry, they operate on very low margins (typically 1–2 per cent of the cost of the holiday), so any new CRM system has to generate significantly more sales to cover the expenditure. One option is to have a 'reactive' system where YTA ensures that the client can easily contact them via email, webchat and social networking sites. The second option is a 'proactive' system where YTA is able to 'track' the client during their trip and offer services as appropriate. The latter would require much more sophisticated systems such as dedicated email addresses, possible apps for smartphones etc., and would need additional staff to monitor these.

1 Conduct a brainstorm amongst your team looking at the ways these two options could be carried out (i.e. means of delivery).

2 Use one of the tools above to show how the new CRM process would operate.

Chapter 10

Decision making in the client context

Lead me, follow me or get out of the way.

George S. Patton

Learning outcomes

The main learning outcomes for this chapter are to:

- appreciate different approaches to understanding decision making;
- understand the basis of the traditional model of rational decision making;
- recognise the limitations of this model;
- recognise the types of *decision-making roles* managers undertake in organisations;
- recognise the ways managers *influence* each other's decisions;
- understand the *dimensions*, including multi-criteria that can be used to define a particular decision;
- analyse the decision-making environment the client organisation presents: to recognise how decision making within the organisation is influenced by *organisational orientation*, *organisational culture* and the *strategy implementation process*;
- appreciate the *naturalistic decision-making* approach and how this can inform the consultant's understanding of managerial decision making.

The study of decision making is now an established subject in its own right, drawing insights from both economics and sociology.

People need to make decisions all the time. Some are significant, others trivial. Some seem hard, others easy. Some people are conscious of making decisions; others are more intuitive. The study of decision making splits into three main areas:

Normative: normative approaches are concerned with what a *rational* decision maker might do. These target some definite objective such as utility or profit maximisation. Rational methods are favoured because they indicate decisions that are *optimal*. This approach is usually somewhat mathematical. It features in finance theory and management science. It can be present in some decision support and planning tools. It is a specialist area, but one in which consultants are involved, especially in financial management, operations planning and risk strategy development.

Descriptive: human beings are rarely rational in the way that normative theory predicts or dictates. Deviations from rationality are rarely random. They are systematic and have a pattern in the way they deviate from rationality (referred to as biases). The study of actual human decision making is referred to as the descriptive tradition. The descriptive tradition is important to consultants because they must work with what managers do, rather than what they should do.

Prescriptive: this tradition is concerned with advising and supporting people (managers, or experts generally) in improving their decision-making skills. This is the approach that is of central concern to consultants.

One prescriptive philosophy is that rationality is best, and so the objective of prescriptive interventions is to make managers more rational. There are, however, a number of issues with this. First, who is to say that rational is best? Rational (normative) models are only best if they take into account all managers' concerns. There is no guarantee that they do so. Second, even if rational is best, to find the rational decision may require a high degree of technical knowledge (or support), be complex, time consuming and difficult. Rationality may not always be conducive with decisiveness. Third, even when they know the rational answer, managers may not actually feel comfortable with what it is telling them to do.

So a manager may prefer a rough and ready – or 'fast-and-frugal' – approach to decision making that is straightforward and rapid that gives 'good enough' (if not strictly optimal) answers to a slow, overly analytical approach. Comfort is found in the space between 'paralysis by analysis' and 'extinction by instinct'. Modern approaches to prescriptive advice and technologies take these concerns into account. Prominent here is the naturalistic decision-making approach discussed further in Section 10.12.

10.1 Decision making in organisations

Organisational decision making goes beyond the concerns of the individual: it involves interactions between individuals.

A decision is a choice between two or more courses of action. Complex psychological processes involving recognition of personal need, cognitive style, cognitive strategy and motivation influence individual decision making. Organisations must also make choices between different courses of action. These interactions include the passing of information, discussion about analysis and the negotiation of outcomes. Individual choices are only part of the process of organisational decision making; organisational decision making occurs at a level above that of individual decision making.

The 'traditional' picture of decision making in organisations sees it as an open process in which the manager seeks information, analyses it in a rational way and then implements the decision through the organisation. Such a picture is represented in the general model of organisational decision making. The origins of such a model go back as far as the work of T.T. Patterson (1969). Models of this type, as illustrated in Figure 10.1, highlight six stages in the organisational decision-making process.

Such models are valuable in that they suggest ways in which decision making may be accessed and influenced. However, they present a somewhat idealised picture of how decision making really occurs in organisations. As with many models of organisational life they depict the 'essence' of a process rather than its reality. The details of decision making are often much more complex than such models suggest. Human issues complicate the matter. Managers do not always sit and plan decisions in detail. Information may be limited. Advice, even good advice, may not be appreciated. The manager does not instigate all decisions; some are forced upon him or her. Not all decisions are rationalised through a formal interpretation of choices. Some are impulsive and based on intuitive understanding. Authorisation may not always be 'official'. Execution may be hindered by political concerns and internal infighting.

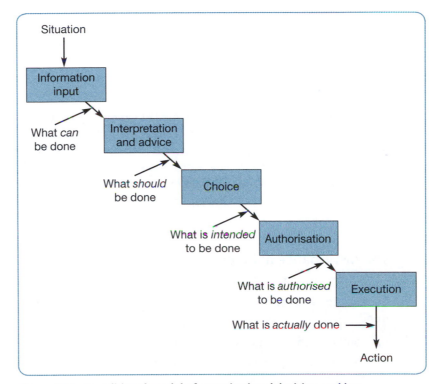

Figure 10.1 A traditional model of organisational decision making

The consultant aims to influence decision making in the organisations with which they are engaged. It is important that the consultant understands how decisions are made in practice. Every organisation has its own style of decision making. If the consultant is to be effective in supporting the client organisation in achieving its objectives then they must be sensitive to this style: the way in which decisions are *actually* made, justified and implemented within a business. To do this, four levels of insight are valuable:

- an appreciation of the *types* of decision a manager is called on to make;
- an understanding of *who* is involved in decision making;
- an understanding of the way in which a decision may be *defined*;
- an ability to define the *styles* of decision making an organisation can adopt.

| 10.2 | Types of management decision-making roles |

Not all decisions are the same and the manager's role may therefore differ.

As stated in Chapter 1, Henry Mintzberg has defined four distinct types of decision-making role for managers. These are the *entrepreneurial*, the *disturbance handler*, the *resource allocator* and the *negotiator*. It is appropriate at this juncture to reflect on the type of decisions these roles entail.

The entrepreneurial

Entrepreneurial decisions are those aimed at generating controlled change for the organisation. They involve the manager in actively seeking out new opportunities and identifying problems that, although not pressing at present, may limit the organisation in the long term. The manager who initiates entrepreneurial decisions and actively promotes them in the organisation is often called an intrapreneur, a term introduced by Gifford Pinchot (1985). Formal evaluation techniques may or may not be used to evaluate and justify entrepreneurial options.

The disturbance handler

Disturbance-handling decisions are those that are forced on the manager by some crisis or organisational 'disturbance'. Such disturbances take three broad forms. They may result from:

(a) conflicts between individuals within the organisation;

(b) some change in the external environment which affects the way the organisation operates;

(c) a sudden loss in some important resource.

Real organisational crises often result from a combination of these three things. Disturbances must be handled quickly and often in a situation of panic and political intriguing. The manager must often act on impulse and insight and may not have time for much formal evaluation of the decision. Decision making in a crisis is often based on a manager's intuitive knowledge and understanding, his or her confidence, judgement and decisiveness.

The resource allocator

Resource allocation decisions are those that involve the dedication of resources to specific projects on behalf of the organisation. These decisions may relate to capital investment, discretionary investment, the purchasing of the factors the organisation uses or the delegation of particular tasks and work programmes. The ways in which such decisions are made and justified depend on the significance of the decision to the organisation and its culture.

The negotiator

Negotiation decisions involve argument over outcomes on behalf of the organisation with the other organisations and individuals with which it comes into contact. Important outcomes include the commitment of resources and sharing rewards gained from joint projects. Negotiations take many forms. Some are seen as 'zero-sum' games in which one party must lose if another wins. The negotiator sees a 'pie' of fixed size that can go only so far. The aim is to get the biggest share. Alternatively, they may be more positive and be driven by a win–win attitude. In this case the negotiator sees the parties to the negotiation as able to work together to make the pie bigger for all.

10.3   The decision-making unit

> A business decision also involves the interaction of managers in groups within the organisation as a whole.

Mintzberg's four roles relate to individual managers. They represent only one dimension of decision making. The group involved in making a decision is referred to as the decision-making unit (DMU). The key players in the DMU are the decision maker, the authoriser, information providers, the resource provider, influencers, implementers and gatekeepers.

The decision maker

The decision maker is the person called upon to actually make a decision. They will be the person who is seen as responsible for the *outcomes* of the decision.

The authoriser

The authoriser is the person who is called on to authorise, modify or sanction the decision made by the decision maker. In hierarchical organisations the authoriser is often the decision-maker's line manager. In team-based organisations it will be the project leader.

Information providers

Information providers give the decision maker the information needed to analyse possible courses of action and to justify the decision eventually made. Information providers may be part of the organisation but are often external experts called in when needed. Consultants are often information providers.

The resource provider

The resource provider is the person who authorises the use of any resources that are required before the decision can be implemented. The resource provider can be the same person as the authoriser but this is not always the case.

Influencers

Influencers are individuals who are in a position to change the opinion of other members of the decision-making unit and develop their attitude towards particular decisions. The influencer's role may be formally defined or it might be informal.

Implementers

Implementers are those individuals who must put the decision into effect. Important implementers are production staff, research and development specialists and sales staff.

Gatekeepers

Gatekeepers are those people who control access to other members of the DMU. Personal assistants, secretaries and receptionists are often important gatekeepers. Different decisions call on different DMUs within the organisation. Their nature will depend on the scope and significance of the decision being made. Routine decisions may be controlled by long-standing DMUs. Non-routine decisions may require the setting up of an ad hoc DMU. Some DMUs are recognised formally – the board of directors, special committees and project teams, for example. Others may be quite informal, such as the clique of managers who meet for a drink after work. It is possible that the organisation may not even recognise that some informal DMUs are functioning, though their impact on the business may be considerable.

10.4 The dimensions of a decision

Decisions have a number of different facets.

The decision-making roles outlined above suggest that all decisions can be described in terms of a small number of features, in particular the significance of the decision, who is involved in making it, how it is justified within the organisation and how it is communicated within the organisation.

The significance of the decision

What impact will the decision have on the business? Is it a major decision defining the future of the business or is it a relatively minor one? What proportion of the organisation's resources will be affected by the decision? How many people within the organisation will be affected by the decision? In general, the more important the decision, the more extensive, and formal, will be the involvement of a DMU.

Who is involved in the decision?

Who is involved in making, authorising and implementing the decision? In other words, what are the structure, function and membership of the DMU that will judge the decision? (see Sections 10.2 and 10.3). Are they necessarily the right people – for instance, the inexperienced brand manager agreeing expenditure or commitment to new product manufacture without authorisation by the finance director, or the marketing director who delegates important sales and operations planning decisions to junior staff?

How the decision is justified

How does the decision maker go about justifying the decision that is advocated? There are a number of ways a decision can be promoted within the organisation. It can be through a process of logical analysis (presenting detailed market data), cost analysis and option evaluation; it can be advocated on the basis of the decision-maker's expertise and past successes ('Trust me – I know what I'm doing!'); it can be insisted upon on the basis of the decision maker's authority ('I'm the boss and I say it's going to happen!'); it can be made to happen through political manoeuvring ('Help me on this and you'll get my support later!'). In practice, many decisions are promoted in different ways to different members of the DMU. Typically, the consultant will be more formal in their decision justification than the organisation would expect its internal managers to be. This is for two reasons. As an outside expert the consultant will be expected to work *as* an expert – and this means formality. Second, the consultant, lacking experience of the internal situation and formal authority, must rely more on overtly logical justification. Process consulting, though, may deliberately avoid an excessively formal approach.

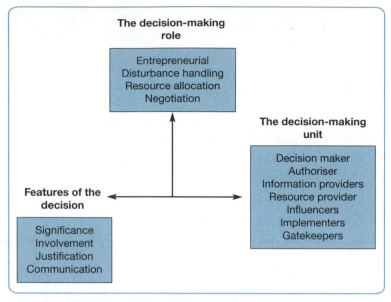

Figure 10.2 The dimensions of a business decision

How the decision is communicated

How will the members of the DMU be informed about the decision? It might be through a formal meeting or presentation. The decision might be communicated in a written format or be part of the recommendations in a report. Alternatively the decision maker may talk it through on an informal one-to-one basis with members of the DMU. It may also travel through the informal grapevine in the organisation. Normally, a consultant will be called on to communicate their ideas in a formal way, through a report or presentation, though effective consultants also know how to use informal channels of communication. A particular decision can be depicted as located in a three-dimensional space, with the axes defined by the decision-making role, the functioning of the DMU and the features of the decision. This decision-making space is depicted in Figure 10.2.

10.5   Multiple criteria decision analysis

Whether in daily life or in a professional context there are multiple conflicting criteria that need to be evaluated in making decisions.

Multiple-criteria decision making (MCDM) or multiple-criteria decision analysis (MCDA) is a sub-discipline of operations research that explicitly considers multiple criteria in decision-making environments. Cost verses price is an obvious example. Some measure of quality is typically another criterion that is in conflict with the cost. Consider purchasing a new vehicle: research has shown that a male's motivation may be for reasons of self-actualisation, such as image, power, styling and the variety of gadgetry, whereas a female may be more concerned with rational considerations such as reliability, safety, fuel economy, storage space and manoeuvrability. Both sets of criteria will need to be taken into account when the vehicle is designed and a compromise will have to be reached between partners when the purchase decision is taken. In terms of cost, it is unusual that the cheapest car is the most comfortable or the safest.

In managing a share portfolio there is a trade-off between enjoying a high return and reducing the downside risk. It is often the stocks that have the potential to bring high returns that carry with them high risks of losing money. In service provision customer satisfaction and the cost of delivering the service are two often conflicting criteria. The Queenswick Adult Social Care case (see Chapter 7) is one such example: can the council afford the cost and disruption of implementing the improved system the consultants have recommended?

In daily life we usually weigh multiple criteria implicitly and we may be comfortable with the consequences of such decisions that are made based on intuition alone. On the other hand, when the stakes are high it is important to properly structure the problem and explicitly evaluate multiple criteria. In making a decision of where to locate a wind farm, commission fracking exploration or establish a site for the traveller community, there are not only very complex issues involving multiple criteria, but there are also multiple stakeholders who will be deeply affected by the consequences.

Structuring complex problems well and considering multiple criteria explicitly lead to more informed and better decisions. There have been important advances in this field since the start of the modern multiple-criteria decision-making discipline in the early 1960s. A variety of approaches and methods, many implemented by specialised decision-making software, have been developed for their application in an array of disciplines ranging from politics and business to energy and the environment.

MCDM is concerned with structuring and solving decision and planning problems involving multiple criteria. The purpose is to support decision makers facing such problems. Typically there is no unique optimal solution for such problems and it is necessary to use decision makers' preferences to differentiate between solutions. 'Solving' can be interpreted in different ways. It could correspond to choosing the best alternative from a set of available alternatives (where 'best' can be interpreted as 'the most preferred alternative' of a decision maker). Another interpretation could be choosing a small set of good alternatives, or grouping alternatives into different preference sets. An extreme interpretation could be to find all 'efficient' or 'non-dominated' alternatives: solutions which have the property that it is not possible to move away from them to any other solution without sacrificing in at least one criterion.

10.6 Decision-making style and influence

Every organisation has its own style of decision making. The consultant must recognise this and be ready to use it.

Consultants should not challenge the organisation's style of decision making (not in the first instance anyway, though this may be the objective of change management programmes). They are most influential when they present their arguments in a way that is sympathetic to the organisation's decision-making style. Even if they are involved in a change management project dedicated to developing organisational decision-making skills, they must still work with the organisation's initial style, not against it. In short, a consultant should go with the flow! This presents the consultant with a challenge. How are they to understand the decision-making style in the client organisation and then use it? There are a number of models that help provide such an understanding. Three which are particularly valuable are the ideas of *organisational orientation*, *organisational culture* and *strategy process*. The following three sections explore these.

10.7 Organisational orientation

> Businesses are sometimes described as having an orientation. This defines the priorities the organisation sees itself as having and the kind of issues it must address.

Three orientations are described: the *production orientation*, the *sales orientation* and the *marketing orientation*.

The production orientation

The production-orientated organisation is primarily concerned with how it makes the things it sells, or delivers the service it offers. The business will prioritise decisions that relate to the developing of products, the setting up of production and the solving of operation problems. These things will be seen to be more important to the organisation than actually creating demand for what it offers. For a business with a production orientation, generating demand for products is secondary to actually making them. The production orientation is often found in new businesses and those that are adopting an innovative approach to production and service delivery. Technologists and operational specialists tend to be important players in decision-making units (DMUs).

The sales orientation

The sales-orientated organisation is primarily concerned with actually *selling* its goods or services to customers. It is interested in creating short-term demand and gaining immediate sales revenues. The business is usually very confident in its belief that what it sells is attractive to its customers – it just needs to get them to buy it! The sales-orientated business can sometimes give the impression that it is seeking power over the customer. Priority is given to decisions focused on sales strategy and (short-term) promotional tactics. The sales orientation is often found in businesses that are in highly competitive markets, those which are underperforming financially or those where demand is latent and requires particular stimulation, such as funeral plans, financial services and charities. Sales managers are usually key players in businesses' DMUs.

The marketing orientation

The marketing-orientated business gives priority to understanding customer demand and developing a means to satisfy it. The business will profess that the customer lies at the centre of the business and that addressing the customer's real needs is the key to performance. It will eschew what it sees as 'hard-selling' techniques as unnecessary. The business is usually concerned with developing a strategic approach to its marketing and to product development. These factors will feature strongly in the decisions it makes. Marketing and development personnel play key roles in DMUs. Many management thinkers advocate the marketing orientation as the 'highest' or 'best' orientation and the key to long-term success. It has been suggested that a business evolves from the production to the sales to the marketing orientation as it grows, matures and learns.

This may be so, but the marketing orientation can only really establish itself in a business that can free its managers to take on the entrepreneurial decision-making roles and engage in long-term, self-instigated projects. Hence the marketing orientation is often found in innovative businesses that have enjoyed a degree of success and in which there are no immediate crises. If a critical issue arises and the disturbance decision-making role is demanded, the marketing orientation can often be dropped in favour of one of the other two. The marketing orientation may be seen as 'unrealistic' or too 'long term', whereas the sales orientation will seem to offer an immediate solution to demand-based problems and the production orientation solutions to supply-based problems that challenge the business. It is a valuable exercise for the consultant to assess the business and determine its orientation. Different parts of the business may have different orientations. This is often the case in larger organisations that have separate production, sales and marketing functions.

10.8   Organisational culture

The idea of culture as a description of the 'way a business does things' can be used to give a good picture of the decision-making environment in a business.

The idea of organisational culture is one of the most important to enter the management lexicon in recent years. It has been advocated most notably by Tom Peters and Robert Waterman in *In Search of Excellence* (2015) as *the* most important facet of the business which can be used to differentiate it from competitors and establish a base for success. Others challenge the way the concept is used by management thinkers and suggest it cannot provide a meaningful management tool. Charles Handy has described four types of organisational culture in *Understanding Organisations* (1993). These are the power culture, the role culture, the task culture and the person culture (or people culture).

Consideration of culture in this way can provide a particularly useful insight to the consultant.

The power culture

The power culture is characterised by a strong, central figurehead who dominates the business. They are the source of all authority in the organisation. Often the authority is based on ownership of the business combined with personal charisma and leadership. Tasks other than the most routine are delegated by this central figure on a 'need to do' basis. Planning is ad hoc and largely concerned with short-term issues. There is little formality in the business. Procedures are ill-defined and bureaucracy low. It is likely that communication will, in the main, take the form of informal discussions. The central figurehead will dominate any DMUs in the business. They may even be the DMU. Power cultures often occur in small, privately owned and entrepreneurial businesses. Power cultures work only in an organisation that is small enough for one person to make all the important decisions.

The role culture

The role culture is characterised by structure and procedures. Individual roles are defined through job descriptions and specifications. An individual's position in the organisation is defined in an organogram. Position bestows authority. The business is likely to be broken up into well-defined departments or functions such as finance, marketing, production and so on. The organisation may engage in formal planning and use it to specify definite goals and future situations. Officially, communication is formalised by the use of regular meetings, reports and memoranda. Informal grapevines are often important as well, though. Decision making in such organisations is routinized as far as possible. DMUs are extensive, with individuals taking on recognised, official roles. Organisations with role cultures are often quite bureaucratic. They are typically well-established medium to large firms operating in a stable environment.

The task culture

A task culture is characterised by the need to get particular jobs done. Achieving objectives is seen as more important than defining what one's job is. The business may be structured around multidisciplinary teams rather than departments. Authority is based on expertise rather than formal position. Teams may be permanent fixtures or set up ad hoc when needed to undertake a particular project. Long-term planning may be engaged in but it is likely to be seen as offering a way of gaining insights rather than specifying a definite path. The organisation attempts to keep bureaucracy to a minimum though formal procedures may be established to monitor and provide resources for the activity of the task teams.

Decision making is centred on the project team which largely constitutes the DMU. The authorisers and resource allocators may nominally stand outside the group, but they will be susceptible to advocacy by the group. Businesses with task cultures are often innovative and fast-growing entrepreneurial businesses that are too large for a power culture. They are effective in unstable and rapidly changing environments where decision making must be delegated.

The person culture

The person culture is characterised by a prioritising of the needs of the individual over those of the organisation as a whole. Organisations with a person culture resist the imposition of formal structures and procedures though informal ones may emerge. The main concern is with the internal environment rather than with the organisation's relationship with the wider world. Decision making is informal. DMUs tend to cluster round influential individuals who may exercise unofficial authority based on expertise and/or personal charisma.

This type of culture is hard to sustain, as it can be difficult to reconcile the needs of the organisation as a whole with those of the individual. Organisations with person cultures can find it hard to focus on well-defined objectives and may tend to fragment. They often need support in obtaining resources. Person cultures can be found in some non-profit organisations such as public healthcare or charities and in religious groupings. Some unorthodox profit-making organisations such as cooperatives may profess or aspire to a person culture. A person culture may also be found in some 'professional' organisations that have a small number of 'highly valuable' people who must be handled with care. Important examples include advertising agencies, legal firms and management consultants.

10.9   Strategy processes

Strategy process is the way a business organises its decision making.

A business strategy has two sides. One is the *content* of the strategy, what the business actually does. The other is the strategy *process,* the way in which a business decides what to do. Henry Mintzberg (2011) has described three basic modes of strategy process: the *entrepreneurial,* the *adaptive* and *planning.*

The entrepreneurial mode

Four main features typify the *entrepreneurial* mode of strategy process. First, it is focused on identifying and exploiting new opportunities. Second, entrepreneurial decision making is concentrated into the hands of a powerful individual. Third, it is concerned with major moves forward rather than incremental or gradual change. Fourth, it concentrates on decisions which offer the possibility of business growth. An entrepreneurial mode of decision making has resonance with a power culture.

The adaptive mode

The adaptive mode of strategy process is reactive rather than proactive. It represents a response to short-term and immediate opportunities and threats. Four characteristics arise as a consequence of this. First, adaptive decision making is made by individuals and small groups and is not coordinated by the organisation as a whole. Second, it is not aimed at achieving well-defined long-term organisational goals. Third, adaptive decision making is incremental. It is concerned with small changes, not with major leaps forward. Fourth, it is disjointed – it may be difficult to relate the logic behind one adaptive decision to that behind another.

The planning mode

The planning mode of strategy making is characterised by systematic analysis and formality. Three features of decision making arise from this. First and foremost, individual decisions are integrated into and related to an overarching strategy for the business. Second, alternatives are carefully evaluated to assess costs, benefits and risks. Formal techniques may be brought in to do this. Third, not least, as a result of the need for the application of formal planning and decision analysis techniques, expert strategic analysts play an important role in the organisation's DMUs.

10.10 Strategy development processes

Goal orientation and process orientation define strategy development.

P.J. Idenberg (1993) has built on these insights by Mintzberg and others and proposed a two-dimensional matrix that defines four types of strategy development processes. These are explained as follows.

Goal orientation

Goal orientation is the *what* of strategy development. It is concerned with the definition of goals, SMART targets and desired future states for the business. It considers the actuality of decisions and their outcomes. Goal orientation decisions are of the 'where do we want to go?' type.

Process orientation

Process orientation is the *how* of strategy development. It is concerned with the rules and procedures by which strategy making is guided, evaluated and monitored by the organisation. It considers how decision making will be controlled, rather than what the actual decisions are. Process orientation decisions are of the 'how are we going to get there?' type. Each orientation may be strong or weak in the way it influences organisational decision making. The options define the matrix illustrated in Figure 10.3. This matrix has four quadrants, each of which represents a distinct strategy-making style.

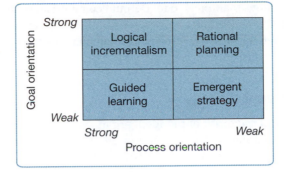

Figure 10.3 The Idenberg matrix for strategy process

Source: Reprinted from P.J. Idenberg, 'Four styles of strategic planning', *Long Range Planning*, 26 (6), 132–137. Copyright © 1993, with permission from Elsevier.

Logical incrementalism

The logical incrementalism style results from the organisation having both a strong goal orientation and a strong process orientation. There is a concern both with *where* the organisation is going and *how* it will get there. Decisions are monitored and evaluated by pervasive control functions in the organisation. The justification of decisions may be formalised by both systematic analysis and review procedures. Critically, decisions are related to each other. The organisation moves forward in a pattern characterised by incremental and rational steps. The business may well mistrust 'entrepreneurial' decisions that demand significant leaps into the unknown.

Guided learning

Guided learning style results from an emphasis on the process of making strategy at the expense of what the strategy is meant to achieve. The business may be active in delegating decision making to local managers. Rather than prescribe targets, the business expects managers to set their own targets and perhaps to engage in planning activity. However, this will be seen as a way of getting managers to explore their environments and the possibilities the business faces and perhaps even their own thinking modes rather than as a procedure for simply defining objectives.

A guided learning style does not mean managers are free to make any decision they wish. Controls still exist. The organisation will be active in developing managers so that they make the 'right' decisions. This control can be explicit, say through training programmes. It can also be implicit. The organisation may rely on its culture – its 'how we do things around here' – to define and limit management decision making.

Rational planning

The rational planning style is characterised by an emphasis on meeting definite goals rather than worrying about how managers go about achieving them. In many respects it parallels

Mintzberg's planning mode. Definite commercial targets imposed on managers from the top define it. Planners adopt systematic decision-evaluation techniques and decisions are reviewed using formal procedures. Top management carefully monitors the achievement of objectives.

Emergent strategy

The final quadrant of the Idenberg matrix strategy development occurs in the absence of both strong goal and process orientations. The business strategy 'emerges' rather than being explicitly developed. As discussed in Section 10.2, managers do not always have the luxury of being able to sit down and plan every decision. Some must be made on the spur of the moment in response to a crisis. Some decision making may not be guided by consideration either of the organisation's goals or of how it should best go about making decisions. Managers use their intuition and take decisions. Entrepreneurs starting a new business rarely consider their decision making in an abstract sense. They are likely to be more interested in using their decision-making skills to chase opportunities and get the venture off the ground. If they are successful and the business grows (perhaps through a power culture, then a task culture phase), they may never explore, in isolation from the actual running of the business, the way in which the business makes decisions about where it is going and how it is to get there.

This is not to say that emergent decision making is a free-for-all. It is just that decision making is controlled by being embedded in the experiences, knowledge and culture of the business and its key personnel rather than by location with reference to externally considered goals and processes. Organisational life is rich and complex. Decision making is an integral part of the organisational tapestry. The three approaches to understanding organisational decision making – organisational orientation, organisational culture and strategy process – simplify the complex picture of decision making. By simplifying it, they make it easier to be understood. However, they also present the risk of caricaturing it. They are best used as frameworks that can guide the consultant's experience of the client organisation, rather than as rigid boxes into which 'facts' about the organisation must be forced. Used in this way they can be a valuable tool that can help a consultant convince the client organisation that their ideas are worth implementing. Evaluation of decision-making style is a critical first step to developing a strategy to communicate ideas to the client organisation.

10.11 External influences on organisational decision making

It is preferable to think of individuals as having a spectrum of relationships with the organisation from intimate to distant rather than to think of those who formally work for it and those who do not.

Management thinking often, and quite metaphorically, pictures organisations as somehow bounded and separated from the outside world. We talk of an 'internal' environment and an 'external' environment. In reality, of course, organisations are not separated from the 'outside' world by any boundary. Organisations are made up of individuals and individuals come into contact with, and share information with, people who work both within the organisation and outside it. People, not organisations, buy. People, not organisations, forecast, negotiate and decide.

This means that the outside world can influence internal decision making in a variety of ways, not all of them formal. The overall PEST/STEEPLE environment impacts on individual decision makers in their private lives as well as in their profession. An increase in interest rates may mean an individual's mortgage will go up. This may influence their attitude to risk for the business in addition to the increase's effect on the firm's cost of capital. A bad experience when travelling in a country while on holiday may impact on a decision maker's attitude towards their firm developing export markets in that country. Comments about a particular supplier made by a friend at a dinner party may have as much, if not more, influence on a decision maker than those made by a professional colleague within the firm. In short, individuals do not compartmentalise their lives, separating their 'professional' from their 'private' experiences. They make decisions based on their overall, and integrated, life experiences. Good consultants must be aware of this and, at times, draw out decision makers' general life experiences as well as their professional ones if their decision making is to be fully understood.

10.12 The naturalistic decision-making approach

An approach that sets aside formal ideas such as outcomes and probabilities can be valuable.

Traditional approaches to understanding decision making, whether normative, descriptive or prescriptive share a number of things in common. They often assume that a decision problem can be broken down into a series of features that the decision maker will value in some way and that the decision maker will consider options on the basis of whether they will deliver these features or not. Orasanu and Connolly (1993) suggest that this approach does not capture many aspects of decision tasks that managers find relevant and take into account. A managerial decision problem is often characterised by having high stakes, being ill-structured, directed at achieving shifting, uncertain and perhaps competing goals, as playing with the interests of people other than self, with the manager paying attention to feedback from earlier decisions and constrained by organisational and social norms in an uncertain and poorly defined environment.

The *naturalistic decision-making approach* considers some more intangible aspects, putting emphasis on:

- mental simulations of decision problems;
- prioritising assessment of the decision situation, rather than decision options;
- calling upon expertise rather than decision models;

- finding 'good-enough' solutions rather than strictly optimal ones;
- trying one option, then another, until one that is good enough is found, rather than simultaneously considering all options;
- being prepared to act before a decision is made, rather than waiting until after the decision to act.

One idea developed by Orasanu and Connolly is that a manager's decision making will depend on familiarity with the decision situation. The recognition primed decision (RPD) model suggests that managers judge situations according to whether they demand:

- **A simple match:** situational cues mean a situation is perceived as typical. This creates expectancies (about what will happen if previously tried actions are taken). Goals are understood and plausible.
- **Developing a course of action:** situation is not typical, but aspects of it can be integrated with previous goals, actions and expectations to produce the innovation of a novel approach.
- **A complex approach:** situation is quite new and has few features, which mean past experience can be directly called upon. The requirement is that the decision maker should simulate possible decisions and outcomes and actively evaluate new possibilities.

The RPD model is useful because managers use familiarity as a platform for decision effort and inventiveness. Familiar situations favour tried and trusted decisions and choices. Novel situations demand a new and inventive approach. The consultant is likely to be engaged with managers involved in all three decision modes, but their expertise is most likely to be demanded when the manager recognises that *simple match* (and probably developing a course of action) is seen as insufficient. Learning to work at the *complex* level both with their own decisions and supporting the decisions of managers is a critical aspect of consultants' skill, knowledge and experience.

Managers often have to deal with *risk*. Engaging a consultant may be motivated by recognition of risk situations. Whatever the objectives of the consulting project, it is likely that risk will enter into considerations and it is inevitable that the consultant will have to consider the risk implications of their recommendations. Much normative modelling is concerned with how risk should be valued. In these models, risk is regarded in terms of the probability that something valued might or might not happen. Descriptive research is clear that risk is not seen in this simple way. Lipshitz and Strauss (1997) suggest that when faced with risk, rather than assess outcomes and their probabilities, managers will engage in what is described as the RAWFS heuristic. This acronym summarises the following ideas:

Reduction	Simplify the situation by concentrating on its critical aspects.
Assumption-based reasoning	Where information is missing, make assumptions.
Weighing pros and cons	Broad-based evaluation of options in terms of good and bad aspects.
Forestalling	Where no clear decision is apparent, make moves that buy time.
Suppression	Where information is complex, or uncertain, neglect or suppress information that confuses and hinders decision making.

The naturalistic approach clearly offers a more convincing narrative of managerial decision making than traditional models (but this does not, in itself, make the naturalistic approach more true or valuable). It does, however, provide the consultant with a 'language' of decision making that managers can relate to and a perspective on decision making that invites supportive intervention. The consultant may advocate a naturalistic approach to theirs and others' decision making and use the naturalistic approach as a framework for analysing client decision making.

Team discussion points

1 Discuss the following statements. Are they true or not?
- 'It is the consultant's responsibility to facilitate client decision making, not change the decisions the client would have made anyway'.
- 'The naturalistic account sounds more like the way in which managers *really* make decisions than other descriptive approaches. It is therefore a better *theory* of management decision making'.

2 Consider the project your team is undertaking. Evaluate the risks the project faces (from both your own and the client's perspective). Analyse the way in which your team has interpreted and reacted to those risks using the RAWFS heuristic.

Summary of key ideas

- The study of decision making is a mature discipline within the social sciences, drawing from insights in psychology, economics and sociology.
- It is split into three avenues: normative, descriptive and prescriptive.
- Decision making in organisations can take a number of forms. It may be explicit, open and rational, or it can be implicit and based on management intuition.
- Businesses adopt a variety of styles of decision making. If the consultant is to see their ideas take shape, they must work within the client's decision-making style.
- Managers take on four distinct decision-making roles: the entrepreneurial, the disturbance handler, the resource allocator, the negotiator.
- Decisions in an organisation are controlled by decision-making units (DMUs).
- There are multiple conflicting criteria that need to be evaluated in making decisions.
- The four features of a particular decision are: its significance, who is involved in making it, how it will be justified, how it will be communicated.
- A number of frameworks can be used to analyse organisational decision-making style.

- Managerial decision making is influenced by factors both outside and inside the organisation.
- The naturalistic decision-making approach draws away from traditional optimisation approaches to understanding and prescribing effective decision making.

Key reading

Idenberg, P.J. (1993) 'Four styles of strategic planning', *Long Range Planning*, 26 (6), 132–137.

Lipshitz, R. and Strauss, O. (1997) 'Coping with uncertainty: a naturalistic decision-making analysis', *Organizational Behavior and Human Decision Processes*, 69, 149–163.

Further reading

Brockman, J. (ed) (2013) *Thinking: The New Science of Decision Making, Problem Solving and Prediction*. New York: Harper Perennial.

Gigerenzer, G. (2002) *Reckoning with Risk: Learning to Live with Uncertainty*. London: Allen Lane.

Handy, C. (1993) *Understanding Organisations* (4th edn). London: Penguin.

Klein, G. (2011) *Streetlights and Shadows: Searching for the Keys to Adaptive Decision Making*. Cambridge, MA: MIT Press.

Köksalan, M., Wallenius, J., and Zionts, S. (2011) *Multiple Criteria Decision Making: From Early History to the 21st Century*. Singapore: World Scientific Publishing.

LeBlanc, J. (1998) *Thinking Clearly: A Guide to Critical Reasoning*. New York: W.W. Norton & Company Inc.

Lipshitz, R., Klein, G., Orasanu, J. and Salas, E. (2001) 'Taking stock of naturalistic decision making', *Journal of Behavioural Decision Making*, 14, 331–152.

Mintzberg, H. (2011) *Managing*. Harlow, Essex: Financial Times Prentice Hall.

Orasanu, J. and Connolly, T. (1993) 'The reinvention of decision making', in G.A. Klein, J. Orasanu, R. Calderwood and C.E. Zsambok (eds) *Decision Making in Action: Models and Methods*. Norwood, NJ: Ablex Publishing Corporation, pp. 3–21.

Patterson, T.T. (1969) *Management Theory*. London: Business Publications.

Peters, T. and Waterman, R. (2015) *In Search of Excellence*. London: Profile Books.

Pinchot, G. III (1985) *Intrapreneuring*. New York: Harper & Row.

Case exercise

Dunwich Marine

Dunwich is a port on the east coast of the UK that has known better times. It once had a thriving trawling and seafood-processing industry. Many marine engineering companies were formed to service the fishing fleets and considerable commercial freight was exported and imported through Dunwich docks.

With the decline in the UK fishing industry in the 1970s, Dunwich was badly hit. Unemployment rose, there was little investment and the port and dock facilities deteriorated. The fish market was used to sell catches trucked down from Scotland and a yacht marina and fishery museum were established. Even though there was still some very limited fishing, the whole port area was decaying and seemingly neglected.

The Dunwich Port Authority (DPA) was created to operate and manage the port facilities, but their ability to do so was conditioned by the availability of public funding. The fish market was revamped but much of the remaining port area was still in disrepair.

Dunwich, however, has a valuable asset that other east coast ports do not: a slipway. Unlike a dry dock, this facility is not dependent on tidal movement, and 60–80 vessels of up to 850 tons are worked upon each year, the work involving welding, engine repair, pressure washing, painting and other routine maintenance. However, it is in a dilapidated state. It has been largely unaltered since its construction in the 1930s and is only capable of working at 50 per cent capacity.

The slipway is rented out from the DPA (at a peppercorn rent) by the Dunwich Slipway Company (DSC), a non-profit distributing company with a dozen or so members. They provide the services of slipping vessels using winches and rails located in the slipway precinct and finance the facility's maintenance and the winch operator's employment. Another organisation, Dunwich Marine Repair (DMR), consists of a similar number of independent small marine engineering companies (some of whom are also members of the DSC) who identify business opportunities for their members. Both organisations also have an equity stake in the DPA.

To its great good fortune, Dunwich is in the right place at the right time. The UK government has announced plans for a massive investment in offshore wind farms in the North Sea. The vessels servicing the wind turbines will themselves need to be maintained at locations as close as possible to their bases, one of which will be Dunwich. The main European wind farm companies have already established a presence in Dunwich and others are to follow.

A consultant was hired by the DPA to recommend how this potential could best be exploited. He found that the DSC were unambitious and survival-focused (perhaps unsurprising given Dunwich's recent history), that DMR were content to leave things as they are, that the slipway needs substantial investment to bring it up to standard and that both the DSC and DMR were by their very conservatism missing many business opportunities such as defence tenders by failing to market and promote themselves.

The consultant recommended that they merge to a single association, to be called Dunwich Marine, with a part-time chief executive hired to promote the slipway and its members' skills. Located in premises in the DPA, he would identify the refurbishment needs, publish a business plan, identify and project manage the work, and seek funding. He would be expected to network with investors and the major customers, represent the company on outward trade missions, subscribe to organisations with details of defence tenders and maintain efficient records. Members of the new company would retain their individual identity and autonomy, but in future a policy of one-customer-one-invoice would be introduced, rather than the complicated system currently operated where the DSC and companies working on slipped vessels invoiced the customer separately. The consultant identified a candidate for the post and he also obtained details of a source of finance, East Finance, an organisation set up to manage residual European and government money to finance local business expansion.

It was therefore with some optimism that the consultant attended a meeting of the DSC and DMR members at the DPA. Copies of his report were made available and a PowerPoint presentation was given. Both the local council and the DPA supported the unthreatening proposals, but the DSC and DMR members turned them down flat. They knew their business and they were not going to be patronised by a consultant. The meeting ended with no next steps. Reflecting on the fiasco, the DMA's chief executive commented with exasperation on the 'history, tradition and politics' which so bedevilled any development plans put forward for the port. He wondered aloud whether it might be better to sell the slipway for an extension to the marina (which was certainly needed) or whether to sell it to a progressive multinational marine engineering company who would have short shrift with the parochial incumbents.

Five years later, the consultant happened to meet the DMA's chief executive at a fishing conference. 'It's just what you said would happen', he told him, 'they've just about gone bust. Most of the companies have gone out of business. Demand has gone way up, the slipway is as bad as it was and it's going to cost a couple of million to put it right. The Council are ready to contribute half the cost, yet still there is resistance from the DSC members. Despite them I'm determined to go ahead!' Perhaps, mused the consultant', I am not a prophet without honour after all'.

1 What next steps would you propose for the client and consultant respectively?

2 How could the consultant have done things differently?

3 How do you think the consultant would view the outcome of the project?

Chapter 11

Managing the project

All things are difficult before they are easy.

Thomas Fuller

Learning outcomes

The learning outcomes from this chapter are to:

- recognise the *key tasks* which contribute to the consulting project;

- recognise how tasks might be *allocated* between team members;

- develop a *plan* for the project with an allocated budget;

- understand how *meetings* with the client can be made effective;

- be able to *monitor* the project and its progression;

- recognise the value of effective time management;

- understand the simple rules which make time management effective;

- be able to use simple systems to support time management and dealing with slippage;

- recognise how a *project log* can help the effective delivery of the consulting project;

- know what to *include* in the log;

- be able to select a log *format* that is right for you and your project.

In Section 3.2 we looked at the key project management skills a good consultant needs. What the client ultimately expects from you is to deliver a well-managed project. This involves ensuring that your team members have not only been allocated a role but the appropriate one for them.

> **All must be effective: just one person not doing their job properly can cause major problems.**

If someone is not doing what you expect them to do, do not assume that they are unwilling. Did you brief them properly? Are they aware of the deadlines? More critically, do they have the appropriate skills? It is better to address these issues sooner rather than later, even if it is a difficult conversation. The longer it drags on, the harder it will be to remedy.

In the excitement and the rush of completing the consultancy assignment, it is easy to let good intentions slip. We have all done it, thinking that we can cut corners, despite meticulous planning upfront. Before embarking on each stage of the process, it is important to step back, review what you have done and think about your next actions. You need to check that you are still on track to deliver the project on time and on budget. A consulting project that is veering off course is like an accelerating runaway train. It gets increasingly difficult to get it back under control.

> **Planning meetings, managing your time and using a project log might seem an unnecessary diversion to the 'real work' but they pay dividends in the long run.**

11.1 Individual roles for team members

> **The advantage of working in a team is that it allows individuals to specialise.**

Differentiating and coordinating activities is a way to make the team more effective. Some teams will be quite homogeneous, with all members engaging in all tasks and perhaps only occasionally dedicating specific types of task. Others will operate with a high degree of formality, even to the point of having individual job descriptions within the team. A number of factors drive specialisation, such as the size of the team, the nature of the task the team is taking on, the expertise of team members, the longevity of the team, the team leader's style and external influences. These factors are explored in more depth in Sections 7.5 and 7.6. Some of the types of role the consulting project will demand are as follows. However, one individual may take on a number of these roles in the consulting exercise.

A team coordinator and leader

They organise the team as a whole, allocate tasks and ensure that deadlines and targets are met. The leadership role will demand assessment and motivation of other team members.

A client contact

This person keeps the client informed and reassures them that the project is progressing well. Ideally it should be a particular member of the team to enable a definite one-to-one relationship to be built with the client. This will be particularly valuable if there is a crisis in the project and objectives need to be renegotiated.

An information gatherer or researcher

They identify what information is needed for the project, receive information requests from other team members and then find sources of that information.

An information analyst

This is the member of the team who takes information from the information gatherer and analyses it so that it can be used to support decision making. It may be formal techniques such as those described in Chapter 6 or more intuitive techniques such as mind mapping and brainstorming (discussed in Chapter 9). In these situations the information analyst may facilitate the analytical creativity of the consulting team as a whole.

A report writer and presenter

A framework for the final report should be laid down early in the project and the details can be filled in as the project progresses. It is useful to assign responsibility for this to a particular team member, not only for producing the report but also for circulating interim drafts at intervals to get the opinion of other team members. This approach to developing the final report is expanded upon in Section 12.4. The report writer may also present the report.

A team coach

Members of the consulting team may occasionally come into conflict with each other. Disagreements may relate to the definition of objectives or the management of the project. Often a conflict can arise if more than one person sees himself or herself as the leader of the project. Such conflicts are a normal part of team dynamics (and are discussed in Chapter 7). However, such disputes need rapid resolution if the team is to work effectively. The team coach is the person who acts as an arbiter and helps reconcile conflicts between members. The team coach can also keep the whole team motivated and interested in the project, especially when the project is going through a difficult patch. Often, but not inevitably, the team coach will be the person who has taken on the leader's role.

11.2 Setting a timetable and the project budget

> Setting a timetable for the project lets the client know when he or she can expect the outputs to be delivered.

It is also a way to set signposts so that it can be seen that the project is on track and to highlight when slippage is occurring. The level of detail in the timetable will reflect the complexity of the project. A simple project may need a list of only a few key events. An extensive project will require a detailed list of activities and their interconnections. It is important to include things such as:

- an initial meeting with the client;
- the preparation of a formal proposal;
- a period for information gathering;
- analysis sessions with individuals and perhaps the team as a whole;
- regular contacts with the client and a period for preparing the final report.

Critical path analysis involves identifying the sequence of tasks that will define the schedule for the project as a whole. These tasks must be undertaken in order, and the time needed for undertaking them determines the rate at which the project progresses. Other tasks can be fitted around the critical path. The individual tasks that make up the project are listed. The time needed to undertake the task (and, if appropriate, its cost) is then assigned. The way tasks connect to each other is analysed. Particularly important is recognising when one task cannot be undertaken until another has been completed. Many tasks will not have a unique time period/cost relationship. One can be played off against another. Many tasks can be done quicker, though only if more is spent. Figure 11.1 shows how the stages of the consulting project described in Chapter 2 are organised into a critical path. The times shown are typical.

Budgeting means assigning expenditure in two dimensions: *over time* and by *type of expenditure*. The timescale will depend on the length of the project. Typically, weeks or months are used as the basis. The type of expenditure will depend on the nature of the project. Some of the most common categories of expenditure on consulting projects are detailed in Table 11.1.

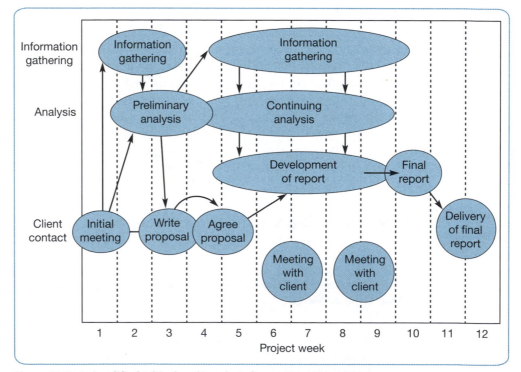

Figure 11.1 **A simplified critical path analysis for a consulting project**

Table 11.1 A typical budget sheet for a consulting project

Expenditure	Period 1	Period 2	. . .	Period N	Category total
Consultant's fees*					
Travel expenses					
Periodicals and reports					
Commissioned market research					
Communications					
Report preparation					
Period total					Grand total

(*Daily rates × number of days worked)

The budget has two parts. Expected expenditure is a forecast of what will be spent. This is money that must be reserved for the project. This is replaced by actual expenditure as the project progresses. Comparison can then be made. Actual expenditure is often different from what was budgeted. However, both under- and over-expenditure should be avoided. Over-expenditure means additional funds must be found while under-expenditure means money that could have been used elsewhere is tied up.

11.3   Organising meetings

The formality of a meeting with the client will depend on:

- the situation;
- the relationship with the client;
- the objectives and significance of the meeting and those present.

Meetings are an important tool in progressing projects and so thought and preparation should go into setting up and running meetings properly. Some key considerations are as follows.

The meeting's objectives

- What will be achieved as a result of holding it?
- How do the objectives of the meeting fit with the objectives of the project as a whole?
- Are all present aware of the objectives?

The project log is a good place to review these issues.

Is the meeting really necessary?

Might a less disruptive and time-consuming form of communication be better? Being called to a meeting he or she does not feel to be necessary will not impress the client.

255

Consider who needs to be present at the meeting

People are easily offended if they are not invited to meetings to which they feel they should have been. However, being asked to attend a meeting that is not relevant makes people think that their time has been wasted. The solution is to advise the client to inform people about the meeting, explain its objectives and ask whether they would like to attend. There will be more commitment to making the meeting successful if everybody attending has requested to be present.

Plan ahead

Recognise that people are busy and diaries fill quickly. Try to give as much notice of the meeting as possible to give people a chance to plan their schedules.

Consider what information will be needed at the meeting

Inform people of the information they are expected to bring to the meeting. If information is to be shared and discussed at the meeting, prepare and circulate it in advance. Consider the way the information might be presented to make it easier to understand and more likely to have an impact.

Prepare an agenda for the meeting

An agenda should detail the points that the meeting needs to discuss and should be distributed in advance, along with the objectives of the meeting and indications of special information that will be required. Make sure that the key roles have been allocated for the meeting. These include:

1 A *chairperson* who has overall responsibility for coordinating and guiding the meeting. This may or may not be the project leader.

2 An *opener* who has responsibility for opening the meeting and giving a short presentation on what the objective of the meeting is and what the background issues are. This person is usually the chairperson but having the same person in both roles is certainly not compulsory.

3 Someone to take the *minutes* of the meeting. Formal minutes detailing everything that has been said are rarely necessary unless the meeting is particularly formal. However, a short statement of the objectives of the meeting and details of the key action points decided upon (and who it has been agreed will follow them up) are useful. The minutes should be distributed to all who attend (plus other interested parties) as soon as possible after the meeting. Even if formal minutes are not required, the project log is a good place to keep personal notes on the meeting.

4 Someone to *facilitate* the meeting. This person acts in a neutral capacity and can either arbitrate in conflicts or move things forward if the meeting has become stuck in irrelevant details. External consultants are often called in to perform this role as they are seen as unbiased.

Plan the venue

Make sure the room is adequate for all who wish to attend and allocate places rather than just letting people sit where they want. If you know that two people are particularly likely to come into conflict, sit them next to one another rather than opposite one another (it is much harder to argue with someone who is sitting next to you!). Before the meeting starts ensure that any equipment is available, set up and working. Are people seated so they can see them properly?

Maintain focus on the key issues

Meetings are a great chance for people to get together and discuss the host of issues they have on their mind. It is easy for the original objective of the meeting to be lost and the conversation to be diverted into discussion of a variety of unrelated issues. It is the job of the chairperson to maintain the focus of the meeting and ensure that it keeps to its objectives, though a good facilitator can also do this. When productive discussion on one agenda point has come to an end, close discussions on it with a summary of the key points raised and move on to the next point. Have an idea of the time available for each agenda point to keep the meeting on schedule. If the discussion has drifted on to an issue unrelated to the core business, first redirect the discussion by summarising the point being discussed and offer to take it to a separate forum.

Involve everybody

An important role for the chairperson is to ensure that space is created for everybody to contribute. If someone is dominating the debate, you need to interrupt politely and end the talk by saying, for example, 'That's actually a very interesting point – how does everybody else feel about this?' or 'Thanks for raising that, A. How will it affect you, B?' The point of these interventions is to move the conversation on while leaving the dominating speaker with the feeling that he or she has made a useful contribution.

Encouraging quiet people to speak is often just a case of redirecting the conversation towards them such as, 'What's your opinion, A?' or 'How will that affect your approach, B?' If someone is particularly nervous about contributing in meetings, it may help to discuss their contribution with them before the meeting and set aside a slot. If an issue comes up which will benefit from the comments of one who has taken a particular role, use this to draw that person into the discussion.

11.4   Organising workshops

Workshops are a favourite tool of consultants. At times, they are little more than a glorified meeting where the consultant seeks to engage with the client by getting the latter more involved. At other times, they are really a training session where the consultant is just imparting knowledge. However, used properly, they can be a powerful tool to get some new thinking on problems and develop radical solutions. In this case, the consultant should act as a *facilitator*. They should not be *telling* but *advising* and *guiding* the client towards a conclusion. To have a successful workshop, you should think about the following:

- What is its purpose, i.e. what are the expected outcomes?
- The design of the session should ultimately be a joint decision between you and the client, although you can make some suggestions.
- The attendees – only invite those who will make a contribution, do not include any just for political reasons (which you might do for a meeting).
- The agenda should be flexible to accommodate unexpected outputs and you should be ready to work with alternative scenarios.
- Venue is critical – strategy workshops are often off-site, so that there are no distractions from daily office life.
- The atmosphere you create has a large impact – even people's dress can affect how they think and act.
- Set ground rules for the day – the most common nowadays is to get people to switch off their mobile phones!
- Work within the agreed timetable, i.e. start and *finish* on time.
- Finish the session on an upbeat message – emphasising all the good work that has been done, so that everyone will view the session as a success.
- If there are to be a series of workshops, ensure that preparations for the next one are communicated to the participants, so that they are well prepared.

11.5 The importance of time management and effective time management

Effective time managers follow a series of simple rules so that they make best use of their time. With a little practice these rules can become second nature. The most important rules are as follows.

Be aware of time

A task may seem a long way off but deadlines loom up. It can quite suddenly become current, especially if the project is a busy one and you are distracted. Be aware of the tasks that are coming up. If you don't have the kind of memory that is good at keeping track of what needs to be done when, a time management system that reminds you (discussed below) can be of great help.

Prioritise and anticipate tasks

The consulting project will demand that some tasks are undertaken before others. Some tasks will be 'bottlenecks'. If they are not done, many other things will be held up.

A critical time management skill is to recognise which tasks are more important at a particular time. The priority of a task will change as the project progresses. A task that is of low priority can suddenly become high priority, especially if it is delaying the rest of the project.

> **Do tasks when you *can* – not when they *need* to be done.**

Assess what jobs can be undertaken now even if they are not an immediate priority.

Avoid putting off jobs

Team working allows people to undertake a specialised role. Even so, there will still be some jobs we don't feel like doing. However, doing them gets them out of the way and leaves you free to take on those tasks you do enjoy doing. Ask why you don't like doing it. Can the task be undertaken in a different way so that it is less onerous?

Break down tasks

If a complex task is broken down into smaller parts, it may be possible to approach it in more manageable stages. This is sometimes referred to as *eating the elephant*. The point is if you approach a large task all at once, it may seem overwhelming – just like eating a whole elephant in one go. However, if you break it down into smaller pieces to tackle, then over time you can complete this project which seemed so onerous at the start.

Ensure deadlines are understood

Make sure that all involved in the project are clear on deadlines. If in doubt, raise the issue. Be ready to plan, discuss and negotiate deadlines, especially for non-critical tasks. Make sure that agreement is finally reached and that all are aware of that agreement.

Be prepared

Preparation for meetings not only means contact time is used effectively, it will also project an overall professionalism that will reassure the client. Before a meeting, decide on the objectives of the meeting. What outcomes are desired from it? Define an agenda for the discussion and stick to it. If information is needed, ask whether the client should be given notice so that it can be collated. If the client will need information, make sure it is taken to the meeting or sent beforehand.

Support others with time management

Someone, whose time management is poor, can let the whole team down. Always make sure others are aware of deadlines. If someone is having problems with time management, advise them on how they can improve. Build in interim deadlines so that outputs can be checked before they become critical.

11.6   Time management systems and dealing with slippage

A time management system has two essential parts. First, it is a guide to breaking down projects into their component tasks (*eating the elephant*). Second, it is a way of reminding you when the task is due to be completed. A third part, a guide to reviewing the task may also be included.

One-page plans

A one-page plan is a flow chart that illustrates the stages of the project. Time is usually depicted along the horizontal axis. Different types of activity are defined on the vertical axis. This may take the form of the critical path analysis discussed in Section 11.2. The project can be monitored as it progresses along the horizontal axis. The jobs coming up, and how they connect to other jobs, can easily be reviewed. The consequences of pushing a task back can also be seen.

Tasks-to-do list

A list of tasks to do is a system that divides the project into intervals (usually weeks or days). Each interval is given a page of its own and on this page the tasks that need to be done can be listed. Some prefer to list only the major task headings. Others like to put in a great deal of detail. It is a matter of how much reminding you need. A simple Excel spreadsheet can be used here.

The project log

The project log can be used as the basis of or to support effective time management. A tasks-to-do list can easily be added to it, as well as a one-page plan. The project log not only allows you to keep track of tasks and make time management more effective, it also provides a forum for their review, thus making time management part of the active learning programme. It should form part of the project files that are kept in a shared electronic system such as Dropbox, so that all members of the team can view it and be kept up to date.

Dealing with slippage

If a project has slipped behind schedule there are a range of options available (ACCA, 2010). These are:

- **Do nothing** – it may be accepted that things are best allowed to continue as they are.
- **Add resources** – if capable staff is available and it is practicable to add more people to certain tasks it may be possible to recover some lost ground. This may require additional funds or the possible sub-contracting of some work.

- **Work smarter** – consider whether the methods currently being used are the most suitable, perhaps prototyping could be used.

- **Replan** – if the assumptions that the original plan was based on have been proved invalid, a more realistic plan should be devised.

- **Reschedule** – a complete replan may not be necessary. It may be possible to recover some time by changing the phasing of certain deliverables or taking activities normally done in sequence and fast-tracking them to be done in parallel.

- **Introduce incentives** – if the main problem is team performance, positive incentives such as bonus payments could be linked to work deadlines and quality. Poor team performance may also need to be addressed through more negative responses, such as disciplinary action. This can apply both within the team and with contractors or suppliers who are involved.

- **Briefings and motivation** – if the project is lengthy it may prove beneficial for the manager to hold update briefings with the team so as to renew their energy and enthusiasm and thereby increase productivity.

- **Change the specification** – if the original objectives of the project are unrealistic given the time and money available, it may be necessary to negotiate a change in the specification. This could be either to reduce the number of activities or to reduce the level of quality required in each activity.

11.7   The function of the project log

A log is a day-by-day record of the consulting project. It summarises the activities, analysis, observations and experiences that occur as the project unfolds. The main benefits are discussed below.

It aids project planning activities

The consultant must have a detailed and up-to-date schedule of the tasks that need to be undertaken. This demands an understanding of how activities support each other and depend on each other. Once this schedule is in place it provides a series of milestones or benchmarks against which the delivery of the project can be monitored. These benchmarks have a 'what' and 'when' aspect: *what* must have been done and *when* it must have been done by. The log offers a ready device for monitoring the *what* and *when* of these outcomes and for triggering remedial action if an expected outcome does not happen.

It provides a summary of information collected

Information is rarely collected as a neat summary. Articles and reports need be sourced. Statistics and facts have to be identified. The log provides a good place to keep key data, a summary of the information collected and references back to primary sources. Ready access to this will make analysis and compiling the final report much easier.

It provides a secure location for notes taken when communicating

A large number of notes will be taken as a result of meetings, taking details from telephone conversations and recording the details of interviews. Taking written notes helps in two ways. First, the very act of writing something down helps reinforce it in our memory. Second, it provides a hard source to refer back to when our memories need refreshing. Using the log as a place to keep these notes means they can be found later.

It provides a forum for analysis

Using the log encourages analysis to be undertaken where and when it is necessary. Doing analysis as the opportunity arises means that its insights are immediately available to guide the project and direct the need for more information. If the analysis is sophisticated and is better left to a later time, the log can still be used. If a piece of analysis is undertaken by the group as a whole, or by one group member on behalf of the group as a whole, copies may be included in other group members' logs. Any analysis performed may well be included in the final report to the client and if so, it will act as at least a first draft that can be accessed easily. This will mean that you will not need to redraft it when writing the final report.

It encourages reflection on the consulting experience

The log, if used properly, can help the development of an active learning strategy, by encouraging reflection and facilitating analysis.

A few questions that you might consider reflecting on within the log include the following:

- What outcomes have been achieved at this stage of the project?
- How do these compare to the project plan?
- How did they compare with my own expectations? (The answer to this question may not be the same as the previous one!)
- How might they compare with other people's expectations? (In particular: other members of the group; the client; the project assessors.)
- What has gone well to this stage?
- What made it a positive experience?
- What might have gone better?
- Why were these aspects not such a positive experience?
- How might this experience be improved in the future?

It acts as a permanent record of the consulting exercise

It is useful to be able to refer back and find out when something happened, what was undertaken or what was said or agreed at a particular point. The log enables quick and productive review of the project as an aid to reflection on it and can be used to establish how much time was spent on a particular activity undertaken on behalf of the project. This can be useful for planning new projects. Information in the log can be used to resolve some of the disputes that inevitably occur when working in teams.

■ It provides a long-term learning resource

It can offer a guide to personal strengths and the areas that might be developed in the future. It can offer insights into what types of tasks we enjoy doing (and why). In this respect, many students, for example, find it very useful as a source of points to discuss at job interviews.

11.8 What to include in the project log and suggested formats

The discussion in the previous section gives an indication of the kind of information that can feature in the log. At this stage it is useful to summarise what might be included. Key headings could include:

- the date;
- the stage of the project;
- the status of the project (actual outcomes relative to objectives);
- a summary of activities undertaken since the last entry;
- the objectives of those activities;
- minutes of meetings/workshops held;
- details of information gathered;
- notes from communications;
- details of analysis undertaken;

and, in addition to these 'routine' headings, for the student consultant:

- reflections on the consulting experience.

The length of the inclusions under each heading will vary and not every heading will be needed for every day's entry. It will mainly be text, but mind maps and other creative devices can also be used (see Figure 11.2).

The project log is a working tool that the consultant team uses to assist in delivering the consulting project. It is not intended to be shown to the client. It is a flow of ideas, comments, notes and reflections. It does not matter if it is rough and untidy in appearance. What matters is that it works as a store of notes on the project and a stimulus to reflection. The project log should not be completely lacking in organisation, though. You want to be able to find ideas later. You could use a standardised form that prompts entries under the points discussed above. An example of how this might be filled in is given in Figure 11.2. A blank electronic form is used in this case. This approach is good because it disciplines thinking about the project.

You may feel that a standardised format is restrictive and prefer the latitude to create entries as and when they are necessary in the way you think fit. Notes from meetings can be added as the meetings happen. Leave some room for later reflection. However, do not be tempted to revise and refine notes to produce a polished document. Rather, let it stand as a honest and immediate reflection on experienced events (which is what they are meant to be).

New strategic direction for W&G Cracking Pie Company
12 June 2015

Key achievements to date:
• First two workshops held
• Vision of where W&G CPC wants to go
• Strategic options identified

Next steps:
• Present strategic options to Board and agreed favoured option
• Objectives for workshop 3

Notes:
• Need to have a 'pre-meeting' with chairman and chief executive to brief them on issues raised

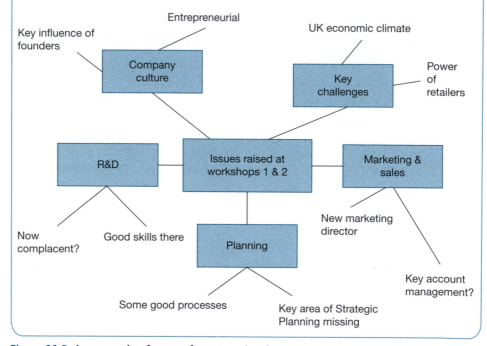

Figure 11.2 An example of a page from a project log

Team discussion points

1 The final report evolves as the project progresses. Using the team roles discussed in Section 11.1, discuss how each role can contribute to the overall development of the report. How might the logistics of this be managed? What will be the time management responsibilities of each role?

2 Consider the formats available for a project log. Decide on one which you think will work for you. Present your format to the rest of the group. Say what you think are its strong points. Invite (positive!) criticism to identify what might be its weak points. After each group member has done this, consider your choice of format. Can it be improved by making some modification? Does another format look better? Select the format you will use for the project. Don't forget, it is an individual choice. It is not necessary that every member of the group use the same format.

Summary of key ideas

- A few simple planning rules can make the consulting project more rewarding and more successful.
- The consulting project will be managed around the key tasks of collecting information, performing analysis, communicating with the client and the overall coordination of the team.
- The team can take on individual roles based on these key tasks.
- Time is one of the consultant's most precious assets.
- An ability to manage time makes the manager more effective, in terms of both productivity and, potentially, leadership.
- A number of simple systems can be used to support time management.
- The project log provides the basis for a good time management system.
- The log should include details on the stages of the project, events and communications that take place. It should consider these in relation to the objectives set and the outcomes achieved. It is also a place where information important for the project may be noted and analysis undertaken.
- Critically, the log is a place where reflection on outcomes, both positive and negative, may be made. The log is a private document. Experiment with formats and find one that works for you.

Key reading

Blanchard, K. and Johnson, S. (2015) *The New One Minute Manager*. London: Thorsons Classics.
Nokes, S. and Kelly, S. (2014) *The Definitive Guide to Project Management* (3rd edn). Harlow, Essex: FT Publishing International.

Further reading

BPP Learning Media Ltd (2010) *ACCA Paper P3 Business Analysis Study Text*. London: BPP Learning Media.
Haverila, M., Bateman, E.R. and Naumann, E.R. (2011) 'The drivers of customer satisfaction in strategic consulting engagements', *Management Decision*. 49, 8, 1354–1370.
Highmore Sims, N. (2006) *How to Run a Great Workshop*. Harlow, Essex: FT Prentice Hall.

Loflin, J. and Musig, T. (2007) *Juggling Elephants*. London: Penguin.

Little, B. (2011) 'The principles of successful project management', *Human Resource Management International Digest*. 19 (7), 36–39.

Newton, R. (2013) *The Project Management Book: How to Manage Your Projects to Deliver Outstanding Results*. Harlow, Essex: Pearson Education Ltd.

Newton, R. (2014) *Brilliant Checklists for Project Managers* (2nd edn). Harlow, Essex: FT Prentice Hall.

Tracy, B. (2013) *Eat That Frog! 21 Great Ways to Stop Procrastinating and Get More Done in Less Time* (Rev edn). London, Hodder Paperbacks.

Case exercise

Siam Lubricants

Siam Industrial Lubricants (SIL) is an autonomous part of a multinational oil company, having been acquired ten years ago as part of the latter's strategy to diversify away from its core business of drilling and refining oil. Having been largely left to its own devices, Siam's Board has pursued its own strategy for growth, based largely on developing strong relationships with its customers. These have ranged from large multinationals to smaller regional players. All have been given the same level of high customer service and typically offered bespoke products to suit their exact needs. The parent company, though, is not happy at the declining profitability of SIL and has brought in a well-known strategy consultancy to review and recommend a new approach. The consultants have delivered their report and one of the areas that they have highlighted is the number of products that SIL now offers. This has mushroomed from 2,000 ten years ago to now nearly 8,000. Without doing any detailed analysis, the consultants believe that this number needs to be significantly reduced, based on the 'Pareto' principle. This is where typically 80 per cent of sales come from 20 per cent of products (see Section 6.2).

SIL's Board think at first that they can do the product rationalisation themselves but on closer examination realise they have no idea where to start. Just getting rid of the low sales products would not be easy. Quite a few were supplied to their major customers. The risk was that by removing some of the products available to these key customers, the latter may take *all* their business away. There was also a culture of innovation, which on the positive side meant that SIL was continually offering new and better products to its customers. On the negative side though, it may be construed as merely tinkering and a lot of supposedly different products in fact fulfilled a very similar function. The board decided that a new approach was needed and has called you in as part of a specialist consultancy.

You meet with the client team, who are all very personable and willing to help, but lack focus and are nervous of the potential changes ahead. Your first task is to break down the very long list of products into more manageable groups. The first split you do is by broad product function i.e. what it does and the second is by customer. The first is a nice short list of 8 but the latter is over 500. The technical team believe that you should use the former as the basis for this product rationalisation exercise but the sales team think you should use the latter. You realise though that both sides have to be looked at in order to come up with the best, i.e. most profitable solution for SIL. You are being pushed by the board to come up with a solution quickly so the changes can take effect in this financial year. You realise that you cannot do this alone and you need to get the technical and sales members of the client team to work with you on a solution.

1 What would be your approach to getting to the optimal solution?

2 Develop a critical path analysis for the stages that you would go through.

APOLLO TECH SOLUTIONS CASE STUDY

Part Three

Sam Arnott was looking forward to his annual summer break and everything seemed to be going well with Project Moon. The analysts, working with their counterparts from Apollo, had amassed a huge amount of internal data and were studiously working their way through it. Allen had appointments for initial interviews with all the senior managers that needed to be seen and together with her consultant colleague had arranged telephone conferences with Apollo Advance's main customers. The attendees for the first workshop, due to be held the week of Arnott's return from holiday, had been chosen and Klingner had promised that one of their ICT experts would be available to attend the critical first two workshops. Just as Arnott was about to leave on the Friday afternoon, Allen came to see him 'just to check that he would be available on his mobile where he was going'. Arnott made it clear that in his absence, all queries should be directed to Jill Davy.

At the start of week four, Arnott returned refreshed from his holiday and was looking forward to the first workshop at the end of the week. He called in Davy to check on progress. When she arrived to see him she seemed a bit nervous, especially when he asked her how things were going. It transpired that some of the critical data about customers for the first workshop looking at 'where are we now?' was not available. This was the task allocated to one of the inexperienced analysts as Allen had assumed that this would be a relatively straightforward task. All the analyst had to do was to ask the respective sales managers for three sets of figures for each customer for the last three years: total sales, sales by product line and total gross margin.

While all the sales managers in AA who were asked for this information, diligently gave some figures, it became clear that some of these were estimates (as managers didn't have any accurate figures) and those that were based on real information used different methods to calculate sales and gross margin. Some sales were booked only when the money was received by Apollo and others when contracts were signed with an agreed fee, for example. Gross margin was even more complicated as just about every customer contract was calculated differently from those including only the cost of providing the product and to those including varying levels of overheads as well. Of more

concern, Davy had only spotted the large discrepancies in the data late the previous week, when she had asked the analyst for the information.

This problem was a legacy of the way the Apollo Advance business had been built up over the years, with many personnel joining Apollo from the acquired businesses. They had got used to 'doing things their own way'. Arnott soon realised that was going to be a major obstacle to progress and told Davy to quickly convene a meeting of her fellow commercial accountants to try and find a common methodology of working out these key figures. He also insisted that Allen should be involved as it was partly Ferguson & Co's fault that this issue had not been highlighted earlier because of the inexperience of the analyst. Davy and Allen were to report back to him by the end of the week with a solution. He then contacted Klingner and asked for his advice regarding the impending workshop.

Klingner's view was that the workshop should go ahead as it was important to maintain momentum and he also didn't want to signal to those outside the project team that there were issues. Klingner convinced Arnott that they could work with the provisional figures that Davy and Allen had promised him. Moreover, the focus of the workshop was less about actual answers but more about how the attendees (some of Apollo Advance's senior managers) viewed the business and how they responded to the challenges made by the industry expert from Ferguson & Co. So preparation for the workshop continued. Arnott hoped that this was the only issue he had to deal with that Monday morning. It was not to be. His PA came in and said that four senior managers from AA who had not been invited to the workshop had individually asked to get a full briefing from him on the project. He was reluctant to do this but realised that at least one meeting with these individuals was needed, so he told his PA to set up the sessions in the next couple of weeks.

While some in Apollo felt they were not being consulted enough, he also had to deal with more communication issues at the afternoon Executive Board meeting. He had hoped to give a positive report on progress but before he could start Irvine (CEO) complained that in the last three weeks, Klingner had insisted on seeing him every time he came to the head office, which was once a week. McPherson also said

Apollo Tech Solutions Case Study (continued)

that both Klingner and Allen had tried to have 'brief chats' to update him. Both asked Arnott whether all this was really necessary as neither Klingner nor Allen seem to give them much new information, rather it felt like a 'fishing trip' for more business for Ferguson & Co. Arnott said that he would talk to the pair and ensure only meetings with the consultants would be those that Irvine or McPherson initiated until the end of the project.

By the afternoon before the workshop, Davy (with Allen's help) had come up with a solution to the customer data problem. Arnott spent the rest of the day with them and other project team members crunching through the raw data to be ready for the following day. It was with some relief that the first workshop went well, even if it was a little uncomfortable for some of the participants. The consultants from Ferguson & Co were very challenging of AA's senior managers who were defensive when presented with the consultant's analysis of their current business. Many of the assumptions they held were shown to be untrue or misguided, such as large customers always being the most profitable.

There were more tensions in the second workshop, looking at 'where they wanted to be'. Many of the managers had grand aspirations for these dynamic new markets but often the industry expert from Ferguson & Co showed up their lack of technical expertise and true knowledge of these markets. Arnott admired the way Klingner was able to identify who was the key stakeholder in the room (seen by their peers as the leader in the field) and test out their true abilities. It was becoming clear that there were those in the organisation who were up to the challenge of turning around this business and there were others that were not.

However, when it came to present strategic options to Irvine, McPherson and Arnott, Klingner and Allen stuck to the 'non-people' issues, such as having a new customer management system, focusing on more profitable customers and investing in the three sectors that had the best long-term prospects for growth. Irvine and McPherson were happy with the outline plan and Project Moon proceeded to its final stage of building a new strategy and understanding the requirements in terms of implementation. The next two workshops ran smoothly and the stage was set to reveal the new strategy at a conference attended by all Apollo Advance's senior managers on the 3/4 September. Arnott and his colleagues from Apollo on the project team were tired because of the relentless pace set by Ferguson & Co but overall were happy with the outcome of Project Moon.

Questions

1 Did Arnott achieve the right balance between controlling the team and delegating the tasks? What would you have done differently?

2 How would you have handled the project shock of the customer data issue?

3 How should the 'people issues' been dealt with in this project?

PART FOUR

Delivering the product to the client

Chapter 12

Communication skills and presenting your ideas

Be sincere; be brief; be seated.

Franklin D. Roosevelt

Learning outcomes

The key learning outcomes from this chapter are to:

- recognise the importance of effective communication to consulting success;

- understand the process of communication;

- be able to establish objectives for communication;

- recognise that communication has rational and emotional aspects;

- appreciate the advantages and disadvantages of verbal, written and visual mediums for communication;

- recognise the importance of delivering your findings to the client;

- understand the means by which those findings can be delivered;

- appreciate some rules which will make the communication of findings and the implementation of change more effective.

You are nearly there, you have done all the analysis, conducted the client meetings and workshops. Now you need to present your ideas and convince the client of the benefits of implementing them. This should be the easy part, but in many ways it can be the most difficult. You could be drowning in information, as many consulting projects bring up many more issues and potential solutions in addition to the ones that were envisioned when the project started. You need to remain focused and clear about what is the 'big picture'. What is the 'big idea' that you want to communicate? It is perhaps a bit of glib 'business speak' but the lift (or elevator) test should be applied. Can you explain the idea to the client, so that he or she understands, in the time it takes to complete a short journey in a lift? The problem is that people generally do not remember large amounts of detail. That is why politicians are fond of 'sound-bites' – short pithy statements which convey their policies. Being able to communicate effectively is an essential skill for the consultant: without it, they cannot do their job properly.

12.1 The nature of business communication

The facility to communicate subtle and complex messages is what enables us to organise tasks:

- to decide what needs to be done;
- to allocate different jobs to different people;
- to discuss how they should be undertaken;
- to agree how the rewards of that cooperation are to be shared.

> **Communication allows us to build organisations and use them to create value.**

If the business is to take the consultant's advice of a new course of action, the consultant must communicate his or her ideas effectively. Communication is primarily about motivating people to act in a particular way. People act as a result of the information they are given and their actions are coloured by the nature, tone and context of the communication as well as by its content.

> **Consultants must understand the *how* of communication as well as *what* is to be communicated.**

Communication is a process, where there is a distinction between the sender of the message and its receiver. It goes through the following stages (see Figure 12.1):

1 The sender decides on what they wish to include in the message that has to be sent.
2 The sender decides on the medium to be used, i.e. verbal and/or visual.
3 Transmitting the message, where it is possible that the message may be confused by 'noise' interfering in the communication.
4 The receiver of the message actually receives it and decodes it.
5 The receiver interprets and acts on the message.

The whole process is governed by a feedback mechanism, whereby the sender knows if the message has been sent correctly depending on the reactions of the receiver.

This model tells us a lot about the nature of communication and how we can go about managing it. It highlights:

- the fact that we never send information directly – it must first be presented in some way;
- that communication can occur only if both the sender and receiver understand and share the language used;

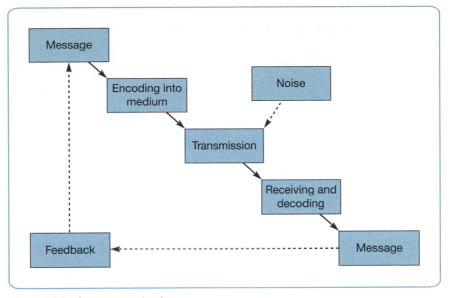

Figure 12.1 The communication process

- that the message may be interfered with by noise in the medium through which it is being transmitted and so the message may be misunderstood;
- that receiving a message is an active part of the communication process, not a passive one;
- that actions are taken as a result of communication.

These are important points that we will need to keep in mind when we start to consider the management of the communication process.

12.2 Communication as a business tool

People cannot make the right decisions in business unless they have the right information to hand.

> Communication is the means by which people obtain and transmit information and indicate what information they need in order to make decisions.

Actions are a result of the decisions that people make. Communication can encourage them to take one particular course of action over others. It is a process governed by feedback. Once initiated, communication leads to further communication. We judge other people's perceptions of our actions by the feedback (response communication) we get. In general, positive feedback encourages or reinforces particular actions. Negative feedback discourages them. Communication, information, decision making and action taking are then linked in a loop. Managing communication effectively and using it as a business tool, is about managing this loop in its entirety (see Figure 12.2).

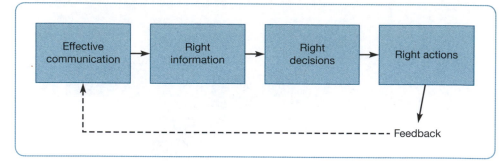

Figure 12.2 Effective communication loop

The extent to which formal and explicit objectives are set will influence the nature of the communication. A major presentation to the client will demand a formal consideration of objectives. A telephone call to check on some facts will have objectives that are implicit and will not need much explicit consideration. The following is a general framework for setting communication objectives. They apply to any communication: not just those between the consultant and client but those between members of the consulting team.

> **Ask yourself: what do I want to happen as a result of this communication?**

The question to be answered is not 'What do I want to say?' but 'What do I want to happen as a result of saying it?' Once this objective has been resolved, the following questions need to be asked:

- Who will be the recipients of the communication?
- What information needs to be conveyed?
- What actions should the recipient(s) take as a result of the communication?

The recipient may, for example, provide you with some information, but this has to be what is wanted or 'What do I want them to tell me?'

The other party may feel motivated or demotivated, so consider how the recipient should *feel* as a result of the communication and what information the recipients need in order to act in the way desired. What is the minimum information the audience will need to complete the actions required and whether it will be a hindrance or help if the recipients have to come back for more information. What level should the information be at? Think about how deep is the audience's understanding (and desire to understand) of specific details. Do they want a broad picture or a highly detailed account? How technically competent are the audience? How much technical detail do they need?

> **Communication is a continuous process, not a one-off exercise.**

What follow-up actions will be needed as a result of the communication to ensure the desired actions occur? This consultant–client communication does more than just transfer information – it is the basis on which an effective and rewarding working relationship is built.

12.3   Types of communication

Communication can be verbal (spoken), non-verbal (visual gestures, tone of voice), written and visual. All need to be used at the appropriate time and place to be effective.

Verbal communication has the following advantages:

1 Flexible – communications can be generated quickly.

2 Relatively low cost.

3 Allowing the communication to be supported by personal contact – persuasion may be easier.

4 Ensures the meaning of messages can be complemented and modified by gestures and non-verbal communication (see below).

5 Gives instant feedback.

There are, however, a number of disadvantages:

1 It does not (usually) leave a permanent record.

2 It can be difficult to control and direct (especially when large groups are involved).

3 Responses are expected quickly: there may be little time to plan and think ahead.

4 It can easily be dominated, especially where there are strong-willed people with opposing views.

Verbal communication often demands an immediate answer to a question unlike written communications. Planning for verbal communication therefore falls into two types: *prior* planning, where what is to be said is decided before the conversation occurs, and *ongoing* planning, which occurs while the conversation is taking place. The latter can be made much easier by a little prior thinking about the conversation that is to take place. Think about:

- What actions do I wish the recipient of the conversation to take?
- What information should be given?
- What should be the tone?
- How should the recipient feel?

Additionally, however, some consideration should be given to the kind of response the recipients might make:

- What kind of questions are they likely to ask?
- What additional information will be requested?
- What kind of problems and objections might be encountered?

The meaning transferred through verbal communication is not just about the words used, it is also how they are used. As an old saying goes: 'It's not what you say but the way you say it'. Attention should be given to the following:

- tone of voice – indicating emotions, for example, anger or expectation;
- timbre of voice – indicating attitude, for example, trembling with apprehension or sneering with condescension;
- timing – particularly important for indicating degree of consideration and conviction.

> We do not only use words when we communicate to one another. We have a whole array of *non-verbal* means of communications.

Non-verbal communication may be instinctive and can, if we are not careful, convey a completely different message from the words we are using. Some of the common ones are:

- Facial expression – some people may smile or laugh if they are nervous: not a good idea if you are delivering bad news.
- Body language – eye contact is important, for instance. Looking up at the ceiling all the time while delivering a message minimises its impact.
- Posture – the positioning of the whole body with respect to what is being communicated can be a form of expression. An open posture (arms relaxed by the side of the body) is more inviting than a closed, defensive posture (arms folded across the chest).
- Gestures – specific movements may add emphasis; for example, pointing, arm opening (indicating welcome) or looking at the watch (indicating boredom). Gesture can mirror meaning. Relaxed body postures are more inviting than tense ones.

The most important pieces of written communication the consultant makes are the initial project proposal and the final report. The consultant's report, whether backed up with a presentation or not, is often seen by the client as the 'product' of the consulting exercise – the thing that is actually being paid for. Consider the pros and cons below when considering whether a written communication is appropriate elsewhere during the project.

Advantages of written communication	Disadvantages of written communication
- There is time to plan the communication before it is delivered. - It is permanent; it can be stored. - It is unambiguous: what's written is written! - It is easily copied. - The receiver has time to analyse the content of the communication at leisure. - It can be supplemented with visual communications (e.g. diagrams, graphs).	- It is slow compared with verbal communication. - There is little opportunity to modify the communication with other means such as tone of voice and facial expression. - Feedback is restricted: there is a limited opportunity for the receiver to explore the communication with the sender (unless verbal communication is used as a supplement).

The visual image can be used to simplify complex ideas and relationships (see Chapter 9). It can also be used to support and add impact to other forms of communication, as images are remembered much more than words. However, without supporting explanation the image may be ambiguous and it may therefore require special interpretation skills. Visual images used in communication can be diagrams, graphs, photographs, sketches or drawings. Visual stimuli can be three-dimensional – for example, models. The visual image therefore should be used when:

- the subject of the communication is primarily visual;
- complicated ideas need to be simplified;
- complex relationships need to be demonstrated;

- the communication requires emotional impact;
- the message needs to be remembered as we remember information in the form of images much better than in a verbal form.

> **Visual communication really comes into its own when it is used in conjunction with other forms of communication, such as written text and the spoken word.**

The visual medium is very effective at representing information in a way that is memorable, draws attention to relationships and has impact. People will tend to remember five to seven pieces of information from a visual image. Try to organise the information that you wish to communicate so that each image has around this number of key points. Include not only facts but also relationships between facts; so not only that this year's sales are £2 million but also that they are larger than last year's and smaller than is hoped for next year.

Be creative with visual images. Graphs are a good way of illustrating facts and the relationship between them, but their impact can be made greater by customising them with bespoke images. Complex arguments can be made clearer by the use of flow diagrams that indicate how different aspects of the argument are logically interrelated. Images can also indicate the way the audience is expected to feel about the information. Imagine a graph of a company's sales performance to which has been added the illustration of a rocket soaring away in flight – or the illustration of a sinking ship! As a test for a visual image, ask the following questions. If the audience were asked to summarise the image, what five facts would they indicate? How would they feel about those facts? That is, would they react positively or negatively?

12.4 Planning the communication

The communication of the findings of the consulting exercise to the client is important as the client is likely to see this as what he or she has 'paid for'. The consulting project will have generated a lot of information and ideas. The main challenge in producing the communication is organising that material so that the message you want to send is delivered in a coherent and convincing way. Barbara Minto, a consultant for McKinsey & Company who went on to specialise in communication, describes one very effective approach in her book *The Pyramid Principle* (2008). The basis is to organise ideas into a hierarchy (a pyramid) so that they are sorted and interrelated. Minto lays down three rules for connecting ideas:

1 Ideas at any level in the pyramid must be summaries of the ideas below them; conversely, ideas at any level may be expanded upon at a lower level.

2 Ideas in each grouping (pathway in the pyramid) must be ideas of the same kind – that is, they must relate in some way and can be grouped together.

3 Ideas in a grouping must be ordered according to some internal logic.

She advocates two ways of approaching the problem: top down and bottom up. The former concentrates on the central theme of Subject, Question, Answer, Situation and Complication.

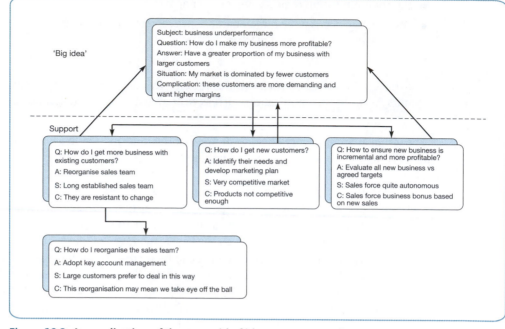

Figure 12.3 An application of the pyramid of ideas

An initial hypothesis is put in for the main Question and Answer. This is 'challenged' first by the top-level Situation and the Complication. Then underneath is the same analysis for the supporting statements. Figure 12.3 is an example.

This approach should be used when you are fairly confident about the main theme or big idea that you want to convey. If you are not, then a bottom-up approach may be a better place to start. Here you list all the points you want to make and then start to work out the relationships between them. Finally you draw conclusions from the relationships. In Figure 12.4, the issues highlighted from a typical consulting project are laid out in this manner as an example. The issues were:

- Sales are growing strongly in the own-label sector (over 10 per cent a year) but we are making no profit in this sector.
- Sales in the branded sector are falling by over 15 per cent a year but we are making a profit here, even if that too is falling.
- The factories are not at full capacity because of the falling sales, particularly in the higher volume branded sector where machinery and labour is often idle.
- A lot of stock is wasted as they are often delivered late to the customer and thus rejected for having too short a shelf life.
- The IT systems are old and it is difficult to communicate customer orders quick enough in order to manufacture on time.
- Raw material costs, including energy, are increasing faster than the price increases we are able to pass on to our customers.
- My management team is dysfunctional: most meetings end up with lots of arguments and no agreements!

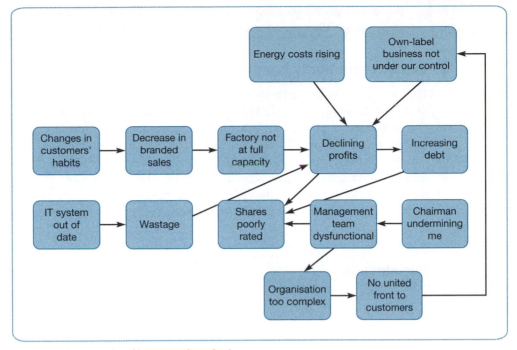

Figure 12.4 Example of how to relate the issues

- The chairman of the board is new and is seeking to assert his authority by undermining me and my efforts to improve the company's position.
- The shares are poorly rated and we have high levels of debt, which makes it difficult to make the necessary investment to update IT systems, for example.
- Our organisational structure is too complex and it is therefore difficult to make decisions; more critically, we do not present a united front to our powerful customers.
- Our products are suffering from the current trends in healthy eating.

From this the following conclusions could be drawn:

- Need to review how we do business with our key customers;
- Have to develop a new more simplified organisational structure;
- Ensure our manufacturing is used optimally across all our businesses.

12.5   The consulting report

A report provides a tangible, accessible and permanent communication of the findings of the consulting exercise. It need not be a long document.

> The consulting report should be a succinct and impactful presentation of the opportunity you have discovered for the business.

Remember your objectives: it should be a call to action. For an example of a consulting report, please see the Appendix. The report may comprise the following sections.

Executive summary

This is a summary of the findings of the consulting project. This will certainly be read in detail and so is the most critical part. It must be short and clear. Use bullet points to isolate and summarise your ideas and recommendations. There are two key questions about the executive summary. First, does it invite the reader in? On reading the executive summary will the reader be motivated to delve further into the report? Second, if the reader reads only the executive summary, what is the message he or she will get? These two questions may seem contradictory but they are not. If the executive summary is both complete and an invitation to go further, it will have impact and set the scene for the expansion of the ideas it relates.

Introduction

The introduction should highlight the context of the report. It should give any relevant information on the business and its situation. It should also specify the goals, objectives and outcomes that were agreed originally as covered by the original project proposal.

Body of the report

This is the part of the report where you can expand on your ideas and develop your case. The body of the report can be given a suitable title. It may be broken down into subsections if appropriate. Don't forget, it is generally better to have a lot of short, well-defined and titled subsections than long sections. They make reading and later accessing easier. The pyramid discussed in the previous section can be used to organise the material for the body of the report. Lay out the skeleton of your overall case first and then flesh out the details later. Be explicit. Tell the reader what your case will be and promise to support it later. Use internal references to signpost where your ideas are going. You may also want to use visual representations of ideas and information.

Summary and recommendations

Remember your objectives. You should close your report with a final call to action with a succinct summary of findings and the recommendations listed as bullet points. This not only repeats the message but also makes the recommendations accessible. It might feel that you are repeating yourselves by saying the same thing in the executive summary, the body of the report and then again in the summary of recommendations, however, this re-enforces the message.

Appendices

Be cynical and assume they won't be read! They are a good place to put any information that you have used to make your case and that might be of interest to the reader in the future but does not need to be in the main body of the report. However, information that will be of use in the implementation of recommendations (say a list of potential customers) should not be hidden away in appendices, it should be highlighted and accessible in the body of the report.

The report is a representation of your efforts and so you should make time for its planning and preparation. Check the copy and make sure that spelling and grammatical errors have been removed. It is usually better to have someone other than the report writer to do the copyediting. A variety of graphics can be used to decorate the report. But ultimately, it is the substance of the report that matters. A simple, well-written, well-laid-out report relating ideas that will have a real impact on the performance of the business is much better than a report rich with graphics but lacking substance.

12.6 Formal presentations

> A formal presentation allows the message to be fine-tuned using both verbal and visual communications, to get instant feedback from the client and to respond immediately to points and questions.

To be effective a formal presentation must be well organised and delivered with confidence. It is worthwhile to take time to plan the visual aids to be used to ensure they are to have an impact. Some useful points to remember are as follows:

- Analyse the audience. What images will they find relevant and will have impact? What interpretative skills do they have?
- Do not make the images too complicated. Clear, simple images have much more impact.
- Consider the relationships you need to communicate. Use images that emphasise the relevant relationships.
- Do not forget you can use a sequence of images to build up ideas.
- Use the pyramid principle to organise your message.

The images in the presentation should be used to support the presentation. They are an *aide-mémoire* for the presenter and add impact to what the presenter says. Colour is an effective stimulus in visual communication and can be used to differentiate relationships (say, by the use of different coloured lines on graphs) but colour information is lost in black and white hard copies. The following are a few points for producing effective visual support of the presentation.

- Remember that the visual material is supporting the presentation, not making it! Do not put text on the screen and read from it.
- Keep the images simple. They should add impact to the presentation, not distract from it.
- Put up bullet points to indicate to your audience the key issues you are identifying. These will also act as an *aide-mémoire* if you are presenting without notes.
- Use lower-case text. Upper-case text is austere and can be difficult to read.

The rules for a presentation are the same as for any other communication. Think about what you want to achieve from it. Be sure of what you want people to do as a result of the communication. Analyse the audience. Some simple rules for an effective presentation are as follows:

- Rehearse and practise the presentation. This is best done as a team. Not everybody need be involved in the actual delivery, but all can add to it.

- Use notes as an *aide-mémoire* but try not to read from a script. It is better to consider the points you wish to make and learn them using the visual stimuli as a prompt.

- Time your presentation. Make sure it is the right length for the time available. Make mental notes of some time points to enable you to time the presentation and make sure it is on track.

- Before the presentation, check that the equipment (e.g. laptops, projectors, microphones) is working. Make sure that the slides you intend to use are in the right order.

- When making the presentation use confident body language. Pace your speech so you get your message across clearly.

12.7   Making a case, answering questions and meeting objections

Being influential with information is a matter not only of identifying the information which makes your case but also of delivering it appropriately to the audience.

Information will be more influential if it:

- is relevant to the decisions the recipient needs to make;
- is pitched at the right level of understanding;
- is presented in a form which makes it easy to understand and digest;
- is supported by impactful visual stimuli;
- is placed in appropriate opinion and feeling contexts;
- is delivered in a situation of good rapport (see Chapter 7);
- is part of an interactive process where the recipient is encouraged and supported to explore the information;
- has key points signposted and highlighted.

If you need to organise the information before presenting it, use the pyramid principle described in Barbara Minto's book.

It is useful to develop some skills in dealing with the questions and objections at the end of the presentation. Listen to the question being asked.

Consider the nature of the question being asked as well as the question itself. Is it a 'head' question, a rational seeking of further information, or a 'heart' question, a more emotionally rooted seeking of reassurance?

Some useful points to remember in answering questions are as follows.

- Summarise the question being asked before attempting an answer to ensure that you have understood the question and that the rest of the audience have understood it. If the question is complex and contains more than one question, break it down into individual questions.

- Answer the question to the best of your ability. If you do not have the necessary information to hand, say so. Take the questioner's details and offer to get back to him or her with the information.

- After answering a question, close the answer by asking the questioner whether the answer is satisfactory by saying something like 'Is that OK?' or 'Does that answer your question?'

Objections are a little more difficult to deal with. Objections may be more heart than head. They may be individual or may summarise what might be the concerns of the entire audience. Meeting objections may require more than fighting fact with fact. If you come up against an objection:

- Start by recognising the objection by saying: 'Thank you. I'm glad you raised that' or 'Right. I can understand your concerns there'. However, do not over-use this as, after a while, it sounds glib.

- Consider the speaker's feelings when meeting objections (even if he or she doesn't seem to be considering yours). If he or she is seeking reassurance rather than information, give reassurance.

- If the objection is clearly emotional or no answer is obvious, ask a question back in a non-threatening way, such as 'This is obviously a major concern for you. Why is that?' or 'Have you encountered this kind of problem before?' This should get the objector to explore his or her objection (forcing him or her to put it on a more rational footing).

12.8 Change programmes and communication

As discussed in Section 8.4, change programmes may fail to be implemented because of 'under-communicating the change vision' with the result that there is resistance to the change. So the importance of the 'change message' in readying the company for change is critical. Armenakis and Harris (2002) look at the five areas that the message needs to address.

- Discrepancy – employees need to feel that something is wrong and needs to change.
- Appropriateness – is the change proposed appropriate for the issues faced?
- Efficacy – will the change work and for individual employees, can I deliver it?
- Principal support – is the company and senior management behind this and willing to devote resources?
- Personal 'valence' – how will individuals benefit or be impacted by the change i.e. 'what is in it for me?'

They then identify what they refer to as three 'message conveying strategies' to create readiness for change.

- Persuasive communication – direct communication efforts;
- Active participation – involving people in activities designed to have them learn directly;
- Managing internal and external information, i.e. making the views of others available.

Of the three, they think that active participation is the most effective as the employees become fully engaged and feel that it is a partnership, rather than a directive.

Overcoming hostility to change

As discussed in Section 8.6, resistance to change occurs frequently and with it comes hostility, so the communication has to take this into account. In the previous section, we discussed how we may overcome objections in a formal presentation, but here we look at more widespread blocking forces that can occur during a change programme. Campbell et al. (2015) have examined the strategies that could be adopted when faced with a hostile challenge; see Table 12.1.

In the study they conducted, they concluded that the 'timing strategy' was the best generic choice for responding to a hostile challenge from a stakeholder. The 'existence strategy' was also highly preferred, while the 'ability' and 'desirability' strategies were the least preferred. In conclusion, Campbell et al. offer six practical lessons to help change agents manage communication and maintain credibility with stakeholders who have made a hostile challenge.

- Lesson 1: Diagnose the source of the stakeholder's hostility in order to determine the component of readiness you need to address.
- Lesson 2: Claim dealing with the challenge isn't timely as your default response strategy.
- Lesson 3: With an efficacy challenge, either deny something about the challenge exists or explain why answering the challenge isn't desirable.
- Lesson 4: Deny something about the challenge exists to deal with challenges to discrepancy and appropriateness, as well as efficacy.

Table 12.1 Five strategies for responding to a hostile challenge of discrepancy: 'why are we changing a successful system?'

Strategy	Strategy description	Sample response based on strategy
Existence	Deny that an item referred to in the challenge exists.	The current system creates a number of problems.
Agency	Deny that you are the agent for answering the challenge.	The internal work group that studied this system can best explain its benefits and efficiencies.
Timing	Deny that answering the challenge is a timely act.	I cannot explain this now; you will have an explanation when our annual report is released.
Ability	Cite reasons for your inability to answer the challenge.	I am unable to explain this because of its technical nature.
Desirability	Cite reasons that answering the challenge is not desirable.	The current system will not continue to be successful – change is necessary for us to stay ahead of competitors.

- Lesson 5: Claim you are not able to handle the challenge with caution and only when dealing with principal support or personal valence challenges.
- Lesson 6: Do not deny you are the right person for handling the challenge.

Team discussion points

1 Go back to the project proposal you have made to the client. Analyse it as a piece of communication. Ask the following questions:

   a   What was the objective of the communication?

   b   Does this objective meet the criteria set for objectives discussed in Chapter 5?

   c   What actions did you want the client to take as a result of reading the proposal?

   d   What is the mix of 'rational' and 'emotional' elements in the communication?

   e   Did you talk the client through the proposal on a one-to-one basis? If not, do you think this might have added to the impact of the proposal?

   Discuss these issues in your team.

2 Prepare a short formal presentation (of five minutes with one or two slides) on the theme of what you feel you have gained from the consulting project experience in terms of learning outcomes, transferable skills and enhanced career prospects. Each member of the team should give this presentation and invite (positive) criticism from the other members of the team.

Summary of key ideas

- An ability to communicate effectively is a critical skill for a consultant.
- Communication is not just about passing information; it is about getting the recipient of that information to act in a particular way.
- Communication has an impact at a rational and emotional level.
- Objectives should be set for communication.
- Communication can take place through verbal, written and visual mediums. Each has its own advantages and disadvantages.
- Verbal communication is influenced by more than just content – paralanguage and body language are also important.
- The final communication of the consulting findings is the 'product' the client is 'paying for'.
- The communication may take the form of a report, a personal presentation or a combination of the two.
- The communication should be planned with the objective of positively influencing the client and getting him or her to implement the ideas presented.
- Using the pyramid principle, organise your message.

- The most important part of the report is the executive summary; this sells the report to the reader and invites him or her in.

- A presentation should be planned in advance. Impact will be gained if the presentation is pitched to the audience, their level of understanding and interests.

- Visual materials should support the presentation, have an impact and reinforce the key ideas.

- Communication is a vital part of the success of change programmes

Key reading

Bourne, L. (2015) *Making Projects Work: Effective Stakeholder and Communication Management*. Boca Raton, Florida: CRC Press.

Minto, B. (2008) *The Pyramid Principle* (3rd edn). Harlow, Essex: FT Prentice Hall.

Further reading

Armenakis, A.A., & Harris, S.G. (2002). 'Crafting a change message to create transformational readiness'. *Journal of Organizational Change Management. 15*, 169–183.

Bowden, R. (2011) *Writing a Report: How to Prepare, Write and Present Really Effective Reports* (9th edn). Oxford: How To Books Ltd.

Bradbury, A. (2010) *Successful Presentation Skills* (4th edn). London: Kogan Page.

Campbell, K.S., Carmichael, P. and Naidoo, J.S. (2015) 'Responding to Hostility: Evidence-Based Guidance for Communication During Planned Organizational Change' *Business and Professional Communication Quarterly*. 78 (2), 197–214.

Hargie, O. (2010) *Skilled Interpersonal Communication: Research, Theory and Practice* (5th edn) London: Routledge.

Pedley-Smith, S. and Robinson, Z. (2010) *A Student's Guide to Writing Business Reports*. Wokingham, Berks: Kaplan Publishing.

Thompson, N. (2015) *People Skills* (4th edn). London: Palgrave Macmillan (Part II).

Weissman, J. (2008) *Presenting to Win: The Art of Telling Your Story* (Rev edn). Harlow, Essex: FT Prentice Hall.

Case exercise

Stanley Consumer Electronics

Stanley Electronics is a large multinational corporation whose main business is in electronic components, which is primarily business to business. However, its division, Stanley Consumer Electronics (SCE), sells final products direct to consumer. This means they are largely independent of the rest of the corporation in terms of the processes they need to be successful. Given their background, SCE are very technologically driven, rather than consumer led. This is a major issue as their main competitors are some of the leading consumer goods companies who are acknowledged as the best in terms of marketing to consumers. From a large strategic review of the SCE's overall business, it is recognised that this weakness in marketing expertise has to change if they are to improve sales and profits. A long-term project has therefore been initiated called 'Creating Marketing Excellence'. It has six key tasks:

- Improve the marketing processes;
- Improve the competences within marketing;
- Improve the learning within the organisation;
- Have better organisational fit to requirements;
- Make better use of the tools available;
- Reset the culture and mindset to a new way of working.

This is a large task and your consulting firm has been brought in to help the senior management at SCE deliver this project over the next 12 months. They are particularly looking for you to provide experience from your work with their main competitors on the latter's marketing processes. Your first task is to understand what SCE does now, so you look at both the 'official' process handbook and also interview key players to learn how the marketing function runs in reality. The senior management want a process imposed that mirrors 'best practice' from the competitors. However, you feel some resistance from the marketing department itself, who feel that the current way of working just needs tweaking, rather than a radical overhaul. After all, they will be the ones responsible for implementing the new marketing planning process and understandably, they believe they know what will work in their organisation.

Mindful of the sensitivities around this area, you prepare for the first workshop. The first part of this will be a presentation by you about 'where we are now' and the 'best practice marketing processes' in order to generate debate on the way forward.

1 Which of these two important areas would you tackle first and why? (Hint: most people would start with the 'now' and go to 'future' but a case can be made for doing it the other way round.)

2 You have identified a number of issues around the current way of working, how would you prioritise and summarise these? The issues are:

- No clear marketing objectives, only sales targets and market share (no idea on profitability by sector/product area).
- Marketing communications not quantified (no idea if they are working!).
- Product portfolio objectives not defined (impossible then to brief R&D).
- R&D decides on which new products to launch (the tail is wagging the dog!).
- Distribution strategy non-existent (just try and maximise shelf space, no idea on what that costs).
- No key account management with the leading retailers (SCE's sales department are often last in the queue to see the buyers).
- Pricing strategy is based on cost of components, not what the market will pay.
- Most of the marketing department have only worked for SCE.

Chapter 13

Learning from success

We become just by the practice of just actions, self-controlled by exercising self-control, and courageous by performing acts of courage.

Aristotle

Learning outcomes

The key learning outcomes from this chapter are to:

- learn how to hand over ownership of the project effectively

- complete a post-project summary and review;

- undertake follow-up projects and key client management;

- use the consulting project as a case study;

- recognise success in the consulting exercise;

- recognise how these successes provide evidence of transferable learning;

- be able to document these successes on a curriculum vitae and use them to support career development.

Handing the project over to client management is an important step, representing the final delivery of the work.

Section 5.5 discussed the importance of the 'control' phase, where ownership of the project is transferred to the client. It is at this stage that the client receives what they feel has been paid for. Hence it is the stage at which expectations are met or preferably exceeded. If this is to happen satisfactorily, it must have been clear from the outset the degree to which the responsibility of the project is about making recommendations or about *implementing* those recommendations. Even if the project is primarily concerned with making recommendations, it is important that these recommendations are presented in an actionable way with clear benefits outlined, so that the client has a clear plan of action to put them into effect and is motivated to do so.

13.1 Transferring project ownership

Consulting exercises can 'fail' at this point because the client does not follow the consultant's recommendations through.

Although the consultant is not exactly at fault because they cannot manage the client after they have left, they do bear some responsibility for not ensuring the implementation phase is adhered to. It would seem illogical that, having paid for the consultants' time, a client would not implement effectively; but any organisation is a group of individuals, not a homogeneous being. The main reasons why the implementation phase goes wrong are:

- The individuals in the client organisation who are expected to carry out the implementation of the project are given other priorities.
- The leadership of the organisation is faced with a crisis or different challenges to those addressed in the consulting project – for example, a major new competitor comes on the scene.
- The sponsors of the project leave the organisation or are assigned different roles.
- The benefits have not been properly communicated within the organisation, so that commitment is half-hearted.
- The forces of resistance and opposition to the project mobilise themselves adroitly to undermine it.
- The funds required to complete the implementation phase are diverted elsewhere.
- The initial momentum is not sustained once the external consultant has left.

Although it is not always possible, a follow-up meeting three to six months after the end of the project is a useful aid to see whether a project is still on track. Ideally, this meeting should be included in the original contract. It can also serve a number of other purposes including providing an opportunity for additional work for the consultant and an opportunity to add to the information in the case study (see Section 13.4). A limited period of free post-project advice would also enable the relationship to be continued.

13.2 Post-project summary and review

A dispassionate assessment of client satisfaction is a key part of the process.

The leading consulting firms recognise that their most profitable business comes from a loyal group of clients. This is because the cost of sales is lower than for new clients, as less work and fewer meetings are needed to achieve a sale. This works only when the client is continually satisfied with the work performed by the consulting company. The way to gauge this is first for the consultants involved to complete a post-project summary, and for an independent review of the project to be undertaken by a senior member of the consulting company. The latter usually involves a meeting with key members of the client company to discuss the project.

The post-project summary needs to include the following:

- the original aims and objectives of the project;
- the project charter;
- the time plan – predicted and actual;
- key successes – what went well;
- key issues – what did not go well or caused problems for the project;
- the end result, i.e. the final outcome of the project.

The project review should be in the form of an interview, as mentioned above. Key areas for discussion should be the overall capabilities of the consultants, where the consultants performed well and areas where they could have done better. Finally, there should be a conclusion as to how successful the project was in the end and whether the client was satisfied with the work and would use the consultants again. In this way, there should be an objective view as to how well the project was undertaken and an assurance that the client remains committed to the consulting company. A positive assessment will of course also act as a testimonial for future pitches to other potential new clients.

13.3 Follow-up projects and key client management

Building a long-term client relationship is an important objective for the consultant.

While some consulting business is gained through previous projects not being completed properly, this is a 'distress purchase' and not really beneficial for a long-term relationship with the client. It may also mean that the follow-up project is harder to undertake as a result, with greater resistance from the client. In short, this type of consulting work should really be kept to a minimum. Instead, consultants should 'build' on their previous work in a positive way, hopefully using the goodwill generated from the previous project.

Follow-up projects can be identified either by the consultants themselves, by the senior managers of the consulting firm or by the client. The key is to maintain momentum. There is little point in conducting post-project reviews a year after a project has been completed, as the client probably would have forgotten about it: it should be done as soon as possible. In addition, it would also be advisable for the same consultants to work on the follow-up to eliminate time and effort wasted on bringing new people 'up to speed'.

For the larger consulting firms, their preferred mode of operation is to have 'key clients'. These are large organisations that are regular users of consultants. Often the consultancies appoint senior managers to also be 'key client managers' for a particular company and their role is to ensure that there is a steady flow of business from their client. A key tool that they use for planning is the 'sales funnel' developed by Miller and Heiman. In order to keep a regular flow of projects, it is important to have potential and actual projects at every stage of the funnel (Figure 13.1).

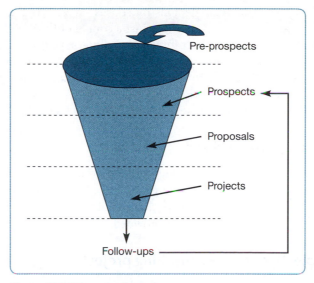

Figure 13.1 The sales funnel

Source: After Miller and Heiman, in Heiman, S.E., et al. (2011) *The New Strategic Selling*, London: Kogan Page.

Table 13.1 The project flow

Sales process	Funnel stage
Step 1 Identify potential targets	Pre-prospects
Step 2 Product offering	Pre-prospects
Step 3 Competitive review	Pre-prospects
Step 4 Promotion of services	Prospects
Step 5 Sales enquiries	Prospects
Step 6 Meeting potential clients	Prospects
Step 7 Project proposal	Proposal

As the likelihood of conversion increases as you move further down the funnel, the number of projects needed decreases. Similarly, as projects move through the funnel, it is vital to introduce new ones at the top to 'feed it'. Managing this funnel successfully is perhaps one of the hardest tasks for a professional consultant but failure to do so means an unstable business with a 'feast to famine' existence. Using the framework developed in Chapter 2, the sales process can be matched against the sections of the funnel (Table 13.1).

13.4 Using consulting projects as case studies

Past experience is an important marketing tool for the consultant.

One of the most important marketing tools for a consultant is past experience. Many new clients want the reassurance that the consultant has been involved in similar work. The best way for a consultant to demonstrate this is via case studies of previous consulting projects. They can be very brief; perhaps just a couple of lines such as 'helped a leading food and drink company with their international marketing strategy that doubled their exports'. However, for the case study to be most useful, the more information the better, although prospective clients do not want to read an inordinately lengthy tome! It is ideal if the information can fit comfortably on one side of A4.

However long the case study, there are some key elements that need to be included.

Description of client

Although the client may not usually be named for confidentiality reasons, a clear description needs to be given including their line of business, their size and possibly their position in their marketplace. Some background information as to why the client needed consultancy expertise should also be provided.

Objectives of the consulting project

These should be the key objectives that were defined at the start of the project and included in the proposal. However tempting it might be, these should not be changed to make the project look more successful, as this is a public document.

Work undertaken

This should be brief bullet points giving the reader an indication of the work undertaken in order to complete the project. This is important as it demonstrates capabilities in certain areas that may be relevant for a future client.

Achievements of the project

Wherever possible these should be tangible, that is, relate to hard facts such as sales, profits, cost savings, outputs, number of products remaining in the case of rationalisation. The figures given should be realistic, that is, reflecting the situation before the project started and a reasonable time after, as effects are not often immediate. Again, it is important not to be over-ambitious with what this project has achieved and to refer back to the original objectives.

It may be noted that some of the case studies outlined in this book refer to real consultancy projects undertaken by the authors.

13.5 Recognising the successes

> Undertaken with enthusiasm and with the correct application of the appropriate tools and methods, a consulting exercise will provide a positive experience.

Value will be created at several levels. It will be an opportunity to develop valuable and transferable skills. It will provide a chance to gain evidence of those skills. A high-level contribution will be made to the progression of a business venture. The consulting experience offers an insight into key senior management responsibilities: decision making at a strategic level and influencing the course of the business.

A successful consulting exercise – indeed, any successful managerial experience – has three aspects. First is the *experience* itself – the actual activities engaged in. These will include elements of the three skill areas essential to effective consulting: analysis, project management and relationship building. Second is the *learning* that is gained as a result of that experience. This is best achieved through the experiential learning cycle: the application of ideas gained through analysis and then active reflection on the outcomes. Such learning is valuable because it is *transferable*. The third aspect of the exercise is the *evidence* that that learning has been used to create value and that it can be used to create new value in the future.

13.6   Success and transferable skills

> A successfully completed consultancy assignment provides evidence of having developed valuable and transferable skills.

The successes achieved in the consulting exercise will provide positive and motivating memories. Yet they have meaning beyond this. Some experiences that will be of value in the future are as follows.

Objective definition

Managers are directed towards objectives. Objectives will be of value only if they are good ones. Indeed, bad objectives will take the venture down the wrong path and reduce value. The consulting exercise will have provided practice in creating objectives that are relevant, well defined, achievable and signposted.

Problem analysis

Usually a business's managers will wish to see it grow. This presents a challenge. Businesses are limited by both external and internal factors. The external ones arise from market and competitive conditions. There is a ceiling on the economic value that can be created, given the business's assets. Internal limitations stem from the way in which managers use those assets. It is rare that a little more value cannot be squeezed out of them by working them harder. The things that limit a business will be recognised by managers as 'problems'. Yet problems do not present themselves. If they are to be managed, problems need to be highlighted, defined and rationalised.

Knowledge and application of academic tools and frameworks

The client, especially a small or medium-sized enterprise, is unlikely to have the same degree of academic knowledge as the consultant. They may well not have heard of Ansoff, Porter, Mintzberg, Harmon and other management theory experts, still less be familiar with their various analytical tools. This is knowledge the consultant will bring to the project, and their ability to apply the right tool to the right situation – what the consultant may regard as obvious and commonplace – can appear almost a revelation to the client. These frameworks have all been developed as the result of studying business problems and solutions, and they genuinely represent a simple methodology to simplify the problem and develop possible solutions. Some of this knowledge should be transferred to the client as additional value beyond the specific nature of the particular project.

Strategy development

A strategy is, at one level at least, just a way of using assets. In particular, a strategy is a way of creating value out of those assets. The development of an effective strategy is one of the great challenges of management. It demands consideration of the internal competencies of the business and the potential of the environment it is operating in.

Project planning

A strategy will create value only if it is put into practice through the right plans. Plans are recipes for action. The project leader or preferably its champion must drive plans. Planning has formal aspects that assist in resource allocation and budgetary management.

External relationship management

Firms prosper only if they can attract external resources. This demands that relationships be built with the external parties who control those resources – customers and investors. Clearly, the ability to manage such relationships is very valuable. A consulting project will be successful only if a good relationship is built and maintained with the client. It presents an opportunity to develop such skills and gain evidence of their possession.

Teamworking

When employers are asked what they consider to be the most essential managerial skill, the answer they give most often is the ability to work as part of a team. The growth in team-working is one of the most prominent features in the development of management practice in recent times. Teamworking demands an ability both to integrate with and to motivate fellow team members.

Leadership

Leadership is perhaps the most precious managerial skill. It is certainly in demand and there are good rewards for managers who possess it. Leadership is a skill. It is not a fixed aspect of personality. Leadership is about behaviour: it is what leaders *do*. It can be learnt. But like any valuable skill it takes practice. The consulting project offers an opportunity both to recognise one's own leadership style and to put it into practice.

Any manager who can combine these skills is offering a great deal to the organisation they work for.

13.7 Knowledge Transfer Partnerships

KTPs are an ideal introduction to consultancy.

One way in which a recent graduate can 'test the waters' of consultancy in a way that will prove their ability is to be recruited as an associate in a Knowledge Transfer Partnership (KTP). Launched in 2003, KTP is Europe's leading programme helping businesses to improve their competitiveness and productivity through the better use of knowledge, technology and skills that reside within the UK knowledge base (universities, further education colleges and research and technology organizations). KTPs enable graduates to apply their degree, start a 'real' job straight away and gain further professional qualifications. They enable academics to lead rewarding and ongoing collaborations with innovative organisations which require up-to-date research-based expertise to succeed and enable firms to access highly qualified people to spearhead new projects, with the expertise to take the business forward with innovative solutions.

This is a government-funded programme which enables firms to recruit for a fixed-term (normally two years) and at a subsidised rate (in some instances 60 per cent of the salary) an associate with knowledge which is external to their competency and which will benefit their business. Once the government agency is convinced that the firm's proposal is appropriate for a KTP, the post is advertised and an associate is eventually selected. This person has the support of a full-time academic for the equivalent of half a day a week throughout the project. In addition, they enjoy free provision of research-based master's level education (such as M. Phil. or M. Res.) and can complete programmes of study leading to vocational or professional qualifications. The strain of working on the project and undertaking further academic study can be very demanding, but there can be no better proof to cite to potential employers than the completion of a successful KTP. Being public-funded there is inevitable bureaucracy involved, which the client organisation may often find tiresome, but the government-appointed advisors bring considerable experience, can provide new insights and enable the associate to utilise a network of expertise to which they would not otherwise have access. Further, the project is fully documented to a prescribed format and an overall assessment is given.

Government statistics show very positive outcomes for KTPs.

- For each £1 million of government spend, on average 112 new jobs are created, 214 company staff members are trained, profit before tax is increased by £4.25 million and £3.25 million investment is made in plant and machinery.

- For the knowledge-base partner, each project on average leads to 3.6 new research projects and 2 research papers.

- For associates, 60 per cent are offered (and accept) a position in their host company at the end of the project, 41 per cent register for a higher degree and 67 per cent are awarded one.

More information on KTPs can be obtained from http://ktp.innovateuk.org.

13.8 Recording successes on your CV and relating them in job interviews

A CV should be considered a personal advertisement.

The curriculum vitae (CV) is a particularly important piece of communication. It promotes the individual and what they have to offer to potential employers and clients. It records the individual's experience and achievements, but its *function* is to enable them to find a job – or at least to be invited to an interview. In today's ever more competitive employment market a good CV is essential. It needs to be accurate and honest, but the author should not under-rate themselves and should avoid modesty. Their ability has to be immediately obvious. The important information to include is as follows.

Personal information

Include name, age, date of birth, nationality, contact address(es), telephone number(s) and email address.

Education

Give details of formal qualifications (date, subject, grade, awarding institution).

Experience

Outline details of any employment undertaken. This should include the employer, the position and a brief summary of key responsibilities. Avoid verbosity. Use bullet points. This is also the place to refer to the consulting project.

Achievements

A potential employer is interested not so much in what the individual has done as in what they might do. Past achievements are evidence of what might be achieved in the future. Achievements should be documented in a positive manner. If possible, quantify the achievement. To illustrate, the following are examples of achievements of a consulting project that might be included:

Key achievements of the consulting project were:

- the development of a strategy which increased sales by 20 per cent;
- a plan which enabled the business to enter an international market worth over £100 million;
- an increase in productivity of 30 per cent;
- a sales brief that was instrumental in gaining new customers worth over £100,000.

Referees

A referee is someone who has experience of the individual's work and who is willing to make a positive statement about it. A satisfied client makes a good referee. The person's title, name, position, employer and contact details should be specified. They need to be consulted in advance as to their willingness to act as a referee, and ideally should be able to view the CV to reassure themselves they are not being asked to support bogus information.

13.9   Learning from failure

Failure provides lessons that can be learned from.

Not everything goes right. A consulting exercise is a complex experience. It presents a rich tapestry of intellectual and human engagements. Many experiences will be positive. But some, inevitably, will be negative. Mistakes and errors of judgement will be made. Information will be misinterpreted. Not all relationships will be good ones. Some people never seem to develop a rapport with each other. There will be disagreements between members of the team over objectives and courses of action. There may even be disagreements with the client.

Such experiences are part of managerial life. They cannot be avoided. But they can be managed. Errors that result from the misinterpretation of information or poor judgment present opportunities to challenge the conceptual models and frameworks being used. Some of these will be explicit. These are easy to revise. Others will be locked into the cognitive strategy being used. These must be reflected on and actively revealed. A good consultant is active in revealing his or her own cognitive approach and recognising how it might be developed.

Errors that result in misunderstandings and conflicts with other people must also be used as learning experiences (although they may be more painful than simple interpretive mistakes). Again the challenge is to analyse the experience and see what it says about how the person should be approached in the future and what it says about how people in general should be dealt with. Consider the message sent. How was it interpreted? How might it have been misinterpreted? It must be borne in mind that a message has paralanguage aspects (see Section 12.2) as well as a formal meaning. Also consider the other party's motivation. What did they want out of the situation? What did they get out of it? The key thing when interpreting a personal exchange is to avoid the temptation to allocate blame – either towards oneself or the other party. It does not help. Analysis should be dispassionate and honest.

Team discussion points

1 For the consulting exercise that you have completed, do a post-project summary and a case study, interviewing the client if you can.
2 What career options have you considered? What skills are going to be valuable to success in these careers? How has the consulting experience given you an insight into these skills? What evidence of their possession have you gained? How might you document this in a CV?

Draft a CV and review each other's as a team.

Summary of key ideas

- Handing over ownership of the project is a critical step. Recommendations should be motivational and action orientated.

- At the end of a project, it is important to do a post-project summary and review to learn from the experience and to help gain further business with the client.

- Follow-up projects can be a cost-effective means of gaining additional business.

- Management of regular clients is called 'key client management' and the use of a 'sales funnel' is a valuable tool to ensure continuity of business.

- A case study is also a useful tool to reflect on the project and to use to obtain new business.

- A consulting project is a great opportunity to develop and use skills that will be invaluable in a future career: managerial experience, active learning, achievements and evidence of achievements.

- Knowledge Transfer Partnerships are an excellent means of taking first steps into consultancy.

- An individual should use the consulting experience to sell themselves: their CV should document quantified achievements.

- Not all experiences on the consulting exercise will be positive. The negatives should be accepted as a proper part of managerial life but they should be learned from.

Key reading

Cope, M. (2010) *The Seven Cs of Consulting: The Definitive Guide to the Consulting Process* (3rd edn). Harlow, Essex: Prentice Hall (Chapters 8, 9 and 10).

Heiman, S.E., et al. (2011) *The New Strategic Selling* (3rd edn). London: Kogan Page (Chapters 17 and 18).

Further reading

Bright, J. and Earl, J. (2015) *Brilliant CV: What Employers Want to See and How to Say It* (5th edn). Harlow, Essex: Prentice Hall.

Cheng, V. (2012) *Case Interview Secrets*. Seattle: Innovation Press.

Eggert, M. (2007) *Perfect CV* (Rev edn). London: Random House Books.

Gertner, D., Roberts, R. and Charles, D. (2011) University-industry collaboration: a CoPs approach to KTPs, *Journal of Knowledge Management* 15 (4), 625–647.

Jay, R. (2013) *How to Succeed in Any Interview* (3rd edn). Harlow, Essex: Prentice Hall.

Kolb, D.A. (2015) *Experiential Learning: Experience as the Source of Learning and Development* (2nd edn). Upper Saddle River, New Jersey: Pearson Education.

Markham, C. (2004) *The Top Consultant: Developing your Skills for Greater Effectiveness*. London: Kogan Page.

Case exercise

Wessex Custom Design

Wessex Custom Design (WCD) was a small/medium enterprise located in Swindon. It had been established for approximately twenty years, with a turnover of £6 million. The company consisted of four divisions: Wessex Corporate Imaging, whose main business was the provision of high-quality outdoor signage; Wiltshire Property Services, a growing shop-fitting business; Wyvern Engineering, providing commodity steel and aluminium fabrications to industrial customers; and PowCo-RX, a business exploiting powder coating technology. Historically, Wessex Corporate Imaging tended to account for around 65 per cent of group turnover.

The strength of the company lay in the quality of its production and creativity. It therefore applied for a Knowledge Transfer Partnership whose objective would be not to address shortcomings so much as to establish how the company collectively could build on its strengths and enjoy healthier levels of growth and profitability. Turnover had stagnated in the region of £5.9–£6.2 million in the three preceding years. Senior management were of the view that the group was under-performing and that fixed costs were at too high a level for the turnover achieved. Productivity was therefore a key issue.

The company's approach was largely product-oriented and its style was opportunistic and entrepreneurial, driven by the talents and instincts of its two senior executives and joint owners. A key weakness was the lack of communication and coordination between the four divisions, some duplication of resource and misaligned accounting and IT systems which frustrated an easy management overview of the operation.

The application was successful and an associate appointed – Maria (24), a talented and vivacious Polish girl who had recently graduated with a first in business studies from the nearby university.

Early into the programme, WCD successfully divested PowCo-RX at a good price, thus generating a cash windfall which helped to ease their borrowings and improve the cash flow. This also meant that the associate could concentrate on the important strategic and operational issues rather than be drawn into the crisis management situation which might otherwise have been experienced.

Maria conducted a detailed analysis of the external business environment, the individual markets in which the various businesses were operating, their competitors and the WCD companies themselves, using proven academic models such as STEEPLE, SWOT, value chain, etc. She was also able, somewhat resourcefully, to source competitor financial information which brought into focus the sub-optimal profitability and relatively high overheads in the group, notably Wessex Corporate Imaging. These findings identified specific strengths and weaknesses for each division, together with recommendations as to the appropriate strategy for each. Some of these were quite radical: Wessex Corporate Imaging's offerings were considered too highly engineered and too high quality for a marketplace which had become more cost-conscious, Wiltshire Property Services were recommended to consider a more up-market positioning focusing on higher added-value opportunities with more carefully selected customers and Wyvern Engineering were encouraged to diversify their client base without prejudice to existing relationships, targeting particular market sectors.

The findings, together with observations on corporate versus divisional branding, operational style, performance monitoring and marketing processes (including website and brochures), were shared with company management in a series of meetings which Maria handled admirably. They understood her analysis and logic and supported her, opting for an incremental approach seeking quickly to introduce a good number of small, important changes as quickly as they could be implemented, rather than preferring a 'big bang' policy. However, it was further down the organisation that Maria had problems: comments like 'why should we change, we've always done it this way', 'what does a girl straight from college know about our customers – and who is she to tell us our products are too fancy?' and 'what are we getting for the money we are paying her?' began to be heard. Thus the proposals foundered for some months, as there was no visible implementation plan owned by the business's leaders.

Fortunately, a new sales and marketing coordinator had been hired from within the industry. He readily appreciated Maria's findings and recommendations and committed to make them happen. Unlike the owners, who were perhaps held back by their long-standing relationships with some of the opponents to her plans, and unlike Maria, who was young, very bright and dynamic – but inexperienced, he could impose change by virtue of the position he had been hired to occupy and his length of time in the industry.

In summary, the group would in due course need to define its vision, mission statement and key values; implement the agreed operating strategy; optimise the potential for investing in new technology; divest off-strategy interests; improve the site environment and reception area; use CRM software as enabling technology; assign responsibility for marketing tasks; create a management information system; use latest view and moving annual total in financial reporting; decide on the key performance indicators to be used to monitor the business' health and invest in leadership development and staff training.

Even by the end of the KTP, Maria could identify additional revenue somewhere in the order of £350,000, quantified savings of £6,000, free publicity worth £1,000, a 15 per cent saving in energy bills and carbon emissions, unquantifiable efficiencies in terms of time saving, improved project management, waste recycling and staff motivation and morale.

In the following financial year, WCD were trading 30 per cent, or £2 million, above the level at which they had stagnated at the time of the KTP application.

1 What were the difficulties Maria would have encountered in identifying and recommending her solutions? How would you have addressed them?

2 How could commitment to implementation have been gained and the proposals delivered more quickly?

3 What could she have done after the end of the project to ensure that her recommendations were not lost and could be implemented?

4 How might Maria have described her KTP experience in her CV?

APOLLO TECH SOLUTIONS CASE STUDY

Part Four

On 1 September, Carl Klingner and Samantha Allen stood once more in front of their key client contacts at Apollo: the Project Moon team, Stephen Irvine (CEO), Tom McPherson (CFO) and Samuel Arnott (Strategy Director). Arnott knew the content of their presentation and was confident that his colleagues would be impressed by the rigour of the analysis and proposed plans. The presentation clearly summarised what Apollo should do in terms of a new strategy. All went fine until Klingner asked for a private word with Irvine, McPherson and Arnott. Then he dropped the bombshell. He casually noted that 'having met your senior managers in Apollo Advance, I do not think they are all capable of implementing the changes we propose'. Klingner then, to his mind, thoughtfully offered Ferguson & Co's services for the next six months to 'help' with the implementation. The cost would be four times that of Project Moon.

Irvine, McPherson and Arnott were in a quandary. They knew that Klingner's analysis was probably right but they were not prepared for this. It was also too short a time to delay presenting the strategic plan at the AA conference. So they decided to carry on with the latter and have a meeting with Klingner after the conference. During the presentation on 4 September, Arnott found himself listening very carefully to the responses of AA's managers to the proposals. He identified three types from their responses:

- The 'eager to please' – worried about their jobs and would agree to anything.

- The 'sit on the fence' – not committing themselves but open to change.

- The 'it's a good idea but…' – refuseniks who were trying to hide their opposition.

While the middle group probably would be able to carry out the change needed, Arnott had serious doubts about the other two groups. Unfortunately the latter comprised of over three-quarters of the managers present. Klingner was therefore right and it was unlikely that Apollo could carry out the implementation of the new strategy unaided.

When he, Irvine and McPherson convened after the conference, Arnott found that his views were shared by his colleagues. They put in a conference call to Carl Klingner to explore how Ferguson & Co could help them. Klingner was indeed happy to help but he wanted to use the existing team to ensure the best possible result. They would therefore have to start immediately.

Arnott said that they needed to think about this and perhaps have some 'reflection time' of, say, 4–6 weeks. Klingner was adamant that they needed to start now as he couldn't guarantee his team would be available then.

They thanked Klingner for his input and discussed amongst themselves the way forward. At the start of the project, Irvine had been keen on the project and was the key driving force alongside Arnott. McPherson had been the sceptic, arguing that it was a lot of money for an unproven project. Now roles were reversed. Irvine urged caution that this was a lot of money to be spent in this financial year and the profit this year was already looking shaky because of the poor economic climate. McPherson, on the other hand, was keen to proceed as a) he recognised that if the implementation failed then the consulting project had been a waste of money and b) this also gave him an opportunity to 'review overhead costs', a euphemism for cutting down the management not only of AA but even the wider organisation.

Irvine and McPherson then turned to Arnott for his views. Did he really think that AA was capable of implementing this strategy on its own? Was the growth projected by Ferguson & Co really achievable given the current leadership of Apollo Advance? Would implementation take just six months or would Apollo face further bills to get the new strategy in place and the business growing? There were more questions than answers and Arnott felt pressured by Klingner's demand that they decide immediately. It was this and the thought that he and his internal team were more than capable of acting as an internal consultants. So, reluctantly he sided with Irvine and argued that they should not engage Ferguson & Co further.

McPherson's 'price' for agreeing to this was a widespread review of the two Apollo divisions with a view to reducing complexity, i.e. costs, as this had been one of Ferguson & Co's recommendations for Apollo Advance.

Questions

1 How could have the senior team at Apollo Tech Solutions avoided the dilemma of having to rush the decision on whether to use the consultants for the implementation?

2 Was it ethical of Carl Klingner to pressurise Apollo into making a snap decision? Should he have handled it differently?

3 How could Klingner and Arnott have managed the knowledge transfer better between the consultant and the client?

Chapter 14

Consulting as a career

The finest eloquence is that which gets things done; the worst is that which delays them.

David Lloyd George

Learning outcomes

The learning outcomes from this chapter are to:

- appreciate the history, structure and dynamics of the global consulting industry;
- know who are the key players in the consulting world;
- understand the common career structures in consulting companies;
- gain an insight into becoming a consultant;
- recognise the opportunity to develop an internal consultant managerial style;
- understand the value consultancy skills offer for non-consulting jobs.

You have completed a consulting exercise as part of your course and you have enjoyed doing it. So, perhaps, you are thinking of becoming a consultant when you complete your degree. This chapter therefore aims to give you a picture of the consulting industry to help you think about your options. You will certainly not be alone: becoming a management consultant remains a popular career move with over 360,000 employed in the sector in the UK in 2013 (source: Keynote *Business and Other Management Consultancy Activities Market Report*, 2015). Being a full-time external consultant is not for everyone and sometimes it is possible to become an internal consultant within a firm, where you can use your consulting skills but in a familiar environment. Though just as every consulting project is different, so is an individual consultant's experience. If you are interested in consulting as a career, then use this opportunity of doing a student consulting project to help guide you. Good luck!

14.1   The history of management consulting

When did management consulting start? Well, if it is defined as providing professional services (or advice) to businesses for a fee, then it is likely to have started not long after people began trading with one another. Someone who could help another make more money would always be in demand! Certainly the expansion of the colonial network of the Western European countries in the seventeenth century relied on the ability of the state-endorsed private trading companies to successfully develop the economies of the new colonies. The dissemination of technical knowledge, such as planting the right economic crops, was therefore vital. The new English colonies in Virginia initially failed to take root both literally and metaphorically when the attempts to grow various crops there ended in failure and resulted in near starvation for the colonists. Only the successful introduction of tobacco in the 1620s ensured its long-term survival and provided the basis for more English colonies in North America.

> **With the industrial revolutions of the eighteenth and nineteenth centuries in Britain, Europe and America, consultants with expertise in improving production processes started to emerge.**

Arthur D. Little, for example (whose eponymous firm, ADL, was founded in 1886), was an engineer who helped businesses make best use of the new technologies such as the telegraph and the railways.

Alongside these 'technical' experts, accountants began to recognise that they could offer businesses additional services to the traditional audit function. One of the first of these was Andrew T. Kearney, who founded his firm in 1926: the same year that fellow accountant James O. McKinsey set up his new consulting business. Their aim was to provide not only financial but also management advice. These early firms provided the training ground for consulting professionals and most of the larger operations today were started by alumni of ADL, McKinsey and A.T. Kearney from the 1960s onwards. For instance, in 1963 Bruce Henderson left ADL to set up the Boston Consulting Group.

> **It was the large mainstream accountants such as Andersen and PricewaterhouseCoopers who came to dominate the consulting business in the 1980s and 1990s.**

Concern was expressed that there was a conflict of interest between their audit and consulting practices with too much overlap. Pressure was put on the firms to set up 'Chinese walls' but doubt remains how effective they are. A few, such as Andersen, eventually split off their consulting business in 2001, which was renamed Accenture.

The market had been very buoyant until 2001, growing in excess of 10 per cent per annum. However, in 2002, for the first time in three decades, the market fell by 6 per cent (Kennedy Information, *The Global Consulting Marketplace*, 2003) due to a tougher IT market and an increased scepticism among consultancy buyers following the Enron/Andersen accountancy scandals. The net result was a reduction in the number of consultants employed (an estimated 15 per cent of consultants left the profession in 2002) and also a reduction in the average fee rate. This proved to be a short-term setback, as the industry continued to grow after a flat year in 2003 due to three main factors. The first was the increase in core demand from 'laggard' industries as trends such as globalisation and information technology increased the complexity and competitiveness of the environments in which businesses operated. Managers recognised the importance of knowledge rather than simply products or price as a basis for competing. Businesses now wanted to stick to their core expertise and so they wanted to bring in specialists to manage non-core activities when they are needed. The continued strong growth in outsourcing is a testament to this (see Section 2.4).

The second factor was the continued demand for IT spending as the use of technology became more critical to effective modern businesses. The Internet had a major impact on the way many established industries operated. It is estimated that digital-led consultancies now account for a quarter of all consulting business in the UK (source: Keynote *Business and Other Management Consultancy Activities Market Report*, 2015). The third factor in the growth of consulting was the increasing demand from governmental and associated organisations (see Section 2.5). In recent years the boundary between the private sector and the state has been pushed back and become blurred. This is a worldwide phenomenon. Increasingly, it is accepted that government has a role only where the market cannot operate but would still like to exercise some degree of influence. As a result, government departments are outsourcing work and offering tenders to private firms for capital projects. However, these have been started to be reined back in recent years.

14.2   The consulting industry today

The size of the consulting industry today depends on the definition of what is or is not a consultancy project.

> **Most definitions of consultancy would include the following: information technology (IT) consulting and system integration; management consulting including strategy, operations management, human resources management, project and change management; outsourcing and other specialist roles, such as training, executive selection and audit.**

In addition, some estimates also include *business advisory services* that include all mergers and acquisitions and public flotations work done by accountants, merchant banks and other financial institutions.

It is estimated that $449 billion will be spent globally on consultancy in 2015 (including business advisory services), an increase of over 8 per cent on 2014 (Plunkett

Table 14.1 The consulting industry's share of business in Europe, 2014

Sector	Market share (2014)	CAGR 2010–14
Strategy	11	0.4
Operations	32	3.3
Financial Advisory	25	0.5
Human Resources	10	2.7
IT	22	2.7

Source: Kennedy (http://www.consultancy.uk/consulting-industry/european-consulting-market, consulted 15 January 2016)

Research). The split of business in Europe between the main areas of consulting is shown in Table 14.1.

The market throughout the early part of the twenty-first century has reflected the cyclical nature of the world's businesses and economies. Up to 2008 the market was very buoyant, with business coming both from the private and public sector. However, the global financial crisis and the subsequent reining back of expenditure meant that there was a sharp drop in consulting work of between 5 per cent and 10 per cent in 2009. When the world economies recovered slightly in 2010 and the early part of 2011, buoyed up by their respective government's financial stimulus packages, demand went up for consulting too. However, as more countries introduced debt reduction programmes that were starting to bite in the second half of 2011, the outlook for consulting again became less favourable, particularly those firms who relied heavily on public sector work.

What has been notable about this most recent economic recovery is that consulting firms have rebounded at the same time as their clients (Kennedy Information, *The Global Consulting Marketplace 2010–2013*). Previously, there was a delay as firms recovered confidence and started spending again on what was deemed 'non-essential' items, such as consulting. This reflects the fact that the consulting market has matured and is now seen as an important part of business operations. This is particularly true for operations management where businesses are continually striving to improve the way in which they operate. There is, however, less emphasis on human resources consulting in the last few years as employers have been shedding jobs, rather than looking for ways to retain or recruit staff. Business advisory services have continued to be an area of growth, reflected in part by government legislation but also because this is a more difficult area to compete in and fee rates have remained high.

All types of business call on the services of consultants. In Europe, in 2012, the top two areas, accounting for nearly 50 per cent of the revenue, came from the financial services industry and the industry sector (see Figure 14.1). Most notable has been the recent drop in market share for the public sector, which is symptomatic of the reduction of government spending across Europe.

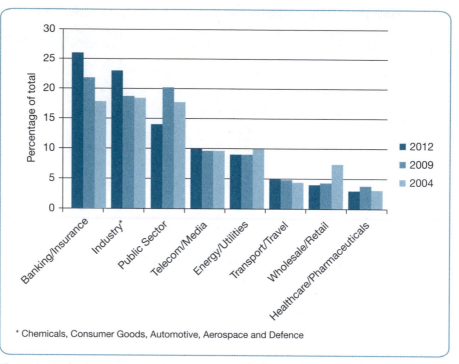

Figure 14.1 The key industry sectors for consulting in Europe, 2012, 2009 and 2004.
Source: Survey of the European Management Consultancy 2011–12 & 2009–10, FEACO & FEACO Survey 2004.

14.3   Key players in the consulting world

The consulting industry is fragmented and includes a number of sectors.

> **The trend is for players to be large with a global reach or small and offering a specialised service.**

The main types of consultant firms are as follows.

IT firms

As the cost of their traditional products (hardware and software) become more competitive and profits are driven down, the IT companies have increasingly looked towards consulting as a means of increasing revenue. At first they tried to achieve this organically but often did not have the credibility or the critical mass. So the trend has been to buy consulting businesses, particularly those from the accounting firms; for example, IBM's purchase of PwC Consulting. However, the sale of AT Kearney by the company EDS to its management team in January 2006 may indicate that the fit between mainstream consulting and IT consulting may not have been that profitable.

Table 14.2 Top 10 consulting firms by revenue and market share (2014)

Rank	Company	Revenue ($m)	Market Share (%)
1	Deloitte	14,674	11.7
2	PwC	12,732	10.2
3	EY	12,056	9.6
4	KPMG	10,743	8.6
5	Accenture	4,079	3.3
6	IBM	3,999	3.2
7	McKinsey & Co.	2,335	1.9
8	Booz Allen	2,051	1.6
9	CGI	1,460	1.2
10	CSC	1,412	1.1
	Top 10	**65,540**	**55.5**
	Others	**59,697**	**47.7**

Source: Gartner. It measures business consulting services, including business process transformation, business process redesign or re-engineering, business performance improvement, corporate compliance, risk management, governance and sourcing advisory.

Accountancy firms offering consultancy

There has been a major change here following Andersen's woes. In response to criticisms, many of the accountancy firms sold off their mainstream consulting operations either to the management or to other consultancies (particularly IT). They have since rebuilt their 'consulting services' businesses and these have become a significant part of their business. For instance, the advisory services of PricewaterhouseCoopers (PwC) earned revenues of $12.7 billion in the year to 30 June 2014, 37 per cent of their total revenues (Company Report, 2014). It was also their fastest growing segment, increasing by nearly 10 per cent on the previous year (ibid). PwC further increased their consulting services business by combining with Booz & Co, a specialist strategy consultancy, in 2014 to form 'Strategy&'.

Major consulting-only firms

These are large firms with a global reach. Their core business has always been consulting and they offer a wide range of services. Table 14.2 gives their most recent revenues available and their market share.

A number of leading consultancy firms issue magazines or journals. These provide a medium for communicating new ideas on themes in management and are promotional devices. They are available online and are worth reviewing, both to keep track of development in management thinking and as a good source of information on individual consultancies, particularly their specialisms and style of working.

14.4 Career structure in consulting firms

All management consultancies organise themselves in their own way. They can be quite hierarchical in their structures, especially the larger firms.

> The large consulting firms' structure provides a definite ladder for gaining experience, building expertise and developing a career.

In practice, teams that cut across levels of responsibility undertake most consulting projects. Being team based, most consultancies operate with a professional, informal culture. Job titles vary, but some of the common roles (in ascending order of seniority) include the following.

Analysts

Analysts are responsible for gathering information and processing it for the consulting team. They would probably have little contact with the client, until they gained more business experience. They would be placed within an industry (e.g. consumer goods) or practice group (e.g. strategy); however, they would not be expected to have detailed knowledge of either. Most graduates would start here straight from university or business school. Only the large firms offer these positions.

Consultants

Consultants undertake the evaluation of the client business and make recommendations on its behalf. They have the most direct contact with the client and would increasingly be given more exposure to the management of consulting projects as they become more experienced. It is at this point that they would start to specialise in a particular area to build up expertise. These are either analysts who have been promoted after a couple of years or those who have been in industry and have moved to consulting as a career change.

Senior consultants or managers

More experienced consultants have responsibility for leading a consulting team undertaking a project on behalf of a client. In addition, they would be expected to have in-depth knowledge of their specialist area, be it an industry or a practice. They would typically have three to five years of consulting experience and would have already demonstrated their ability to take on the responsibility of running small consulting projects. They would also be more involved in dealing with members of the client team and building key relationships to gain repeat business.

Business development managers

Business development managers within the consulting business are responsible for developing the firm's products and building its relationship with clients. They will also be involved in some large, complex consulting projects at a strategic level. Most at this level would have five to ten years of consulting experience.

Directors (or partners)

Directors (or partners if a private firm) are the most experienced consultants, who take on responsibility for the development of the organisation as a whole and who lead its strategic development. They will also maintain contacts with senior personnel in the client companies and will have overall responsibility for projects. As the most senior in the organisation, it would be expected that they would have at least ten years of experience in this field.

14.5   Becoming a consultant

As has been discussed above, new graduates can join the larger consulting companies as an analyst straight away. Otherwise the normal entry into consulting is after a period working in 'client companies'. Many join after completing an MBA from one of the prestigious business schools, such as Harvard or INSEAD, which require candidates to have at least five years' working experience.

> **Both joining as a graduate or with some business experience has their merits and any individual needs to think carefully about the route they follow that would be best suited to them.**

If one wants to be a 'career consultant', then starting as an analyst makes the most sense. If, however, the long-term goal is to use a period as a consultant to hone general business skills, then an individual may be better to start as a graduate in industry, possibly complete an MBA, and then apply to be a consultant.

Whatever route is followed, some key questions need to be addressed before a candidate identifies which consulting firms they will apply to:

1 Does the firm offer positions at the level that is appropriate to me?

2 Is their area of consulting of interest to me?

3 Do I have the right skills (and experience) for this firm?

4 What is the balance of work at office versus on client site (an indication of how much one would travel)?

5 What is the experience of previous new employees (i.e. does this sound like a firm I would like to work for)?

6 What is the remuneration package – not only salary but other perks such as pension, private healthcare, car allowance and holiday entitlement?

7 What is their training programme?

You may also want to consider the company's 'style' of consulting. Many have a distinct 'culture' such as McKinsey (see McDonald, 2014) that you will need to 'fit' into. There are those such as the specialist strategy consultants who prefer to use standard tools and employ what is best described as a top down approach. From years of experience in similar situations, they start from the perspective that they know the broad answer before they start and then use the relevant information to validate it. At the other extreme are operations consultants, for example (also known as 'performance enhancement' consultants), who analyse everything in order to find the answers. While these two examples above are at either ends of the spectrum, most consultancies tend to be either on one side or the other. Neither approach is wrong, but you need to think about whether you are a 'big picture' person or one more comfortable with lots of detail.

In the previous chapter we discussed putting together a good CV, which is vital.

Many consulting firms also use the 'case question' technique as a means of recruitment.

Case questions are used in addition to the normal questions about a CV that candidates normally face and typically it can take up over half the time spent at the interview. The types and examples of case questions are detailed in Biswas and Twitchell's book *Management Consulting: A Complete Guide to the Industry* (2002). They have defined ten broad types, together with examples, which are given below:

- **Brain teaser** – why are manhole covers round?
- **Business strategy** – should a food retailer offer other services, such as insurance?
- **Human resource management** – what should banks do with their counter staff as ATM networks expand?
- **Market entry** – how should a gourmet coffee chain locate its stores?
- **Market sizing** – how many people surf the web in a single weekday?
- **Mergers and acquisitions** – should a gin distillery buy a beer company or a snack company?
- **New product introduction** – should a food company offer olives with stones, or without?
- **Opportunity assessment** – should a soda bottler backward integrate into the manufacturing of syrup?
- **Pricing** – how does the Post Office price a first-class stamp?
- **Profitability loss** – a pharmaceutical company is losing money; what should it do?

From the above, we can see that the questions can be varied and it is important not to think that there is a 'right' answer. Instead the interviewer is trying to establish how good your consulting skills are in tackling the question. So they will be looking for good analytical, project management and relationship skills of the type that have been detailed in this book. As with all things, practice here is key and the more of these 'case questions' you tackle, the better you will be at doing them. Biswas and Twitchell have a good section on examples for a candidate to work through, including some sample answers, as well as Victor Chang's website (www.caseinterview.com). Another good source of information are websites **vault.com** and **wetfeet.com**.

Although you will need to find what works best for you. One approach to the case question could be to approach it as a mini case study. Give yourself enough time to think about each stage before proceeding to the next.

Stage 1 – Listen to the case question	Ensure you understand it – repeat it back if appropriate
Stage 2 – Ask further questions	These should be to clarify the question and elicit more information
Stage 3 – Analysis of the case	Look at using some of the tools in Chapter 6 but do not 'force fit' any just for the sake of using them
Stage 4 – Framework	Decide on what framework you will use and present this to the interviewer
Stage 5 – Answer the question!	Summarise your thoughts and make your conclusion in a clear and precise way. Remember the Pyramid Principle!

14.6 The internal consultant

The changes that are driving the demand for consultancy services are also changing the way in which internal managers work.

The old way in which businesses operated, with fixed structures defining hierarchies in which people worked, are no longer appropriate. Businesses need to be flexible and responsive to developing customer needs requiring multifunctional teams. Managers must forget about the jobs they are *supposed* to do and look towards the tasks they *must* do in order to make their businesses more competitive. William Bridges has suggested in his book *Jobshift* (1995) that managers must learn to thrive in a workplace without jobs, or at least jobs as they were understood. The internal consultant is simply a manager who develops the role and approach of a consultant while employed in a permanent capacity. The following characterises the approach of the internal consultant.

Awareness of the resources needed by the organisation

External resources such as the goodwill (and hence spending) of customers, investors' valuable capital, the support of suppliers and distributors, human expertise and information are vital. As discussed in Chapter 1, attracting these resources is the way in which the consultant creates value for the client. The internal consultant is as keenly aware as the external consultant of the resources he or she is obtaining for the organisation, the value of those resources and the management of the relationships critical to obtaining them.

Constant redefinition of job

The role of the consultant changes with the challenges he or she meets. For the internal consultant, the job he or she does similarly undergoes constant evolution. This means a constant redefinition of roles, responsibilities and relationships, both internal and external. External relationships are managed to maintain resource flows; internal ones so that the whole organisation recognises the developing role.

Demand for change

As the environment and competitors change, the business must change in response. The internal consultant will not only accept change positively, he or she will actively demand it and lead that change.

Constant development of skill profile

Internal consultants must evaluate the skill demands of the tasks they face, assess personal competencies and identify any skill gaps and source a means of developing those skills.

Intrapreneurial planning

Entrepreneurs are managers who drive *significant* change. An *intrapreneur* is simply a manager who behaves entrepreneurially within an established firm – that is, leading the organisation so that it can change to exploit significant new opportunities. Effective entrepreneurship demands planning. An opportunity must be identified and its value evaluated. A strategy to exploit that opportunity must be devised. That strategy must be put into effect. These are all tasks for the internal consultant.

Team discussion points

1 Each person in the group should seek out one or more of the websites of the major consultancies. Imagine that you have been taken on to undertake a recruitment drive for that firm at the analyst and consultant level. What would you look for in prospective candidates? Give a short presentation (of five minutes with two slides) of your findings to the rest of the group. Give them a one-page summary advising them how to approach that firm to discuss career prospects.

2 Taking one of the case questions outlined in Section 14.5, work in a team to come up with a solution, not forgetting to use the key skills required of a consultant.

Summary of key ideas

- The formal consultancy business has been around for over a hundred years, helping businesses deal with an ever changing world.

- The growth of the industry continues, despite dips due to economic downturns – it seems that consultants have become an essential part of the corporate culture.

- The consulting business is quite fragmented with a few very large firms but many medium-sized and one-person operations.

- Becoming a consultant can take place at any stage in one's career but the key consulting skills need to be demonstrated in successful interviews.

- Changes in established organisations mean that the internal consultant will have an ever more important managerial role.

- Consultancy skills are general management skills. A person with consulting skills can look forward to success in a wide variety of roles and organisations.

Key reading

Biswas, S. and Twitchell, D. (2002) *Management Consulting: A Complete Guide to the Industry.* New York: John Wiley and Sons (Chapters 5, 7 and Appendices).

Fombrun, C.J. and Nevins, M.D. (2003) *The Advice Business: Essential Tools and Models for Management Consulting.* Upper Saddle River, NJ: Pearson Prentice Hall (Chapters 1, 25, 27 and 28).

Further reading

Bellman, G. (2001) *The Consultant Calling*. Chichester, West Sussex: Jossey-Bass Wiley.

Bridges, W. (1995) *Jobshift: How to Prosper in a Workplace Without Jobs*. London: Nicholas Brealey.

Cheng, V. (2012) *Case Interview Secrets: A Former McKinsey Interviewer Reveals How to Get Multiple Job Offers in Consulting*. Seattle: Innovation Press.

Cosetino, M.P. (2013) *Case in Point: Complete Case Interview Preparation* (8th edn). Needham, MA: Burgee Press.

IMC (2015) *The Inside Careers Guide to Management Consultants 2015/6*. London: Cambridge Market Intelligence Limited.

Johnson, M. (2009) *Starting Up on Your Own: How to Succeed as an Independent Consultant or Freelance*. Harlow, Essex: Pearson Education.

Kipping, M. and Clark, T. (2012) *The Oxford Handbook of Management Consulting*. Oxford: Oxford University Press.

McDonald, D. (2014) *The Firm: The Inside Story of McKinsey, The World's Most Controversial Management Consultancy*. London: Oneworld Publications.

Sturdy, A., Wright, C. and Wylie, N. (2015) *Management as Consultancy: Neo-bureaucracy and the Consultant Manager*. Cambridge: Cambridge University Press.

Xu, Z. (2013) *Breaking and Entering: The Graduate's Guide to Management Consulting*. London: Zedex Schumann Ltd.

Case exercise

Grey Consulting Ltd

Grey Consulting Limited (GCL) was established by two family members. The brain-child of Gerard, who persuaded his brother Michael to join him in the venture, the business was set up originally as a boutique consultancy to serve one primary target market – boards and board directors. The plan was to work only with and for boards using staff that could hold their own with individuals and groups at this level offering 'trusted advisors acting with high integrity'.

GCL was created as a virtual consultancy. It had no buildings or offices and used virtual support mechanisms as much as possible: telephone answering services, meeting places, accountancy help. Anything not considered mainstream or central to the business was out-sourced. This was not considered detrimental to the business as, for example, offices rented by the day or even hour could be chosen for particular meetings.

It was soon decided that the two brothers working alone might be an issue – it might be sometimes difficult to separate the professional from the family – so a third board member, Ian, was invited to join who had been known to Michael for many years but shared some background with Gerard. Ian brought with him other complimentary skills to the mix. Gerard had occupied main board roles in large multinationals, often focusing on the technical side of some high-tech businesses. Michael, on the other hand, had the greater consultancy experience grounded also in technology companies but of a different nature. Ian brought innovation expertise, some good contacts and, like Gerard, was old-school educated with their attendant networks.

Beyond this, GCL was to be staffed by associates chosen to bring complementary skills to the core team, such as in-depth knowledge of particular sectors like technology, retail or of disciplines like human resources. Any associate had to be known to at least one of the core team and to be used only as and when dictated by a project. A website was established –

a vital portal for the business – in which all associates were shown as well as the three core directors. The website was designed to demonstrate the long and experienced history of the team to demonstrate the equality of the team to board directors. The site also advertised some of the published work of team members related to board roles and board activity.

GCL was set up to help boards and executive teams through major, challenging transitions such as creating and executing new strategies, reorganisation, innovation, mergers and disposals. Products and services included preparation for and subsequent company sales, board governance assessment (based on the Combined Code – a set of principles of good corporate governance aimed at companies listed on the London Stock Exchange) and board dynamics (which focuses on the psychology of board operation). These assessment tools were empirically derived and owned by GCL.

Initially, GCL's business came from immediate industry contacts the three directors enjoyed from their previous careers. In time a more systematic approach to identifying and targeting market segments was taken, with the aim of broadening the base business. Typical targets included:

- The remotely located divisions of multinationals,
- Family firms,
- Managing Directors with MBAs (a very 'consultant-savvy' group),
- The venture capital and private equity community who needed to source high quality directors and uses consultants for due diligence work and to support major changes in investee companies.

The focus on boards and their members was designed to play to the real strengths the team and associates had working at that level. The assumption was that there would be more than sufficient demand from this group to 'feed' the machine. Though there were some successes here, it was quickly realised that board members of blue chip companies have their own favourite consultancies or rather consultants within the largest consultancies with whom they preferred to work. Greater success followed when the focus changed to small- and medium-sized companies though their ability to pay the fees the team were used to was much more limited.

Originally conceived on a broader basis to appeal to boards and directors in all types and sizes of firms, it was quickly realised that the bigger, blue chip operations preferred the safety of the known big consulting outfits and would, therefore, not easily be converted to the 'new kids on the block'.

Being an open-minded team, they decided to call you in and ask for a review of the business.

1 What do you think of the target niches – too narrow and too well targeted (available verses addressable markets)? What might be the issues with this level of targeting?

2 What issues do you imagine might have been associated with running a consultancy of this nature? How might it differ from, say, a large-scale consultancy?

3 What critical assumptions do you think the team made that may have been invalid?

Example of a consulting report: New strategic direction for W&G Cracking Pie Company

Executive summary

The consulting project aimed to:

- identify the strategic options available for W&G Cracking Pie Company (W&G CPC) for the next five years;
- develop a new strategic planning process that works for W&G CPC;
- create a framework to develop specific internal project teams to deliver the strategy.

The key findings from the project were:

- While W&G CPC had some good planning processes in place, they were ad hoc and uncoordinated.
- The two founders (the Chairman and Chief executive) had different aspirations for the business from the other key stakeholders, principally the key shareholder (private equity firm) and other members of the senior management team.
- Its main product, W's Self-Heat Superpie, as it was a market leading product, had led to some complacency and a relative poor research and development programme.
- The tougher economic outlook for the UK economy meant that the company needed to start considering other markets.

Key outputs:

- There is now an agreed new strategic direction that has been accepted by all key stakeholders, including the private equity firm who have committed their support for a further five years.
- The framework for the strategic planning process is in place and will start next month to set targets for the individual business units for them to make their plans.
- Key areas of weakness in new product development, marketing and key account management are being addressed by their respective project teams.

Introduction

Since its establishment in 2005 by its two founders, W&G CPC has grown rapidly from its initial base in the north of England and now covers the whole of the UK. Its main product, W's Self-Heat Superpie accounting for 75 per cent of its sales, is now stocked in all branches of the leading supermarkets. However, over the last year sales growth has slowed and profitability has reduced. The private equity backer has expressed concern over the company's forward plans and whether they will continue to invest in the business. Therefore there was a need to develop a strategy for the next five years, which would both increase the market share in the UK with new products and look for overseas opportunities either directly or with a partner organisation. This has to be achieved not only in terms of increased sales but also profits as well to satisfy the continued support of the financial backers.

The approach taken was to build a new strategic planning capability using our unique and tried and tested tool, the *Strategy App®*. In Stage 1, working with senior members of the management team, we built a number of initial strategic options through in-depth interviews, workshops and a review of the available marketing research. These options were then presented to the board together with the recommendation of a favoured option. In Stage 2, the project team comprising of our consultants and selected members of the client team put together the new strategic planning process and prepared a new strategic plan. In Stage 3, the joint team identified the areas and the personnel involved for the internal project teams required to carry out the new strategy.

Key events in the project were as follows:

Stage	Activity	Timing
One	Background research and interviews	April 2015
	Workshop 1 – 'Where we are now'	May 2015
	Workshop 2 – 'Where do we want to be'	June 2015
	Presentation of strategic options	July 2015
Two	Workshop 3 – 'Building a new strategic process'	September 2015
	Presentation of new process	October 2015
Three	Workshop 4 – 'Building the project teams'	November 2015

As a result of this consulting exercise, it was envisaged that W&G CPC would be able to:

- deliver the required sales and profits for the key stakeholders;
- run an annual strategic planning process;
- have an ongoing five year strategic plan;
- measure progress against a defined set of objectives.

Summary and recommendations

Output of Workshop 1 – 'Where we are now'

- Very dynamic business, driven by the enthusiasm of the two founders, although their aspirations are different to the private equity firm and senior management.

- Good place to work with managers feeling that they had a good amount of autonomy, although occasional feeling of a lack of coordination.
- Some of the more recent senior recruits had brought in a more planned way of working, which has been beneficial.
- Its main product, W's Self-Heat Superpie, because it was a market leading product had led to some complacency and a relative poor research and development programme.
- The key customers (supermarkets) are getting harder to deal with.
- One of their main rivals has just brought out a new product that could seriously impact on W&G CPC's sales.
- The new marketing director, who has come from a large FMCG (fast moving consumer goods) company, thinks the marketing strategy and process should be improved.
- Targets are set but not in a structured or measurable way.

Output of Workshop 2 – 'Where do we want to be?'

- In five years' time, want to have doubled sales and profits.
- Aligned strategic priorities with key stakeholders.
- Do not want to lose the 'entrepreneurial spirit' by too much bureaucracy.
- Have a process that aids rather than hinders.
- In new markets, with the next generation of products.
- Have leading edge new product development, sales and marketing.

Output of Workshop 3 – 'Building a new strategic process'

- Scenarios explored and their impact – 'business as usual', 'organic growth' and 'growth through acquisition or alliance'.
- Strategic options identified using the *Strategy App*® and key recommendation identified.
- A draft top-line process ('straw model') and shown in the Appendix, to be presented to the board.

Output of Workshop 4 – 'Building the project teams'

- New product development, marketing and key account management are identified as areas for the new project teams.
- In addition, there will be a fourth team which will look at cross-functional processes to ensure consistency.
- The teams will have core team members drawn from their respective departments and will be led by a member of the senior management team, who will act as their sponsor at board level.
- They will remain in place for at least another year to ensure implementation.

Recommendations

- This is a large change in both the processes and the mindset of the company, so it is important to get staff ownership.
- While a new strategic direction has been made for now, it is important that in the planning process, this is challenged in the future as the world can change!
- Realistic and measurable objectives must be set in order to monitor progress.

Index

Page numbers in *italics* indicate figures and tables